With the Compliments

of

CHARLES H. MOLLOY

DAVID McKAY COMPANY, INC.

750 Third Avenue
New York, N.Y. 10017

THE JUDAIC HERITAGE

By the same author

THE ETERNAL FLAME

HOW DID IT BEGIN?

MEXICO—A COUNTRY OF CONTRASTS

THE JUDAIC HERITAGE

Its Teachings, Philosophy, and Symbols

by
R. BRASCH, O.B.E.
Rabbi, Ph.D., D.D., J.P.
Chief Minister, Temple Emanuel, Sydney, Australia

Have we not all one Father?
MALACHI II, 10.

DAVID McKAY COMPANY, INC.
New York

THE JUDAIC HERITAGE: ITS TEACHINGS, PHILOSOPHY,
AND SYMBOLS

To

FRED MENDEL—

benefactor, philanthropist,
and my friend

Library of Congress Catalog Card Number: 69-20209

MANUFACTURED IN THE UNITED STATES OF AMERICA

VAN REES PRESS • NEW YORK

FOREWORD

This book is meant for Jew and Christian alike. It gives a description of Jewish faith and the Jewish way of life. Its purpose is not solely a presentation of the oldest monotheistic faith on earth but, in addition, to make a contribution to present-day spiritual life. It is written with a love of Judaism and the conviction that the Jewish religion can give much help and guidance in this distraught world.

A modern thinker described Judaism as "the unknown sanctuary." Indeed, few Jews today are fully aware of the totality of their heritage; of what it means to belong to the people whose task on earth is to search for God and, by force of example, spread faith. Even fewer people outside the Jewish fold realize the meaning and essence of Judaism. This book seeks to offer to all of them, whatever their religion, an introduction and an explanation. Its scope is the life of a Jew from birth to death. Touching upon his essential beliefs and the sacred books of Judaism, it explains Jewish customs and symbols, their origin, and their present-day meaning.

Less than one-hundredth of the world's population belongs to the Jewish faith; yet Jews have always been a creative minority. *The Judaic Heritage* discusses the unique place of the Jew in the world—his impact on civilization and on society—and in the realm of the spirit.

Perhaps the greatest contribution made to modern life by the Jews—not as individuals, but as a group—will arise out of the creation of the State of Israel, whose potentialities have still to be fully developed. Knowledge of its history and unique insti-

v

tutions is fundamental to the proper understanding of Judaism, and therefore they have their rightful place in this work.

A recurrent theme is the outstanding features of the Jewish faith which reveal themselves in many and diverse ways: whether in the creation of a holy tongue, a unique fast for man's atonement, or the village of the blind in the Holy Land. All of them proclaim the Jew's rational outlook, his warmth of nature, and his universalism. In our ecumenical age, this volume discusses frankly where Judaism and Christianity meet and diverge and presents the Jewish viewpoint on Jesus, the Gospels, and the story of the Crucifixion.

It was Einstein who said that it is far easier to smash an atom than to smash a prejudice. Perhaps no people have been more misunderstood than the Jews. All through the ages they have suffered because of wrong notions about their life and faith. Jews are not a race. Pharisees were not hypocrites. God's name never was Jehovah. How, then, did these and many other fallacious ideas arise, and why were they perpetuated? The pages that follow present the facts on all these and on other questions which still confuse the minds of so many people.

Religion is like a lighthouse sighted by a ship in a stormy sea. The lighthouse cannot save the ship, which needs its own power to reach harbor safely. But the lighthouse points the way to salvation.

In this age of affluence and automation, in which loneliness, vulnerability to hurt, frustrations, ever-renewed fears, and a sense of helpless insignificance beset many, it is faith alone that can give life purpose and happiness again.

Threatened as we are by the dangers of materialism, it is essential that we should have a spiritual anchor to save us from drowning in a sea of moral bankruptcy. A world without values it a world without meaning.

It is my hope that this handbook on Judaism may be not only a source of information but an inspiration to Jew and Christian alike and contribute to their mutual understanding and friendship. It aims at giving the Jew a deeper comprehension of his faith, and the Christian, an appreciation of his Jewish heritage. If they wish for an insight into the Jewish way of life and the many Jewish practices that are so much a part of the Jew's religion, this book will help them to understand. And we need that understanding.

R.B.

ACKNOWLEDGMENTS

Grateful acknowledgment is extended to the following authors and publishers for their kind permission to quote:

Behrman's Jewish Book House: *Talmudic Anthology* by L. Newman, 1947.

Bloch Publishing Company: *Hasidic Anthology* by L. Newman, 1944.

Harper & Row and Hodder & Stoughton: *A New Translation of the Bible* by James Moffatt—the rendering of Isaiah LVIII, 13.

Hebrew Publishing Company: *Kitzur Shulchan Aruch* by S. Ganzfried, translated by Hyman E. Goldin, 1927.

Routledge & Kegan Paul Ltd.: *The Teachings of Maimonides* by A. Cohen, 1927, and *The Guide for the Perplexed* by Moses Maimonides, translated by M. Friedlander, 1956.

World Publishing Company and Meridian Books: *A Rabbinic Anthology* by C. C. Montefiore and H. Loewe, 1960 and 1963.

Thomas Yoseloff—A. S. Barnes & Company: *The Golden Peacock* by Joseph Leftwich, 1961—the rendering of the poems "Burn Out, Burn Quick" and "The You-Song."

As with all my books and my entire work, my wife has stood by my side as a true helpmate and a tower of strength in the writing of this volume. With alert mind and inexhaustible energy she has participated in all its stages: from the earliest draft and the typing of the manuscript to the making of the index. No words of mine could ever adequately express my appreciation.

CONTENTS

ix

PART I

The Jewish Way of Life

Chapter 1

THE FAITH OF THE JEW

Judaism is the religion of the Jewish people. Yet, in a wider, historical sense, it may be seen as the origin and basis of all that the world possesses of ethical, religious civilization.

It was more than four thousand years ago, in the days of the earlier Egyptian dynasties, that in Ur of Chaldea a desert princeling named Abram revolted against the prevailing vice of his idolatrous age. Essentially a man of action, Abram gave the world his superb concept of one God, a Supreme Being and Universal Father.

Thus did Judaism begin, and from it, thousands of years later, sprang the two other great contemporary religions, Christianity and Islam, like Judaism founded on the spiritual belief in one God and the ethical principles of the Ten Commandments. Surely it was divine inspiration that changed the name of Abram, the first Jew, to Abraham, the father of multitudes.

Judaism is rational, logical, and moral. It is not a creed, but a way of life. It demands righteous living, not the acceptance of dogma. Beliefs as such are significant only if they serve as a means to foster goodness and holiness. Judaism has neither an ecclesiastical body with an authority over the souls of the people nor any hierarchy. It knows of no division between priesthood and laity. The rabbi is a teacher, but not a priest. He is merely one of the people, an ordinary man with a vocation and training in the field of religion. His task is to set an example by his life, to expound the faith and explain it from its very sources.

The teachings of Judaism are based on two fundamental

1

works: the Bible (the Old Testament of Christianity) and the Talmud. These have been variously supplemented, developed, or summarized by other books. Outstanding among these were the collective works of the Apocrypha ("hidden books"), which found no place in the biblical canon, and the Midrashim, containing the gist of thousands of sermons preached in Babylonia and Palestine some two thousand years ago. Classics by individual authors are Moses Maimonides' twelfth-century philosophical interpretation of Judaism, *The Guide for the Perplexed,* and Joseph Caro's sixteenth-century annotated *Shulchan Aruch,* a complete compendium of rabbinical Jewish law, arranged so systematically and with such orderliness that its name likened it to a perfectly "Prepared Table."

Judaism teaches that there is one God, Who is universal and yet most personal. He is the Father of all men, Whom we must love with all our heart and serve in all our ways. He is absolute unity, which cannot be divided in parts or conceived in different forms. Though always the same, His creative energy manifests itself forever in an infinite variety of ways within the universe, which is His creation.

To the Jew, God is not a philosophical abstraction, but an ever-present reality. He is all-powerful, spiritual, and eternal. Both mercy and justice belong to His Being. Life and this universe are not just an interplay of blind forces or a product of chance and fate. God gives them meaning and purpose. Though often inscrutable, a divine plan shapes this world. Man has the sacred duty to act as God's partner, who can hinder or foster the realization of His purpose.

All men are God's children. Every human being is equally near to Him and can approach Him directly. Judaism denies the need of any mediator, priest, or church. Man must worship God out of love, not fear. Judaism is inherently opposed to racial discrimination. The Bible allegorically tells of the creation of one first man from whom all people and races have descended. Sharing a common ancestry, no one people has the right to consider itself superior to any other. For this reason, the command "Thou shalt love thy neighbor as thyself" from earliest times has been regarded as a basic tenet of Judaism and been paraphrased in the Talmud as implying: "Thou shalt love thy neighbor—for he is as thou." Not selfish love, but the knowledge of equality, must be the determining factor in a human relationship. The fatherhood of God implies the brotherhood of man, which allows of no differentiation or discrimination.

Life is distinguished by its colorful and unending variety, which must be maintained, and not abolished. Judaism teaches that everybody has a rightful place and is chosen for a specific task. Everyone is needed and is irreplaceable. Without him, this world would lack something. A famous rabbinic simile claims that every human being is "coined for himself," a unique creation of infinite value.

Judaism believes that man was "created in the image of God." A divine spirit dwells in every individual. This endows him with potentialities for good, a yearning for the infinite, and a longing for an ideal. Through it, God and man are no longer far apart, but become closest and nearest.

Judaism does not believe in "original sin." Man is born pure. Sin is the result of his freedom and a condition of his moral responsibility. Man's will is unfettered. He himself chooses between right and wrong, good and evil, and must therefore be ready to accept the consequences of his choice. Yet there is always the possibility of return. No evil is final. Suffering is not merely punishment but a means of purification and a test of faith. Nothing in man is innately evil. Even his instincts and passions can be made instruments of sanctification. Judaism teaches neither asceticism nor celibacy, nor does it know monasteries and convents. It demands the control of passion: not its mortification, but its consecration.

The rabbis taught that "everything is in the hand of God, except the fear of God." He cannot compel man to be religious and to obey His Law. But in his freedom, man possesses immeasurable possibilities. Although unable to choose the circumstances of his existence, he can master them and determine the moral quality of his life. Judaism is a world-affirming, optimistic faith. It does not consider the world dismal and evil. It insists that our God-given existence can be made great and beautiful through our own efforts.

Hillel, who was born seven decades before Jesus, accepted the challenge of a pagan to summarize Judaism in the shortest possible form: "What is hateful to yourself, do not unto your fellowman." This, he asserted, was the whole of Judaism. Everything else was mere commentary. Judaism is not a religion of personal salvation, but of social justice. There is no true Judaism without love of humanity. This must never expend itself in abstract sentimentalism, but be expressed in definite and ever-renewed individual action. To help the needy and weak is not a voluntary act, but a sacred duty. It is the essence of Judaism, which does not know the word "charity," with all its condescending benevolence. In its place, the genius of the Hebrew language has created the unique, untranslatable word *mitzvah,** which embraces both "helpfulness" and "commandment." To help is both a privilege and an obligation. Anyone who is hardhearted denies his divine origin.

Judaism believes in the immortality of the soul. Death is not the ending, though it is the limit of human vision. A detailed understanding of immortality exceeds man's power. It certainly is not restricted to special faiths or groups, but belongs to all human beings. It is a spiritual state, and not a matter of Paradise, Heaven, or Hell, with their physical connotations.

The final goal, the destiny of man, will be achieved not by supernatural interference or miraculous action. Man's own work alone, here on earth, can attain it. This has been variously described from age to age. At times, Jews emphasized the coming of a personal Messiah. In other periods they spoke more distinctly of the Messianic Age. But the aim was always a righteous society in which each individual developed to the fullest his spiritual qualities and maintained his dignity and freedom. In the "end of days" the Jew visualized a peaceful coexistence of all men and races, freedom from fear and want, cessation of war

---

* In order to avoid an excess of italic type, Hebrew and Yiddish words are presented in italic the first time and thenceforward in roman. Such terms already adopted into English according to modern dictionaries are in roman.

and preparation for war, a complete change of heart: positive, constructive effort supplanting all destructive and negative thought. This vision gave man his duty. It taught him to think in terms of centuries and never to tire in his pursuit of holiness and in the Messianic quest.

Jews are not a race, but a people of religion. They were chosen to be God's messenger to all men and by their teachings, their lives, and even their mere existence to testify to His Being. Their being chosen implied not privilege, false pride, or conceit, but obligation, humility, and even suffering. As a "nation of priests" their task is to build God's Kingdom on earth by spiritual endeavor, ethical living, and social action. This is the Jews' sole justification for existence. The name of the Jews' faith is no accident, but a fundamental characteristic. Buddhism and Christianity center on the figures after whom they were called: Buddha and Christ. Judaism never singles out an individual, asserting itself as Abrahamism or Mosesism. It grew out of the soul of a people to whom God revealed Himself in numerous ways and through many inspired personalities, priestly, prophetic, and rabbinical. Judah Halevi, Spanish philosopher-poet of the eleventh century, rightly commented that "the Jews did not derive their eminence from Moses, but Moses received his for their sake. The divine love dwelt among the descendants of Abraham, Isaac, and Jacob. We are not called the people of Moses, but the people of God."

Hardly one-hundredth of the world's population belongs to the Jewish faith. Everywhere, except in the State of Israel, the Jew constitutes a small group within a wider community. The proportion may vary from country to country: it is infinitesimal in Spain, average in England, and maximal in the Argentine. Yet the Jews are what Arnold Toynbee has called "a creative minority." They gave humanity its ethical monotheism, the belief in the supremacy of the spirit and in a moral world order. Theirs is the duty to be the conscience of mankind, the torchbearers of progress, and the advocates of the downtrodden and forgotten.

Leo Baeck, one of the outstanding twentieth-century Jewish figures and interpreters of Judaism, described as the very core of Judaism the anxious quest "to discover the soul of every being." That is why the Bible commands that "you shall know the soul of the stranger" and claims that "the righteous man knows the soul of his beast." In the Hebrew language, every person is called a "soul."

The Jew possesses a sense of the categorical. In his zeal he feels compelled to fight for the true and just. In him there must never arise spiritual apathy, moral indifference, or neutrality to the question of right and wrong. Merely to stand by when evil is done, to be lukewarm in the face of suffering anywhere, would be a denial of his Jewish duty.

The Jew is the eternal pioneer, the seeker of the way for a better world. His is the task "to make a highway for the Lord in the desert." Just as the first Jew, Abraham, left his home in Mesopotamia in search of the right way of life, so Jews throughout the ages never ceased in this quest. They will have justified their existence only at the hour of its final attainment. Then, and only then, with their mission fulfilled, can they find rest and lose their identity.

Jews do not try to convert other people to their faith, though Judaism is open to anyone who, from inner conviction, desires to embrace it. It is the Jewish teaching that the righteous of all nations and faiths will inherit eternal life. Man is not judged by his creed, but by his life. Loyalty to one's own religion hastens the day of God's Kingdom on earth. Obligatory upon all men is adherence to seven basic laws, "the precepts of the sons of Noah." They demand justice and prohibit idolatry, blasphemy, immorality, bloodshed, robbery, and cruelty. By accepting this way of life the righteous non-Jew is considered equal to the most pious Jew.

Jews are allowed to read everything. It is inconceivable to the Jewish idea of man's God-given mind to ban any book. There is no Jewish censorship nor a Jewish index of forbidden writings. Jewish scholars have not only studied but even written commentaries on the Gospels.

The Jewish religion stresses the importance of both Christianity and Islam and the role they have played in establishing monotheistic faith on earth. The Jew, however, considers Jesus a great religious personality, but not the Messiah: a man, but not God incarnate. He was born a Jew and lived all his life as such. Even his very last words were a quotation from Hebrew Psalms: "My God, my God, why hast Thou forsaken me?"

Once again Jews, Christians, and Moslems have united in the Holy Land. There, in the State of Israel, they are all Israeli citizens. This modern miracle has great meaning for the Jews throughout the world. Israel is the birthplace of their faith, the home of their ancestors, and a haven of refuge to millions of homeless and hounded victims of man's inhumanity to man. However, while the Jew of today believes himself almost unbelievably privileged to see the fulfillment of prophecy in the rebirth of the Jewish national state, he is bound both by inclination and religion to give his wholehearted and undivided loyalty to the land in which he lives. The principle is enunciated many times in Jewish writings, but never, perhaps, more concisely than by Jeremiah when he bade the Jewish exiles in Babylon to pray for and seek the welfare of the country where they were to live and make their homes.

Judaism does not have any sects. It knows only different sections: Orthodox, Reform, Conservative, and Reconstructionist movements.

Orthodox Judaism believes that God revealed Himself completely on Mount Sinai. Then and there Moses received His Law in both its written and oral forms. It is divine and contains the final revelation of God—the highest wisdom and absolute truth. Therefore, it is unalterable for all times and of equal value in each of its parts. To live according to it is the Jew's supreme duty. It is neither necessary nor possible to develop or alter the Law, whether in regard to its ethical legislation or its ceremonial customs. If the Law is truly understood and interpreted, Orthodoxy further maintains, it offers the answer to every situation in life.

Reform Judaism, which started in the early nineteenth century in Germany, whence it spread to America and then all over the world, is also referred to as Liberal or Progressive Judaism. It believes in a progressive revelation throughout the ages and thus does not accept the binding authority of Bible and Talmud, but reinterprets ancient tradition and rabbinical law for present-day circumstances. To make religion understood and relevant to the modern generation is one of its main endeavors. Reform Judaism sees in the early religious documents not only divine inspiration but also human elements conditioned by the limitations of the time when they were written. Customs are kept only if they still fulfill a religious purpose. Reform thus stresses the spiritual aspect. Symbolic of its aspirations and teachings is the name chosen for its American headquarters: The House of Living Judaism.

Conservative Judaism (also described as traditional, historic Judaism) was born as the result of the search for a middle road between the old and the new. Considering Jewish Law of divine origin, it continues to observe many of the Orthodox customs. Nevertheless, it shares with Liberalism (Reform) a belief in the need for adapting the ancient tradition to modern times by developments and modifications, but insists that these have to be introduced slowly and in moderation. "When it is not necessary to change, it is necessary not to change" could describe its philosophy. The aim to *conserve* as much of the tradition as possible explains its name. Conservatism in its modern form owes its existence to Professor Solomon Schechter, who arrived in America from England in 1902.

Reconstructionism was founded by Mordecai M. Kaplan, a graduate and teacher of the Conservative Jewish Theological Seminary of New York. It views Judaism not merely as a religion in the conventional sense of the term but as an evolving and dynamic religious civilization, composed of all the elements that make up the life of a people. Its aim is to promote a positive ideology for all Jews to meet and work together and thereby to *reconstruct* the Jewish religious civilization. The revitalization of Judaism and the replenishment of Jewish culture require that the belief in God be interpreted in terms of universally human and of specifically Jewish experience. When established in 1940, Reconstructionism was particularly addressed to the American

Jewish community. It was not meant to create a fourth movement in Judaism. In spite of the small number of its adherents, Reconstructionism is exerting a notable influence on all other branches of Judaism.

Though these various sections of Judaism thus differ in interpretation of revelation and thereby in appreciation and emphasis of the ritual of the synagogue, they share all essentials: the fundamental teachings of Judaism, the consciousness of mission, and the purity of faith.

Chapter 2

THE JEW AND THIS WORLD

The Jew views life as something that is good and should be enjoyed. Because the world is part of God's universe, it must be essentially good.

Judaism believes in immortality and sees in this life only a stage in the development of the human spirit. But instead of losing itself in speculation on the beyond, the Jewish faith—and this is the outstanding characteristic of all its philosophy and practice—puts the emphasis on this world, on appreciation and improvement of it. The world is not to be superseded, but to be redeemed. Every human being is entrusted with this charge: "it is not thine to complete the task but neither art thou free to exempt thyself from it."

To escape from life, instead of enjoying its beauty, would both deny God's wish and defy it. It would amount to rebellion against His will. At the most solemn season of the year, the Jew prays, "Remember us unto life, O King, Who delightest in life."

Not only does man have a right to feel happy but it is his duty to seek happiness. He is commanded to rejoice—to rejoice before the Lord. He must miss no opportunity of sharing in the joys of life, but at the same time he must recognize that each one of them has been sent by God. That is why the Jew considers it a privilege and a religious duty to join with others in their moments of happiness and why he has devised numerous special benedictions with which to praise God for the manifold gifts and pleasures of life. Still contained in the prayerbook of our time are blessings to be uttered on such diverse occasions as the sight of the year's first blossom, the donning of a new garment, the eating of fruit, or the smelling of the fragrance of a plant. One rabbi

10

even asserted that "in the hereafter every man will be called to account for the earthly pleasures he had rejected."

God's world needs cheerfulness and optimism, not gloom and melancholy. A talmudic legend tells of how, on one of his frequent visits to earth, the prophet Elijah came to a big city. There he met its rabbi, who was anxious to know who of all the citizens was most worthy of eternal bliss. Elijah confounded him by pointing to a couple of men who certainly had never distinguished themselves by religious observances. Later, when the prophet had departed, the rabbi approached the men and asked them what they had done and could say for themselves. He then found that their outstanding merit lay in the fact that they had made people laugh and had brought gladness wherever there had been sadness and grief.

Happiness is a state of mind which is dominated by the feeling that life is worth while. Small wonder, then, that length of life was considered a blessing. For that reason, the Jewish attitude toward heart transplants, or, for that matter, the transplant of any organ, is clear and definite. The saving and the prolonging of life supersede all other considerations. When the historic first South African heart transplant (on a Jewish patient) was about to be performed, an urgent message was sent to Anglo-Jewry's then newly appointed Orthodox Chief Rabbi, Dr. Immanuel Jakobovits, a recognized authority on Jewish medical ethics. He was asked whether the operation was legal, whether it conformed with Jewish tradition. His cabled reply left no doubt as to the Jewish position. It said: "Judaism cannot but enthusiastically applaud medical triumph in service of human life. Operation sanctioned provided prior death of donor definitely established."

Throughout the ages, and even at the most dismal moments of his existence, the Jew's toast was, "To Life." Exaggerated, perhaps, yet true to Jewish sentiment, is the traditional wish to live "up to 120." Strangest of all, and unparalleled anywhere else, is a Jewish custom of affirming the goodness of life even at the hour of death. It is then that some Jews express their condolences by wishing the bereaved "a long life."

Suicide is viewed with abhorrence. God has given us this life, and only He is permitted to take it away. We are placed on earth as sentinels and must not relinquish our posts until we are released.

Man's most precious possession is his immortal soul; yet even this is bound up with his body. Indeed, physical well-being is an aid to spiritual strength, and true holiness is unattainable without a state of earthly happiness. Both body and soul need each other, and neither must be neglected at the expense of the other. The rabbis spoke of a blind man and a lame man in an orchard who both desired to eat of its fruit. Clearly, neither of them could obtain it unaided. Only by a combined effort were they able to achieve their wish. The blind man thus lifted the lame man on his shoulders, and together they picked the fruit.

It is natural that Judaism knew its moments of negation and self-denial. But they never prevailed. They were exceptional and short-lived. The Bible rejected the Preacher's claim (in the book of Ecclesiastes) that life was vanity of vanities and vexation of spirit. The Nazirite who practiced abstention from legitimate enjoyments, even for a limited time, was called a sinner and was in need of God's pardon.

However, man's physical needs and mundane desires must never become ends in themselves. They must be employed as tools for the development of man's spiritual being and happiness. It is therefore sinful to indulge one's appetites. This would degrade man, denying his dignity and divine heritage. A man who afflicts his body for his soul's sake has his motive to plead for him. But the sensualist can give no justification and forfeits his character as a child of God.

Man must control his instincts. Only he who rules himself is able truly to enjoy life. Thus, Jewish philosophy adopted the principle of intelligent moderation which must be the result not of calculated prudence, but of self-reverence. Enjoyment of life must not be confused with what is commonly called "having a good time." Every pleasure must be restrained and dedicated; it must contribute to man's appreciation of the sanctity and the value of this world.

Judaism therefore knows of the limitation of joy. It has its dietary laws, which prohibit and restrict, and it supplements its feast days by fast days. But instead of killing and denying, it lifts the worldly into the realm of the sacred. Man must be stronger than matter: he must learn to be master, and not slave, of his instincts. Similarly, to strive for earthly goods is not evil in itself. Judaism has never aimed at the abolition of property, but demands its moralization. Wealth must not be hoarded, but used for the good of all. Every enjoyment of the good things of life, given us by God, must thus be accompanied by a sense of obligation.

One of the distinctive characteristics of Judaism is its stress on action instead of belief. As the rabbis said, "It is not the doctrine but the deed which is essential." In order to be able to experience true joy, we must enable our neighbors—and especially those who are least regarded and most in need—to rejoice with us. This conviction gave the Jew his social conscience and his passion for social justice and righteousness. His faith taught him to serve God in this world: to hallow His name on earth in the life of humanity.

Life has its frustrations, disappointments, and tragedies. There is much in the world that is imperfect. Job's words that "man is born to trouble, as the sparks fly upward" still hold true. But this evil is not inherent in the nature of things. Because of the limitation of our minds, we may not be able to explain it. Possibly suffering is at times sent to us as a discipline, though often it is the result of man's conduct and therefore accidental and avoidable. Whatever its origin or reason, evil must not paralyze us, cause us to flee this world, or make us fatalists. On the contrary, it is our task to change despair into hope.

Jewry's greatest thinker, Moses Maimonides, lucidly and frankly discussed the experience of the evil things from which no one is spared. He knew that people may easily adopt a wrong attitude. Coming face to face with the ugly facts of life, such as greed, jealousy, selfish ambition, and lust, they may say, "I want to get away from it all," and then, going to the other extreme, they may despise all the pleasant things of life, reject comfort, stay unmarried, become vegetarians and teetotalers. But Maimonides pronounced such a world-denying attitude as un-Jewish and contemptible. To turn our backs on life because of its obvious faults and temptations is sinful. Despair denies God. Evil in this world is meant as a challenge. We must neither ignore nor escape from it: "thou shalt remove the evil from the midst of thee."

However, the mere negative pursuit of subduing all that is bad is insufficient. Indeed, it is far easier to flee from evil, or even to resist it, than to attain the good. The world's stability is based on three principles: truth, justice, and peace. A world without righteousness can never be at peace; the result of righteousness is quiet faith and undisturbed, confident living.

It is one of the great paradoxes of Jewish existence that a people whose whole history is saturated with suffering and persecution never lost the will to live or the love of life. Even periods of utmost agony could not quench this innate Jewish optimism. Typical was the reaction of German Jewry's saintly leader, Rabbi Dr. Leo Baeck. When he was asked, after his liberation from a concentration camp, how he had endured all the humiliation and torture, how he had been able to keep up his spirit in this slough of despond, he replied, "Some of us were determined to demonstrate that the goodness of man can be victorious over brutality and bestiality." This answer echoed the heroic optimism of the Hebrew prophets, uttered thousands of years earlier and expressed succinctly in the words "and yet." The circumstances of the moment may weigh heavily on us; through man-made misery, life may seem utterly dismal and disheartening; "and yet" life is meant to be good, and light will overcome darkness.

The Jew believes that right must prove itself right and that in the long run it is, in fact, might. He is convinced that all things can be made new and better. Perhaps the finest lesson of the story of the Flood is that even a corrupt world is not doomed, that a new beginning is always possible. That is why the Jew never accepted tragedy as final, but felt that sorrow was only temporary, and not the essence of existence. From Abraham's days onward, the Jew has striven to make the wilderness blossom, and with this aim in his heart he became a champion and a pioneer.

Judaism, thus believing in the ultimate goodness of the world and of man, is certain of the possibility of progress. This, however, is not inevitable, but depends on man himself and gives him his special duty.

We are meant to make this world a place worthy of God. We can do so by our lives and the joy we weave into the lives of others. God's Kingdom does not exist above this world, nor will it be bestowed on us as a gift or appear by a miracle. It is to be built here on earth by our own effort, by working for our neighbor. And everyone is our brother, the child of God.

Chapter 3

THE LIFE OF A JEW

The Jew believes that only a "God-centered" life is worth living. Without awareness of God and spiritual content, human existence is virtually an empty shell, possessed only by sensuous lusts and selfish instincts. The life of a Jew is meant to be "God-intoxicated." That alone gives meaning to his being, which is why the Jews were called to be "a kingdom of priests and a holy people." Without his religion, the Jew is like a ship without a rudder, or a clock without its hands—useless, without a purpose.

From birth to death, from early morning till late at night, Jewish thought, feeling, and action must be directed toward God. It is only too true that for most people, modern secularization of life has made just a legend of far-off days of all this inspiring ideal, or a goal too great and too difficult, it appears, to be achieved. Yet this is how Jewish teaching commands the Jew to live if he wants to realize his duty toward mankind.

At the moment of awakening, the Jew is asked to give his very first thought to God to thank Him for having kept him alive throughout the night. His last thought, immediately before falling asleep, should be God's sanctification, expressed in the ancient words that speak of God's unity and humanity's oneness.

Man becomes all too easily accustomed to the blessings of life. Things for which he should be eternally grateful he takes largely for granted, bringing them to mind only when he has lost them. That is why the Jew is asked to utter daily at least a hundred benedictions on a hundred different gifts with which life has blessed him. At no time should he lose consciousness of the fact that in all his being he depends on God. There are "ready bene-

16

dictions," so to speak, waiting to be applied on the most diverse occasions, so that the fumbling mind should not tarry in seeking for the appropriate words. The religious genius thus prepared benedictions on such varied subjects as the beauty of nature, the eating of a crust of bread, the meeting of a philosopher—Gentile or Jew. Not to utter them, when called for, would amount to religious negligence.

Three times every day—morning, afternoon, and evening—the Jew instituted synagogue prayer meetings. They are still kept in every Orthodox community throughout the world, requiring a minimum attendance of ten male people. Only he who has completely turned away from his mundane occupation and united those three times with his brethren in prayer has fulfilled his duty as a Jew. Throughout the day and throughout the world, therefore, the Jew maintains and generates unceasingly spiritual powers. He can never be overwhelmed by the anxieties, cares, or pleasures of life. "Know before Whom you stand!" is his continuous reminder.

Even at mealtime, when man too easily can lose his dignity, the command to bless God before partaking of food, the duty to say grace afterward, and—most of all—the conscientious observance of dietary laws throughout the meal, with every dish and course, never permits the Jew to forget God's presence.

Such a life, if earnestly and eagerly followed, could establish the Jew as God's witness on earth. By united effort of all Jews everywhere, a tremendous spiritual force could thus be released into humanity's soul, lifting it up out of the slough of materialism to the heights of inspiration.

As on every single day of his existence, so on numerous special occasions throughout his earthly life, God's presence and man's destiny are brought near the Jew.

On the eighth day after birth, the Jewish boy is initiated into the Covenant of Abraham by the act of circumcision, the symbol or reminder that the Jewish life is one of dedication to the service of God and of mankind. Apart from this religious aspect, the act of circumcision is seen to have an important social or sociological significance, impressing on man the sanctity and importance of family life and ever reminding him of his obligation to remain master, and never to become slave, of his passions and desires.

As soon as the child was ready to absorb the elements of learning, he was taken to the synagogue to receive his first lesson. This consisted of verses from the Law of Sanctity, from the Third Book of Moses, Leviticus. There was a beautiful—if not always hygienic—ancient custom, by which the tablet from which the child learned his first letters and scriptural verses was covered with honey, which the child was allowed, and even invited, to taste, so that from the very beginning there should be an association of pleasantness and beauty with religion and God's Law.

On his thirteenth birthday the boy is deemed to have so far progressed in his knowledge of God's Law—the Torah—that he is ready to be admitted to the congregation with full adult responsibility for his religious life. The outward recognition of this occasion takes place in the synagogue on a Sabbath morning when the boy is summoned to come forward in public and, like any other adult male, to read the appropriate blessings and to chant a passage from a handwritten Scroll of the Law. He is also presented with a praying-shawl, the symbol of Jewish worship, its white cloth standing for purity of thought and the blue of its stripes for the sky, leading the mind heavenward. From now on he will don it whenever standing before his God, and one day it will accompany him into his grave.

Now he is a bar mitzvah, a "son of the commandment," with all that this word implies. He prays to God:

On this solemn and sacred day, which marks my passage from boyhood to manhood, I humbly raise my eyes unto Thee, and declare with sincerity and truth, that henceforth I will keep Thy commandments, and undertake to bear the responsibility of my actions towards Thee. In my earliest infancy I was brought within Thy sacred Covenant with Israel; today I again enter, as an active responsible member, Thy congregation, in the midst of which I will never cease to proclaim Thy Holy Name in the face of all nations.

Progressive congregations, anxious to stress the equality of both sexes, have introduced also a ceremony of bat mitzvah in which girls of thirteen become "daughters of the commandment." In the United States and Britain, notably, Reform and Conservative Judaism have a confirmation service for both boys and girls of a more mature age, generally around the sixteenth birthday.

In the life of the average Jew, marriage is the next special religious occasion. In the rabbinical writings, marriage is regarded almost as an essential public or civic duty. Without it, man is incomplete and would fail to fulfill his purpose: "No man without his wife and no woman without her husband; and they both never without their God." Only family life can guarantee happiness, as it in turn is the only secure foundation of any community. Divorce, though deeply regretted, is permitted.

At the marriage service, the Jew once again is reminded of life as a holy task, and not a mere mundane existence. To sanctify God is his mission. When husband and wife join each other and the bridegroom ceremonially places the ring on his bride's finger, he pronounces the formula: "Be thou consecrated unto me with this ring as my wife. . . ."

"Consecration" is the meaning of the Hebrew word for marriage. Twice drinking out of the same cup of wine during the ceremony, bride and bridegroom promise to share alike all the joys and sorrows that life may bring them. They stand under a canopy representing the presence of God and reminding them that only constant awareness of His will can ensure lasting happiness. At the end of the service the bridegroom breaks a glass. Just as this action is irrevocable, so the marriage has become final and perpetual. "For whither thou goest, I will go. . . . Thy people shall be my people."

Birth, marriage, and death are the three milestones of human existence. At hours of anxiety, religious faith proves itself even more than at moments of joy. When death enters his home, the Jew submits to God's will reverently and without bitterness. At the very hour of death, the essential beliefs of Judaism find supreme expression. It is the sincere wish of every Jew to die with the declaration of his faith, the *Sh'ma,* on his lips: "Hear, O Israel, the Lord our God, the Lord is One." If the dying person is unable to pronounce the words, he who is nearest and dearest to him utters them within his hearing.

All men are equal. Hence it is forbidden for the coffin to vary for rich and poor. Every Jew is buried in exactly the same kind of casket, made of simple boards and lacking any adornment. All are wrapped in the same kind of white linen garb and then in the praying-shawl.

At the funeral service the Jew speaks of God as "The Righteous Judge."

The Rock, His work is perfect, for all His ways are judgment, a God of faithfulness and without iniquity, just and righteous is He.

The Rock, perfect in every deed, who can say unto Him, What doest Thou?

When the coffin has been lowered, the male relatives and friends perform the last possible service to their departed dear one by assisting, symbolically, to fill the grave. Then the nearest kinsmen join in the recital of one of the most unusual prayers that have been devised by the religious genius of any faith: the kaddish, or "sanctification." This is a formalized prayer of praise to God, and its recital must, in the circumstances, be regarded as a sublime act of abnegation, of resignation to the divine decree. "Extolled and hallowed be the name of God," says the mourner, "throughout the world which He has created. . . . Just is He in all His ways. . . . Praised be the Lord of Life, the Righteous Judge." No reference to the deceased, no mention even of death itself; yet in the circumstances under which it is recited, the kaddish has come to be known as the prayer for the dead.

In the hour of grief the Jew testifies once again to his faith; thinking of his loved one, his heart heavy, his mind aggrieved, he still praises God. Even bereavement can hallow our lives and make us dedicate ourselves anew to the service of man and God.

Once every year, on the anniversary of the death of his father and mother or a close relative, the Jew keeps the *Yahrzeit,* as the day is called in its German-Yiddish term. For twenty-four hours, a candle or oil light is lit in the home, the flame being the symbol of the soul. The Jew goes to the synagogue to join with the other mourners there in the prayer of the sanctification of God, the kaddish, which he first uttered at the funeral of his loved one. Even the Jew who has broken every other association with his religion keeps this one custom. He does so every year to the very moment when he, too, is called to life everlasting and others start "saying kaddish" for him. In Hebrew, the word for cemetery shows the link between finite man and infinite God. It is called "The House of Eternity."

This is the life of a Jew—in its ideal—from the moment of his initiation into the Covenant of Abraham, his very first ancestor, to his being wrapped in a simple shroud. Constantly he is mindful of man's duty and destiny: to do justice, to love mercy, and to walk humbly with his God.

Chapter 4

THE JEWISH CALENDAR

As with everything else connected with his daily life, the Jew has a calendar which is fundamentally religious in its significance and practical application. The earliest calendars were inscribed on tablets of clay. This fact is commemorated by the use, to this day, of the word *luach,* literally "tablet," in reference to the "Jewish calendar." Incidentally, archaeologists working in modern Israel have found examples of very ancient clay calendars.

The chronology of the luach is reckoned from a period 3,761 years before the beginning of the current civil era. This date, according to talmudic tradition, marks the creation of the world. It was based on genealogical data quoted in the Bible (see, especially, Genesis XI—the "begats"). By careful research the rabbis tallied the number of years quoted for each generation, starting with Adam and coming down to a historically known character or event. Accepting the Torah as being literally true, the rabbis concluded that their answer correctly indicated the full span of human existence and therefore, from Genesis I, of the age of the world.

Western nations observe the solar year, based on the time the earth takes to run its course around the sun. The Jew, throughout history, has followed the lunar year. His month is regulated not by the sun, but by the moon, which herself is responsible for the word "month." It was a most obvious and easy way of reckoning the passing of time. The phases of the moon could easily be recognized by everybody. The new moon indicated the beginning of the new month. The month lasted twenty-nine or thirty days, based on the period of 29½ days it takes the moon to encircle the earth, but avoiding counting half a day into one month.

22

Twelve lunar months form the Jewish year, which counts 354 days. Their names were adopted in the Babylonian exile, 2,500 years ago, and have not changed since:

1. Tishri
2. (Mar)Cheshvan
3. Kislev
4. Tevet
5. Sh'vat
6. Adar
7. Nisan
8. Iyar
9. Sivan
10. Tamuz
11. Av
12. Ellul

The difference of length between the Jewish lunar and the Christian solar year created an obvious difficulty. Being eleven days shorter, the Jewish calendar in its original form could not always observe the seasonal festivals (bound up with the movement of the earth around the sun) at their proper time in the Holy Land: Passover as the season of the barley harvest in the spring, and Tabernacles as the feast of the gathering of fruit in the fall. To solve the problem and ensure that the holy days should fall at their appropriate season, the Jew introduced his unique leap year, adding not just one day but a whole month. Seven times in every cycle of nineteen years it is inserted after the sixth month, Adar. Having no name of its own, it is called just the month of "Again Adar" or "Adar II" (in Hebrew: *V'Adar* or *Adar sheni*).

The calendar is further complicated by additional rules devised to prevent certain festivals from occurring at forbidden or inconvenient dates. For example, the Day of Atonement is not permitted to fall on either the day before or the day after the Sabbath, since this would make the necessary preparation and celebration quite impossible.

The very nature of the Jewish calendar, with its shorter months and its recurring leap years, naturally causes Jewish dates to vary from those of the civil calendar. Solar and lunar dates coincide only once in every nineteen years. During that cycle they may differ by anything up to thirty days.

The Jewish day begins at night, when three stars can be clearly seen by the naked eye. This has its origin in the biblical story of creation, where evening preceded morning: "And God called the light day, and the darkness He called night. And there was evening and there was morning, one day." Thus, Sabbaths and festivals are celebrated from sunset of one day to sunset of the next, and the actual hour of their commencement varies according to the seasons.

The Luach does not possess any special names for the days of the week. They are simply called "the first day," "the second day," and so forth. However, so important is the sacred seventh day that the previous day is known as "eve of the Sabbath" and the day itself as "Sabbath."

For many centuries there was no written calendar. Though the "new moon" could be observed by every individual, to prevent any mistake or doubt the duty of fixing the new month was assigned to a rabbinical council in Jerusalem. Their decision was subject to the testimony of two reliable witnesses. As soon as their report had been received and checked by astronomical calculation, an official message was sent out by chains of fire signals. When these were observed in outlying communities, the "new moon" was celebrated there.

This system was continued—the Jews are deeply conservative —until the second century of the current era, when, infuriated at being refused recognition as Jews, the Samaritans adopted the mischievous practice of lighting fires on hilltops a few days before new moon so as to confuse and annoy Jewish settlements and cause them to celebrate their festivals on wrong days. To counter this, Rabbi Judah the Elder instituted a system of "dispatch runners" in place of the fire signals.

While this no doubt frustrated the Samaritans, it created another difficulty. Given alert watchers, the fire signals could traverse the length and breadth of the Holy Land in a very short time. Messengers, however, were much slower, so that settlements near or beyond the boundaries usually did not receive their signal until the following day, which added to the confusion caused by the Samaritans. On the other hand, to permit the remote settlers themselves to proclaim their own new moon would be an intolerable slight to the proper tribunal and an infringement on its privilege.

The dilemma was resolved, as in the modern fashion, with a compromise. Village elders were authorized to watch for the new moon, to announce it, and to prepare for its proper celebration. These arrangements, however, were dependent on the arrival, the following day, of the official messenger. Thereupon, to show proper deference to the central authority, the village concerned had to repeat the celebration.

This strange custom explains why, to this day, Orthodox Jews living outside Israel add an extra day to their festivals, observing Passover for eight days, instead of the seven ordained in the Bible, and two days of Shavuot instead of one. Being in all things realistic, however, the authorities made an exception in the case of the Day of Atonement. To abstain from food and drink for twenty-four hours is something of an affliction, but to extend this to forty-eight hours could be dangerous to health. It is of interest to note that some ultra-Orthodox Jews at the conclusion of the Atonement service have a speedy and frugal meal and immediately renew their fast for a second day.

With the destruction of the Jewish State (in 70 C.E.*) and the eventual elimination of the centralized rabbinical court (the Sanhedrin), the Jewish people were dispersed far and wide throughout the known world. This meant that the messenger system could not be operated, and accordingly publication of a fixed calendar was needed. Calculations based on astronomical forecasts had to take the place of visual observation. The work was put in hand; and finally the calendar, in its present form, together with the basic rules, previously jealously guarded secrets, were published by the second Rabbi Hillel in the year 359 C.E.

With the publication of a more or less fixed calendar, there was no need to celebrate an additional festival day. Nevertheless, most Jewish communities, simply to preserve a tradition, continued the practice. In more modern times, Reform congregations, fully aware of the origin of the custom, like the Jews in Israel, keep only the precise number of days as prescribed in the Bible.

* C.E.: Common (or Current or Civil) Era.

In ordinary life, Jews naturally follow the civil calendar of the countries in which they live. But in every religious respect, they still observe their own "reckoning." This determines not only the celebration of all festivals but also the date of the attainment of religious maturity (the bar mitzvah), the commemoration of the anniversary of the death of one's parents (the Yahrzeit), and the dating of the marriage certificate and tombstone.

The Jewish calendar has had and still retains some influences on other religions. The Moslems, for example, adopted the Jewish system of the lunar year, but did not introduce the corrective leap year with its extra month. Thus, the festivals of Islam fall at times which (according to the current calendar) vary from year to year. Christianity, while regulating almost all its religious events in accordance with the civil calendar, still fixes Easter according to the Jewish system of chronology.

Interestingly, it is recorded that on his voyage of discovery, Christopher Columbus used a Hebrew almanac, specially translated and prepared by the Spanish Jewish astronomer Abraham Zacuto.

Jewish worship has its special prayer for the blessing of the new moon. The beginning of each month is sanctified with a special service and a reading from the Scroll of the Law. The rabbis stressed that it was not accidental that the Jew's attention was focused on the moon. Her fate was identical with Jewish existence. Both are often reduced to almost an invisible minimum; yet they are indestructible and in due time regain their waned strength.

It will have been noted above that the phrase "before" or "after the Current (or Civil) Era" was employed in place of the usual abbreviations "B.C." or "A.D." While these are normally used in a quite perfunctory manner, it is true that the former represents Jesus as Christ the Messiah, while the latter identifies him as Dominus the Lord.

The Jews recognize the Jew Jesus as a great religious figure of his day, but to be consistent with their own theology, they deem it proper to use the clear but not contentious terminology "B.C.E." or "C.E."

Chapter 5

THE CYCLE OF THE JEWISH YEAR

Only religion can give human existence unity, meaning, and value. Every day in Jewish life, therefore, has its moments of devotion and its requirement to seek God in its many and varied events and happenings. But the turmoil and cares of life make such occasions, if at all observed, rare, intermittent, and short-lived.

To ensure religion its rightful, permanent place, Judaism introduced its holy days. Like a sacred bond they girdle the year. They make man pause in his daily work to confront reality and to renew faith. To a mere succession of days they impart rhythm and purpose. On holy days all work has to stop, and the world of material things is replaced by the world of the spirit. Holy days are the powerhouses that renew spiritual strength and the lighthouses that give life its direction.

This is the aim of all Jewish holy days, Sabbaths and festivals alike. In addition, though varied in their emphasis and occurrence, other features are distinct. The "appointed seasons" of the year celebrate significant events in the history of the Jewish people, evaluating their eternal message. They foster within the Jew a consciousness of his mission and a vision of history as the working out of divine providence.

The rhythm of nature enters the meaning of three of the festivals. Religious celebrations marking the harvests—of barley, wheat, and fruit—are meant to teach the Jew to be thoughtful in life, grateful for its gifts, and aware of man's dependence on God, Who gives food to every being.

As each festival has its own meaning and definite message, so its symbols and moods differ, contributing a kaleidoscope of color

27

to Jewish existence. Solemnity and awe alternate with exuberance of joy; total abstinence from food, with delicious festival dishes; somber darkness, with the kindling of lights. Even the holy day melodies vary according to their message and meaning. But all Jewish festivals share the beauty of holiness. They are all essentially religious in nature. At no time do they deteriorate into mere secular holidays. They center on God and the Jewish people as a people consecrated to Him.

THE JEWISH HOLY DAYS

Sabbath

Rosh Hashanah (New Year)	Tishri	1 & 2
Yom Kippur (Day of Atonement)		10
Succot (Tabernacles)		15 (for 7 days)
Shemini Atzeret (Feast of Conclusion)		22
Simchat Torah (Rejoicing of the Law)		23
Chanukah (Feast of Lights)	Kislev	25 (for 8 days)
Purim (Feast of Lots)	Adar	14
Pesach (Passover)	Nisan	15 (for 8 days)
Shavuot (Feast of Weeks)	Sivan	6 (for 2 days)
Tishah b'Av (The Fast of Av)	Av	9

Israel and Reform Jews keep Pesach only for seven days, join Simchat Torah with Shemini Atzeret, and celebrate Shavuot solely on 6 Sivan. Rosh Hashanah, though observed in Israel for two days, is generally kept by Reform Jews only on the first day of the New Year, 1 Tishri.

The Sabbath

Every seventh day is the Sabbath. It is the most important holy day, the bond between God and man. Ahad Ha-Am, great Jewish essayist, rightly remarked that "more than the Jew has kept the Sabbath, it was the Sabbath that has kept the Jew." Its importance is so great that it was the only festival mentioned in the Ten Commandments. Its meaning is manifold and never-aging.

The social significance of the Sabbath is outstanding. It gave freedom to everybody. After six days of work, which were equally commanded and considered a human privilege, everyone, without distinction, had a right to rest. Even the dumb animal, as one of God's creatures, was included in this social legislation. Just as man's work-a-day week expressed the dignity of labor, so the rest on the seventh day established the dignity of his personality. At least one day a week every man could call his own.

All men are free and the same before God. On the Sabbath, master and servant meet as equals. Significantly Judaism has related the Sabbath to the redemption from Egyptian slavery. Weekly it should remind the Jew of his very distant past, when he himself, at the very cradle of his existence, was nothing but a rightless slave. All the more should his heart understand and go out in sympathy to those in need of rest.

The Sabbath frees all men from the burdens and anxieties of life. Forgetting them for one day a week, even the most unfortunate can find joy. The rabbis spoke of the "Delight of the Sabbath" (in Hebrew, *Oneg Shabbat*), words which became the name of one of its modern celebrations. Delight is achieved not by cheap amusement, but by this inner freedom, banning all sorrow and care. The Sabbath is the weekly recurring divine protest against oppression, injustice, and inequality.

This seventh day also serves as a continuing source of spiritual progress. It renews in man his faith in life and in the supremacy of spirit over matter. It reminds the Jew of his freedom of will, with its implicit responsibility. It does so by linking the Sabbath with the work of creation as related in the Bible—not its scientific data, but its religious message.

This world is not just an aimless assembly of atoms or the outcome of inevitable mechanical force. It is the purposeful work of God, Who is above nature and its master. According to a talmudic legend, matter once almost got out of hand, but divine will halted it. Putting it in its place, He called out: "Enough. So far and no further!"

Man in his creative force has been given divine power which he is meant to hallow and use constructively, but not to debase and abuse. Like God, he should be the master of work, and not its slave. Work must never overwhelm him and crush his soul. To cease work one day a week ensures man's freedom from enslavement to joyless toil and the world of machines. It asserts his status as a free, creative being. He is not just a cog in a wheel. But above all, to stop work, at the sacrifice of worldly gain, losing monetary profit for the sake of spiritual betterment, denotes true maturity.

The Sabbath is not simply a stoppage of work. Its aim is not negative rest, but the enobling of life. It is true that physical labor is banned (sometimes, in the past, even in its most minute expression). But all energy is now concentrated on intellectual and spiritual enrichment. This is yet another of the many unique properties of Jewish life. Not an intellectual elite or a priestly class, but all the people observe the Sabbath with devout worship and intense study. One day a week, throughout the year and throughout life, is set aside for the whole community to study its sacred books and fill the mind with inspiring thoughts and exalting ideas. The proud rich and the humble poor join together in this sacred task. Even the laborer who spends the six-day working week in toil becomes an intellectual and God-seeker on the Sabbath.

The Sabbath molded the Jew. No legislation anywhere else had ever succeeded in making a people abandon work, not to idle but to gather together in joyful study of religion and of its application in life, for religious inwardness and spiritual regeneration. The Jewish Alexandrian philosopher Philo, two thousand years ago, emphasized this phenomenon, unparalleled in history, that every seventh day "there are spread before the people innumerable lessons in prudence, justice and all other virtues, so as to improve the quality of life of every one."

The Sabbath introduced a system of universal adult training: not in the arts of war or in book learning, but in the art of living and the improvement of man's spiritual being. The day taught the Jew to achieve moral freedom from enslavement to self. From a mere day of rest and social equality, it became a day of holiness.

Babylonians knew a Sabbath. It recurred on the 7th, 14th, 19th, 22nd, and 28th days of certain months. But it was a day of gloom and fear on which the king and certain privileged classes abstained from work out of terror.

To the Jew, from the beginning of his history, the Sabbath

was a day of joy and universal rest. According to tradition, even the patriarchs and the Israelites under Egyptian bondage kept it! In biblical times desecration of the Sabbath became a punishable offense. The manna itself stopped falling on the seventh day, so that the Israelites should rest even in the desert.

It was the day when the people called on the "man of God," to be led spiritually, and to be inspired. They visited the Temple, where on the Sabbath twelve loaves of bread were newly placed on one of the golden tables.

The early neglect of its sanctification is apparent by the emphasis laid on this very point by the prophets: "If you refrain from doing your own business upon the Sabbath, on My sacred day, and hold the Sabbath a delight, and the Eternal's sacred day an honour... not doing business, and not talking idly, then you shall have delight in the Eternal's favour." On their return from Babylonian exile, the Jews' religious consciousness had deteriorated to such an extent that in Jerusalem itself the Sabbath became the weekly market day. Only sternest measures by Nehemiah eventually succeeded in restoring the Sabbath observance.

By the time of the Maccabees, the Sabbath had become one of the outstanding symbols of Judaism. In his campaign to destroy the Jewish faith, Emperor Antiochus IV of Syria realized the Sabbath's importance and made its observance punishable by death. Thousands of martyrs chose to die rather than to profane the Sabbath. In their "wars of liberation" the Maccabees had first refused to take up arms on the Sabbath. Only when the enemy took advantage of the undefended Jewish positions did bitter experience establish a new ruling which permitted fighting on the Sabbath in self-defense. Later again, the postbiblical talmudic period further anchored the Sabbath in the Jewish soul as a day of sanctification and rest. Every means was devised to embellish the day, to increase its sacred joy and keep out any profane influence. Houses were decorated with myrtle, white Sabbath garments were worn, and most of the day was spent in the synagogue or in the house of study. Sermons were preached then, two thousand years ago, and eagerly listened to by men and women alike. Many volumes of collected addresses of that early period (the Midrashim) are still in existence, giving even the names of the preachers. An additional (third) meal was introduced to honor the day, and people felt that "the spice of the Sabbath" made it taste different and much better.

To ensure a complete day of rest, much legislation was enacted. Thirty-nine categories summarized prohibited activities. The observant Jew did not write, ride, light a fire, or carry anything on the Sabbath. His walks were restricted. Even meals had to be prepared on the preceding day, giving equal rest to women, whose work in the house otherwise never ceased. The Sabbath was a day of joy, and therefore all mourning ceremonials were suspended.

Then the Middle Ages brought the ghetto, with its harsh discrimination, humiliation, and persecution. Barred like cattle behind high walls, the Jew was sustained by the Sabbath alone. On that day he forgot his troubles and anguish. Hounded throughout the week, on that one day he became a free man. The Sabbath was announced from a high roof by the blast of the ram's horn, repeated three times at long intervals. At this joyful signal, shops and workrooms were closed, and the community, arrayed in Sabbath garments, assembled at the synagogue to say a welcome to "Sabbath the bride" and to thank God for Sabbath rest and peace. Then they returned to their homes in happy family unity around the spotless Sabbath table, gleaming in the light of the Sabbath candles—too gentle to reveal the ghetto walls, but clear enough to illumine the signs of God's goodness and providence.

With the era of emancipation the ghetto walls fell. The Jew now mixed freely with his fellow citizens and became largely one of them. Of necessity, Sabbath observance again changed, but the Sabbath eve at home remained, with its beauty and charm. Orthodoxy, stressing the immutability of Jewish law, demanded the Sabbath's complete, traditional observance. Reform Judaism reinterpreted the old laws for the present day.

The creation of the State of Israel renewed the force of the Sabbath. Once again it became the national day of rest. As in olden days, it is announced by the blast of the ram's horn, and an atmosphere of dedication suddenly envelops everyday life.

From Israel itself, a new way of celebrating the Sabbath has spread all over the world. It is called by the biblical word Oneg Shabbat. It consists of informal assemblies, with intellectual debates, spiritual discourses, and communal singing. It owes its origin to Chaim Nahman Bialik, greatest modern Hebrew poet, who introduced it soon after his arrival at Tel Aviv in 1923. On the Sabbath afternoon the community assembled first in his home and later in a specially donated building.

Bialik himself explained the Oneg as having been created out of the necessity to build modern Israel on the strongest foundation of Judaism. No form could be found loftier or more profound than the Sabbath, "which preceded the giving of the Torah and was observed by the children of Israel while they were still in Egypt. The Sabbath is indeed the cornerstone of Judaism, and it is not without cause that it is called the 'sign of the Covenant' between God and the children of Israel."

Thus, the Sabbath has been part of Jewish life from its earliest history to the present day. It is no exaggeration to say that it was the gateway to Judaism. Neglect of it inevitably weakened the Jew's spiritual heritage, while observance of it gave him strength, joy, and survival.

Judaism early realized the importance of the home. Friday night is family night. The Sabbath eve unites parents and children in family prayer. The festive table, the starched linen, the finest crockery—all contribute toward the glory of the Sabbath. The father blesses each of the children individually. He praises his wife with the ancient song from the book of Proverbs: "Many women have done worthily, but you surpass them all." The mother lights the candles, which are the symbol of joy. At least two in number, they are a recollection of the twofold message of the Sabbath: God's creative power and man's social duty. The father sanctifies the holy day by blessing a goblet of wine. He breaks the bread and thanks God for his daily food. Two loaves are used as a reminder of the double portion of manna that was gathered in the wilderness on the eve of the

Sabbath. They are called challah, which was the original name of the piece of dough taken from each baking as a gift for the priests. German tradition calls them *Berchos*—a word possibly derived from the Hebrew for "benedictions" (*brochos*), but also explained as a corruption of the German Berchta, goddess of vegetation, who was honored by German women by the presentation of twisted bread.

The poor or homeless are invited to share the family meal on Friday night and to join in their songs and joy. To have his coffin made out of the boards of the very table at which he entertained the needy on the Sabbath, used to be the host's sacred wish.

Special services "sanctified" the Sabbath in the synagogue. Additional prayers and readings from the Torah and the prophets explained and emphasized its message.

Each Sabbath certainly was a day eagerly looked forward to throughout the week and then never forgotten. As the Kiddush (the "sanctification" of wine) introduces the Sabbath, so a special ceremony of *Havdalah* (distinction) marks its ending. A cup of wine, filled to overflowing, is a hopeful symbol of richest blessing; a spice box, whose perfume is inhaled, a last gift of the passing day; and the shining flame of a braided taper, a reminder of the light that came first in creation and must shine throughout our lives. The Sabbath over, Jews wish each other "Gut Woch" (A good week).

It is rarely realized that it is to the Jew that humanity owes its weekly universal day of rest. Indeed, the Sabbath is perhaps the greatest contribution Judaism has made to civilization and happiness. The institution of the Sabbath was so new in the non-Jewish world that at first it was met not only with ridicule but with bitter opposition. Seneca, political philosopher of the first century, complained that its wide adoption among the Romans wasted one-seventh of the working life of man!

Both Christianity and Islam adopted the Sabbath. At first they, too, celebrated it together with the Jew on the seventh day. Then, to stress its separate identity, Christianity replaced it with the Sunday (but not until the fourth century) and the Moslems with the Friday. Today, the Ethiopian Church and the Seventh-Day Adventists still continue the original tradition of keeping the Sabbath itself. The Christian sect of the Sabbatarians derived their very name from its strict observance. Modern social legislation, with its guaranteed days of rest, perpetuates the Jewish idea of the Sabbath.

The Jew has long employed a special form of greeting dedicated particularly to the Sabbath and festivals. When Jews meet just before or during any of these days, their greeting, inevitably, is "Good Shabbos" (Sabbath) or "Good Yom Tov" (holy day).

There is no corresponding greeting in the general community. It is, of course, the custom to say "Merry Christmas," but one does not hear, for example, "Happy Easter," and certainly never "Happy Sunday."

There should be food for philosophical thought in this sharp distinction between the adherents of two great religious systems.

The Jewish New Year—A Solemn Season

The annual cycle of holy days commences with a two-day celebration (one day in Reform) of the New Year, usually falling during September or October.

It might seem reasonable to think of the festival as having lots of fun, drink, and noise. But, on the contrary, it is a most solemn day, distinguished by reflection, prayer, and penitence. It is not a national festival or historical celebration. It is a day of universal significance: a holy day, not a holiday. The Jew looks back on it, sums up his failures and failings, and then looks forward, striving to take new bearings.

New Year deals with man's soul and humanity's future. Jews assemble in their synagogues all over the world. They ask God's forgiveness for man's sin and pray for the unification of mankind. "Unite all of us in the bond of brotherhood," commences one of its many beautiful, thousand-year-old prayers.

In Hebrew, the Jew calls his New Year Rosh Hashanah (the head of the year). This is not just a manner of speech, but a deliberate choice of words. The first day of the New Year bears the same importance to all other days as the head to the rest of the body. It has meaning only when joined to all the other days as the source of spiritual and moral regeneration and universal renewal of life.

The New Year aims at man's realizing his sins and resolving to mend his ways and return to God. Learning from past errors, he must have the honesty to admit them, the courage to begin again, and the faith that divine love always gives man and humanity—if determined on a better life—another chance. All New Year customs and prayers express this idea and pursue its attainment, even in the way the Jew counts his years.

Christian nations commence the era of their calendar with the birth of Christ, and Moslems with Mohammed's flight from Mecca to Medina. The ancient Greeks used the Olympic Games as their measuring rod of time, while the Romans counted their years from the foundation of Rome. Applying parallel principles, the Jewish calendar might have commenced with Abraham's birth, Moses' flight from Egypt, or Joshua's conquest of the Holy Land. Yet none of the dates of these events was chosen. The Jew related his calendar not to any part of his own history, but to the universe, counting his years "from the creation of the world."

Certainly, everyone knows today that not a mere five thousand, but uncountable millions of years have elapsed since that mysterious moment. But geological and cosmological facts belong to science. Religion is concerned with the essence of man. Though the actual figure of the Jewish year as a scientific statement is quite fictitious, its importance as a religious symbol is most vital.

Here, history is contemplated not from the narrow, national point of view, but in the perspective of eternity. Life is seen not in fragments, but in its totality; mankind not as separate races, nations, and peoples, but as one humanity. Rosh Hashanah therefore teaches humility and the unity of man. Compared with the grandeur of the universe and the length of time, our individual existence is "like the grass that withereth, the flower that fadeth, like a shadow that moveth on, a cloud that passeth by, a mote of dust that is blown away, a dream that is no more."

Yet within man there is a spark of eternity, raising him above time and mortality. On this day of creation man and nations must give account of how they have used their God-given faculties. Regret at failure and sin is not enough. Even reparation of the damage done does not suffice. Judaism demands positive and constructive action. "Repentance" in Hebrew really means "return"—to God's ways.

Divine forgiveness must be preceded by, and can never be attained without, human reconciliation. A world at war, or man at strife—unjust, hard of heart, and divided in himself—cannot find peace in God. Man must first right all wrongs, must ask and obtain forgiveness from those he has hurt. On these days of awe the Jew prays for humanity, a better world, and the rule of righteousness. He asks for the destruction not of the wicked, but of wickedness. God does not desire the death of the sinner, but "that he return from his evil way and live."

In its universal vision, Rosh Hashanah stresses the importance of mutual responsibility. We all are our brother's keeper and must bear his burden and share his sin: "Our Father, our King, we have sinned before Thee." The rabbis wisely admonished that "if one prays for happiness in the year to come, one must be prepared to give that for which one prays."

New Year is the judgment day for each individual and all nations. On this day, God determines "how many shall pass away and how many shall be born; who shall live and who shall die; who in the fulness of his days and who before his time; who shall be tranquil and who shall be harassed; who shall be brought low, and who shall be raised." The decision is neither arbitrary nor final. It is not the outcome of an autocrat's whim or of inevitable, impersonal fate. It is the result of man's own actions. Life or death, annihilation or reconciliation, are not forced on but freely chosen by him.

Man can avert "the evil decree" in a threefold way: by a total reorientation of his ways, returning to life's lasting values; by a united spiritual effort led by prayer; by loving-kindness expressed in social action.

On New Year, the Jew sounds the shofar. The oldest-known wind instrument being a ram's horn, its blowing during the service has a deep and manifold symbolism. It is considered so important that the festival itself has been called "The Day of the Clarion Call." Even the horn's bent shape has been interpreted as conveying that only the humble and contrite in heart, never the arrogant and proud, can find God.

From ancient days, the sound of the shofar has been a rallying call to the community and has announced all its significant days. In specially prescribed notes and sequence, the same sounds are heard on Rosh Hashanah in every synagogue the world over. Only a man of outstanding character is permitted to fulfill the sacred task, "to blow the shofar." Far from being tuneful and soothing, its sounds are rousing and shattering. They are meant to stir man to the very depth of his being, to call to his conscience to renew his faith and to return to God.

To be ready always to answer His call and to trust in Him even in the face of the incomprehensible is a further lesson of the shofar, derived from the day's special biblical passage, dealing with Abraham's trial. In it, the ram's horn is closely associated with the supreme example of unqualified obedience to divine will. Abraham, asked by God to offer his only and beloved son Isaac as a sacrifice, did not realize that he was being subjected only to a test of faith. Yet he never wavered. Even at the hour of greatest anguish, unquestioningly he obeyed God's will, believing that everything God did must have its purpose. The trial over and Isaac's life saved, Abraham suddenly perceived a ram caught by its horns in a thicket and sacrificed it instead of his son. That is why the sounding of a ram's horn, the shofar, has become the symbol of supreme loyalty, knowing no exception and denying no sacrifice. It signifies unshakable faith in God's love, which, though often inscrutable in its ways, shapes man's destiny. New Year is the most universal of all anniversaries and unequaled as a time of self-scrutiny and judgment, repentance and return to God.

Strangely enough, the name Rosh Hashanah itself is not mentioned in the Bible. It first occurs in the Talmud. In the Torah, it is called the "Day of Memorial" and the "Day of the Clarion

Call." Though now celebrated as the beginning of the year, in the biblical calendar the festival falls at the commencement of the seventh month. Emphasizing its message, varied and even strange customs have become associated with it. One of the more beautiful is the tradition that still persists of starting the meal on New Year's Eve with a dish of fresh apples, sliced and dipped in honey. This is intended to symbolize the universal hope that the coming year may be one of sweetness and joy. The same thought is further expressed by the avoidance of any dish that is peppery or bitter, such as the popular condiment made from horseradish and beetroot.

There was also a custom according to which whole families —men, women, and children—went on the afternoon of New Year's Day to the banks of a flowing stream into which, with simple symbolism, they cast their sins. Despite strong opposition from rabbinical authority, this practice persisted for many centuries.

There is symbolism, too, in the customary Jewish New Year greeting, "May you be inscribed for a happy year." This is used during the ten days from New Year to the Day of Atonement, but toward the end of the period it is changed to "May you be inscribed and sealed for a happy year." This is based on the talmudic tradition that while on New Year's Day God writes the destiny of man in the Book of Judgment, yet, waiting for man's repentance, He keeps it unconfirmed until the Day of Atonement, when finally it will be sealed.

The Day of Atonement

The Day of Atonement, Yom Kippur, is the climax of the ten days of penitence with which the Jewish year commences. This is the most sacred day of all, a day for self-searching, for purification, for turning from sin—the "Sabbath of Sabbaths."

The religious philosophy of the day is indicated by the English form of its name. By his sins, man has lost his sense of unity with God and by his self-centered life has not only drifted away from his Maker but also separated himself from his fellow men. Yom Kippur comes to urge him to "penitence, charity and prayer." By these, he can again become *at-one* with the Almighty and with his brethren.

Before the eve of the holy day, Jews kindle a light in the home. This is intended to burn for the whole twenty-four hours as a memorial to dead kinsmen. In the synagogue, pious men enrobe themselves in white shrouds which serve not only as symbols of purity and equality but also as a reminder of the Day of Judgment, when all men must at last meet their God face to face. The service opens with the famous and often misunderstood prayer Kol Nidre, sung to a glorious, soul-stirring melody which has been an inspiration through the ages and throughout the world. In fact, the whole evening service has been called by the name of this one prayer.

All day long the Jew remains at the synagogue in continuous prayer. All adults, men and women alike, fast for twenty-four hours until the "concluding service," which ends with a united reading of the Jewish declaration of faith, the *Sh'ma Yisrael*. Finally, the sound of the shofar announces that the Day of Atonement has come to its close.

During its long history, the Day of Atonement has passed through various stages of development. At the Temple in Jerusalem, the high priest used to offer special sacrifices to make atonement for the sins of the whole community. The climax of this service came when, alone and filled with awe, the high priest entered the Holy of Holies and, prostrating himself before the Ark, called on the name of God. Later, in a ceremonial which is recalled in the word "(e)scape-goat," the high priest symbolically loaded the sins of the people on the head of a sacrificial goat, which was then driven out into the wilderness to "escape" there.

In the early rabbinical era, Yom Kippur was not the solemn day of our modern age. The knowledge of God's grace and the hope of forgiveness gave it a joyful note. During the afternoon the happy communities gathered in the vineyards outside Jerusalem, singing and dancing. Maidens, all attired alike in white garments, addressed themselves to the young men, calling on them to choose their partners without too much concern for outward appearance: "Give not attention to beauty of face: heed rather the beauty of our souls."

After the destruction of the Temple, the people felt more strongly than ever that it was not a ritual of expiation, but an inner change of heart alone that could ensure forgiveness of sins. Rabbi Yochanan ben Zakkai comforted the people by quoting the words of the prophet Hosea: "God desires mercy and not sacrifice." The prophetic lesson read on Yom Kippur morning itself emphasizes self-sacrificing love as the truest kind of fasting. Maimonides, centuries later, said, "Repentance atones for all iniquities."

Talmudic teaching early stressed the importance of the understanding of the real meaning of atonement: "If one says, 'I will sin, and the Day of Atonement will bring me forgiveness,' the Day of Atonement will bring him no forgiveness. For sins of man against God, the Day of Atonement atones, but for transgressions against a fellow-man, it does so only after one has first become reconciled to him." The "penitential days" preceding Yom Kippur have thus become a period of sincere reconciliation. All grievances must be made up and any bitter feeling within one's heart be forgotten. To right the wrong and to forgive one's enemies are indispensable conditions of the efficacy of the Day of Atonement.

The vital need is a real change of heart and mind, to be achieved by repentance and regeneration. To renew life, man must first become conscious of his failings, which only too often have become second nature to him. Then, regretting and amending them, he must determine never to repeat them. After he has completely broken with his sinful past, the Day of Atonement, so to speak, renders him "a new creature." The Jew denies the necessity of any mediator; man himself confronts his God.

Yom Kippur does not speak only of man's individual sin. It stresses corporate responsibility. Mankind is one, and therefore all men are bound up with each other. A collective confession of sins is one of the most distinctive features of the service on the Day of Atonement. This takes the form of a "litany" of sins, expressed in the first person plural and arranged in alphabetical order. Reading in unison, members of the congregation make confession of *"our* sins," whether committed under compulsion or willingly, in ignorance or through folly, openly or secretly, in thought, word, or action, knowingly or in error. Almost every possible aspect of sin is included in this unique list of man's failings. Among them are mentioned contentiousness, hardness of heart, sensuality, pride, envy, laxity of morals, stubbornness, hatred, breach of trust, and confusion of mind. After each paragraph the whole community pleads: "O God of forgiveness, forgive us, pardon us, grant us remission."

Such all-embracing confession makes everyone fully aware of his own sins but also emphasizes his share of guilt in the wrongs committed by others. Here, again, Jewish universalism extends its concern to all humanity. On Yom Kippur, nothing is restricted merely to Jewish fate. All its prayers aim at the salvation of mankind. One of its lessons, the book of Jonah, specially includes even the pagan in divine grace and forgiveness.

The Jew's fast on this day is unique of its kind. When a Moslem fasts he abstains from food and drink for a whole month from sunrise to sunset, but during each night renews his strength. A Roman Catholic does not eat meat. But the Jew on the Day of Atonement for twenty-four hours continuously neither eats nor drinks!

However, the mere act of fasting does not ensure forgiveness. One of the teachings of the book of Jonah is that it was not when the Ninevites fasted and put on sackcloth that God forgave them, but only when they turned from their evil way. The passage from the prophet Isaiah which constitutes the other reading of the day goes even further when, almost in a paradox, it explains that the true fast is to feed the hungry and to give drink to the thirsty.

Yet the fast can serve to achieve religious aims of great importance. It leads to mental concentration and higher spirituality. By it, the Jew asserts his will against his appetites. He shows that he can be stronger than his desires. At the same time, such exercise strengthens his willpower, so essential in the fight against evil without and temptation within. But his fast represents, especially, an act of repentance for man's sin. It is the greatest united and regularly recurring spiritual effort for mankind.

The Jews' setting apart of one day in every year to concentrate to the utmost of their ability on the spiritual advancement of man is without parallel in the history of humanity. The fact that all Jews everywhere, on the very same day, unite in this fast is tremendous. That they have done so year by year for centuries is immeasurable in its significance. The Jew has contributed in many ways and in almost every field to the happiness of man. He has done so unconsciously, perhaps merely by chance. But on the Day of Atonement, the Jew strives with keenest intention and concentration to help mankind, a task which to him is the only purpose of his existence. He battles to bring nearer the time when God's Kingdom will be established on earth for all men, with discord, disunity, and disbelief replaced by reconciliation, faith, and atonement. The rabbis declared that even if all other holy days should no longer be observed, the Day of Atonement, so universal and human, will always remain.

Succot—The Feast of Tabernacles

On the very night that Yom Kippur ended, the observant Jew of former times used to start building the *succah*, which symbolizes and gives its name to the next festival, starting five days later. The succah is a simple, one-roomed booth or hut built, without nails, of branches, twigs, and leaves and decorated with fruit and flowers.

"Tabernacles" lasts seven days. For the whole of this period the Jew was meant to spend most of his time, and certainly to take all his meals, in this frail hut. Once every home possessed its own succah, and all the family participated in its building. Now, all too often, the succah may be found only at the synagogue, and Jews merely gather there after the service. Yet its multiple symbolism is undying.

Succot commemorates the Jews' wandering through the desert, where for forty years they dwelt in flimsy tents and yet were securely rooted in the knowledge of God's love. The succah itself, a temporary and insecure dwelling, serves to remind the Jew of the many transient homes from which in his unhappy past he was driven forth and that though he was scorned and humiliated by man, he ever had the guidance and protection of God. Furthermore, this ramshackle booth, continually reminding the Jew of his humble origin, teaches him to be modest and to be mindful of those who are still friendless and homeless.

Tabernacles, also named "The Season of Our Rejoicing," further commemorates the feast held in the fall in ancient Israel to mark the harvest of fruit and vine, and the succah is the counterpart of the shelters built in the fields and the vineyards so that the workers could find shade from the burning sun.

In grateful joy the Jew expresses his thanks for God's innumerable gifts. He knows only too well that without divine help he would labor in vain. At the synagogue services for this festival, the worshipers hold aloft the lulav and etrog. These consist of a citron, a shoot of the palm tree, three twigs of myrtle, and two willow branches and serve as reminders of the great variety of vegetation with which God has blessed this earth.

Succot, like Passover and the Feast of Weeks, is one of the "three pilgrimages" in which the Israelites of old formed joyful processions from all corners of the Holy Land and marched to the Temple in Jerusalem, taking thanks offerings from their flocks and from the harvest of their fields.

The Feast of Tabernacles, the historical and agricultural thanksgiving of the Jewish people, also has its universal message. It speaks of the power of faith that sustained even pursued fugitives. The succah is deemed to be built properly only if the stars are visible through the roof. Its very frailty is intended to remind man not to waste his life in the pursuit of shadows, but to dedicate his God-given faculties to lasting values. It calls on humanity not to put their trust in physical strength, but to remember that it was the power of the spirit alone that sustained the Jews throughout their storm-tossed existence.

The rabbis saw in the succah a guide to happiness, which cannot depend on material things, but can surely be found in a simple hut, provided only that kindness and love are also to be found there. That the succah had to conform with definite measurements, which could neither be exceeded nor lessened, should teach man to build his life wisely, neither on too grandiose a scale nor too subservient a pattern.

From individual life, the Feast of Tabernacles then turns to human existence. In the days of the Temple seventy different sacrifices were offered for the well-being of all the nations of the world, then believed to be seventy in number. The lulav and etrog are pointed in turn to the four quarters of the compass, toward heaven and toward the earth, to proclaim God's omnipresence. Even the four kinds of plants, so different in value, appearance, and aroma, were to the rabbis symbolic of the brotherhood of man, which must unite all different kinds and conditions. Only if etrog and lulav are held close together is the Jew permitted to pronounce the benediction. Likewise, the rabbis pointed out, God's blessing can rest on mankind only if its many and diverse races, peoples, and colors have found unity.

Succot not only stressed this unity of man across all frontiers but defied all class distinction. To God, people were not rich or poor, but only good or bad. A special "water libation" implied a protest by the masses against those who claimed that the costlier the sacrifice, the more acceptable it would be to God. The offering of water, obtainable free anywhere, democratized religion. Both rich and poor had an equal opportunity of serving God, Who was not concerned with the price of the gift, but with the sincerity of the giver.

Tabernacles thus has a manifold message of the personal and universal, the historical and eternal. The Jew can truly pray on these seven festive days, so full of gladness and joy, that the Tabernacle of Peace may spread over all the children of God, whoever and wherever they may be.

The month of Tishri is crowded with festivals. Twelve of its days (apart from the Sabbaths) are holy days. Now, with the festival of Tabernacles over, the Jew holds a special holy day to celebrate the completion of all festivals and calls this Eighth Day of the Assembly (Shemini Atzeret) or The Feast of Conclusion. On the following day comes the last scene in this cavalcade of holy days, The Rejoicing of the Law (Simchat Torah). (Reform Judaism combines the two days.) Most recently introduced of the holy days, it probably originated in the ninth century of our era. On each Sabbath throughout the year, the Jew reads a section of the Torah of such length that he completes the Five Books of Moses within one year. This cycle of weekly portions is so timed that on Simchat Torah he reads the last verses of Deuteronomy and the first verses of Genesis, symbolizing the truth that to the Law of God there is neither ending nor beginning. Like God Himself, His word is eternal.

All the Scrolls are taken out of the Ark and in joyful procession carried around the synagogue. A lighted candle is put in their place, as the Torah itself is a symbol of light. Children, carrying miniature Scrolls of the Law and waving flags above their heads, join in the marching and singing. Later in the service, all men and boys, regardless of age, are called forward to the Ark to read a blessing over the Torah. A special honor is reserved for two men selected on the basis not of wealth or position, but of religious merit and communal service. Termed, respectively, "bridegroom of the Law" (chatan torah) and "bridegroom of creation" (chatan b'reshit), they have the distinction of blessing in turn the ending of one cycle and the commencement of the next.

A most joyful celebration thus closes this season of concentrated, spiritual effort. The song in which cantor and congregation join on this day is its very leitmotiv: "Let us rejoice and be glad with this Law, for it is strength and light for us."

Chanukah—The Feast of Lights

Chanukah lasts eight days and falls during December. It means "consecration," as it commemorates the rededication of the Temple in Jerusalem in 165 B.C.E. after it had been desecrated by three years of heathen worship. It celebrates the supremacy of spiritual values over material forces and the right of every people to lead its own life freely, according to its conscience. After a life-and-death struggle against the overwhelming odds of the Syrian invaders, a small band of undaunted fighters—

the Maccabees—defeated this most highly organized army of occupation. They freed the Holy Land not only from the foreign invader but from the rule of pagan materialism. The Maccabees were the first army in history to take up arms not for the enlarging of their border nor for booty, but for an ideal.

Nightly at this season the Jew lights the Menorah, as the eight-branched candelabrum came to be called, after the original seven-branched candlestick of the Temple: the first night one candle, the second night two, and so forth, until, on the last night, all eight lights together shine forth as a symbol of the ever-growing triumph of the forces of light over the powers of darkness. This ceremony has been carried out in myriads of Jewish homes throughout the world for almost 2,200 years.

Chanukah is a minor festival, which means that during its eight days the Jew is permitted to carry out his normal, daily work. Nevertheless, as a national occasion with a background of great patriotic heroism, it is widely celebrated to this day; and especially since the establishment of modern Israel, the Menorah is kindled with as much enthusiasm as ever in the past. It has an appeal particularly to the children and, perhaps to fix it in their minds, is associated with a special type of pancake (latke), with spinning-tops (dreidels), and with the giving of presents (Chanukah-Gelt).

Historically, the festival of Chanukah owes its origin to an early, would-be dictator, Antiochus IV of Syria, who proclaimed himself "Epiphanes" (The Divine), but came to be known as "Epimanes" (The Madman). Ignoring or underestimating the value of spiritual faith, Antiochus set forth to conquer the world and by force of arms to impose his pagan ideals on the subdued people. Nation after nation succumbed, but the tiny and apparently insignificant Jewish people dared to offer resistance to the onslaught which aimed to destroy not only their bodies but also their souls.

Taking personal command, Antiochus issued ruthless edicts, to be enforced by brutal bands of trained officers—the brownshirts of those days. The observance of Judaism was totally prohibited, and it was made a capital offense to observe the Sabbath, to initiate a man-child into the Covenant of Abraham, to hold public worship, or to give religious instruction.

The Temple of Jerusalem was desecrated. A statue of Zeus was erected in the Holy of Holies, and the altar was defiled with the blood of swine.

The reign of horror was not satisfied with the prohibition of Judaism. It aimed at forcing the Jewish people to worship heathen idols. In public, they had to prove their loyalty to the new state religion, not by verbal affirmations but by deeds. The animal most obnoxious to the Jewish mind was used for this purpose. All over the country, Syrian soldiery erected pagan altars, coercing the whole population to worship there and to eat the flesh of swine. The campaign, fiendishly planned and efficiently executed, reached even the smallest villages.

Panic seized the population. The weaklings yielded in fear, but thousands died the deaths of martyrs. Others, attracted by pagan ideals or the promise of material gain, cooperated with the occupation forces. A program of total Hellenization and de-Judaization was in progress, eagerly supported by Quisling priests. People changed their Jewish-sounding names into Greek ones and tried to remove from their bodies the seal of Abraham so that they could appear as equals in the gymnasia opened up in the Hebrew cities. Modern Greek literature took the place of Holy Scriptures. To appear Greek in speech, dress, and custom became the fashion of the day.

The combination of complete assimilation and merciless persecution seemed likely to achieve its aim, when, in the small village of Modin, north of Jerusalem, Mattathias, an ancient priest, and his five sons rebelled. Proudly they proclaimed that even if all the people of the empire obeyed the tyrant, never would they recede from their faith. They slew the local Quisling and destroyed the pagan altar, killed the enemy soldiers and called on all the zealous to join them in their fight for freedom.

Their fame rapidly spread abroad. They came to be as much feared by the Syrians as they were watched with hope by the Jews, under the name of the Maccabees. The origin of the word is uncertain. Some hold that the most valiant of the five sons, Judas, was nicknamed "Maccabeus" or "The Hammerer." Others, however, claim that the word was derived from the initials of the four Hebrew words which comprised the battle cry of the brethren: "Who is like unto Thee, O Lord, among the mighty?"

They established their headquarters in the hills of Judea from where they maintained Judaism and directed a continuous guerrilla warfare. At last, after three years of stratagems and battle, they triumphed. The untrained and poorly equipped amateur fighters finally overthrew the efficient, professional army of Antiochus. Occupying Jerusalem, the Maccabees reconsecrated the Temple on 25 Kislev, three years to the day after its desecration. For eight days the liberated Jewish community celebrated this victory of an ideal over brutality. They kindled lights, sang psalms of praise to God, and bore branches and flowers. Judas Maccabeus, the hero of the first war of liberation, "ordained by common statute and decree that every year those days should be kept by the whole nation of the Jews" as a perpetual memorial to be marked by the kindling of the Menorah as a symbol of the light of freedom that must shine for all the peoples of the world.

A talmudic legend adds further beauty to this custom. It records how the perpetual lamp, symbol of God's continuous care, had been extinguished by the Syrian conqueror. When rededicating the Temple, the priests' first concern was to rekindle the light. Yet, only one cruse, sufficient to last one day, was found in the debris of the Sanctuary. But miraculously it burnt for eight days till new oil was ready for use.

The story of Chanukah is not found in the Bible, though some traces of it can be discerned in the book of Daniel, but in the books of the Maccabees, which have become part of the library of "hidden books"—the Apocrypha. The Menorah itself, modeled on the ancient seven-branched candlestick of the Temple, has become one of the finest symbols of Judaism. When lit in Jewish homes during Chanukah, it is put in the window to proclaim abroad that light is stronger than darkness and that history is made "not by might, nor by power," but by the spirit of God.

The founder of modern Zionism, Theodor Herzl, visualizing

the rebirth of the Jewish State, saw in the Menorah the symbol of the enkindling of a nation and the Jews' mission on earth:

When there is but one light, all is still dark, and the solitary light looks melancholy. Soon it finds one companion, then another and another. The darkness must retreat. The light comes first to the young and the poor, then others join them who love Justice, Truth, Liberty, Progress, Humanity and Beauty. When all the candles burn, then we must all stand and rejoice over the achievements. And no office can be blessed more than that of Servant of the Light.

It was on Chanukah, 1917, that Lord Allenby led the British and Australian forces into Jerusalem, ending centuries of oppressive Turkish rule. This was yet another prophecy that a new light was to shine from the Holy City. Today, in modern Israel, Chanukah has become an eight-day children's festival dedicated to the heroes of Jewish history. From vantage points in the cities huge Menorahs shine forth to illumine the night. Torchlight processions are held, and special outings of thousands of children center on Modin, the village of the Maccabees.

Chanukah falls on 25 Kislev and Christmas on 25 December, a coincidence revealing an early connection of those dates. It is believed that the lighting of Christmas candles is borrowed from Chanukah, just as the celebration of Christmas Eve maintains the Jewish tradition of commencing all festivals at night.

Purim—The Feast of Lots

Purim, the other minor festival, is a joyous occasion which normally occurs during March. The literal translation of the word Purim is "lots" or "ballots," a recollection of the "lottery" drawn by Haman, Jewry's arch enemy, to fix the date most propitious for their total annihilation within the Persian Empire. Offended in his vanity by one Jew's refusal to extend to him divine homage, he was determined to take vengeance on the whole people. But divine intervention, through the person of Queen Esther, changed a day of mourning into a day of rejoicing.

The story of Purim is told in the book of Esther, which is part of the Bible. For convenient use on the festival, it is reproduced in the form of a scroll (Megillah). It is read out on the eve and the morning, often accompanied by appropriate acclamation and noise from the congregation.

Purim is the most hilarious day in the cycle of the Jewish year, the most secular of the Jewish holy days. It is a Jewish carnival and Guy Fawkes Day in one. Effigies of Haman are burned in public. Dramatizations of the Purim story are performed, the actors wandering through the streets and calling on each Jewish home, where they are made welcome. Children are given rattles, which they take even to the services, turning them loudly each time the name of Haman is mentioned. In the Middle Ages, when the Jews could look for consolation only to some happy episode in their history, the parties reached heights of great exuberance and were given the name *Adloyada,* which means, literally, "until he did not know!" This possibly refers to the mental confusion following excessive or unaccustomed use of intoxicating drink, as a result of which the celebrants could scarcely differentiate between the cursing of Haman the fiend and the blessing of Mordecai the deliverer. Presents are exchanged at this time within the Jewish community and especially sent to the poor. The Jewish table is enriched with triangular pastries stuffed with poppy seeds, called Haman taschen—a recollection of the fiend's three-cornered pocket (or hat).

Purim has been celebrated for twenty-four centuries. In days of suffering it was the feast of hope and trust in divine help. In times of peace and tranquillity it became a thanksgiving and a memorial. When all suffering has ceased on earth, Purim will be like a tombstone on the grave of the dark past for the happier generations of the future.

Pesach—The Feast of Passover

Passover (following a month later) is the birthday of the Jewish people and at the same time the first V-Day of humanity. Egypt's Pharaoh had thought that might was right. He had created a slave society of which the pyramid was the symbol: one dictator, the apex, at the top, and thousands of slaves at the base, trampled under foot. Passover teaches that man's inhumanity toward man cannot last. It commemorates the Israelites' liberation from the yoke of Egyptian bondage. It is called "The Season of our Freedom." Liberty is affirmed as the inalienable right of every human being. The name Passover itself is derived from the biblical story which relates how the angel of death, when killing the Egyptian first-born, "passed over" the homes of the Israelites. But it was also the description of the Paschal lamb, sacrificed by the Jews as an offering of thanksgiving.

For eight days (seven days in the case of Reform Judaism and in Israel) the Jew abstains from eating bread and instead partakes of unleavened cakes (matzah). Many consider this a delicacy, but its real meaning is just the opposite. It is intended to remind the Jew of the bread of affliction he had to eat in ages gone by. Only through God's grace is he free. "Because we were slaves, and if the Most Holy had not delivered our ancestors, we and our children would still be in bondage to the Pharaohs of Egypt," reads one of the main prayers of Passover. Very few former slaves like to be reminded of their past, but the Jew considers it his duty to remember the days of his bondage.

Religion must start at home. Unless the family observes it, it is useless to send children to Sunday school or even to services. The first two nights of Passover are therefore celebrated at home. The family reads together the 3,000-year-old story of the exodus from Egypt. It is contained in a book, richly illustrated and beautifully produced, named, simply, Haggada (story). The two nights are called Seder, which means "order," as the home service follows a definite routine. After the sanctification of the festival by the father with a goblet of wine, the child starts off the celebration by asking four traditional questions regarding "the difference between this night and all other nights." Then follow an extensive discussion, fervent prayers, and a festival dinner. The evening ends with joyful songs. Modern Israel has produced most up-to-date Haggadas, which include modern Hebrew songs and which, apart from the ancient exodus from Egypt, celebrate the modern-day liberation from human bondage.

Numerous symbolic dishes are eaten on Seder nights. Bitter

herbs (maror) are a reminder of the bitterness of past history. A dish consisting of apples, almonds, and cinnamon (charoset) is meant, by its brick color, to lead the Jews' memory back almost 3,500 years to the days of Pharaoh, when "we were slaves in Egypt" and under forced labor conditions had to make bricks, even without straw. Salt water represents the tears which the Jew shed in the agony of his suffering. A shank bone and a burnt egg speak of the ancient glory of the Temple, with its sacrifice and burnt offering. To the thoughtful, hard-boiled eggs are a lesson of immortality. To the superficial eye, the egg appears dead; and yet out of it new life can arise. In history, likewise, often when man could see no hope, divine help was near, and in the darkest night the light shone forth.

All these symbols and ceremonies are not simply historical memories. They are meant to renew within the Jew a passion for freedom and social justice. On Passover, his thoughts are focused on the needy and poor, the still unredeemed stepchildren of humanity. On the Seder night, he opens his doors at the very beginning of the reading from the Haggada and, as part of the service, invites all those that are hungry to enter and eat and all that are in need to come also. He lifts the matzah like a beacon of hope. After all, it is not only the sign of affliction but also a symbol of ever-present hope. In their 430 years of Egyptian bondage, the Israelites had almost lost faith in the possibility of freedom. Then liberty came unexpectedly and suddenly. They had not even time to bake their normal daily bread and had to leave carrying unleavened loaves.

The Seder nights do not only look back to the past. They point to the future. A glass of wine symbolically waits for Elijah, the messenger of the Messianic Age, who may come at any moment and for whom the doors are opened during the night. He will bring freedom for all men, who will be united in the service of goodness.

Passover is also a festival of thanksgiving for the barley harvest in the Holy Land, where it starts the cycle of the agricultural year. It is spring, and the reading of the Song of Songs, with its description of the reawakening of nature, adds to Passover a note of joyful expectancy.

Even though Pesach is a festival of rejoicing and a celebration of freedom, fiendish foes of the Jewish people often rendered it an occasion of gloom and tragedy. It was usually then that the ritual murder libel (with which once the Romans had victimized the early Christians) was raised against the Jews. In vain did popes and kings, leaders of church and state, try to halt the mass hysteria which was fanned by expectancy of loot and lust for bloodshed. Passover became a time of apprehension not only in the Middle Ages but in Czarist Russia and Nazi Germany. A relic of the days of witchcraft and black magic was then resuscitated by devilish minds as an excuse for plunder, arson, and expulsion. When on the Seder nights, during the service, the Jew opened the door of his home, it certainly was an invitation to the stranger and a symbol of Messianic hope. But it became also a means to look for any enemies hiding outside, ready to commence their nefarious work!

Perhaps more than any other Jewish festival, Passover has left its traces in the Christian religion. Christ is called the Paschal Lamb. His last supper is the meal on the Seder night of his own Passover celebration. The bread and wine of the communion service are the unleavened wafer (matzah) and the cup of sanctification—Motzeh and Kiddush—of that very Seder night.

Shavuot—The Feast of Weeks

Exactly seven weeks after Pesach follows Shavuot (The Feast of Weeks). Its name indicates the time difference which is also responsible for the English designation of the festival Pentecost, meaning the "fiftieth" day (after Passover).

The seven-week interval is known as the period of the omer, or the sefirah (the "counting"). The Israelites waited anxiously from the day of their physical redemption for the coming of the day of spiritual freedom and expressed this longing by counting the days. Omer is the Hebrew word for a sheaf or measure of grain. In ancient days, when the Jews were an agricultural people, they celebrated the beginning of the harvest by bringing to the Temple an omer of barley on the second day of Pesach, as an offering of thanksgiving. Recollecting both these traditions, observant Jews still count each day as it passes, starting on the second Seder: "This is the first day of the omer," and continuing for the whole forty-nine days.

For the Orthodox Jew, it is a time of national mourning, when no wedding should be celebrated and no public festivities arranged. This commemorates two historic tragedies during the omer. The first was the death of over half a million Jews in an abortive rising against Roman tyranny in 135 C.E., and the second an epidemic among Rabbi Akiba's students which wiped out about 24,000 scholars.

This plague was halted on the thirty-third day of the omer, which is now excepted from the period of public mourning. The day is called Lag of the Omer, the Hebrew equivalents of the letters L and G, representing the number 33. For obvious reasons, Lag b'Omer is also sometimes called "the scholars' holiday."

There are other reasons for permitting relaxation on this day. It was believed that the manna which nourished the Israelites in the desert on their long journey from Egypt to Palestine came down for the first time on Lag b'Omer. It was also the day which marked the beginning of Haman's downfall, when he had to lead Mordecai through the streets of Shushan.

Most of all, Lag b'Omer is linked with the great Jewish mystic, Rabbi Simon ben Yochai. He had refused to obey the Roman decree against the study of the Torah and continued to teach his pupils. His life was in continuous danger. He succeeded in escaping to a cave in the mountains of Galilee, where he hid for thirteen years, during which time he is reputed to have written the Zohar, Judaism's mystic Bible. Annually, his students visited him on Lag b'Omer. Lest the Roman soldiers should suspect them, they disguised themselves as hunters and carried bows and arrows. Tradition adds that Rabbi Simon died on Lag b'Omer. His last request to his disciples was that the day of his passing be observed by celebration, rather than by mourning. Thus, Lag b'Omer became the only Yahrzeit in Jewish life and history distinguished not by a mood of sadness, but by happy rejoicing.

Annual pilgrimages are held to the rabbi's burial place at Meron, in northern Israel. His grave is decorated and illuminated, and after a religious commemorative service, excursions, bonfires, and games for children (most prominent among them with bows and arrows) become the order of the day—an oasis of joy during seven weeks of dejection.

Passover celebrated the birth of the Jewish people, their attainment of physical freedom. But this in itself was not enough. Vitally important is the use man makes of his God-given freedom. Liberty and law must go together. The rabbis said: "There is no freedom except through law." That is why Shavuot, as it were, completes Pesach and the Jew counts the days "in-between." What began with Passover was concluded at Pentecost by the revelation on Mount Sinai and the giving of the Ten Commandments. Shavuot is the birthday of the Jewish religion. To serve God and to obey His commandment, then, became the highest kind of freedom.

No religious document has exercised greater influence. In a mere 120 concise Hebrew words, the decalogue covers the whole sphere of conduct. It asserts God as an ever-present reality (first commandment), Who demands of man unqualified loyalty, with no idol of any kind ever taking His place (second). Religion must remain pure and never be abused for selfish purposes, using its name for worldly gain or power (third). The duty of work and the privilege of rest are inalienable birthrights of every living being (fourth). The honor of one's parents is a sacred obligation without which personal happiness is unattainable (fifth). Any kind of killing is evil (sixth). The sanctity of family life (seventh), honesty (eighth), and integrity in human relations (ninth) are basic laws for all men. Even the mere desire to possess anything belonging to others is the negation of God's will (tenth).

The two tablets of stone, once carried in the Ark through the wilderness, contain what have become basic ideals of humanity. That their replicas now decorate the Ark in every synagogue is symbolic of their central place in Judaism.

On Shavuot, once again, the Jew expresses his thanks to God for the blessings of nature, this time for the wheat harvest in the Holy Land. He knows well that whatever he gathers in his field is not the result of his own work alone. The synagogues are decorated with flowers and plants. The book of Ruth, with its harvest setting, is read. Reform congregations throughout the world (ever since 1831) have made Shavuot the season also for the confirmation of young boys and girls. As the time of the revelation on Mount Sinai, it was considered the most appropriate occasion to confirm Jewish youth in the faith of their fathers.

The Ninth Day of Av

The most ominous day in Jewish life concludes (sometime in July or August) the cycle of the Jewish year. Its date, Tishah b'Av (the ninth day of Av), became its name. On this date, both first and second Temples were destroyed (in 586 B.C.E. by Nebuchadrezzar and in 70 C.E. by Titus), the last resistance against the Roman invader collapsed (in 135 C.E.), and the Jews were expelled from Spain (in 1492). Was it just a coincidence that the first world war of this century also commenced on that day of accumulated woe?

Tishah b'Av is a day of mourning and fasting. The synagogues are deprived of all adornments, even the curtain in front of the Ark and the silver candlesticks being removed. In plaintive tunes the cantor intones the biblical Lamentations as well as special dirges composed by the Jews in the dark ages of their history.

The rebirth of the Jewish State has raised the question, even in many Orthodox quarters, whether it is desirable that Jews should go on mourning the destruction of Jerusalem in ancient days and keep the Fast of Av. Suggestions that they should cease doing so have been strongly opposed.

The Ninth of Av commemorates all the misery and anguish of the ages, which were never God-sent but always man-made. The day, therefore, prepares the Jew for the solemn period of the New Year with its note of regeneration and hope of a better world.

Chapter 6

JEWISH MYSTICISM

Mysticism has been defined as the type of religion which puts the emphasis on the immediate awareness of God, on direct and intimate consciousness of the divine presence. "It is religion in its acute, intense and living stage."

Understanding of Judaism is incomplete without a knowledge of its great mystical force. This left its early traces in Bible, Apocrypha, and Talmud, but it also created its own invaluable writings. Far from being a mere literary movement, mysticism molded the lives of millions of Jews in eastern Europe. Strangely enough, it even introduced into Judaism belief in reincarnation! In modern days it has found its fervent exponent who sees in a return to the best of Jewish mystical ideas the greatest hope of a renewal of faith.

Kabbala is an early name of Jewish mysticism. It means "tradition," as it carefully preserved and handed down teachings on the mystery of God and the universe. Not science or revelation was its source, but religious ecstasy and deep, mystical speculation. Only the initiated could understand its secrets, which were guarded preciously. The world was seen not as a material entity, but as an essentially spiritual form. God was not isolated outside the universe, but was an ever-present Reality, "boundless" and "without ending." All existence flows out of Him, partaking of His perfection and infinity, just as sparks are part of the flame. Evil is nonexistent as a power in itself; it is merely the negation of good. Man is God's highest creation and the completion of the universe. But his body—skin, flesh, blood, veins, nerves, and tissues—is only the outer garment of the real man: his soul.

Jewish mysticism has its own specific character. It knows the rapture of total absorption in God. But it stresses equally the importance of action. Even here, in utter spiritual ecstasy, the meaning of life must be manifested in deed. The joyful experience of the divine must not exhaust itself in abstract emotion, but be expressed in the sanctification of every action. The Jewish mystical ideal was never the isolated recluse, but the inspired, pious man living within the community.

Mystical thoughts appeared early in the Hebrew Bible. They became more strongly pronounced at the beginning of the current era, when we meet with a variety of mystical speculation and the first works of Jewish mysticism. Its literature then grew throughout the centuries. The Book of Twenty-two Letters, for instance, deals with the hidden power of the Hebrew alphabet, giving each letter cosmic significance. The Zohar (Brilliance) became the Bible of mysticism. Ostensibly a commentary on the Torah, it sums up all previous speculation, and all later Jewish mystic efforts are indebted to this classic. It appeared in Spain at the end of the thirteenth century. It describes the world as a battlefield between good and evil. Man's soul migrates from one existence to another until, perfectly purified, it is ready to be reunited with God.

The anguish of the Jewish soul after the persecutions of the seventeenth and eighteenth centuries renewed the fiery stream of mystical consciousness and brought to white heat the Jew's quest for God. This led to the establishment of the most modern and complete system of Jewish mysticism, called Chassidism, which means "pietism," teaching a world-accepting, world-enjoying kind of piety.

Its founder was Israel ben Eliezer. Born in Poland in 1700 and orphaned early in life, he was adopted by a pious family. He was a wayward child, often playing truant from school to wander far in forest and field, meditating in solitude. For a short time he was a pupil-teacher; then in turn he became the beadle in a synagogue, a merchant in clay, and finally an innkeeper! But always his main desire was to seek communion with God. In his thirty-sixth year he abandoned his secular life and revealed himself as a preacher and a teacher. He was simple, spontaneous, and never sanctimonious. Not the mortification of our instincts, but their sanctification, was his aim. He knew how to express the feelings of inarticulate masses, who soon recognized him as their guide. Thousands flocked around him. When he spoke, each felt himself personally addressed. He needed two secretaries to cope with his correspondence; yet no work of his is in existence. His life was a lesson. As Socrates had his Plato and Johnson his Boswell, so Ben Eliezer's pupils preserved the legend of his life, which became the foundation of Chassidism.

Martin Buber rediscovered this great movement, which flourished over a century. He stressed its vital importance in our present world: "For now is the hour when we are in danger of forgetting for what purpose we are on earth, and I know of no other teaching that reminds us of this so forcibly."

God fills every nook and corner of the universe. He is in mind and matter, in the star and in the stone, in good and evil. This conviction was vividly expressed in the composition of one of the great mystics, the "You-Song."

> Almighty God, Lord of the Universe,
> Almighty God, I shall sing You a You-song.
> Where can I find You?
> And where can I not find You?
> You-You-You, You-You.
>
> For wherever I go—You!
> And wherever I stand—You!
> Always You, only You, again You, forever You.
>
> If things are good—You!
> Alas, bad—You!
> East, You! West, You!
> North, You! South, You!
> Above, You! Below, You!
>
> You-You-You, You-You-You, You-You-You!
> Wherever I turn, wherever I move,
> You-You!

Man can find God's divine fire everywhere and in everything. Yet he must release it from its prison. Every act and every word of ours can be sanctified by its presence. To make the hidden light of God shine wherever we are is the ultimate meaning of our existence. It does not matter what we do, but how we do it. Even a cobbler, with each stitch of his awl that draws together the upper and lower leathers, can join God to his world. "Where is the dwelling of God?" a rabbi asked some learned men. They smiled condescendingly. Did not God's glory fill the universe? But the mystic differed in a significant way: God dwells only where He is admitted by man. Without man's conscious effort, God will remain unredeemed. Thus, Chassidism pronounced the principle of man's responsibility for God's fate on earth.

Every man is unique and necessary in the working out of God's destiny. Each one of us is called upon to bring something to its completion which, without this individual effort, would remain unfinished. Jewish thought rejects the mystic who, absorbed in God, forgets man. We must walk with Him in the midst of this world, taking part in the life of the people, but raising them up to God. We need one another, and God needs us all. Jewish mysticism thus demands not the abandonment of external reality, but its affirmation. Joyfully, we must face life and its obligations. It was the founder of Chassidism who said: "It is the aim and essence of my pilgrimage on earth to show my brethren by living demonstration how one may serve God with joy and gladness. For he who is full of joy is full of love for men and all fellow-creatures."

Life needs not doctrine and learning, but redeeming love. When a man sees that his neighbor hates him, he must love him more than ever before to make up what is lacking, for the community where there is love of all people is the vehicle of God's presence, and each crack in it hinders it from rising out of its material shell.

Only if he serves God with all his being can man be redeemed. Lukewarm allegiance is insufficient. Like a drowning man battling for air, we must yearn for God. A prayer without fervor is mechanical and wooden, unable to lift man to Divinity. But every human action can be a prayer if it is saturated with the holy desire for union with God. If our soul is aflame, it will unify the multiplicity of our being. Humility is essential. There is no room for God in him who is full of himself.

A pious man desired to abstain from food and drink a whole week, from one Sabbath to the next. When the last day came, his thirst was unbearable. In utter despair he went to the well, but there he suddenly realized that by drinking, a whole week's effort would be wasted. Only a few hours were left, and then he could attain his goal. By tremendous self-control he did not drink. Now a feeling of pride filled his heart. When he realized this, he was ashamed; to fall a prey to pride was far worse than to break his fast. Thus, he went back to the well. But when he was about to drink, he found that his thirst had vanished. When, at the beginning of the Sabbath, he entered his teacher's home, conscious of his completed fast, the rabbi met him disapprovingly. "Patchwork," he said.

We must be all of one piece. Wholeheartedly and with a united soul, we must serve man and thus find God.

Chapter 7

THE BOOK WHICH GREW
A THOUSAND YEARS

The Bible is the main source of Judaism, its very foundation. It unites God's testimony in the legends of the forefathers, the words of the men of God, and the teachings of the prophets.

It recounts the early history of the Jewish people, from its very beginning down to the time of the Maccabees (165 B.C.E.). It presents the spiritual interpretation of life, as well as its origin and meaning. Describing a pattern of life inspired by God, it regulates everyday existence with a vision of the days to come. Accepting man as he is, with all his faults and weaknesses, it still proclaims his God-given, moral power to do the good and to achieve the right.

The word "Bible" is of Greek origin and means simply "The Book." It has not been found necessary to give it any specific or descriptive title. It stands as *the* Book, because no other book ever produced has been read by so many people or played so significant a part in the history of humanity. It has been translated into well over a thousand languages and dialects, and more than 200 million copies have been distributed during the past hundred years.

The Hebrew Bible is not just one single book, but a collection of thirty-nine books, an anthology of godliness. It contains poetry and philosophy, ritual law and social legislation, history and metaphysics. The Bible did not suddenly appear. It is a book that grew for a thousand years. Its oldest passages stem from the days of Moses (1200 B.C.E.), and its newest from the Maccabean era (165 B.C.E.).

At least one hundred authors wrote the Bible. They included priests and prophets, social revolutionaries and conservative aristocrats, seekers after personal piety and strivers after national unity and regeneration. Some lived halcyon days in isolation, communing with God in the solitude of nature. Others had their place at the crossroads of history and in the arena of battle. A few enjoyed the placidity of a serene faith; others were confronted with inexplicable suffering and national catastrophe. Whoever they were, and wherever they lived, they all shared a passionate faith in God and an unshakable determination to establish His Kingdom on earth.

The Bible, as the unique volume of Jewish sacred writings, was created by force of historical circumstances. Originally, there existed a vast quantity of Jewish literature in the form of pamphlets, scrolls, and books. This collection had been growing for over a thousand years. Then the development of Christianity and the publication of many heretical views created the utmost confusion. A definition of "Jewish writings" became an urgent necessity so that the unenlightened and ignorant could be sure which books were sacred and the revelation of God's word, and which profane and the effusion of man's mind. To remove any uncertainty, rabbinical conferences were convened at the beginning of the second century of this era, to select the works which they considered to be inspired and divine, the word of God, and which alone would represent the authoritative Jewish point of view.

It was not an easy task. Prolonged and heated debates took place. Strong objection to the inclusion of several writings was overcome only after much discussion and by the help of interpretation or even interpolation. At last the list of "holy writings" was final. It was called "the canon," a Greek word of Hebrew origin meaning "standard," since, naturally, all thirty-nine books chosen conformed to a definite norm of God-inspired truth and unquestioned authority. All other religious writings were declared to be, at best, inspired but not divine; at their worst, they were characterized as heretical, blaphemous, and atheistic.

It is this canon which constitutes the Hebrew Bible as it is known today. Its thirty-nine separate "books" fall into three distinct divisions. (1) The Five Books of Moses (often known by the Greek word *Pentateuch,* or fivefold book) which contain the Law; (2) The Prophets; (3) The Writings. The totality of these, the Jewish Scriptures, are given the Hebrew name *T'nach.* This is a word coined from the initials of the three foregoing sections, which, in Hebrew, are called *Torah, N'viim,* and *Ch'tuvim.*

The three sections did not come into existence simultaneously, but represent three successive stages of collection and canonization, started in the time of Ezra the Scribe in 444 B.C.E. and completed by the conferences at the beginning of the second century of our era. The actual order in which they were then arranged, almost two thousand years ago, persists.

The term Old Testament, commonly applied to describe the Jewish Scriptures, is never used by Jews. The word "testament" means "covenant." When Christianity ceased to regard itself as a new sect of Judaism and emerged as a new religion, its leaders claimed that the Old Covenant which God had made with the Israelites had been superseded by a New Covenant. Accordingly, they gave the Jewish Bible the name Old Testament, and to their own Gospels, which told the story of their new covenant, they gave the name New Testament. For obvious reasons, the Jew does not accept this terminology and continues to use the name "The Bible."

The Arabs rightly called the Jews "the people of the Book." The Bible has been their "portable fatherland." It was the only possession man could not take from them. They meditated on it day and night "when lying down and when rising up."

To the rabbis, the Bible was an inexhaustible mine of wisdom and inspiration: man's complete guide in his search for God and the good. With loving care they studied its pages. Though apparently written in the language of everyday life, its words, as the inspired word of God, really meant much more. Every phrase, word, and even letter disclosed to them some hidden truth. The Bible taught them lessons of infinite beauty and lasting value. Ben Bag-Bag, one of the teachers of the *Ethics of the Fathers,* summarized this passionate belief in the Bible as the book containing all the answers: "Turn it—turn it over again—for everything is in it. Meditate on it, grow old over it, never stir from it, for you cannot have a better rule for life."

The Bible cannot be studied merely with the intellect. It is not meant to be read only as literature. It must be approached with reverence and love. Apart from all theological speculation or conviction, the quality of ever-renewed meaning renders the Bible a book of everlasting value. It is the work of religious genius.

It is one of the characteristics of any genius that his words convey much more than he originally intended them to mean. Though apparently limited by the circumstances of their time, they are never-aging, inexhaustible in depth and meaning. Each new generation discovers more of their truth and message. This applies to any work of genius: to Beethoven's music, Wordsworth's poetry, Rembrandt's paintings, and Shakespeare's dramas. Time-bound, they are eternal; dealing with subject matters of definite dates and specific places, they are ageless. But no work possesses this quality of perpetual renewal and unending meaning more than the Bible.

The loyalty of Ruth, who was prepared to go anywhere just to keep faith; the trust in God of David, who feared no evil even in the valley of the shadow of death; the endurance of Job, who in spite of all suffering knew that his Redeemer lived—they all were time-conditioned, the outcome of historical circumstances; and yet, immortal in their value, they still speak to us with undiminished, dynamic force. God's call to guilt-stricken Adam and Eve —"Where art thou?"—as well as Cain's brazen refusal to recognize his social responsibility—"Am I my brother's keeper?"— these are not merely echoes from the dream-distant past but possess shattering present-day reality.

The Bible tells the early story of the Jewish people. Yet it is totally different from all other history books. Only too often they select the pleasant and omit the ugly; they see all the good in their own people and all the bad in others. Not so the Bible. This is yet another of its unique features. It is a book of complete and unvarnished truth. We meet Moses as the meek servant of God and yet hear of his anger, heartaches, and disappointments. The Jewish people are described as "a kingdom of priests and a holy nation." But no anti-Semitic literature could have spoken more fiercely of them than that very same Bible, calling them also a stiff-necked people and a seed of evildoers! Without shame, King David's ancestry is traced back to a foreign nation and a pagan convert. The Jewish people themselves are described as descendants of slaves. This passion for truth, indeed, gives the Bible its special greatness.

It is a book of religion, and not a manual of science. The Bible does not purport to furnish scientific data, propound cosmological theories, or supply biological explanations. What matters in the story of creation, for instance, is not whether the world was called into existence in six days of labor and one day of rest, but its religious message. There, in the first chapter of the Bible, we learn the fundamental truths of Judaism. We meet God as the Force behind the universe, its Creator and perpetual Guide. The cosmos is described not as the outcome of fortuitous circumstance, but as the result of a purposive mind; and this world is pictured not as a jumble of haphazard, disconnected happenings, but a moral order ruled by man's freedom with its implicit chain of cause and effect.

Certainly science can contribute greatly toward a better understanding of the Bible and is doing so on an ever-increasing scale. Confounding antibiblical arguments of the last century, it is confirming the statements of the Bible and leading to an ever greater appreciation of its beauty and historical authenticity.

A multitude of exciting facts have been discovered. The finds of ancient manuscripts, seals, and inscriptions have given the philologist a means of illuminating the dark passages of the Bible. For example, a certain word that had been considered corrupt was suddenly proved to be correct by the discovery of a simple (and forgotten) weight, unearthed by the excavator's spade.

Historical statements of the Bible have been not only confirmed and explained but enlarged. The archaeologist has proved the actual occurrence of a flood of devastating dimensions and unearthed examples of the Tower of Babel. Archaeologists have proved the existence of Pithom and Ramses, the store-cities of Exodus. Even the name "Israel" was discovered in hieroglyphics on a monument erected by Pharaoh Merneptah, who in the thirteenth century B.C.E. boasted of having exterminated the Jewish people for all time.

Excavators have laid bare the stables in which King Solomon kept his horses and established the "wailing wall" as an authentic remnant of the Temple in Jerusalem. Clay tablets in cuneiform script, containing parallels to the Mosaic Law, have helped to put into relief the unique nature of the Jewish philosophy of life. It has been established that a Greek inscription from the days of Herod's Temple served as a poster to Gentile worshipers at the Jews' sanctuary.

Egyptology has explained the background of Israel's sojourn in Egypt and shown Moses as an Egyptian word meaning "the child," found in numerous names of pharaohs. Historians identified the pharaoh of the Bible with Ramses II, whose mummified body now lies in Cairo's National Museum!

Further evidence of the truth of biblical history was provided in 1868, when a Prussian missionary discovered a large, inscribed stone in the possession of Arabs living in Moab, east of the Dead Sea. It was of obvious antiquity and importance, and by his excitement the finder aroused the greed of the Arabs. With tortuous Oriental logic, they argued that if one stone was valuable, a hundred stones were a hundred times more so. Accordingly, they shattered the priceless relic; but fortunately, though they offered the pieces to various buyers, almost all the fragments were collected and the stone was restored.

The inscription proved to be an account by King Mesha of Moab of the battles in which he was defeated and his country subdued by Omri and Ahab, kings of Israel, as related in II Kings III, 4–27. This relic, nearly three thousand years old, now rests in the Louvre in Paris. It is of black basalt and three and a half feet high.

The Bible tells how Hezekiah, King of Judah, constructed a

special underground pipe line from outside Jerusalem into the city. Anticipating a siege by the Assyrian enemy, he hoped thereby to secure the city's water supply. In 1880, children bathing in a rock pool found a tablet inscribed in ancient Hebrew characters. It dated from the time of Hezekiah and was affixed there 2,500 years ago to commemorate the completion of this very conduit. Twenty-five centuries had elapsed until the biblical report was confirmed by this outstanding discovery. The tablet, which is known as the "Siloam inscription," is preserved in the Turkish Museum at Istanbul.

The search amid the "sands of time" for further evidence of the truth of the Bible has been greatly intensified, especially since the reestablishment of the State of Israel, by the Hebrew University through its Institute of Archaeology and its Faculty of Oriental Studies. Much material of inestimable importance has been found, adding to the grandeur and knowledge of this book of books.

Rabbi Dr. Nelson Glueck, President of the Hebrew Union College–Jewish Institute of Religion, Cincinnati, who pronounced the priestly benediction at President John F. Kennedy's inauguration in Hebrew and English, using the Bible as his guide, located the long-lost copper mines of King Solomon and identified the site of Ezion-Geber, Solomon's port on the Red Sea. His belief in God never depended on "proving" the Bible. However, he was elated that his diggings confirmed the Bible's "almost incredibly correct historical memory" and that "no archaeological discovery ever controverted a biblical reference," even in the realm of geography.

Yigael Yadin, Israel's renowned general-turned-archaeologist, excavated Hazor, near the Sea of Galilee, and by the artifacts he unearthed supplied evidence of the sack of that city in Joshua's times, as recorded in Holy Scripture, confirming and supplementing the biblical story.

Nothing surpasses the sensation created by the find of the Dead Sea Scrolls in 1947. Certainly, we owe a debt of gratitude to that Bedouin shepherd who, in search of a stray goat, accidentally brought to light the treasure from a cave north of the Dead Sea, in an area known as Qumran. The scrolls contained manuscripts of the Hebrew Bible more than a thousand years older than the earliest documents previously known. They proved the accuracy, antiquity, and essential authenticity of the text of the Bible, as we now possess it. For instance, an entire book, the prophecies of Isaiah, was found on a twenty-two-foot-long scroll, untouched for more than two thousand years. Its sixty-six chapters tally in text almost word for word with the traditional printed Hebrew version which has come down to us through the generations. More significant still, the scrolls have helped to explain biblical passages which had baffled the expert. As well as these works, the caves yielded copies of Jewish literature formerly wholly unknown, among them a scroll named "The War of the Sons of Light Against the Sons of Darkness."

The exploration of the Dead Sea region has continued, resulting in more and more finds. Those at Masada, the last stronghold in the Jews' revolt against the might of Rome, which fell in 73 C.E., are most famous. The excavation was carried out by a nucleus of professional archaeologists under the direction of Yigael Yadin. They were assisted by two thousand volunteers from thirty countries. For eleven months during two seasons in 1963–1964 and 1964–1965 they dug up eight miles of walls and moved and sifted thousands of tons of earth. Among the great treasures discovered in this whirlwind "campaign" were the Bar Kochba letters and fragments from parchment scrolls dating back to the time before the destruction of the Temple to the first half of the first century C.E. The finds included parts from the books of Genesis, Leviticus, Deuteronomy, the Psalms, and the prophet Ezekiel and the first Hebrew text ever obtained of the apocryphal book of Jubilees, hitherto known only in the Ethiopian, Greek, and Latin translations and a first-century B.C.E. copy of the lost Hebrew original of the book of Ben Sirach. It was a most spectacular archaeological adventure, and, with a flair for the dramatic, Yadin had invited the whole world to participate in it. It made Masada, a name hardly known before 1963, a glorious concept.

Even psychology, by its interpretation of legends as truth-revealing dreams of a people, has greatly contributed to the understanding of the Bible. Thus science, once considered the enemy of religion, has become its great friend and helper. It confirms the Bible's narrative and sheds light on the unexplained and unexplored.

THE BOOKS OF THE BIBLE

I. *THE FIVE BOOKS OF MOSES*

1. Genesis
2. Exodus
3. Leviticus
4. Numbers
5. Deuteronomy

II. *THE PROPHETS*

A. *Earlier Prophets*

6. Joshua
7. Judges
8. Samuel I

9. Samuel II
10. Kings I
11. Kings II

B. *Later Prophets*

(a) Major

12. Isaiah   13. Jeremiah   14. Ezekiel

(b) Minor

15. Hosea
16. Joel
17. Amos
18. Obadiah
19. Jonah
20. Micah

21. Nahum
22. Habakkuk
23. Zephaniah
24. Haggai
25. Zechariah
26. Malachi

III. *THE WRITINGS*

27. Psalms
28. Proverbs
29. Job
30. Song of Songs
31. Ruth
32. Lamentations

33. Ecclesiastes
34. Esther
35. Daniel
36. Ezra
37. Nehemiah
38. Chronicles I

39. Chronicles II

THE FIVE BOOKS OF MOSES

First in the order of the Bible and importance stand "the Five Books of Moses," known as the Torah, usually translated as "The Law." Their place in the Jewish mind is revealed by their vernacular name, the Chumash, or "The Five"—as though this number could have no other significance.

They not only commence the canon but contain the fundamental ideas of Judaism. They describe the beginnings of the world and the formative history of the Jewish people, ranging from the very first Jew, the creator of monotheistic religion, to the death of Moses. There we find the Jewish declaration of faith in the one God, Whom we must love with all our heart; "Thou shalt love thy neighbour as thyself," the passage which has been called the basic tenet of Judaism; and the Ten Commandments.

The books of the Torah are not written systematically, as in the modern style. They contain a blend of history, biography, legend, law, narrative, and poetry, freely intermingled, leading one into another according to no discernible plan. The rabbis declared that this intermixing was deliberate, designed to indicate that each section is as important as any other. Yet the five books broadly follow a chronological sequence.

The English Bible calls each one according to its main theme, while in Hebrew one of the characteristic opening words always supplies the name.

Genesis

The first book is called in English by a Greek name, *Genesis* (the birth). In Hebrew it is named after its opening word, *B'reshit:* "In the beginning."

In the account of the creation with which it starts, Genesis conveys the vital lesson, foreshadowing all that is to follow, that God is the creator of the entire universe and that the many nations and varied people of the world actually belong to one family—the children of God.

The rabbis who established the canon might, reasonably and justifiably, have excluded the early chapters of Genesis and started the Bible with the beginning of Jewish history. That they did not do so illustrates the essence of Jewish universalism, which contemplates history against the background of eternity.

Genesis supplies an answer to many of the problems of thinking man. It does so not historically, but religiously. It searches after the meaning of existence, the origin of the diversity of language, and the causes of man's antagonisms. It teaches the unity of man, his moral task, and the inevitable chain of cause and effect in history.

Having dealt in its first eleven chapters with humanity and its problems, the book proceeds to the beginnings of Jewish history: the story of the fathers of the Jewish faith. We accompany Abraham, destined to become the "father of many," from Ur of the Chaldeans into the Holy Land. We share with him and his son Isaac the crisis of their lives, in which both were tested and found out the right way of serving God. We follow Jacob and his twelve sons into Egypt, where Joseph's statesmanship and ingenuity rescued a large nation from famine.

Apart from its narrative, Genesis embodies the early aspects of Jewish religious belief, referring *inter alia* to the institution of marriage, to the Sabbath, and to the "Covenant of Abraham," or circumcision.

The book ends on a high note, with Joseph's brethren and his people living in honored security and Joseph, with his authority and his dignity, peacefully dying amid the mourning not only of his own people but even of the Egyptians, who "embalmed him and placed him in a [doubtless vice-regal] coffin."

Exodus

The book of Exodus, called in Hebrew after its second word, *Sh'mot* (Names), is full of dramatic tension and immortal teaching. It tells of the "going out" of the Israelites from Egypt.

A new generation in Egypt had forgotten the country's debt to the Jews. The new pharaoh was determined to enslave and thereby to exterminate them. But they found a deliverer in Moses, who molded from the subjugated race of slaves a freedom-loving people with a great mission. Undaunted by setbacks, whether due to the despotism of the pharaoh or the backslidings and apostasies of his own people, Moses liberated Israel under God's guidance.

This book leads from the depths of Egyptian slavery to the heights of Mount Sinai, from Moses' defiance of tyranny to the revelation of the Ten Commandments. It teaches the supreme value of freedom under the law.

Exodus also contains the introduction of the Jewish calendar and of the three festivals of pilgrimage to the Temple in Jerusalem: Passover, Pentecost, and Tabernacles.

Leviticus

The priestly class of the Levites and their service in the sanctuary gave the Third Book of Moses its name, Leviticus, which in Hebrew is called after its opening word, *Va-yikra* (And He called). Just as it forms the center of the Torah, so it stresses the central idea of Judaism, the law of holiness as an activating force. This has found expression in the book's detailed description of sacrificial service as much as in its lofty, ethical legislation. Both the functions of the priests and the duties of the priestly people, as related in Leviticus, aim at the sanctification of life on earth.

The ideas of the interdependence of man and of the joint responsibility of all the members of the community are expressed here and symbolized by the congregational sacrifices. We read of the introduction of the Day of Atonement and of the dietary laws. The book affirms that a religious basis alone can ensure national welfare.

Leviticus, however, does not teach just general ideas of holiness. It gives their application in all spheres of life. It bears out William Blake's belief that to speak in generalities might easily lead to hypocrisy, but that a religious and purposeful life demands minute details.

Fear of God is expressed in not cursing the deaf or putting a stumbling block in the way of the blind; in being righteous in judgment and respecting the person of the poor. Indifference to the fate of others, standing idly by while they suffer, and secretly bearing a grudge against one's neighbor or hating him even in one's heart are denial of God's law.

In the unparalleled abundance of its ethical legislation, Leviticus demands of the people that they keep away from superstitious customs, that they never lust for revenge or speak untruth. Anything that gives hurt to a person, mentally or physically, or makes him feel inferior is forbidden as ungodly. The law of holiness commands that in every foreigner the Jew must see a brother and never do him any wrong, but rather treat him like a "homeborn." To look after the needs of the stranger, the poor, and the friendless was not a matter of personal mood, but a sacred obligation. To leave them the gleanings of one's field and its corners was not a humiliating charity, but their rightful due.

No wonder that a book full of such unsurpassed ideals was made the first reader for the young Jewish child, thus launching it on a life of purity and love.

Numbers

The census of the people, taken in the wilderness, constitutes the major part and thereby originated the name of the book of Numbers, called in Hebrew *B'midbar* (In the wilderness).

Once again history and law are interfused. We find enactments on jealousy. We read of the lighting of the seven-branched candlestick, the Menorah, one of the symbols of the Jewish faith. The book contains the "threefold benediction" which has become part of both Jewish and Christian service.

We follow the Israelites on the remainder of their forty years' wandering through the Arabian desert to the borders of the Holy Land and their encounters with unfriendly neighboring states. We hear of Korah's rebellion against Moses' leadership, of the introduction of the advisory council of seventy, of the exploration of Canaan by representatives of the people, and of the legislation preparatory to its conquest.

Deuteronomy

Moses was aware that he would not be permitted to enter the Promised Land, but only to gaze upon it from a distant mountaintop. Already he had appointed Joshua as his successor. A new generation had grown up in the wilderness. Anxious that they keep the covenant of their fathers, he was determined to impress its message on them once again. For the last times he addressed his people, now ready for the conquest, giving them a summary of all previous teachings and then bestowing on them his blessing.

The "fifth book" contains this "repetition of the Law" and is therefore called, by those words (in their Greek rendering), *Deuteronomy,* while its Hebrew name is *D'varim* (Words).

Here, in the last Book of Moses, is the place of the Sh'ma: "Hear, O Israel, the Lord our God, the Lord is One." We hear of man's free will, with its implicit responsibility, and how personal and national existence and happiness depend on moral action, on the observance of Divine Law by both individual and people. Moses, in his final song, reasserts God as "The Rock," in Whom alone men and mankind will find stability.

The closing stages of the book are full of pathos. The aged Moses was burdened with the cares of a leadership he had not sought. Though his magnificent constitution had prevailed so that "his eye was not dim nor his natural force abated," he had completed his task.

His sole reward was, however, still to be granted. Calling him to the summit of Mount Nebo, God permitted him to survey the whole of the Holy Land and repeated His promise to give it to the seed of the patriarchs. And then he died, this man who was known not as the ruler or leader of his people, not even as the lawgiver, but humbly and simply as "the servant of the Lord." Alone and unattended, save by God Himself, he died in an alien land, and "unto this day, no man knoweth the place of his burial."

This ends the majestic cycle of the five books. Dedicated to, and according to Orthodox belief actually written by, Moses, they form an epitaph worthy of that great universal and eternal figure whose name they bear.

The Torah was the earliest part of the Bible to be canonized. Belief in its divine origin invested it with sanctity. Every effort was made to preserve it in its totality: every phrase, word, and letter, unusual spellings or writing, or even a single letter inverted, magnified, or falling out of line, was considered of importance. To fix and safeguard the text for all time, a special tradition, called the Massorah, counted the letters and in marginal notes and separate works laid down all the spelling, the division into verses, paragraphs, and chapters. Nothing was left to chance.

As the Torah was held to be the basic foundation of the Jewish faith, to know it became the imperative duty of every Jew. It was the basis of general as well as religious education, and the introduction of every Jewish child to the principles of his faith began with the study of the Torah.

It was not only a "holy book" for the use of a priestly class but a code of life for the whole people. It follows that it was universally studied, a fact which gave to the Jewish people the distinction of being the first to establish a system of adult education. Throughout the dark ages of the current era, the Jews remained literate.

Apart altogether from individual study, the regular, constant, and systematic reading of the Torah was instituted within the synagogue, where the reading of the Law was given a central place at each major service. For this purpose, and independent of the division into chapters, the Torah was divided into a cycle of fifty-four "orders" (Hebrew: *Sidras*), designed to be read in rotation each Sabbath throughout the year. Each Sidra was given its own name, chosen from among its opening words, and eventually each Sabbath came to be designated by its own Sidra.

The cycle of the annual reading of the Law ended and began on the same day (the Feast of the Rejoicing of the Law) as a symbol of its perpetual importance and endless observance. Appropriate passages were selected for the lessons on holy days and new moons, while on Saturday afternoons and Monday and

Thursday mornings, parts of the following Sabbath's Sidra became the regular feature.

Although it is customary to speak of the "reading" of the Law, it was normally sung or chanted to a traditional melody. This was designed partly to indicate the meaning of the text, or to emphasize special phrases, but mainly—and because the melody was reserved exclusively for the Torah—the chant served to create an atmosphere of consecration. Mistakes in the singing were not to be tolerated, any more than a mistake in pronouncing the words. To prevent any such error, a special system of musical notation was devised and written into the text.

It is interesting to know that the basic melody for Sabbath differed from that sung on high holy days and that for the reading from the prophets (the "second lesson") yet another basic tune existed. Since, however, the musical symbols were incorporated into the text, it follows that one and the same sign conveys a different musical phrase according to the text it accompanies and the day on which it is to be sung.

In theory, all Jewish men should be able to read (that is, chant) from the Torah and thus share in the annual reading of the Law. In practice, this is not the case, and to avoid humiliation it became the practice to call on each member in turn (usually on some special anniversary) to stand beside a trained reader (normally the cantor) while his portion was read. This act of "calling up to the Torah"—known in Hebrew as *aliyah,* or "going up" to the raised dais—is regarded as a privilege. The man so honored pronounces a benediction, proclaiming the sanctity of the Law and expressing gratitude to God for having entrusted the Jew with the guardianship of His Holy Torah. This distinction is reserved for those of religious maturity. It is, indeed, first conferred on a youth to mark his bar mitzvah, of whose celebration the aliyah forms the central feature.

The customs surrounding the reading of the Law and its external trappings all aimed at emphasizing its holy nature. For use in service no printed book could be employed, but only a copy handwritten on a scroll of parchment specially prepared from the skin of a ritually perfect animal. The text of the Scroll omitted all vowels, musical symbols, and punctuation marks. Consisting thus of consonants alone, it followed that only a person who had proved his merit by constant study and thorough knowledge could read it.

The Scroll is enveloped in an embroidered mantle of silk or velvet adorned with a breastplate of hand-beaten silver. Silver ornaments (sometimes in the form of a crown as a symbol of majesty) also are placed on the top of the two wooden rollers on which the Scroll of the Law is rolled. Some congregations, notably of Spanish (Sephardic) descent, house the entire Scroll in a silver case.

In the course of his reading the cantor follows the words with a hand-shaped pointer (called, in Hebrew, a *yad,* or "hand"). This is to prevent the writing from becoming blurred or sullied by the touch of the human hand. In every synagogue the Scroll is kept in an Ark at the eastern end, facing, symbolically, toward Jerusalem.

When called to the Torah, many Jews show their reverence by kissing the Scroll, but, lest they defile it, not directly with the lips. Instead, they touch the Torah with the fringe of their tallit (see Chapter 18), and it is this which they kiss. The accidental dropping of the Scroll on the ground imposes a fast on the whole congregation present.

Decrepit or worn-out copies may not be destroyed. They are either kept in a storeroom (called geniza), set specially aside for this purpose, or buried with sacred ceremonial in the cemetery.

In ancient Greece and Rome, the writing of any book, even the most "holy," was the duty of slaves. To the Jew, however, the writing of the Torah is a sacred task reserved for the most pious in the community. The "Torah scribe" (in Hebrew, *sofer*) has to be a man of integrity and God-fearing habits, and his work must be done in the most scrupulous manner. Should he make a single mistake in the writing of God's name, no erasure is permitted. The entire sheet has to be rewritten. It is an arduous duty, but joyfully undertaken. Its completion is an occasion for great rejoicing for the whole community.

To Orthodox Judaism the Five Books of Moses are God's unalterable, eternal, and final revelation, given to Moses and handed down from generation to generation. All its 613 commandments, combining 248 positive rules and 365 prohibitions, are of equal importance. The very fact of their divine origin excludes any need of explanation. The unqualified and unquestioned acceptance of the whole of the Torah is the expression of true faith. No one has the right to pick and choose. Every passage has its meaning and message, as the Torah is the supreme authority of the Jewish faith.

Reform Jews hold the Torah in equal love and veneration as a transcendental document of divine revelation and inspiration. However, they believe that the five books were not the work of Moses alone, but comprise numerous religious documents written by several authors. From this it is argued that, being the work of men, the Torah may bear the impress of human workmanship and reflect the author's own outlook and the knowledge of his time. Thus it may show many levels of religious inspiration which reveal an evolution from relatively simple ideas and ideals up to the final stages of supreme ethical and spiritual concepts.

Reform Judaism, therefore, does not consider the word of the Torah to be sacrosanct, but differentiates between various parts, assessing their importance in accordance with their inherent spiritual value. It does not require (though equally it does not forbid) adherence to laws and customs which, with the passage of time, have lost their spiritual significance. It does, on the contrary, deem as sacred and binding its eternal message and all directions which still conduce to the purity and sanctification of life.

Many of the world's greatest artistic masterpieces were directly inspired by the Torah. Among them may be mentioned Michelangelo's sculpture "The Horned Moses"; Rembrandt's painting "Jacob Wrestling with the Angel"; Haydn's oratorio "The Creation"; and Shaw's metaphysical Pentateuch "Back to Methuselah."

The Five Books of Moses became the source of the major teachings of Christianity and Islam. Jesus was quoting the Torah when he propounded the laws which form the basis of all true religion, love of God and love of fellow men. Mohammed himself named Abraham as the father of Moslem faith.

The Torah has enriched the literature and even the language of almost all nations. As three unusual English examples, the word "cider" is used in the Torah for "intoxicating drink"; the word "jubilee" is Hebrew for the trumpet or horn sounded to mark the commencement of the fiftieth year which brought freedom to servants and remission of debts; and the "scapegoat" of the Authorized Version is the goat that escaped into the wilderness on the Day of Atonement after the high priest had symbolically loaded it with the sins of all the nation.

Last, holy though it be to worthy men of all religious faiths, the Torah has not escaped the unhappy lot of being used as a weapon with which the Jews could be persecuted. The ambiguity of its description as "The Law," based on its first Greek translation, was seized on. Originally chosen to suggest majesty, solemnity, and authority, it was wrongly interpreted in its narrowest and lowest sense to decry Judaism as a religion of rigidity and legalism.

Worse still, because of the awe with which the Jew regarded it and the power it exerted over his life as the source of his religion, his enemies made it the special aim of their attacks. Rabbis were wrapped in the Torah to be burned alive. Scrolls were made into sacks which, filled with sand, Jews were forced to carry. The desecration and burning of the Torah marked the Syrian persecutions at the time of the Maccabees—more than 2,100 years ago—as much as the Nazi hordes' terror of the twentieth century. This could not destroy Jewish faith, but only confirm and strengthen it. In a moving simile, the rabbis expressed the conviction that though the parchment was consumed by fire, its words escaped out of the flames heavenward. Picturesque and imaginative as this may be, it still serves to illustrate that the words of God, written in His Torah, are indestructible, imperishable, and eternal.

THE PROPHETS

"The Prophets" make up the second part of the Hebrew Bible. It was completed and canonized before 200 B.C.E. and falls into two sections: a historical narrative and an anthology of divine revelations. These are called "the earlier prophets" and "the later prophets."

The Earlier Prophets

By "the earlier prophets" are meant the books of Joshua, Judges, Samuel, and Kings. They tell the history of the Jewish people over a period exceeding five centuries, from Joshua's conquest of the Holy Land to the destruction of the first Jewish commonwealth by Nebuchadrezzar of Babylon.

The books describe the rule of the judges, the creation of Jewish monarchy, and the division of the one nation into two separate states. We follow their individual destiny, leading to the annihilation of the "kingdom of Israel" by the Assyrian power in 722 B.C.E. and the destruction of the first Temple and the exile of the "kingdom of Judah" by the Babylonian conqueror in 586 B.C.E.

The books contain documents of great value. Without them, little would be known of many a phase of early Jewish history. But they are not just a record of events or a one-sided account prompted by national pride or prejudice. On the contrary, they view the history of the Jewish people critically, presenting it as the training of a kingdom of priests. They consider the ups and downs of their fate as the direct result of observance or violation of the laws of God. In the same way, they judge the importance of rulers and kings not by their conquests and material power, but by their spiritual life and moral strength. The "earlier prophets" certainly portray history in a unique way. Their religious outlook and evaluation, truly, express the spirit of the Bible.

The Later Prophets

Jewish prophecy presents a phenomenon in the history of mankind. It has no parallel anywhere or at any time. The prophets were not seers, like the Greek oracles. Their task was not to foretell the future, but to forthtell Truth. They were the conscience of the people. Undaunted, they spoke up in the face of mighty potentates, powerful priests, and raving multitudes, always ready to take the consequences.

The prophets played a significant role in the development of Judaism and the history of the Jewish people. Two types existed. We know of dynamic figures like Nathan, Elijah, and Elisha, about whose actions we read in the historical books which, because of them, are known as the "earlier prophets." But these God-inspired men themselves did not leave any written work. Then there were the "later prophets," men of tremendous literary power and sublime oratory. Many of their speeches are preserved. They themselves, or loyal and enthusiastic contemporaries, wrote them down. These writings, now contained in the Bible, are not their complete work. Much has been accidentally lost or even purposely destroyed. When the biblical canon divides them into "major" and "minor" prophets, it does so not as an evaluation of their importance, but merely of how much has survived of their writings. All twelve "minor" prophets together have only one more chapter than just one of the three "major" prophets.

These "later prophets," "major" and "minor" alike, lived during more than three hundred years (from the eighth to the fifth century B.C.E.) during historical events of great and grave importance in Jewish and world history. They witnessed the rise and fall of great empires in east and west (Egypt, Assyria, and Babylonia), the annihilation of the State of Israel (comprising the northern ten tribes), the destruction of the first Jewish state (the kingdom of Judah), the exile of her people, and their return. To the prophets, history was not the study of chronicles, but a direct and often tragic experience whose inner meaning they strove to evaluate.

The prophets' philosophy of history recognized a moral world order. World history was world judgment. Obedience to God's teaching was the supreme law for all men and nations. If disregarded, no alliance, army, or prayer could save. The spirit of religion had to direct public policy as much as personal life.

No ruler was beyond good and evil. The least citizen and the most powerful king were equally bound by and subject to the same moral law. The prophets realized the interdependence of man and the unity of the world. Jonah traveled hundreds of miles to speak to the people of Nineveh, far east of Palestine. Obadiah scathed the Edomite nation beyond the southern frontier of the Holy Land. Deutero-Isaiah saw in Cyrus, King of Persia, an instrument in God's hand.

With integrity of heart and sincerity of purpose, the prophets demanded truth and justice in every sphere of life and by everyone. They knew of no compromise. To establish the right, they had first to uproot the wrong.

They fought unrighteousness, injustice, and hypocrisy wherever they found them. They spoke to the masses in the market place and to individuals in the streets. Uninvited and usually unwelcome, they entered the Temple and the royal palace. Their aim was to clean up the intrigues of politics, corruption in public life, dishonesty in commerce, and vested interests anywhere. They fought a religion that had become externalized and taken the place of sincere and true faith. They attacked the idle rich, who lived on the exploitation of the poor. They reminded small Israel, buffeted between two world powers in east and west, to remember her mission to be a people of religion and refrain from meddling in power politics.

To drive their message home, the prophets used every possible means. For three years Isaiah walked about naked in the streets of Jerusalem to shock the people and then to make them realize that unless they returned to God's ways they would be denuded and stripped of everything. Jeremiah appeared in public wearing a heavy yoke on his neck. The very sight of him was meant to stir the unbelieving multitude and drive home to them the message of inevitable enslavement, should they continue to put all their faith in military power.

Amos was well aware of the psychology of the mass. To catch the people's ears, he first criticized all other nations bitterly before attacking the Jews' own depraved lives. Jeremiah, when banned from public appearance, wrote down his message and had someone else read it out in his stead. When the manuscript was destroyed by the king himself, Jeremiah did not hesitate to dictate his words all over again.

Unlike priesthood, prophecy was not an occupation, but a call. Not of their own choice were men prophets. An inner voice compelled them to speak, sometimes even against their own wish. Jonah refused to answer the call, but was forced to do so nevertheless. Jeremiah struggled against his mission, considering himself too young. Yet there was a burning fire within him which he could not subdue. Isaiah felt that he was not pure enough to be God's mouthpiece, but he could not resist the divine, all-consuming fire.

The prophets differed in the way of their inspiration and in the manner of their receiving God's word. Some heard it as an inner voice that could not be silenced. Others saw visions of tremendous power. Mystical experience lifted yet others into realms beyond space and time. The psychology of prophecy opens up a wide and most interesting field of study. The prophets received God's message not only by extrasensory apperception. It spoke to them also out of world-historic events, their personal fate, and even the small incidents of everyday life.

In the experience of his own passionate yearning for his unfaithful wife, Hosea recognized God's undiminished love for disloyal Israel. Jeremiah, watching a potter at work, suddenly realized that it represented most vividly God's repeated attempt at reforming the Jewish people. The faulty jar had to be broken, but its very clay could be used again to remake a better vessel. When Isaiah noticed a reed pierce the hand of a man who tried to support himself by leaning on it, he saw in the incident a revelation of the futility of leaning on foreign powers instead of relying on God!

The reading from the prophetic writings became an integral part of Jewish public worship on Sabbath and festivals. It is called Haftarah, a Hebrew word meaning "conclusion," because it completes the reading from the Torah. It is sung according to a special traditional tune different from that of the Sidra. In benedictions which precede and follow it, the Jew thanks God for the gift of prophecy and its words of undying truth.

The readings of the prophets do not follow a systematic order like those of the Torah, which are selected according to the sequence of its individual books. Passages from the prophets are chosen because of their content, which must bear some relevance to the part read from the Scroll. Tragic historical circumstances may account not only for this parallelism of theme but for the very introduction of the "second lesson." Oppressive laws in an era of persecution forbade the Jews to study the Law at public worship. The Scrolls of the Torah were duly confiscated or hidden away. Police spies visited the services to see that the ban was strictly observed. But the inventive genius of the Jew replaced the prohibited reading from the Five Books of Moses by the still permitted study of the prophets. To remind the congregation of the real lesson, the rabbis applied the psychology of association. They chose as the prophetic reading a passage whose subject matter or text, even if only by a mere phrase or word, immediately conjured up in the worshiper's mind the original but suppressed "lesson" or conveyed a similar message. Later, when the ban no longer applied and the reading from the Scroll again became part of Jewish service, the prophetic reading remained, though the reason for its introduction was no longer valid; a substitute thus became the "second lesson."

Others claim that the Haftarah stems from much earlier times: as far back as the inclusion of the books of the prophets in holy writing. A third theory asserts that the Haftarah was added as a protest against the theology of the Samaritans, an early Jewish community who recognized the Torah alone as a holy book inspired by God.

The Christian church adopted this Jewish custom of the two lessons, but instead of selecting passages from the Torah and the prophets chose readings from the Old Testament and then the Gospels or the Epistles.

Each prophet has his characteristic note and message. These reflect his individual, personal background and psychological pattern, as well as the exigencies of his time. There are obvious differences in style, inspiration, and language. We find the visionary and the realist, the calm thinker and the emotional firebrand. Some prophets appeared just once, delivered their message, and then vanished forever; others were active throughout their lives. Yet, whether of royal, priestly, or common descent, whether speaking in exalted poetry or everyday prose, they all aim at the realization of the highest in human life, individual, national, and international. Their teaching not only molded the Jewish faith in their own time but has most potent present-day application.

Major Prophets

ISAIAH

Isaiah's prophecies extended over almost forty years. He was a man of aristocratic birth, and his speeches reveal a sense of dignity and power. In uncompromising earnestness he lays bare the decay of morals, the hypocrisy in religion, and the dishonesty in state affairs. He condemns those who "join house to house, that lay field to field, till there is no room." He points out the futility of sacrifice as a substitute for righteousness, which is the essence of faith and without which no people can endure. He defines God as complete holiness: exalted and transcendent and yet at the same time most personal and near.

Beyond the doom Isaiah visualizes the dawn: "The people that walked in darkness have seen a great light; they that dwell in the land of the shadow of death, upon them hath the light shined." He pictures the ideal human community without war and preparation for war, where righteousness and justice reign supreme and take the place of power politics. His description of the ideal ruler has often been interpreted as a prophecy of the Messiah. Isaiah passionately believed in the ultimate redemption of the Jewish people, who, though decimated by cruel fate, would be reestablished by the "remnant that is saved."

Unsurpassed in grandeur, both of style and content, is the message of comfort of the "great unknown" prophet. Though living two centuries later in the Babylonian exile, his speeches have been attached to the writings of Isaiah (from its fortieth chapter onward). He is, therefore, commonly known as the "second Isaiah" or, in Greek terminology, "Deutero-Isaiah." In exalted poetry and with unforgettable pictures, he gives comfort and hope. "Comfort ye, comfort ye, my people. . . . Every valley shall be exalted and every mountain and hill made low; and the crooked shall be made straight. . . . For a small moment have I forsaken thee, but with great mercies will I gather thee. . . . Everlasting joy shall be upon their head . . . and sorrow and mourning shall flee away."

Deutero-Isaiah knew of God's majesty and mystery. Before Him, all flesh was as grass and as the flower of the field. Compared to His greatness, whole nations were just like a drop falling from a bucket and a speck of dust in the balance. No man could ever penetrate His mind or understand His ways. "For My thoughts are not your thoughts. . . . For as the heavens are higher than the earth, so are My ways higher than your ways, and My thoughts than your thoughts." And yet, God—so omnipotent, universal, and eternal—was a God of love. They that waited on Him would "renew their strength, run and not be weary, walk and not faint."

God has entrusted the Jewish people to be His witness among the nations. This is why they are dispersed all over the world. They are God's "suffering servants." Downtrodden, despised, and ridiculed, their martyrdom throughout history is vicarious. They suffer for the sins of mankind and for the sake of proclaiming God's truth to the ends of the earth.

The poems on the suffering servant have been interpreted by Christian theology as applying to the life of Jesus.

JEREMIAH

No prophet was more outspoken on his personal life than Jeremiah. From early childhood he dedicated himself to his people, who despised and persecuted him. Though he passed through times of despondency, when he even cursed the day of his birth, he remained "an iron pillar," "a brazen wall." Sensitive and introspective, he yet defied the world of his day. He never married, never knew the joys of family life.

Son of a priest from a small village near Jerusalem, he became a most prominent figure in Judah's capital. He was a fearless fighter against spiritual blindness and hardness of heart of a corrupt priesthood and a self-righteous people. Recognizing the Jews' task as a people of religion, he bitterly opposed their intrusion into world politics. God demanded righteousness, and not ritual. His "new Covenant" was not an external code, but inwardly written in the heart of man. Only in the spiritual salvation of the individual lay the salvation of the people.

Speaking for peace, when the people were ready for war, Jeremiah was imprisoned as a traitor; he was saved from certain death only by the intervention of an Ethiopian, a member of a colored race. For years, he had to live in seclusion, if not in hiding. When history proved him true, he did not rejoice. On the contrary, he grieved with the people and stayed with the most lowly and forsaken. Then his prophecy of doom changed into words of comfort.

An inescapable moral compulsion drove him on. No personal suffering ever stilled his compassionate love for his ungrateful and uncomprehending nation. In a letter to the exiles in Babylon, he directed them to serve the country of their domicile loyally, a principle followed ever since by Jewish communities throughout the world.

Jeremiah's prophecies of doom, together with the assertion that the Lamentations were written by him, created the word "jeremiad" as meaning a pessimistic outpouring of the mind. The picture of death as the reaper occurs, for the first time in world literature, in Jeremiah's writings.

EZEKIEL

Ezekiel was an exiled priest turned prophet. A mystic personality, a cataleptic, and a clairvoyant, he experienced visions of great intensity and spiritual power. In Babylonia, he shared the fate of his people. He taught them to seek the cause of their suffering in themselves, and not in the failings of a former generation. He made religion a personal faith. God cares for each individual, who himself bears the responsibility for his action. God does not desire the punishment of evildoers, but their return to ways of goodness.

In his vision of the valley of dried bones restored to life, Ezekiel foretells the return of a regenerated Israel to the Holy Land, even from the ends of the earth. In the last eight chapters of his writings, he describes the "new Jerusalem." His utopia is not a political commonwealth, but a religious community, a theocracy based on spiritual values. Superabundance of the land's produce makes taxation unnecessary. The state's executives are not government servants, but God's ministers. The nations of the world, witnessing this perfect state and inspired by its greatness and purity, will inevitably become one humanity. They will be united by the worship of God. Ezekiel's priestly tradition makes him express his views in the terminology of "holy" and "clean," "profane" and "impure," and to elaborate a sacrificial service as a means of purification.

Minor Prophets

HOSEA

Love is the dominating force in Hosea's passionate prophecy. He saw the relationship between God and Israel in the picture of husband and wife. Even in the people's unfaithfulness, God still longed for them, ever ready to receive them back, with compassion and in forgiveness. But first, they had to realize that the essence of true religion consisted of an all-consuming, consecrated love, and not of sacrifices and burnt offerings.

The oldest colony of modern Israel (established in 1878), through which the modern Zionist metaphorically reentered the Holy Land, is named Petach Tikvah (The Gate of Hope), a phrase used by Hosea (XI, 17). When, in the morning, the Orthodox Jew winds the tefillin three times around the middle finger of his left hand in the simile of a spiritual marriage, he consecrates himself daily to God as the object of his devoted love, with the recital of Hosea's undying words:

I will betroth thee unto Me forever;
Yea, I will betroth thee unto Me in righteousness and in justice,
  in lovingkindness and in compassion.
And I will betroth thee unto Me in faithfulness.
Thou shalt know the Lord.

JOEL

Apart from his short (three-chapter) book and the name of his father, nothing whatever is known of the prophet Joel. Even the period of his life and the date of his prophecy are matters of conjecture. His graphic description of a plague of locusts has been the source of numerous interpretations. It has been understood as a realistic account of an actual, natural disaster sent by God as a punishment of the guilty nation. Figuratively, it has been viewed as a powerful picture of repeated attacks of a ruthless enemy, or of sensuous man being assailed by lust and passion.

The prophecy of Joel deserves to be remembered if only for two phrases which both occur in its second chapter (verse 13). The first is a pithy, telling admonition to those who rank ceremonial above spirituality. "Rend your hearts and not your garments," he cries, and with an eternal message of hope for the dispirited, he adds, "Turn unto the Lord your God, for He is gracious and merciful, slow to anger and of great lovingkindness."

AMOS

Justice and righteousness were to Amos the qualities most desired by God, Whom he saw as King and Judge.

Seek good, and not evil, that ye may live;
And so the Lord, the God of hosts, will be with you. . . .

A shepherd and dresser of sycamore trees, he left his peaceful peasant existence in the kingdom of Judah to raise his voice against corruption, immorality, and paganism in the northern State of Israel. An advocate of the simple, natural life, he denounced those who indulged in the vices bred by the comfort and luxuries of so-called civilization. He taught the moral and ethical significance of religion, which demanded social justice between man and man and righteousness among nations.

That the Jews were chosen by God to be His servants did not entitle them to any privileges, but rather imposed special responsibilities and obligations.

Amos lived about 760 B.C.E. He was the earliest prophet whose writings have been preserved. His lofty conception of God and his passionate fight for social justice have never been surpassed.

OBADIAH

The inclusion of Obadiah among the "minor prophets" can scarcely be disputed, for his is the shortest book of the Bible, comprising one chapter of twenty-one verses. It deals with the depravity of the people of Edom. Their cruelty and treachery became so proverbial that later generations applied their name to any oppressor of the Jewish people. In talmudic literature, it is used to describe the Romans.

There is something of sublimity in his warning to the mighty and the proud of heart who say: "Who shall bring me down to the ground?" The prophet, speaking in the name of God, replies: "Though thou shalt exalt thyself as the eagle and set thy nest among the stars, even thence will I bring thee down!"

JONAH

Jewish universalism and belief in a moral world order have found supreme expression in the book of Jonah. It centers on the fate of a non-Jewish people, the Ninevites, and shows God's concern for them. Destined to be destroyed because of their wickedness, they yet were pardoned as they returned to God's ways. Jonah, God's mouthpiece, tried to run away from his duty, but had to learn that his mission was inescapable, for God was everywhere.

The fate of every nation depends largely on the kind of life led by its citizens. Even to the last, God hopes and waits for man's return to goodness and the divine will. Not outward gestures, but only a change of heart will satisfy Him.

The story of the "big fish," often misrepresented as a whale, has fascinated young and old of all religions and thereby, unfortunately, only too often overshadowed the lofty truths in the book. Yet Jonah's significant message on sin, repentance, and forgiveness induced the rabbis to introduce it for reading on the most sacred day of the Jewish year, the Day of Atonement.

The rabbis saw in the book of Jonah an allegory of the Jew's fate, his insecurity in the battle for survival, and his final redemption. They found in the book, also, the lesson of the Jew's inescapable duty to act as God's messenger to the ends of the earth.

Christian theologians interpreted Jonah's restoration after three days' sojourn in the darkness of the fish's belly as a prophecy of the resurrection of Jesus on the third day after his death.

MICAH

Micah combines in himself the ethical fervor of Amos and the tender love of Hosea. He is fearless in his denunciation of the corrupt politician, the opportunist priest, and the heartless rich man. He shows up their selfishness, ostentation, and hypocrisy. His deep sympathy goes out to the poor, the downtrodden, and the dispossessed. A society built on tyranny, corruption, and false standards, Micah asserts, is doomed. His is the definition of true religion in its simplest and highest form:

> It hath been told thee, O man, what is good,
> And what the Lord doth require of thee:
> Only to do justly and to love mercy, and to walk humbly with thy God.

The arrogant, the unjust, and the unfeeling deny the existence of God, if not in words, by their very lives.

Micah castigated so-called religious leaders whose message was dictated by political and personal expediency and who created a false sense of security when they should have roused the people to a realization of the facts. He himself defied all attempts by the ruling powers, ecclesiastical and secular, to intimidate him.

Micah believed in the ultimate victory of the right and just, when all men will recognize God as their father. Then universal peace will be established, not by the power of tyrants, but by the rule of righteousness. His picture of the Messianic Age (paralleled in the book of Isaiah) makes the positive way of life predominate among men and nations. Constructive achievement will then take the place of destructive power. Not just a decrease of armaments but the total abolition of war and the complete cessation of military training will ensure lasting peace.

> And they shall beat their swords into plowshares,
> And their spears into pruning hooks;
> Nation shall not lift up sword against nation;
> Neither shall they learn war any more.

In a poetic picture, Micah speaks of the wiping out of Israel's sin by God's forgiveness: "Thou wilt cast all their sins into the depth of the sea." The literal interpretation of this passage originated an Orthodox custom. A ceremony called the tashlich (Thou shalt cast), after the first Hebrew word of this verse, takes place on the afternoon of the first day of the New Year. Men and women go to a running stream. Throwing bread crumbs into it, they recite this verse three times, symbolically drowning their sins. The earliest mention of the tashlich custom occurs in the fourteenth century. It corresponds to a German tradition of throwing herbs into the flowing Rhine on St. John's Eve, in hope that the New Year will sweep away all troubles and anxieties, just as the herbs were carried away by the river.

NAHUM

Nahum has been described as the prophet of outraged humanity. His name (meaning "comfort") conveys his message of consolation to nations suffering under the heel of ruthless world conquerors. The book contains an ode of triumph on the fall of Nineveh in 612 B.C.E.: "this city of blood, filled with falsehood, abounding in violence," this empire that "sold nations for harlotries and peoples for witcheries." Nahum's prophecy is the vindication of righteousness. It pictures the downfall of the mighty empire of Assyria, whose heartless potentates had perpetrated all manner of crimes and shown no mercy in their ambition to rule the world.

In extraordinarily (and almost untranslatable) powerful expression, Nahum interprets the lesson of history of his time for all ages. Nineveh had to perish because she had ignored the inherent rights and needs of humanity and had applied her power barbarously and tyrannically. The world is ruled by moral principles. Nations denying or ignoring them sooner or later have to suffer the inevitable consequence.

HABAKKUK

Habakkuk was one of the very first to pose man's eternal question of why the innocent should suffer and the wicked prosper. He challenged God's justice. How was it possible, he asked, that an all-powerful and righteous God could permit injustice in the world? His answer that "the righteous shall live by his faith" was considered by the rabbis as the final summing up of all 613 commandments of the Torah. It was understood by some to mean that the triumph of evil was never lasting; the faithful will prevail in the end, if only they stay loyal to God's precepts and do not despair even in times of greatest adversity. Others explained the passage as an expression of Habakkuk's conviction of the importance of the inner life of man. His character and spiritual qualities could never be influenced by external fate.

ZEPHANIAH

Zephaniah is the only one of all the prophets claimed to be of royal descent. His book speaks of "the day of the Lord," which will inaugurate the millennium. Then, God's final judgment on Israel and all nations will right all wrongs. The people, saved, chastened, and humble, will possess true religion. Single-minded, sincere, and forthright, they will live in a world governed by Truth.

HAGGAI AND ZECHARIAH

The books of Haggai and Zechariah are speeches to a disheartened and disillusioned community of exiles returned from Babylonian captivity. After the initial enthusiasm and joy of homecoming, they experienced the frustration of a hard and insecure life aggravated by the hostility and jealousy of foreign settlers in their midst. The two prophets were anxious to inspire the nation with new hope and confidence. They admonished the people to concentrate on the work of God, and not to be preoccupied with their own welfare. Only by basing their new existence in the old country on spiritual values would they find stability and hasten the Messianic Age, with its promise of prosperity and peace for all nations and people.

Zechariah pictured the "new Jerusalem" thronged with happy crowds, her children playing in the streets and her old men and women secure and unafraid. He reminded the people that God's return to the Temple had to be preceded by the people's return to God. Fasting and religious observance cannot take the place of a righteous way of living. Not material force, but the spirit of God alone guarantees a people's and humanity's survival: "Not by might nor by power, but by My spirit, saith the Lord of hosts."

Haggai's mind is clear. Zechariah uses obscure language in the description of his night visions of the Messianic Age. Yet it was due to the urging of both these prophets, so different in their emotional make-up and prophetic inspiration, that the Temple, whose construction had been delayed and interrupted, was completed and dedicated (in 516 B.C.E.). Apart from their time-bound historical significance, their religious message of the supremacy of the spirit belongs to all ages.

MALACHI

Malachi is the last of the Jewish prophets, in the sequence of the books of the Bible as well as in time. His name has been assumed to be merely his title—"My messenger"—and no definite time is mentioned, but the contents of the book place it around 450 B.C.E., in a period of skepticism and indifference. People did not care any more about religion. They questioned whether it really mattered if they worshiped God. Life seemed to prove anything but the existence of a God of Justice. Laxity in religion had brought on a total lack of moral standards. Immorality was rampant, divorce and intermarriage common.

Malachi battled to revive religion and rouse the people from their apathy. Denouncing moral looseness, he stressed the importance even of formal religion as a means to generate the spirit of faith.

His style is that of rhetorical questions. His theme is that in spite of the people's indifference, God has not ceased to love Israel. Calling for a return to God, he foretells a final reckoning, when evil will be consumed root and branch and righteousness prevail.

Closing the cycle of Jewish prophecy, Malachi, a "minor" prophet in the volume of his writing, is outstanding in the grandeur of his vision. His intense belief in the fatherhood of God and the brotherhood of man makes him call out fervently to all humanity, of whatever race, color, or creed: "Have we not all one Father? Hath not one God created us? Why do we deal treacherously every man against his brother, profaning the covenant of our fathers?"

THE WRITINGS

Hagiographa is the name of the third and last division of the Hebrew Bible, containing "sacred writings" of such diversity as hymns, aphorisms, philosophical dialogues, and historical chronicles. While the rabbis of the Talmud considered the Torah and the prophets as direct and actual divine revelation, they held that the "writings" were only inspired by God. Indeed, the final codification of this third section of the Bible was not an easy task and was preceded by much controversy as to the value of some of its books.

The literary expression of the "writings" ranges from simple prose (Chronicles) to magnificent poetry (Job), the time of composition from the days of King David's dynasty (Psalms) to the Maccabean revolt (Daniel)—altogether a period of more than eight centuries!

PSALMS

The book of Psalms is the oldest prayerbook. It heads the third part of the Bible. In Hebrew, it is called "Songs of Praise"

(T'hillim or, in shortened form, Tillim). It is a matchless anthology of religious poetry.

There are 150 psalms. They were written by many authors at different times, but 73 of them are ascribed to King David, known as a lover of music and an active musician whose playing soothed King Saul in his melancholy.

The psalms vary in thought, style, and length. The shortest consists of just two verses (Ps. CXVII); the longest, of 176 (Ps. CXIX). Sometimes the caption of a psalm indicates its specific type, whether it is emotional or intellectual, a meditation, a lesson, a prayer, a praise, or a philosophical speculation. We find psalms that are the expression of most personal religion and others that are the outpourings of a people's soul. Qualities of pious devotion alternate with those of national sentiment. Some psalms refer to specific events, such as King David's flight from Saul, the exile in Babylon, and the return to Zion. Others reflect the eternal experience of the human heart.

The psalms contain the principles of Jewish faith, which are not found in any systematic theology, but are implicitly expressed. The psalms are prophetic teaching in lyrical form. The awareness of God exists in them not as an abstract idea, but as an ever-present, most vivid reality in nature, history, and personal life. "The Lord is my Shepherd, I shall not want." Only "the fool says in his heart: 'There is no God.' " God is the Father of all men. He therefore cares for them and is never unmindful of their fate, even though He might "hide His face." No one can escape from His presence. Nothing can succeed in life unless based on the consciousness of God. "Unless the Lord build the house, they labour in vain that build it."

Compared with the majesty of God and the immensity of the universe, man appears infinitesimal, a speck of dust. Yet the divine spark within him gives him supreme power. The purpose of his existence is the use of his God-given opportunities and faculties: not to subdue and destroy, but to enrich and ennoble life. The most perfect praise God desires can never be confined to words, but lies in the truthfulness and holiness of man's everyday action. The psalms teach the right way of living and warn of the pitfalls awaiting every man. They tell of the way toward life eternal and of a humanity united in love and the service of God.

The universal appeal of the psalms has rendered them the property of all lands and people. History may change, but the emotions of the heart are always the same. Its anguish and joy have found everlasting expression in the psalms. There is the questioning of the innocent, who suffer injustice, and of the oppressed, who cannot understand the triumph of the evildoer. We share the solitude of the lonely, longing for some sign that they are not forgotten. We experience the joy of him who is elated by the glories of nature and of the one who is grateful for God's help. We find uneasy awareness of sin and the jubilant note of forgiveness.

The Psalter has rightly been called the hymnbook of humanity. No other book of the Bible has exerted a greater influence on man's thought and worship.

Countless generations of Jews were inspired and sustained by its words. With these, they cried out of the depths unto God, lifted up their eyes unto the hills, and, walking in the valley of the shadow, feared no evil. Nations were roused by the stirring accents of its hymns. "O God, our help in ages past, our hope for years to come" is a paraphrase of Psalm XC.

Out of the psalms arose Beethoven's "Creation Hymn" and Handel's "Hallelujah Chorus." Both synagogue and church have made the Psalter an important part of their worship. Jesus' last words are a quotation from it. The Authorized Daily Jewish Prayer-book contains seventy-four psalms. The beginning of every benediction and the central thought of the kaddish, the most widely known prayer of the Jewish people, originate from the psalms.

For every occasion of personal or communal life, a special psalm was added. Psalms were recited at the birth of a child, at marriages, for the dedication of a new home, and on setting out on a journey. To say Tillim for the dying became a sacred duty. The Shir ha-Ma'alot (Ps. CXXVI) is sung before grace after meals. The songs of the Hallel (Pss. CXIII to CXVIII) are intoned on the festivals of Passover, Pentecost, and Tabernacles.

The Psalter, indeed, is the most quoted work of the Bible. Its word pictures have become part of world literature: the sparrow and swallow that have found their nest to lay down their young, and the young hart that pants after the water-brooks as we must yearn for God. Expressions such as "the apple of one's eye," the truth coming forth "out of the mouth of babes and sucklings," and man's life span being "three-score years and ten" all originate in the psalms.

The psalms are written in Hebrew poetry. This differs widely from Western verse. It knows neither rhyme nor meter. Its most regular characteristic is "parallelism." This consists of a verse's being divided into two halves, each expressing the same idea, though in different words, or one half reinforcing the thoughts of the other by stating its contrast (antonym). Another distinguishing mark of Hebrew poetry is its rhythm, obtained by a regular recurring beat on an accented syllable. Some of the psalms have an alphabetic acrostic, an artistic type of Hebrew poetry in which each verse begins with one of the twenty-two letters of the alphabet in their proper order. The recurrence of a refrain marks another variety.

All the psalms were meant to be sung. Music played an important part in Temple worship. There were a special choir of Levites and an orchestra of wind and string instruments. The word "psalm" means "to be sung with string accompaniment." The parallelism of Hebrew poetry facilitated a special musical form of responsive (antiphonal) chanting between two groups of singers. Many words in the text of the psalms, often misunderstood, are merely directed "to the choirmaster" (*Lamnatse'ach*). "Selah" is not a religious exclamation, but a musical direction that the orchestra should start playing. Titles often indicate the tune to which the psalm should be sung, though they are frequently misunderstood as giving the name of the author.

The Psalter is a compendium of Jewish faith and a historical document of early Temple worship with its music, poetry, and communal participation. It is the book of the Bible which contains the largest element of personal religion. The love of God is its central theme, His recognition by all living beings the final aim: "Let everything that has breath praise the Lord."

PROVERBS

Throughout history the Jew has shown the greatest respect for knowledge. To find truth has always been his ambition, expressed with almost religious fervor. He feels that all knowledge of whatever kind comes from God.

The book of Proverbs—this collection of collections of aphorisms—centers on the idea of the greatness of wisdom. Without it, there cannot be true happiness and success. If man is only induced to grasp the beauty and glory of goodness, of necessity he will love and pursue it and despise and eschew evil.

Nothing, therefore, surpasses the importance of education in the right kind of living. Wisdom is the very source of life, of all that is vital and great. It leads man to industry and truthfulness, cheerfulness and justice, self-respect and forgiveness. It will make him avoid false friends, fools, quarrelsome men, flatterers, and gossips. But its very essence is the fear of God.

A man who thinks wisely cannot fail. The common-sense philosophy of Proverbs is applied to every aspect of life. Pithy sayings abound. They are striking in thought, and once heard, they are never forgotten: "Pride goeth before the fall. . . . Hope deferred maketh the heart sick. . . . Righteousness exalteth a nation. . . . A fool's mouth is his ruin. . . . A merry heart is the best medicine. . . . Where there is no vision, the people perish. . . . As a jewel of gold in a swine's snout, so is a fair woman without discretion."

The whole book is universal in outlook. It speaks always of man, and never only of Jews or Israelites. Its ideals are not chimeras, but practicable, sound philosophy. They are expressed not in abstract generalizations, but in everyday language, with a definite message and application: "Train a child in the way he should go; and when he is old, he will not depart from it. . . . Boast not thyself of tomorrow, for thou knowest not what a day it may bring forth. . . . Go to the ant, thou sluggard; consider her ways and be wise. . . . If thine enemy be hungry, give him bread to eat."

Solomon's biography in the Bible relates that he wrote three thousand proverbs. His judgments and his quest for an understanding heart above all things reveal him as a man of profound reason. It was thus only natural that the book of Proverbs, containing pearls of wisdom, was named after him, though not all its chapters were of his composition.

Many of its maxims and phrases have become the common property of humanity. The Proverbs' poem on the ideal wife is read in the Jewish household on every Sabbath eve. The eighth chapter, on the virtue of wisdom, became the fountainhead of a whole literature that inspired numberless thinkers.

The book of Proverbs, with its down-to-earth quality and memorable expressions, belongs not to any one people or any one age, but to all mankind and all time.

JOB

The book of Job is unequaled as a discourse on the problem and philosophy of human suffering. Here, a tortured world asks after the meaning of its agony. It is one of the great dramatic poems of world literature and a masterpiece in the realm of religion. Grappling with the fundamental issues of life, the book of Job discusses them without restraint and without fear. Old theological theories are boldly challenged. Religion is shown not as dead dogma, obediently and blindly accepted, but as an experience and a victory attained out of the crucible of adversity. The book asserts the right of man to question and to doubt. In stark realism and with intellectual honesty it rejects platitudes and refutes self-righteous hypocrisy. The very existence of this book and its inclusion in the Bible testify to the breadth of vision and freedom of thought inherent in Judaism. Jewish universalism is once again made apparent by the choice of a non-Jew as the central figure.

Like Plato's philosophy, Job is written in the form of a dialogue. Yet this is not based on the aim of philosophers intellectually to solve the mysteries of existence. It is the outcry of the soul, suffering without knowing the cause, unable to understand how such fate harmonizes with a belief in God, Who is all-loving and all-powerful.

After repeated attempts on the part of his wife and four friends to comfort him in his misery and to help him in his quest, Job at last finds the answer—not through human agencies, but in spiritual experience.

The prologue of the book describes Job's integrity and original happiness. We hear how the eternal skeptic, symbolized as Satan, disbelieves in the innate goodness of man. He asserts that Job's righteousness is not disinterested, but expedient and selfish. Its cause, he claims, is the expectancy of prosperity in return. "Doth Job fear God for naught?"

As a test, this happy family man, blessed with much property and good health, has to experience the loss of all his worldly possessions, the death of his children in the prime of life, and the tortures, physical and mental, of leprosy. But he never falters. "What! Shall we receive good at the hand of God, and shall we not receive evil?" To the end he keeps faith.

> Though He slay me, yet will I trust in Him. . . .
> Till I die I will not put away my integrity from me.

Even before the actual discussion starts, the book gives a first answer to the problem of suffering. It is the only valid test of disinterested goodness. Fair-weather religion is shallow and empty, but to remain faithful in the face of the agonies of one's heart proves true religion.

Now the narrative changes into poetry and dialogue. First, three of Job's friends suggest that his suffering is punishment for sin. Even the most just cannot be pure in the eyes of God. Failings of which he was not even aware caused his fate. His very stubbornness in asserting his innocence proves his guilt. All three men express this thought. Different in temperament, they vary only in the style and the vehemence of their arguments, their dogmatism and sympathy. In the beginning, they just pity Job; then, their anger roused, they accuse him of hypocrisy.

Then the fourth friend arrives: young, pompous, verbose, and certain of his own wisdom. To him, Job's suffering is not a punitive, but a purgative measure. His anguish is a means of purification, a moral discipline to refine and deepen his nature.

> Behold, happy is the man whom God correcteth;
> Therefore despise not the chastening of the Almighty.

Job rejects all their arguments in turn. They fail to supply any satisfactory and adequate reason why a good and just God should destroy him. At last, he receives the answer, but not from a human source. Divine revelation lifts him up from the level of mere philosophical discussion to the sphere of pure faith. Intellectual struggle is overcome by spiritual experience. Suddenly, Job is made to realize God's omnipotence and absolute wisdom. Compared with His majesty and power, man is insignificant and utterly ignorant. He can only humbly submit and acknowledge his inability to understand God's will or to fathom His infinite mysteries. Standing in awe, he must accept his destiny without ever doubting God's wisdom.

> I had heard of Thee by the hearing of the ear;
> But now mine eye seeth Thee;
> Wherefore I abhor my words, and repent,
> Seeing I am dust and ashes.

Overwhelmed with the eternal mystery of life, Job finds peace at last in a supreme affirmation of faith.

The test is over and Job's torture ended. The epilogue (changing once again from the poetry of the dialogue to the prose of narrative) rounds up the book. Job is blessed anew with a life of plenty, domestic happiness, and joy.

Throughout, the book teaches truths of profound significance. Religion demands honesty of thought. Man is meant not to ignore, but boldly to face the problems of life. Genuine goodness knows of no ulterior motive. To be righteous because it pays is Satan's philosophy. To see in suffering the result of guilt is an immature and unfounded point of view. To regard it merely as a test of true and sincere goodness, or a moral discipline in the molding of character, also is not a complete and satisfactory answer. Man must face the fact that, to his limited understanding, undeserved suffering is an insoluble paradox, which allows of no rational explanation. Its solution lies beyond time and space in the eternal and infinite.

Deep and diverse has been the influence of the book of Job. An unsurpassed spiritual epic, it is the supreme drama of the soul. It still offers the only possible answer to the problems of suffering and misfortune. Commentators and translators found in the book the germ of belief in immortality. The Sephardic rite of the synagogue made Job part of its liturgy on the Ninth of Av, the anniversary of the destruction of the Temple. The funeral service uses Job's words of submission to God's inscrutable will, praising Him, even at the hour of greatest anguish: "The Lord hath given and the Lord hath taken away, praised be the name of the Lord." This certainly is the supreme expression of true faith.

The introduction to Goethe's *Faust* was suggested by the prologue in Job. The music of Handel's *Messiah* has exalted Job's unshakable conviction in God's redemption: "I know that my Redeemer liveth." The book deeply influenced both Dante's *Divine Comedy* and Milton's *Paradise Lost*. William Blake was inspired by it in his mystic art. The description of a monstrous creature, the leviathan, gave rise to much mystical speculation and supplied the title to Hobbes's political philosophy.

Job's very name has become an epithet of the innocent sufferer. The English language has been enriched by immortal phrases of the book, such as "to escape with the skin of one's teeth" and "when the morning stars sang together."

Neither the author nor date of the book is known. Perhaps this is more than just accidental. The book belongs to everyone, and its problem is of all ages. It is the most outspoken work of the Bible, combining reverence and truthfulness. In powerful language it grapples with man's most bitter experience. Its Hebrew includes unique and unusual words. Its tense and dramatic dialogues arrest and challenge the mind.

SONG OF SONGS

Only those writings were accepted for the canon of the Bible which could be conscientiously regarded as the inspired word of God and as presenting true Jewish teachings. For this reason the rabbis gave most anxious thought to the admissibility of the Song of Songs, even though its authorship was ascribed to King Solomon.

Superficially, the book appears to be an unabashed poem of love presented in the form of a dialogue between a country maiden and her royal lover. To him, his sweetheart is his dove. Her lips are a thread of scarlet. Fair as the moon and clear as the sun, her love is a ravishing of the heart. In his eyes all other girls are but thorns around a lily.

The girl, describing herself as "dark but comely," returns his passion and his longing. "Let him kiss me with the kisses of his mouth, for your love is better than wine." Even in her dreams she seeks him.

Both know that "many waters cannot quench love, which is as strong as death," just as jealousy is as cruel as the grave. For the first time in world literature, we hear of the lovesick heart.

In every chapter the book breathes an atmosphere of beauty and happiness. It is a spring song of the human heart as well as of nature:

> For lo, the winter is past,
> The rain is over and gone;
> The flowers appear on the earth;
> The time of singing is come.

Being required to differentiate between the sacred and the profane, the rabbis were deeply concerned by its rather outspoken realism. It was finally admitted to the canon, and thereby perhaps saved for posterity, by the realization that it was capable of interpretation as an allegory. It was seen as a dialogue not between bride and bridegroom, but between God and man. In later centuries, when Christianity had to face the identical problem, it interpreted lover and beloved as Jesus and the church. Every verse had to be considered not literally, but as a picture.

The new way of reading the book made a deep impress on the Jewish mind. Definitely now part of sacred literature, it was specially chosen to be read at the festival of Passover, at springtime in the seasons of the Holy Land, and in the history of the Jewish people. On Passover, too, God had elected His people, just as the lover chooses his bride.

Centuries later, the Song of Songs inspired Solomon Alkabetz, a sixteenth-century Oriental mystic, to see the Sabbath as Israel's bride and to write a hymn which has become the signature tune of the Sabbath eve. He used the very words of the Song of Songs, "Come, my beloved," in Hebrew, *L'cha dodee*. It has been called "perhaps one of the finest pieces of religious poetry in existence."

Neither the faith of Israel nor God is mentioned in the Song of Songs. Authorities differ as to whether it is an anthology of lyrics or a rustic dialogue, of royal authorship or a composition of the people. Yet it is a document of sublime beauty, so much so that one of the great scholars of Judaism, Rabbi Akiba, could declare that if the other books of the Bible are holy, the Song of Songs is "holy of holies," giving voice to the strongest and most sacred emotions of the Jewish heart.

RUTH

The book of Ruth is an essay on true loyalty. That it has found a place in Jewish Scripture is an indication of the universality of Judaism. Ruth was a non-Jewess who embraced the Jewish faith. Of foreign birth, she was made welcome in the Holy Land. Yet from this convert sprang the ancestors of King David, out of whose house, it was foretold, the Messiah would arise.

It is a simple story, told in plain words, about ordinary country people. Naomi, at a time of famine, had left her home in Judah. She had gone abroad to Moab with her husband Elimelech and her two sons, Machlon and Chilion. Misfortune befell her. All three men died, and Naomi—which means "the lovely one"— now called herself Mara—"the bitter one"—as sad fate had embittered her life. Her two sons had married girls of Moab, Ruth and Orpah, who were now widowed.

Ten years later, when the famine had ceased in Israel, Naomi decided to return to Judah, begging her daughters-in-law to stay behind with their families in their own country. After some persuasion, one of them agreed; but the other, Ruth, was not to be persuaded, and when further pressed by Naomi, she replied in impassioned words, unsurpassed as an expression of unshakable eternal loyalty. "Entreat me not to leave thee," she cried,

> For whither thou goest, I will go;
> And where thou lodgest, I will lodge;
> Thy people shall be my people,
> And thy God my God.
> Where thou diest, will I die,
> And there will I be buried.
> The Lord do so to me, and more also,
> If aught but death part thee and me.

Thus, Ruth accompanied Naomi back to Bethlehem, where they arrived at the time of the barley harvest. There she married again—a kinsman of her late husband, Boaz, "a mighty man of wealth," whom she had met while gleaning in his field. Their great-grandson was David, King of Judah.

To this day, female converts to Judaism choose Ruth as their Hebrew name. Her undying words are incorporated into some forms of the marriage service. The book itself, because part of its action takes place at the season of the reaping of barley, is read during the harvest festival of Shavuot.

The book describes the simple life with its selfless love, unaffected goodness, and genuine, religious spirit, welling up out of the people. There is the beauty of family life with its care for the weary and worn. We find how, without self-righteousness, the people look after the poor and needy, who are invited to glean in the fields—without shame or expectation of thanks. The alien is made welcome and treated like one's own. Everyone shares in the joys of the happy and the anxieties of the homeless. Ruth's sickle is antiquated. It has given way to the huge harvesting machine. Her loyalty is still unsurpassed.

In the Hebrew Bible, Ruth is included in the "five scrolls," as it was originally inscribed on a scroll of parchment. The Christian Bible (following the early Greek translation) combines it with the book of Judges, where, chronologically, it belongs.

It may appear strange that this short romance of only four chapters should have survived at all, let alone in so prominent a place. True, it proves to be a link in the genealogy of King David, but more important than that, perhaps, is its explicit lesson of the permanence of unselfish love and even more the implicit suggestion that the Bible is concerned not only with the lives of great men but equally with the misfortunes and fortunes of simple, homely people. In the book of Ruth, as clearly as anywhere else in the Scriptures, is demonstrated the fundamental democracy of the Jewish faith.

LAMENTATIONS

The Lamentations are elegies written on the fall of Jerusalem and the conquest of the Holy Land by the Babylonian forces under Nebuchadrezzar in 586 B.C.E. They are songs of deep sorrow.

The first Jewish State had been completely and ruthlessly wiped out. Of the people who survived, the finest had been led into captivity. The land was ravished; the Temple, the Jews' pride, was burned to ashes. Jerusalem, once the envy of all, was destroyed:

How doth the city sit lonely, that was full of people!
How is she become as a widow, that was great among the nations!

Orphaned children hungered, and none took pity. Hope and happiness had given place to humiliation and sorrow. Former allies had proved to be fair-weather friends and had joined with the enemy in exulting at the humbling of Israel.

Worse still was men's indifference to all this innocent suffering. No one cared.

Is it nothing for you, all ye that pass by?
Behold and see if there is any sorrow like unto my sorrow?

National disaster and personal suffering could not destroy faith. Even in his sorrow the Jew must believe—and hope. Suffering was not just punishment for sin, but a discipline.

It is good for man that he bear the yoke in his youth.
Let him keep silence, for God has laid it upon him.

Even in his torment he must not consider himself abandoned by God, but examine his ways and return to Him even more fervently. The Lamentations end, therefore, not in despair or defiance, world negation or denial of God, but with a prayer for God's love and renewal of faith.

The Lamentations are magnificent Hebrew poetry, written in mournful cadence. In four out of the five chapters the twenty-two verses begin with successive letters of the Hebrew alphabet.

These elegies have become part of the liturgy of the Ninth of Av. The Hebrew Bible calls them after their initial word, *Echa* (How!), and places them among the scrolls. The English Bible, once again following the Greek translation, joins them with the writings of the Prophet Jeremiah, whom tradition claims as the author of these five songs of haunting beauty. They are truly the outpourings of a grief-stricken heart and a nation's martyrdom. But they are also an affirmation of unconquerable faith.

ECCLESIASTES

King Solomon is said to be the author of a fascinating philosophical inquiry after the meaning of life. It is known by three names, each describing in a different language "One who speaks in an Assembly": *Kohelet* in Hebrew, *Ecclesiastes* in Greek, and simply "The Preacher" in English. The book reads like a magnificent sermon addressed to humanity. It seeks to discover what really gives lasting happiness and what should be the aim of all striving. This is its summing up.

Those who think to find true happiness in the pleasures of the table are doomed to disappointment, nor can satisfaction be found in riches. Pleasure and amusement are "vanity of vanities." To seek fulfillment and happiness in the building of pretentious houses and the planting of showy gardens is equally "a striving after wind." To wield authority over people and make them slaves for oneself cannot give enduring joy. Knowledge neither gratifies nor gives peace of mind. The writing of books is unending, but leads nowhere. To try to make the crooked straight is futile. Folly triumphs over wisdom and vice over virtue. History is like a vicious circle. There is a monotony of sameness and nothing new under the sun. The most up-to-date is merely the old remade. That which has been is that which shall be. All progress is an illusion.

Yet to deny life, to long for death, would even be more senseless, for "a living dog is better than a dead lion." Man must learn to differentiate between the false and the true, between passing shadows and permanent reality. To recognize the spiritual values in life and to fulfill God's commandment, "this is the whole duty of man."

Ecclesiastes was the last book admitted into the canon of sacred writings. Its mood of melancholy and skepticism and its bitter reflections on life aroused strong opposition and, in some authorities, determination to exclude it from the Bible.

Many rabbis objected to its negative attitude. They resented its recurring theme of the vanity of things. They rejected its claim that life was ruled by chance and that existence was lacking in purpose. They denied that an equal fate awaited both good and evil. To them, the fatalism and pessimism in the book were totally un-Jewish. Finally, other rabbis stressed the innate qualities of the admittedly skeptical confessions of a man whose soul was tormented with doubts. After all, the book showed a zeal for truth and an intense belief in God's supremacy and man's moral duty. In its demand for reverence and obedience, its final note was not futility, but faith.

Thus, after all the controversy and despite all the opposition, Ecclesiastes became part of the Bible; indeed, it is read in the synagogue each year during the festival of Tabernacles, when its autumnal mood is appropriate to the season.

There remained, however, another problem. Solomon was credited with the authorship of three books: Song of Songs, Proverbs, and Ecclesiastes, representing, respectively, such different states of mind as passionate love, mature wisdom, and almost cynical resignation. How could one man, no matter how great his genius, possess such diverse tendencies and write in such varying moods? After prolonged and profound debate, it was agreed that all three had indeed been written by Solomon, but at different periods. In the ardor of youth he wrote of love; in the prime of his life his thoughts were turned to rules of rational living. Finally, toward the evening of his life, he sought to find a balance between his sense of resigned tolerance and his deep, surviving faith in God.

Ecclesiastes is a sad but sincere book. It proves that man cannot live by reason alone, or by debating life's problems, but, in addition, needs faith and a moral will. The inclusion of Ecclesiastes in the Bible once again testifies to the Jew's zeal not to stifle thought, but awaken reflection; not to impose opinions, but to foster the striving after truth.

ESTHER

In the sequence of scrolls, Esther takes fifth and last place. In popularity it certainly comes first, so much so that it is normally called just the Megillah—"The Scroll." Its story, though referring to definite events in Persia under King Ahasuerus, commonly identified with Xerxes (485–465 B.C.E.), is typical of the perennial fate of the Jew. It tells how a personal grudge led to general persecution, but how, finally, God's providence saved a doomed community.

Ahasuerus felt slighted when his wife disobeyed his command to display her beauty at a public banquet. Dismissing her, he soon afterward married again—this time Esther, a Jewish orphan who, however, concealed her origin and her faith. About the same time, Mordecai, cousin, guardian, and counselor of Esther, discovered a conspiracy against the king and thereby saved his life.

Haman was an upstart who had become the king's prime minister. In his pride of office and lust for power, he demanded almost divine recognition. But Mordecai, as a faithful Jew, refused to bend his knee, an act of reverence due only to God. Haman, hurt in his pride, thirsted for revenge. To punish Mordecai alone would not satisfy his vanity. He therefore determined to destroy all the Jews and, after the pagan custom, cast lots to ascertain the most propitious day.

With his plans ready, he confronted the king. Saying nothing of his personal grudge, he informed him in a general way (not even mentioning the Jews by name) that the empire harbored a most disloyal people, who were not conforming to Persian law. Without any further investigation the king gave his trusted minister full authority to proceed with any necessary measures.

Losing no time, Haman had orders posted throughout the 127 provinces calling on the whole population to exterminate the Jews and confiscate their property on 13 Adar, the "allotted" day. The Jews were panic-stricken. They who had felt so secure now fasted and mourned. At Mordecai's request, Queen Esther, in the presence of Haman and at the risk of her own life, pleaded with the king for her people. Revealing her identity, she proved the Jews' innocence and Haman's guilt. Hearing the facts, the king recognized his minister's corruption and treachery. The day appointed to become the Jews' doom was changed into a day of deliverance. Haman was executed, and his offices and dignities were conferred on Mordecai, whose services were at last acknowledged. A festival was instituted as a perpetual reminder of the Jews' redemption.

Even this "scroll of Esther" provided much difficulty when the rabbinical authorities discussed its suitability to become part of the Bible. The absence of any direct mention of divine power caused strong opposition. True, Esther is a "God-less" book insofar as the name of God is not mentioned once. Yet it is a deeply religious document, since, in spirit, the sense of divine providence is ever-present. The whole narrative testifies to God's working in history. Seemingly chance occurrences are shown up as links in the evolution of a definite pattern.

Scholars have queried the historicity of the book. No work, however, could have more strikingly presented Jewish experience throughout the ages: the innocent suffering of a whole people as the result of the ill will of one individual; the insecurity of Jewish existence even in times of apparent peace; the fickle psychology of the crowd who, by decree of the state, can be led to hate or to love at a moment's notice; the inability of a Jew, no matter how exalted his position or standing, to divorce himself from his people or escape their fate; the fact that the resentment of the action of one individual Jew may lead to the condemnation of the whole people; and that one single Jew's failing causes suffering to all his brethren.

The scroll of Esther came to be regarded not as the property of the synagogue alone; many homes pride themselves in possession of precious copies, written on parchment, lavishly illustrated, and kept in magnificent silver cases.

A joyous festival was instituted to commemorate the dramatic events and their happy outcome (for all, of course, but Haman). This was given the name of *Purim,* which is the Hebrew word for the "lots" cast by Haman. The Megillah of Esther is read in the synagogue amid scenes of revelry that sometimes exceed the normal decorum of Jewish worship.

That the time of origin and the author of the book of Esther are unknown really does not matter. Its message is timeless and universal. It speaks of the eternal miracle of Jewish survival in the face of almost insuperable odds.

DANIEL

Daniel is often considered merely a book of exciting tales of faithful men being rescued from the lion's den and the fiery furnace and of awe-inspiring visions of mysterious writing on the wall and a colossus with feet of clay. In reality it is a documentary story of dramatic circumstances with a message ever relevant when humanity has to fight for survival.

Written at a time of confusion and terror, of religious persecution and brutal power politics, it was meant to encourage dauntless fighters for freedom. It presents an affirmation of faith in the power of the spirit and a call to persevere even in the face of grievous persecution.

People were impressed by the majestic appearance of a colossus of military power. But the book showed up its feet of clay. All its might lacked true foundation and could collapse because of a small stone—not of human hands! Loyalty must be unqualified; without shame and embarrassment, Daniel refuses to eat food prohibited by his religion, even when a guest of the royal family. Though forbidden to pray, he continues to worship God. He and his friends (exiles from the Holy Land) choose imprisonment and the death sentence rather than, even in pretense, to bend their knees in a state-commanded idol worship.

Thus, the book emphasizes the insufficiency of human power and material things and the supremacy of God. His sovereignty will finally be established as an everlasting kingdom, not of this earth alone. Then "the wise shall shine as the brightness of the firmament; and they that turn men to righteousness as the stars forever."

Though dealing with personalities of the early Babylonian exile (of the sixth century B.C.E.), the book was probably written at the height of the Maccabean battle against Syrian dictatorship (in the second century B.C.E.) and distributed in pamphlet form as an encouragement to the fearless fighters. Its apparent antiquity was a clever means to camouflage its burning importance from enemy spies, but at the same time to inspire the contemporary community by the example of history. Its language is both Hebrew and Aramaic, with a few Greek words interspersed. The book is divided equally into narrative and vision.

The impact of Daniel has been immense in the most diverse fields. It contains the only biblical reference to the resurrection of the dead, though no details are given. Christian theology was greatly influenced by the book's account of Michael and Gabriel, the angels of Heaven. It saw a Messianic prophecy in the description of the son of man, coming with the clouds of Heaven to the Ancient of Days. Daniel's reference to specific numbers, animals, and angels gave rise to numerous speculations and intrigued mystics of all ages. Its visions and stories inspired poets and painters. Its dream interpretation and cryptograms were welcome material for modern psychologists and for psychical research. Vegetarians read with great satisfaction the report of how Daniel and his friends, while keeping a strict vegetarian diet, surpassed all others in good health and clear thinking.

The name Daniel literally, and appropriately, means "My judge is God." The book is outstanding in its dramatic power and its value as a historical document: in the inspiration it gave to countless generations in their determination at all costs to preserve their faith.

EZRA—NEHEMIAH—CHRONICLES

The Bible concludes with a unique kind of historical survey. This starts with Adam and leads to the return of the Jewish exiles from Babylonia and their early fate in the reestablished Jewish commonwealth. It consists of dry, genealogical lists and exciting, eyewitness reports, quotations from state archives and excerpts from other biblical writings. The reports concentrate on the fate of Jerusalem and the Temple, its worship and priesthood. They are contained in the books of Ezra, Nehemiah, and Chronicles. They appear in this sequence, though chronologically their order should be reversed, as the Chronicles end with the beginning of the book of Ezra. Again, the language alternates between Hebrew and Aramaic.

The Chronicles commence with the presentation of history in the form of genealogical lists, which fill nine chapters. Then follows the history of David, Solomon, and the kingdom of Judah. The Babylonian exile and King Cyrus' permission to the Jews to return to the Holy Land conclude the "Words of the Days," as the Hebrew Bible calls these two books. They consist of many excerpts, which are presented with definite, priestly leanings. God's intervention in human affairs is their continuous theme.

In Ezra, history changes into memoirs. Important documents are now included, among them King Cyrus' decree of 538 B.C.E. and a list of some of the fifty thousand returned exiles. We accompany Ezra the Scribe back to Jerusalem. We witness the rebuilding of the Temple and the frustration of early attempts to interfere with it. Another list of historical value gives the names of the families who, at Ezra's urging, agreed to dissolve their mixed marriages, which had assumed dangerous proportions.

Nehemiah's autobiographical report follows. An official of the Persian King Artaxerxes, in 444 B.C.E. he is granted leave of absence to visit Jerusalem in the capacity of a royal governor of the district. His special assignment is the restoration of the city's fortifications, the walls and gates having been destroyed by enemy raiders. This task completed, the whole people assemble, and Ezra reads to them the Holy Law. Now God's Covenant is renewed: to guard and keep forever "the Law of Moses which the Lord had commanded to Israel."

Tabernacles is celebrated, and the walls are dedicated. His mission fulfilled, Nehemiah goes back to the Persian court, to return to the Holy Land several years later when once again the religious life of the people has gravely deteriorated and needs a strong hand to be righted. At that point, and with a special invocation of God, the book ends.

Chapter 8

HIDDEN BOOKS

It is not generally realized that there is in existence a fascinating Jewish library of "hidden books," which were concealed about two thousand years ago by the spiritual leaders of that epoch. They have come to be known by the general title of Apocrypha, from the Greek word which means "hidden." It should be stated at the outset that the books were not hidden from the Gentiles. On the contrary, it was due solely to the foresight of the early Christian fathers that they were preserved for posterity.

Actually, it was from the general Jewish community that the books were hidden. There were two reasons for this unusual action by the rabbinical authorities. An examination of these, the main causes of the birth of the Apocrypha, reveals some interesting facets of Jewish history, outlook, and belief.

The first reason relates to the codification of the Bible by the rabbinical synods in the second century of our era. Some of the books examined were deemed to fall short of the required standards of sanctity and scholarship, while others were received too late to permit them to be adequately considered. To prevent any misunderstanding as to their validity and holiness, it was decided to withdraw them from general circulation. They thus did not become part of the official canon of the Bible, but were put away out of the reach of the community at large.

Second, it is claimed that the original Apocrypha consisted of spiritually dangerous books, dealing with the supernatural. It was to protect the average Jew from any mental ill effect that these were hidden.

Judaism has always been a democratic faith. The Jewish outlook does not envisage the exclusive saint, but an all-inclusive "kingdom of priests." Each and every Jew was close to God, and each could find the way direct from his individual soul to the Divine Master. Any distinction between men as consecrated and profane, or initiated and uninitiated, was alien to Judaism.

The Torah itself expressed this idea dramatically when Moses gave his impassioned reply to friends who, in great anxiety, informed him that two men in the camp had suddenly been overcome by ecstatic visions. "Are you jealous on my account?" he cried. "Would that the people of the Eternal were all prophets!"

Yet there were periods within the history of the Jewish faith when certain individuals made an immense effort, either in religious fervor or intense longing for true knowledge, to penetrate the mysteries of life. It was only then that Judaism experienced the phenomenon of esoteric religion; but even in these circumstances it did not become the property of a distinct caste, although, as a precautionary measure and to guard the people's spiritual health, research was restricted to initiates.

"To enter Paradise" became the rabbinical term describing speculation on the innermost secrets of existence. In guarded language the Talmud tells of four rabbis who embarked on this quest of the humanly unknowable. Their fate became a warning. One alone escaped unharmed from "Paradise." "Only Akiba," the Talmud says, "remained safe and sound." Ben Azzai, seeing more "than one is permitted to see," paid with his life. Ben Zoma lost his mind, and Elisha ben Abuya his faith. To safeguard others from a similar fate, the rabbis admonished the inquisitive: "If you direct your mind to four things, it were better you had never been born: what is above, what is below, what was before the creation, and what will take place at the end of the world." It is here that agnosticism enters faith.

To go beyond the horizon of human vision, indeed, implied great danger to man's soul and mind. Such speculation easily led to confusion of thought, destruction of faith, and disintegration of personality. Only very few, feeling themselves sufficiently fortified, could safely set out on this great adventure. Books dealing with such dangerous possibilities had to be kept away from the masses. They were concealed—in the Apocrypha. But paradoxically they were lost (or removed) again, for the books contained in this collection as it exists today, although of great historical importance, are spiritually innocuous.

A third explanation asserts that as some apocryphal writings included revelations of ancient biblical personalities—such as Solomon, Baruch, Jeremiah—which were meant to reach the Jewish people only in later epochs, they had to be hidden until that appointed time had arrived. Yet, knowing that the claimed authorship was totally fictitious and that these books were not the work of biblical figures, but of anonymous modern writers who only assumed the revered ancient names in order to be read and believed, this interpretation of the Apocrypha can be discounted.

Incidentally, the continued use of the name Apocrypha is a classical example of the phenomenon of a word's persisting even when its original significance has vanished. No longer secret or hidden, the books of the Apocrypha are freely available to all who wish to study them.

The Apocrypha are not just an ancient library of forgotten books—a find for the philologist and theologian. They have left their mark in many ways. They became a source of inspiration to dramatic art (*Tobias and the Angel*) and pictorial presentation ("Judith and Holofernes"). They added moving passages to Jewish liturgy and supplied the historical background of one of the most popular holy days.

The very story of the fate of these books, their concealment, preservation, and publication, is fascinating. We can discover in them the result of a combination of Jewish religious genius and Greek philosophical thought. They are a link between the Bible of Judaism and the Gospels of Christianity, the bridge between the Old and the New Testaments. Within these volumes are unique historical information and passages "so inspiring as to be inspired."

The Wisdom of Ben Sirach

The Wisdom of Joshua, the Son of Sirach (also called Ecclesiasticus), is perhaps the most famous book of the Apocrypha.

Its author lived in the second century before the common era. His work was modeled on the Proverbs of Solomon. He aimed at halting and overcoming the moral decay rampant in his time. This expressed itself in lax morals, disintegration of family life, and utter neglect of social obligations.

Written in Hebrew, the original was lost, and for many centuries the work was known only in its Greek, Syraic, and Latin translations. Then, in 1897, Dr. Solomon Schechter, searching in a forgotten, walled-up storeroom of an ancient synagogue in Cairo, discovered a medieval manuscript of the missing Hebrew text. In 1965, Yigael Yadin was even more fortunate. Among other precious apocryphal manuscripts, he found at Masada a first-century B.C.E. copy of the Hebrew original made only a hundred years after the actual composition of the work.

The pattern of life presented in The Wisdom of Ben Sirach aims at the renewal of spiritual and ethical values in a secularized materialist age. It describes the proper conduct of the individual within the family circle and, in the wider community, his duties to God and society. Steadfastness of character, moral and physical health, wisdom and righteousness, are praised as the expression of a life dedicated to God. Selfish friendship, greed, rashness, immorality, and loss of temper are condemned as socially and personally harmful.

In numerous ways Ben Sirach expresses deep worldly experience. "In the day of good things, there is forgetfulness of evil things; and in the day of evil things, a man will not remember things that are good. . . . The affliction of one hour causes forgetfulness of delight." A man is best known by his children. An enemy is never to be trusted. "Though he humble himself, and go crouching, take good heed, and beware of him." A man associates with those who are like him. When a rich man speaks, all keep silence. "What he says is extolled to the clouds." But when a poor man voices his opinion, people ask: "Who is he, anyway?"

A man's dress, his laughter, and his gait reveal his character. "Sand, salt and a mass of iron are easier to bear than a man without understanding." Three things beautify life: concord in the family, friendship of neighbors, and the complete unity of husband and wife. A wife is the most precious possession: she is a helpmeet and a pillar of rest. The foolish man changes like the moon. One that casts a stone on the truly high throws it on his own head.

Ecclesiasticus surveys every aspect of life and is always ready with wise counsel. Patience with and deep concern for one's old parents is true religiosity. To make oneself beloved within the community must be an ever-present aim. Single-mindedness is an essential of honest living. "Winnow not with every wind and walk not in every path. . . . Let thy word be one." To strive for truth unto death will assure God's help. Ben Sirach warns never to envy the glory of sinners or to be impressed by outward appearance. "The bee is little . . . but her fruit is sweetest." Excess is always harmful. Carefulness in one's speech is an expression of wisdom. "A slip on the pavement is better than a slip of the tongue. . . . The heart of fools is in their mouths, but the mouth of wise men is in their heart." But above all, no greatness exceeds the fear of God.

Tobit

The book of Tobit describes simple piety, its trials and final vindication. The old father, an exile from Israel, forthright and unafraid throughout his life, excels in the giving of alms and in loving deeds to those in need. Yet he is afflicted with blindness, he experiences penury and loneliness, and he is shunned by his former friends. Tobias, his son, sent to collect an outstanding debt, does not return and seems to be lost.

Tobit's piety appears to go unrewarded; the unjust seemingly flourish while the righteous wilt. But Tobit never questions God's wisdom. He submits to His inscrutable will. He knows that one day he will understand the reason for his afflictions. Eventually, his faith triumphs. His son returns, bringing riches and a happy wife, and he is able to cure his father's blindness. "And now my children, consider what the giving of charity does and how righteousness does deliver."

The Wisdom of Solomon

The Jewish belief in immortality has found its most comforting and moving expression in another part of the Apocrypha, The Wisdom of Solomon. Written by an Alexandrian Jew mainly as a warning against the folly of atheism, the book gained greatest importance by its sublime assurance of the deathlessness of the human spirit:

The souls of the righteous are in the hands of God, and no evil shall touch them. In the eyes of the simple, they seem to have died, and their departure is accounted to be their hurt. But they are in peace, and their hope is full of immortality. Having borne a little chastening, they shall receive great good; for God has made trial of them and found them worthy of Himself.

The Books of the Maccabees

Among the best-known and most familiar of all the Jewish historicoreligious writings are the Books of the Maccabees; yet comparatively few realize that these do not form part of the Bible, but are included in the Apocrypha.

They tell the story of a war of independence successfully fought more than 2,100 years ago by the aged Mattathias, his gallant sons, and a band of inspired followers. They also relate some of the world's most moving stories of martyrdom—of Hannah and her seven sons and the aged Eleazar—who preferred death to apostasy.

It is one of the many strange aspects of Jewish history that to be able to read of this stirring tale of Jewish heroism and patriotism, the very origin of the Feast of Chanukah, the Jew had to go to the Christian Bible in which the books of the Apocrypha, excluded from the Jewish canon, were safeguarded for posterity.

It was thus the Christians who preserved for the Jews the passionate declaration of Mattathias' faith: "If all the nations fall away each one from the worship of his fathers . . . yet will

I and my sons and my brothers walk in their covenant. . . . We shall not forsake God's law. . . . He who is zealous, follow us!"

Ben Sirach and Solomon's Wisdom, the story of Tobit and the Books of the Maccabees, represent the three different kinds of literature found in the Apocrypha. Each in its own way calls for piety, wisdom, and courage, especially in the face of undeserved suffering, alluring temptations, or ruthless and unjust force.

Among other books of this remarkable collection are the drama of Judith, the story of Susanna, and Jeremiah's letter to the exiles. The very diversity of its writings gives it a most colorful pattern, a blending of fact and fiction, wisdom and superstition, philosophy and theology. The student of the Apocrypha will be rewarded with expansion of knowledge and enrichment of soul.

Chapter 9

A BOOK OF TWO THOUSAND AUTHORS

Although the Bible is known all over the world, the Talmud still forms one of the great mysteries of literature. Yet it is the second foundation of Judaism.

The Talmud is an almost unique document. The word simply means "learning." It is a university in writing. Usually consisting of twelve huge folio volumes, it counts more than three million words and took five centuries to compile (from before the time of Jesus to the sixth century). It is a book written by two thousand authors. They included professors of theology, physicians, philosophers, farmers, astronomers, shoemakers, and smiths, ranging from the God-intoxicated mystic to the free-thinking atheist. The book deals not with one specific subject, but with every aspect of life: from astrology to zoology, from numismatics to dietetics.

Its language is Aramaic, with Greek, Latin, and Persian words interspersed. Like every Semitic book, the lines of the Talmud are written from right to left, and the first page is what would be the last in a European book.

It is the most democratic book ever published and a monument to the spirit of freedom of expression. No opinion is ever suppressed. The view of the minority is specially mentioned, often without stating a preference. Everything is recorded. The erudite conclusions of theological scholars find their place next to facts and fancies from the man in the street.

The Talmud has another fascinating feature. Every edition is alike in its pagination. Millions of copies have been published. Yet, whichever edition you open, whether in Jerusalem, New York, Amsterdam, or Sydney, you will find the same passage and the same word on the identical spot of the same page. This applies to the earliest editions, when the copyist burned the midnight oil in his loved, sacred task, as much as to the product of the modern printing press, with its luxury editions and compressed volumes on India paper. The leaves, not pages, are counted. The numbering recommences with each of the Talmud's sixty-three treatises. The simple addition of the letter A or B indicates whether the number refers to the front or back of that leaf.

The style of the Talmud is most concise. Containing a minimum of words, it is written in a kind of thought-shorthand. Sometimes whole sentences are indicated by a single word. Each passage, therefore, needs not so much a translation as an interpretation. The Talmud cannot be read. It must be studied. That is why each of its pages is printed with two large commentaries on either side of the text, which is arranged in a central column. A whole dictionary of terms and abbreviations is needed for its full understanding.

The discourses in the Talmud do not proceed in the Western way of systematic reasoning, but rather are based on associations of ideas. Points are not developed in a logical sequence, but discussion of one subject easily leads to another through the name of an author, a quotation from Scripture, or the occurrence of a certain term. This was not only the Oriental way of reasoning but an aid to memory, for in the earliest days the whole Talmud—with its thousands of debates, laws, interpretations, and parables—was transmitted by word of mouth.

This implied a tremendous feat of memory. It molded the mind to an acute stage of receptivity and made the Talmud's ethical precepts and ideas part of the life of every Jew. This "encyclopaedic philosophy, centered on the study of God's law," not by a select few but by the whole of the population, became the property of all the people.

Learned by heart, it was called the "oral Law." Tradition claimed that when God handed Moses the Five Books on Mount Sinai, He also simultaneously revealed this oral tradition. Yet today it is written down. This is a paradox with a historical explanation.

The origin and history of the Talmud reflect the fate of the Jewish people, their dynamic spirit of a living faith, and the conviction that religion concerns the whole of life.

The rabbis believed that the Bible was God's revelation for all times and that implicitly it contained the answer to every problem. Facing the new issues confronting their community, they sought guidance in God's word. They thus adopted and adapted the teachings of the Bible for their own epoch. Generation after generation continued this work.

The Bible commanded that the corner of the field should not be harvested, but left for the poor. How big was such a corner? Every morning the Jew should affirm his faith in the oneness of God. When did the morning begin, and how long did it last? The Sabbath was to be honored by total rest; work was prohibited. A definition of work was essential. The Bible permits divorce, but the specific circumstances and legal procedure had to be laid down. On numerous occasions the Bible demanded the statement of witnesses. Who could act as such, and who was disqualified? For seven days the Jew was asked to dwell in booths during the festival of Tabernacles. But what constituted a booth, and did "dwelling" imply the totality of everyday existence? All these questions, left unanswered in the Bible, were discussed by the rabbis of the Talmud in their academies.

New situations demanded reexamination of ancient laws. The Bible decreed the cancellation of all debts every seventh year, "the year of release." This had been possible in a simple agricultural community with hardly any poor and an abundance of harvests. But when society had become complex and trade had taken the place of agriculture, the law had to be reconsidered. A number of poor harvests had added to economic stress, and an ever-increasing number of people applied for loans. It was natural that fear (and experience) of the year of release canceling all debts resulted in the freezing of all funds. To overcome the crisis and reestablish credit, the rabbis introduced the *Prosbul,* an important document of social legislation. The word is Greek and means "before the council," as the document had to be deposited at the council of the city. It contained a simple declaration that annulled cancellations of debt at any time. Though contradictory to the letter of the Bible, the Prosbul preserved its spirit and maintained its ethical ideas, enabling the poor to raise funds in dignity. Once again the rabbis had adapted the words of the Bible to the demands of the hour.

This process of interpretation and development continued without interruption. Then, in 200 C.E., material had become so unwieldy and grown to such an extent that Rabbi Judah the Prince, a well-educated, liberal-minded scholar and the leader of Palestinian Jewry, felt it necessary to collect and systematize the teaching, utterances, and opinions of the rabbis. He made use of some earlier, similar attempts. He called the resulting work *Mishna,* a Hebrew word meaning "repetition," as by repetition it was committed to memory.

Judah divided his Mishna into six sections. They dealt with agriculture, holy days, family life, civil and criminal law, Temple service, hygiene, and purity. Each section was subdivided into treatises, sixty-three altogether, dealing with such specific questions as the meaning of prayer, the problem of divorce, the celebration of the Sabbath, and procedure at courts of law. A hundred and fifty different authorities are quoted in this fundamental work, written in colloquial Hebrew.

All over Palestine and Babylonia students met to study religion at special academies. These Jewish universities were an outstanding institution. Every aspect of life was studied there in relation to God. The ideal was not pure or applied science, but applied religion. The universally accepted textbook, after the year 200 C.E., became Rabbi Judah's Mishna! Almost every one of its sentences was considered and became the subject of heated, learned, and often long debates conducted in the vernacular of that time, Aramaic (the language Jesus understood). This went on for hundreds of years. Each generation added its own wisdom and folly, heartaches and problems, its special prose and poetry of life.

Then persecution closed the Jewish academies, first in Palestine in the fourth century and next, a hundred years later, in Babylonia. In Palestine, disaster came suddenly. In great haste scholars prepared a digest of all the discussions to enable future generations to carry on the study of God's word. About 750,000 words summed up the results of four hundred years of study. With the text of the Mishna, this digest constitutes the Palestinian Talmud.

The Babylonian academies learned from Palestine's experience. Two rabbis sifted, classified, and edited the accumulated material, so that when in 500 C.E. Babylonia's Jewish universities had to suspend activities, five hundred years' study had been summarized in 2,500,000 words, which, with the Mishna, make up the Babylonian Talmud.

Both the Palestinian and Babylonian digests of the discussions are now called the Talmud. It is a concise and concentrated report of all the debates held: a rabbinical Hansard!

The Talmud's horizon is worldwide. Its concern is every phase of activity. It expresses real religion, which must never be anything apart from life, but a guide and inspiration to the totality of existence.

The future of mankind is the continuous care of the Talmud. "By three things is the world preserved: by truth, by judgment and by peace." Charity is not merely a matter of philanthropy but a command. "When a poor man stands at your door, God Himself stands at his right hand." Utter honesty in thought and action is demanded. "God condemns a person who says one thing with his mouth and another in his heart."

Humility exalts. "Whoever runs after greatness, greatness flees from him; and whoever flees from greatness, greatness runs after him." "Whoever exalts himself . . . is like a carcass flung into the street, from which passers by turn their noses. . . . One coin in a bottle rattles, but a bottle full of coins makes no sound."

We must always be ready to forgive. "A man should be soft as a reed and not hard like a cedar. . . . If two men claim your help and one is your enemy, help him first."

The way we treat our animals reflects our own character.

"A man must not eat his meal before giving food to his cattle."
Work does not degrade, but bestows dignity. "No labour, however humble, is dishonourable. . . . Greater even than the pious worshipper, is he who eats what is the result of his own toil." Moderation is good counsel at all times. "Three things are good in a little quantity, but bad in large: yeast, salt and hesitation. . . . More people die from over-eating than from undernourishment. . . . Teach your tongue to say 'I don't know' lest you invent something and be found out. . . . Eat vegetables and fear no creditors, rather than eat duck and hide."

Law must be inspired by justice. It must never be mechanical, but humane and understanding. "Silence is equivalent to confession. . . . Judgment delayed is judgment voided. . . . Two scholars who dislike each other shall not sit together as judges at a trial."

Common-sense rules distinguish the Talmud. To tell the truth is not only ethical but practical. "The penalty for the liar is that even when he tells the truth no one believes him." Caution is always wise. "Your friend has a friend and your friend's friend has a friend—be discreet. . . . Quarrel is like a stream of water. If it has once opened a way, it becomes a wide path."

Empty words and unfulfilled promises are more than dangerous in a child's education. "Do not threaten a child: either punish or forgive him. . . . Do not promise to give something to a child and then forget all about it, because that is how he is taught to lie." Great is the power of wisdom. "He who has understanding has everything." But knowledge implies responsibility. "He who learns and does not teach is like a myrtle which grows in the desert: no one receives enjoyment from it." To teach gives even greater satisfaction than to learn. "A calf may wish to drink its mother's milk, but the cow wishes even more so to give suck."

Great is the power of the mind. Resistance against temptation strengthens the moral will. "If a man guard himself against sin once, twice, or three times, God will guard him henceforth." On the other hand, the repetition of an immoral or unsocial act quickly deadens man's conscience. "When a man commits some offence twice, it seems to him already permissible." People who give many reasons show the weakness of their position. "When a debater's point is not impressive he brings forth many arguments."

Religion needs spontaneity. "Don't pray mechanically, but let your prayers be a heartfelt plea before God." We are all God's children, and therefore every individual has his value and purpose. "Despise no one and consider nothing impossible, for every man has his hour and everything its place."

Studying any part of the Talmud soon makes two totally different forms of expression apparent. Though one often leads into another without any line of demarcation, their diverse quality is obvious.

On the one hand, we find strict legal arguments, dry, terse, and cogent. They regulate the affairs of everyday Jewish religious existence. The rabbis called them the Halacha, meaning "the trodden path," as with their definite rules and regulations they refer to the religious guidance of the people. They are the prose of the Talmud.

Exact laws regulate the relationship between employer and employee. "The worker engaged by the day must receive his wages the same night." The pursuit of justice within the community is a specific religious duty. To be appointed judge, a man must possess the following qualifications: knowledge, humility, integrity, good repute, and popularity. Health and hygiene are the aim of special legislation. "A man must teach his children to swim. . . . It is forbidden to reside in a place where no baths are available." Every citizen must fulfill the obligations of his communal responsibility. "Do not separate yourself from the community." No one is exempt from contributions toward the upkeep of the poor. "Even the beggar, who is maintained by charity, must himself practise charity." Trade laws ensure honesty to the most minute detail. "The shopkeeper must wipe his measure twice a week, his weights once a week, and his scales after every weighing."

We find religious ideas and ethical concepts expressed in the language of parables and legends. These are called Haggada, meaning "narrative" or "story." This is the poetry of the Talmud. While the Halacha is the outcome of a battle of wits, the Haggada grew forth from the heart. Its beauty and aptness are unforgettable.

Goodness is indivisible. "A good man of evil speech is like a mansion built near a tannery; the one defect destroys all its grandeur." To listen to evil is evil. "Why have fingers been made flexible? So that we may stop our ears with them when evil is being spoken." With all his advance and advantages, man must never become overbearing. "Why was man created on the sixth day? To teach that if he is ever swollen with pride, it can be said to him: 'A flea preceded you in creation!' " Self-reliance and independence are a virtue. "Say to the bee: 'I want neither your honey nor your sting.' "

True civilization manifests itself in the ability to postpone the gratification of one's desires and to work for future generations. Honi, a wheelwright, watching an old man planting a tree, inquired when it would bear fruit. Hearing that it would take seventy years, he wondered: "Do you expect to live so long and to eat the fruit of your labour?" The old man replied: "I did not find the world desolate when I entered it. As my father planted for me before I was born, so do I plant for those who will come after me."

Forbidden fruits always tempt. All but one of the trees in the Garden of Eden were allowed to Adam and Eve. They forgot all about the many, and their mind was fixed on the one whose fruit they were not meant to taste. On the Day of Atonement, the great fast of the Jewish year, a rabbi visited a sick friend. The patient was weary and complained of unbearable thirst. In spite of the fast, the rabbi permitted him to drink. When he returned within an hour and inquired after his friend's thirst, the sick man replied: "As soon as you permitted me to drink, I was no longer thirsty."

Thinking mind and feeling heart thus mingle in the pages of the Talmud—its Halacha and Haggada. The fusion of critical spirit and warm emotion render the Talmud a true reflection of life and human experience.

The influence of the Talmud cannot be overestimated. Judaism owes its very survival to the dynamic spirit of the Talmud. It gave new meaning to old forms and interpreted the spirit of Judaism to the circumstances of new epochs and different generations.

When a religion grows older, its symbols easily harden into dogmas. The rabbis were determined to prevent that from happening. They not only handed on the legacy of the past but applied and adapted it to the needs of the hour. They instituted the Prosbul, abolished capital punishment, and pronounced the belief in the immortality of the soul. The Talmud transformed the Day of Atonement from a priestly ritual into a spiritual experience and enunciated the inspiring thought that the Jew's suffering may be afflictions of love.

Thus the rabbis of the Talmud applied its principles to every new situation and maintained religion as a vital force. It was a tree of life that went on growing, its roots firmly embedded in the traditions of the Bible. Judaism was not a creed, but a way of life. The rabbis rendered the Talmud not only a religious document of unsurpassed significance but an instrument for making Judaism "a religion that lives."

While Reform Judaism considers the Talmud a supremely important religious work, presenting a phase in the development of the Jewish faith, the Orthodox Jew sees in it a ritual code of permament and decisive value.

To deprive the Jew of the Talmud became almost synonymous with robbing him of the source and repository of his faith. Especially in medieval Europe, when he was imprisoned behind the ghetto walls in the west, and, later, in the pale of the east, the Talmud provided him with the only freedom.

Unfortunately, there were seeds of calamity within the Talmud itself. It is a vast compendium, and it contains, without restriction and without censorship, thousands upon thousands of sayings and opinions. It follows that while many, perhaps the majority, were gems of beauty, of wisdom, and of wit, others put the views of isolated individuals, misanthropic or antisocial.

This was clearly recognized; but, from its essentially democratic nature, the Talmud could not or would not exclude such passages. The thoughts had been expressed. Sometimes they were even the reaction of a tormented soul and a persecuted people and so had to be faithfully reported.

The tragedy arose from the fact that there were a few renegade Jews. Familiar with the Talmud and eager to damage or destroy the faith they had abandoned, these traitors accordingly quoted the rare and exceptional passages of doubtful merit and presented them to the hostile world as being typical of the Talmud as a whole.

The result was inevitable. Public burnings of the Talmud became state occasions. Thousands of manuscript copies were consigned to the flames. In 1242 in Paris on a single day, twenty-four cartloads of the Talmud were destroyed. Forced disputations were staged with the Talmud on trial, and its burning was the inexorable judgment. One such disputation at Tortosa, in Spain, lasted a year and nine months. Only one complete manuscript of the Talmud, published in Munich in 1334, escaped the flames.

Even in centuries and countries where the Talmud was not prohibited, a strict censorship was introduced. Only copies with many deletions were permitted by the authorities. As a result a sole, uncensored edition, printed in Holland, has been preserved. Truly, no other book ever experienced such trials and exerted such influence on the lives of a whole community.

The Talmud molded the Jewish mind and the Jewish character. For almost two thousand years the Jewish people concentrated on its study. No day passed without "learning" at least one leaf of its 5,894 folio pages. To complete a whole treatise was an enviable feat celebrated by a joyous "concluding feast."

The study of the Talmud was not restricted to the young or the specialist. Early in their history the Jewish people had established a complete system of general as well as adult education. The young confirmand showed his attainment of religious maturity by expounding a difficult talmudic passage. The aged passed the evening of their lives by delving even more deeply into the inexhaustible treasure of the Gemoro, which became the favored (Aramaic) description of the talmudic discussions. Illiteracy was thus unknown among the Jewish people. The Talmud gave them an all-round knowledge. It became almost a conviction that "the uneducated cannot be religious."

Education based on the Talmud inevitably had a spiritual outlook. This textbook of the Jewish people was an encyclopedia of a God-centered philosophy of life. It looked at all existence in the perspective of eternity. Its aim was the hallowing of life and the attainment of righteousness on earth. Its continuous study made its teachings and ethics the property of the entire people. Other nations had introduced compulsory military training; the Jewish people, abhorring war, used the Talmud for the training of the human spirit, not for a limited period of months or years, but for a lifetime. The best books are those which best teach man how to live. The influence of the Talmud gave the Jew his compassion and social conscience.

The very study of the Talmud also exerted a tremendous influence on the intellectual power of the Jewish people. Once, at its oral stage, knowledge of the Talmud was merely a matter of memory training. Now, with the oral law written down, the effort to understand its subtleties and intricacies, and to penetrate beyond its succinct and almost abrupt style, exercised thought to the utmost. Like pure mathematics in our time, it was the finest way to train the mind. It demanded hard thinking, exactitude, and concentration. The Einsteins of the Jewish people are not the outcome of chance, but of the Talmud.

The rabbis spoke of the "ocean of the Talmud." No better metaphor could describe its unique character. Vast in extent, it is unfathomable in depth. Some of its parts are smooth and calm, of polished thought and serene reflection. Others are full of tempestuous debates: thrust and counterthrust, doubts, questions, statements, and denials. Like an ocean, it contains a multitude of forms of life. Some are known and easily understood; others, still mysterious and unexplored.

Chapter 10

RASHI—THE WORLD'S GREATEST COMMENTARY

For centuries, no Jew would dare to admit that he had not read Rashi: to know Rashi was a "must" for every self-respecting member of the "people of the Book." The Bible was not studied, nor could the Talmud be understood, without knowing what Rashi said. His writings became, if not authoritative, indispensable in the comprehension of Holy Writ. Even more, they became the sure guide without which the people would get lost in the ocean that was the Talmud. Not surprisingly, then, the first book ever printed in Hebrew was Rashi (in 1475 at Reggio).

The script used for his writings was more rounded and liquid than the square characters of the ordinary Hebrew from which it was developed. Though in existence long before him, it came to be known as the "Rashi script," to his honor, and has remained a standard type for the printing of every other commentary since, whoever the author. (See illustration, The Hebrew Alphabet.) It was a unique acknowledgment of debt, expressed not in a foreword, which only too often remains unread, but conspicuously displayed and implicit in every letter, word, and line of the whole text from beginning to end. Writings which preceded that of Rashi were thus shown to be his mere forerunners, while books that succeeded his acknowledged their obligation to Rashi's work.

Rashi's commentary has been translated into Latin, German, and English and has even been published in illustrated editions. Students wrote "supercommentaries" on his commentary, and more than a hundred of them are still in existence.

136

Rashi's Life

As if the work should speak for the man, little is known about Rashi himself. He was born in 1040 in Troyes, situated in what was later to become the French province of Champagne, which bordered on Germany. Located in a vine-growing district, the city was famous for the manufacture of parchment and twice yearly was the scene of a celebrated fair. These circumstances were not without their influence on Rashi's life. Writing material, still a rare commodity at the time, was freely at his disposal. The fairs were a welcome opportunity for Jews from afar to meet the rabbi and carry away with them his inspiration.

He studied at the famous rabbinical schools of Worms and Mayence in Germany. He was married while still a student and settled in his native town at the age of twenty-five. While a rabbi there he did not accept any remuneration, but, it is believed, supported himself and his family by cultivating a vineyard.

He opened a school, which soon attracted a vast number of students from all over Europe. It became a center of learning which was to eclipse all other academies. For forty years he led the quiet life of a scholar, lecturing daily and corresponding with other scholars and communities far afield. The permanent result was his commentaries on the two fundamental books of Judaism: the Bible and the Talmud.

Hardly any personal data are included in the tremendous volume of his writings, and only occasionally a few facts about himself can be gleaned from his letters, preserved by his family and his pupils. He had no sons, but three daughters, all of whom married men of great learning.

Rashi died at the age of sixty-five in the city of his birth. His work was uncompleted and was continued by his grandsons and disciples. Though toward the end of his days he was greatly agitated by the sufferings inflicted on Jewry by the Crusades, generally his life was poor in incident and undisturbed. All the greater, in consequence, were the blessing and riches he gave to uncounted generations. It was through Rashi that Jewish life

THE HEBREW ALPHABET

NAME OF HEBREW LETTER	PICTURE	ANCIENT HEBREW	MODERN HEBREW (SYRIAN) SCRIPT	RASHI SCRIPT	GREEK	LATIN	NUMERICAL VALUE
Aleph	ox head	𐤀	א	ƒ	A	A	1
Beth	house		ב	נ	B	B	2
Gimel	camel		ג	ר	Γ	G	3
Daleth	doorpost		ד	ר	Δ	D	4
Hay	window		ה	נ	E	H	5
Vav	hook	Y	ו	ר			6
Zayin	spear	I	ז	ר	Z	Z	7
Chet	fence	H	ח	⊃	H		8
Tet	snake		ט	ט	Θ	T	9

138

Yod	hand			I	I	10
Kaf	palm of hand			K	K	20
Lamed	goad			Λ	L	30
Mem	water			M	M	40
Nun	fish			N	N	50
Samech	prop			Ξ	S	60
Ayin	eye			O	O	70
Peh	mouth			Π	P	80
Tsade	fishing hook					90
Koof	back of head				Q	100
Resh	head			P	R	200
Shin	tooth			Σ	S	300
Tov	cross			T	T	400

was invigorated and the Bible became a book more beloved than ever before.

The name by which Rashi became famous throughout the world paradoxically was not his real one, just as his book is not a real book. Rashi is merely an abbreviation of his title, his name, and his father's name, *Rabbi Sh'lomo Itz'chaki*—Rabbi Solomon, the son of Isaac.

That Rashi's books are not really books is readily understood if it is remembered that it is more natural, and more helpful to the reader, for a commentary to be published not in separate volumes, but together with the text to which it refers. This was especially necessary in Rashi's case because he did not deal with every verse of the Bible or the whole of the Talmud, but only with those passages which, to his mind, required explanation. His biblical commentary thus followed the Hebrew Bible page by page, while his talmudic annotations accompanied the text as an inner column on every leaf. To assist the student, Rashi prefaced each of his individual expositions by the word or phrase he sought to explain.

Rashi Legends

The life of the man so beloved by the people and so outstanding in achievement soon became the subject of numerous legends and even miraculous stories. This was a development aided by the fact that so little was known about his personal life.

For instance, the Rashi Chapel in Worms, which was claimed to be the place of his daily worship and study, actually was built centuries after his death. The awed visitor would be shown a niche in the synagogue's wall which, it was explained, had appeared miraculously to save the life of the unborn Rashi. Walking nearby while pregnant, his mother was almost run over by a stampeding coach. To save her life, she threw herself against the synagogue's wall. In her panic she would have crushed the child in her womb had not the stones given way and created a hollow to protect him.

In 1840 the owner of a butcher shop added immunity from flies to the list of Rashi's miraculous qualities. He claimed to occupy the site of Rashi's former home, a fact sufficient to keep out all insects.

Another legend has it that Rashi visited Spain because of a vision in a dream. Toward the end of his life he had become preoccupied with immortality. His mind had dwelt on the destiny of his soul. Then one night God had revealed to him that in the world to come he would share Paradisal bliss with a certain Spaniard by the name of Don Abraham Gerson, "the righteous."

Rashi imagined the man to be a saintly figure. He pictured in his mind a scholar bent under the weight of studies, pale-faced, bearded, and with sunken eyes from which shone learning and the love of God. Rashi had never heard of the man and was anxious to meet him while still in this world. He departed for Spain to seek him out.

Great was his disappointment when eventually he traced him to Barcelona. He did not find the ascetic scholar of his fantasy, but a most worldly man. Blessed by all the fortunes of life, the wealthy Don Abraham had turned his back on all that was sacred to Jewish tradition. To him, the synagogue was an alien place and the Bible a closed book.

Puzzled that such a renegade Jew should be his companion in Paradise, Rashi wondered whether God's choice was perhaps a punishment and disgrace for some unknown failings in his own past. In sincere self-examination he considered all his actions, but to no avail. Determined to find an explanation, he sought to meet Don Abraham himself.

The Spaniard's splendid home was of palatial dimensions, with a wide, marble staircase, and displayed only the finest and most precious that money could buy. Rashi's antagonism against Don Abraham grew. Here was the typical example, he thought, of a man to whom only worldly possessions mattered and who, blinded by his own wealth, had lost all appreciation of true values and the way of God. But all his preconceived ideas and intense dislike vanished in the interview that followed.

Don Abraham received him with charm and grace. There was nothing of the cold and calculating manner Rashi had expected. On the contrary, the Spaniard showed deference to Rashi's knowledge. Soon it became evident that, though rich, he had not lost the warmth of a Jewish heart, but had used his wealth for the happiness of others.

Joyously he told the rabbi of his forthcoming marriage, inviting him to be his honored guest. At that moment, their talk was dramatically interrupted. A woman forced herself into their presence. Her oldest son, she related, was losing his mind, and only Don Abraham could help him. The girl who had given him her heart, and who, indeed, was the ideal of all his dreams, suddenly was not to be his. A rich man, solely through his wealth, had caused all this misfortune and was now going to marry the girl.

Abraham, though fully appreciating the mother's agitation, was at a loss to make any suggestion. Then the woman, out of the agony of her heart, called out to him, "You are the man!" and left.

Rashi had been greatly embarrassed to witness the incident. As a man who had seen much of life, and not to placate his host, he spoke of the impermanency of the passion of the young. Even if the boy thought that the world had come to an end, with the passage of time he would recover from his shock and possibly be all the happier and wiser for it. To Rashi's surprise, Don Abraham did not agree with his opinion, making rather light, as it did, of the young man's distress. Wholeheartedly he shared the lover's conviction that no one could ever take the girl's place, as she was as unique as the sun in the sky. On parting, Abraham asked the rabbi to be sure to join him at his wedding next day.

It was a fabulous affair. Crowds of people came to watch. Everyone's eyes centered on the wedding canopy, which was exquisitely ornamented with flowers. All was ready for the ceremony. A thrill passed through the people when at last, in solemn procession, preceded by musicians and torchbearers, the bride entered the court. At that moment Don Abraham halted the proceedings. The awed guests heard him explain that everything was in order except one detail, which had to be corrected: the bridegroom's name was not to be his own, but that of Abraham ben Manuel, the poor mother's son. He himself had only acted as the young man's matchmaker.

While the people conversed excitedly about the sensational turn of events, Rashi's voice could be heard. Unable to restrain himself, he called out to Don Abraham: "Indeed, you are worthy to be my companion in Paradise." He then related his dream to his newly won friend, who certainly had been at a loss to understand the implication of the rabbi's words. Don Abraham listened quietly, and when Rashi had completed his story, with deep emotion and utter sincerity, the Spaniard said that nothing could give him greater joy than to know that in the world to come he would share the company of so great a man as Rashi. "Especially so," he added—and the simple words expressed both the beauty of his character and the grief of his heart—"as I shall come single."

Even occult powers and the gift of prophecy were attributed to Rashi, and this, strangest of all, in connection with the fate of one of the famous Crusaders. Godfrey of Bouillon, the story goes, considered Rashi one of the wisest and most pious men of his age. Convinced of the rabbi's power to penetrate the mysteries of the future, he summoned him on the eve of his departure for the Holy Land. Only the rabbi, he felt, would be able to reveal to him beforehand the result of his campaign.

When his call to Rashi remained unanswered, Godfrey did not hesitate to visit the rabbi himself. But, knowing the Crusader's cruelty and afraid of his wrath, Rashi made himself invisible. Only when he had been assured of Godfrey's good intentions did he materialize. Then the Crusader described to the rabbi his plans for the conquest of Jerusalem, even including a detailed account of the troops to be used and the strategy to be followed. When he had finished, he asked Rashi's view as to the outcome of the Crusade.

Victory was certain, Rashi assured him, but Godfrey's rule over the Holy City would last a mere three days. On the fourth day his forces would be routed, and he himself would escape with only a few of his soldiers and return home with three horsemen.

Godfrey was aghast. He had expected encouragement and the prophecy of a lasting victory. His disappointment soon turned into anger and threats. "Beware, Jew," he thundered; "should your words not come true in every detail, and should I return with even only four horsemen, death will be your fate and that of your people!"

Rashi's words came true, with one exception. Godfrey returned not with three, but with four of his men. The rabbi and his people seemed to be doomed. Having failed in his mission in the Holy Land, the Crusader was the more determined to wreak vengeance on the Jews, considering that he was fully justified because of the warning he had given.

And yet even here his plans went awry. When entering the city a stone fell from a roof and killed one of the horsemen. Thus, there remained only three, exactly as Rashi had foretold. Humbled, Godfrey was now convinced that the rabbi was not an ordinary man, but that divine power was his. In a totally changed attitude, the Crusader was now anxious to pay homage to Rashi. But it was too late. The rabbi had died in the meantime. Godfrey bemoaned his passing and honored the memory of a man whose like he was never to meet again.

So runs the legend. However, fact and fiction do not tally, for in reality Godfrey never returned home, but died in Jerusalem five years before Rashi's death.

Rashi as Commentator

Two books dominated Jewish life: Bible and Talmud. It was felt that nothing could ever take their place, and to contribute to the understanding of either was therefore the finest task any man could choose. Ever since the Bible's codification and the Talmud's publication, successive generations concentrated on the study of these two works. No wonder that the outstanding scholar and rabbi, Rashi, who was posthumously awarded the title of "The Light of the Exile," made it his life's work to comment on both these books. Their inherent differences necessitated varied approaches.

Two distinct methods were employed by the rabbis in their

interpretation of the Bible. One aimed at eliciting the simple and genuine sense of a passage. Appropriately, it was called the *p'shat,* "the plain meaning." To discover this, they used every scientific means at their disposal: knowledge of grammatical construction, comparisons with parallel passages, study of context and historical background, and a scrupulous investigation of style, vocabulary, accentuation, and vocalization.

Then—and this second method at times became more popular —there was the allegorical interpretation where often fancy had free play. It became known as *drash,* "the scriptural exposition," derived from a verb that implied "to seek" and "to search." It ranged from beautiful and fitting illustrations, which indeed did bring out the meaning of a passage more clearly, to contrived explanations that were sometimes so farfetched that they did great violence to the verse. As a consequence, it no longer served as text, but as pretext for the expression of certain religious ideas and laws.

While these interpretations actually read into the passage a meaning that was not there, their authors sincerely believed that the meaning was implicit. The rabbis were fully aware of the dangers of such a method. To safeguard against its abuse, they decreed that no interpretation that was incompatible with the plain meaning of the text was permissible.

A great deal of literature was at Rashi's disposal. It consisted of both kinds of interpretation, p'shat and drash, each of which he considered legitimate and used freely. He always chose with care the explanation which seemed to his mind most appropriate and best clarified the actual meaning of the text. This was no small task, and there are passages in which we can detect Rashi's difficulty in making the final choice or in striking a balance. On occasions, his common-sense approach yielded to the contemporary fashion of figurative and fanciful interpretation.

Rashi never prefaced his work nor tried to summarize his method. Yet within the commentary itself he expressed some of his guiding principles: "A passage should be explained, not apart from its setting, but according to the context." "A verse cannot escape its simple meaning, its natural sense." When he felt that no other way was open than that of allegorical exegesis, he said so expressly: "This verse requires an interpretation according to the Midrash [the method employing the drash], and it cannot be made clear in any other way."

No commentary can be compared with that of Rashi. It rendered the Bible, more than ever before, a book of the people. He wrote for the average man. He did not want to shine as a philosopher, which he was not, or to write for an intellectual elite. Free from mysticism, he was clearheaded, sober, and rational. His style was terse and to the point.

Brevity, indeed, was one of his outstanding characteristics. The story is told that once when he was ill, a pupil (his own grandson, in fact) offered to write on his behalf so that the great work on the Talmud should suffer no delay or interruption. But when Rashi had recovered and examined what his grandson had written, he weighed the huge volume of sheets and smilingly remarked, "If you were to write a commentary on the whole Talmud, your work would be heavier than a cart." Wits said that Rashi valued every drop of ink like gold, so sparing was he in the use of words. With a minimum of explanation he shed light on the darkest passages and in everyday language helped people to understand and appreciate what the Bible said.

For rare words, whose comprehension was beyond the knowledge of the average reader, Rashi supplied within the text of his commentaries a translation, mostly in French, but in more than a dozen cases in German also. Altogether, both his works contain 3,157 such translations, always spelled phonetically in Hebrew letters. A total of 967 of them is found in the biblical commentary and 2,190 in his work on the Talmud. They present a vocabulary of more than 2,000 different words. While in his biblical explanations the translation is accurate in every grammatical detail, giving the correct tense, person, and gender, in his talmudic commentary he gives the general meaning of the word only.

Apart from this unique feature in a Hebrew commentary, Rashi unknowingly contributed to the general knowledge of language. Through his translations alone, many medieval French words have been preserved which otherwise would have been totally lost. And his phonetic spelling in the Hebrew transcription is a valuable source of the knowledge of their pronunciation. Strange it is that the science of philology (especially in the case of students of the medieval French as spoken at the time of the Crusades) thus owes an immeasurable debt to a rabbi's Hebrew commentary on Jewish literature.

The way in which Rashi wrote his commentaries on both Bible and Talmud is interesting. As neither is complete, it can be assumed that he worked on both simultaneously. While in his biblical explanations he followed the order in which the books occur, he did not do so when dealing with the Talmud. There, it appears, he selected the treatises not according to their usual sequence, but in the order in which he discussed them at his college, where he had introduced the custom of commencing with a new subject on the first day of every month. This was an ingenious arrangement for an age when curricula and timetables were not published. It enabled students from widely dispersed areas to join the school at the proper moment, at the beginning of a discourse, thus avoiding delay or recapitulation.

In spite of his achievements Rashi remained humble. He avoided dogmatism in his views. When a passage did not make sense to him, he was not afraid to admit it: whenever a verse was beyond his comprehension he did not just ignore it, but said so plainly. He felt that the fault was not in the text of the Bible, but in the limitation of his own understanding.

He did not resent it when people pointed out to him mistakes he had made. On the contrary, he gratefully acknowledged their correction. Still, he fought opinions which he deemed wrong. He never tried to force his views on others; neither did he welcome their acceptance merely out of deference to his authority. He wanted people to see his point and adopt it out of conviction.

Because to Rashi the whole Bible was the word of God, he considered its text perfect and authentic. Thoughts of criticism never entered his mind. He believed that unusual spellings and grammatical anomalies were not the result of a faulty text, or of a copyist's mistake, but intentional. With sufficient insight, their reason could be discovered. Repetitions, contradictions, superfluous clauses, and lack of logical or chronological sequence were never real, but only apparent. Here, too, deeper knowledge would resolve the difficulties and reveal their purpose and meaning.

Christianity regarded the Hebrew Bible as the foundation of its own faith and the "New" Testament as the fulfillment of the "Old." Verses which in reality had a totally different meaning were adopted by the Christian church and explained as referring to Jesus, his birth, life, death, and resurrection. Rashi was well aware of such interpretations and felt the need to refute them. Objectively, he examined the original texts and pointed out their true sense. Indeed, they contained no reference to Christian doctrine or history. Typical portions are the story of Adam and Eve and their fall, Jacob's blessing, "Messianic" Psalms, and Deutero-Isaiah's prophecy of the suffering servant.

The Teachings of Rashi

A wealth of wisdom and knowledge can be gleaned from Rashi's explanations, whether his analysis of mere words or his inquiry into the meaning of passages. Always alert, his intellect and warm heart never failed to reveal permanent truth, beauty, and depth in whatever the Bible says. Since by its very nature his commentary lacks system and classification and merely follows the text, it is well to consider some of its aspects methodically.

Of all books, the Bible must never be read unthinkingly. Its study needs unflagging concentration, not only on its text but on each of its words. There is profound reason for their specific choice. Rashi never tired of inquiring after their significance and why certain words were employed and not others. To him, their very selection often reflected a deep philosophy of living and the Jewish way of life.

The command to *love* the Lord teaches that Judaism is a religion of joyous dedication, not of dread and trembling. We must obey His commandments out of love, not from fear. To be religious because one is afraid denies the very essence of faith and changes a house of worship into a prison.

The use of identical words in the description of the effect on God of the sacrifice of both an animal and a bird prompted Rashi to say that it was not the value of an offering that made it acceptable to God, but only the spirit in which it was brought.

The name of the Red Sea has been interpreted in many ways. It has been connected with the name of a fabulous king, the color of a people's skin, and reddish corals said to abound in and around its waters. Rashi, however, presented a totally different explanation. He understood its name not to be the Red Sea, but the Reed Sea, as the water had once been overgrown with reeds.

Names, indeed, were not chosen haphazardly, but by their very meaning conveyed a message. The left pillar facing the entrance of the Sanctuary was called *Boaz,* meaning "in it is strength," because, Rashi commented, through the Temple's service strength would come to Israel.

Adopting rabbinical tradition, Rashi frequently added to the significance of passages by examining the etymology, grammatical structure, and spelling of individual Hebrew words. A typical example concerns the prohibition of the taking of interest. He discovered in the root of the Hebrew word for "interest" the verb "to bite," which was spelled with the same consonants. He explained that this connection was significant, as the money charged for the use of money lent is that which "bites." The victim of snakebite may not notice it at first. But then the wound swells, and the poison penetrates the whole body. Similarly, a borrower paying interest may not at first feel any hardship. But, little by little, the sum mounts and eventually becomes a crushing burden.

Rashi examined the spelling of every word. If a letter was missing or doubled, he was convinced that this could not be a mistake and sought for the reason. For instance, the omission of the letter *vav* in the Hebrew plural of the "tablets" of the Law, inscribed with the Ten Commandments, was to him not a faulty spelling, but intentional. The Bible used the singular form, he believed, for the express purpose of impressing on the reader that, though there were two tablets, they had to be considered as one. The commandments contained on each of them were of equal importance, whether relating to God or to man.

As to style, Rashi explained the use of specific expressions and similes. Thus, that the permanent bond with God was called "an everlasting covenant of salt" was based on the ancient belief that salt never decayed.

Nothing the Bible mentions is superfluous. Every additional word or clause which at first sight may appear unnecessary, redundant, or even detrimental has its purpose and value.

Even today special rules prevent the publication of certain information regarding people who have committed an offense. When the Bible recorded the immoral conduct of Zimri, was it really necessary to mention his princely status, Rashi asked. After all, his name should have been sufficient. Yet there was purpose in revealing that he was a prince, for God's moral law applied to all alike, the rich as much as the poor and the famous as much as the unknown. No one was exempted from it. To vindicate God's honor and maintain a moral order, punishment must be meted out in equal measure to all citizens, whoever they are.

Why, people may ask, should the Bible, when relating a man's blasphemy, add that he was the son of an Israelite woman and even give her name? After all, it was his sin and no one else's. Rashi commented that this special mention aimed at impressing on the reader the fact that whatever people do does not affect them alone but reflects glory or shame on their families. A man's life is not his own, to do with it as he pleases. His honor or disgrace is shared by his family and people.

Thus, the Bible is a book in which every word has its deep significance and is chosen wisely and purposefully. Nevertheless, only by considering the whole context of a passage will its true and total meaning become clear.

A fact soon obvious to the critical reader is the Bible's lack of logical sequence throughout. In the eyes of the average student, trained in the Western way of thinking, laws and narrative follow each other almost haphazardly. Rashi demonstrated the fallacy of such an opinion. Even here he discovered the genius of the Hebrew Bible, which knew of a deeper unity and continuity than just the tidy classifications and superficial arrangements which might satisfy the philosopher or logician, but had no application to life. The Bible is not a philosophical treatise or a legal document, only to be referred to or to be used as a compendium of decisions. The experience of life, and not cold logic, determined the way of its arrangement, the succession of its sections and themes. For instance, that the chapter dealing with an unfaithful wife was followed by regulations concerning the Nazirite, who vowed abstention from wine, plainly indicated the causal chain between intoxication and immorality. Nothing more than an association of themes thus warned people of the risk of indulging in drink and even tried to persuade them to become teetotalers.

Rashi was aware that, in their awe of Holy Scripture, people might be led to misunderstand some of its pictures. Instead of taking them—as intended—as ordinary metaphors of speech, they would interpret them literally. The most obvious case to hand was the Bible's description of the Canaanite cities, still to be conquered, as being "fortified up to heaven." Superfluously, to our mind, Rashi explained that the Bible used hyberbolical language, a figure of speech not to be taken literally, but employed for the sole purpose of producing a strong impression. Equally, the law of "an eye for an eye" most definitely was never meant to be applied literally, but referred merely to the payment of just monetary compensation. The injunction not to let the blind go astray went far beyond the meaning of the actual words. It warned against misleading any one who was inexperienced.

Rashi was not unaware of apparent contradictions, repetitions, and inconsistencies in the Bible. Its very first chapter presented a problem: "In the beginning God created the heaven and the earth . . . and the spirit of God moved upon the face of the waters." If God had really created heaven and earth first, how, then, was it possible for His spirit to dwell on the waters, of whose creation nothing had been said previously? Anticipating modern critics, Rashi commented that the story of creation did not follow a definite chronological order and that in actuality the waters were created before the land.

As there was only one God, how could it ever be possible to

serve other gods beside Him? They simply did not exist. Rashi recognized the obvious difficulty in the traditional rendering of the second of the Ten Commandments, which demanded that "thou shalt serve no other gods." It was out of the question that the Bible could ever assume the existence of other powers "beside God." He overcame the problem by showing that the phrase did not refer to "other gods," but meant, properly rendered, "gods of others," the worship of objects which others had deified.

The passage speaking of God as "visiting the iniquity of the fathers upon the children" has distressed readers of many generations. God is loving and just. How, then, could He make the innocent suffer for other people's sins? Naturally, Rashi could not have known the law of heredity, often applied in modern times to the understanding of the phrase. However, he revealed deep psychological insight when he pointed out that certainly the evil which parents did lived on in their children, who inevitably were influenced by their example and trustingly followed their lead. Their children's happiness is bound up with their own way of living.

While in the Book of Exodus the Bible commanded that during the feast of Passover unleavened bread should be eaten for seven days, a parallel passage in the book of Deuteronomy reduced the number of days to six (though the present-day Orthodox Jew observes it for eight days). Rashi resolved the contradiction by stating that only during the first six days was eating unleavened bread obligatory, but not so on the seventh, although naturally even then no one was allowed to partake of leavened bread.

Traditional belief considers the Five Books of Moses, as indicated by their title, a work completely written by Moses himself. Yet its last eight verses seem to contradict this assumption, for they tell the story of his death and burial and praise him for his unequaled prophetic powers. It was natural to question whether Moses himself could have written this, though some authorities claim that his power of vision and unbiased objectivity accounted for his having done so. Rashi once again realistically solved the difficulty by attributing these last verses not to Moses, but to Joshua, his successor. Thus in this way also he anticipated modern critical views.

Yet, side by side with his advanced opinions, Rashi preserved an implicit faith in the veracity of ancient legends and traditions which at times appears almost naïve. The Bible, for instance, relates that in spite of continuous exertions, plus dirt and dust, the garments of the Israelites did not wax old during their wanderings in the desert. "How was this possible?" the reader may ask. What happened to the clothes of the many growing children who accompanied their parents or were born in the desert? Rashi, usually so rational, adopted here a miraculous interpretation. He explained that divine clouds of glory sent to shelter the people at the same time cleaned and bleached their clothes, while the children's garments grew with them.

Readers of the Bible have always wondered why it was that Noah was asked to take two of each unclean, but seven of each clean species of animal into the Ark. Bible critics have asserted that the combination of two different texts accounted for the variation in number. Rashi, however, suggested that as Noah was expected after the Flood to sacrifice a thanks offering of clean animals, it was obviously necessary that more of them should survive the deluge.

A deep and tragic knowledge of history and human nature is revealed in Rashi's explanation of the passage referring to the "new pharoah" who did not know Joseph and all that he had done for the Egyptian people in the time of their plight, when his foresight and talent for organization alone had prevented a major disaster. In reality, the Egyptians could not have forgotten him. Pharaoh's ignorance was merely feigned and just another case of the ever-recurring ingratitude of rulers who knew people only so long as it served their purpose.

Nothing is hidden from God. The thinking reader may well ask why, on the eve of the tenth plague, when God's messenger was about to slay all the Egyptian first-born, the Israelites were commanded specially to mark their homes so that the angel might recognize and pass over them. Rashi's interpretation answered the question ingeniously. Indeed, God knew everything. His request had nothing to do with the proper identification and protection of Hebrew homes. It was to serve as a test to see whether the Israelites were ready to obey Him, as only then would they be worthy of being saved.

Similarly, God was not seeking information which was unknown to Him when in various parts of the Bible He is said to have asked for the whereabouts of people: of Adam and Eve after their fall in Paradise and of Cain when he had murdered his brother. The sole object of the inquiry was to stir their conscience and make them realize their guilt.

The Bible is the foundation of Judaism, a textbook for all its beliefs and observances. It was natural therefore, that Rashi shared the traditional view that everything was contained in it. Even later rabbinical laws and regulations, he was convinced, must have their origin or explanation in Holy Scripture. Tracing them in it was an important part of his study. Adopting the methods of rabbinical exegesis, he found them expressed or implied in peculiarities of grammar, spelling, or style. It is here, especially, that Rashi abandoned his usual common-sense approach and independence of thought and, following sanctified tradition, ventured to discover in the Bible references to laws and beliefs which in reality were not there.

In the Hebrew text, used by Rashi, which ordains the fixing of God's words on the entrance of the Jewish home, the word "doorpost" occurs in the singular. This was to him an indication that the "scroll on the door"—the mezuzah—was to be attached to one post, not to both.

The prohibition of work on the Sabbath demanded further definition. It was essential to know what could be considered work. The rabbis of the Talmud had classified it under thirty-nine categories. In his commentary on the relevant passage, Rashi added that the stopping of work did not refer to actual execution of duties alone. Even to think of work was wrong. At the commencement of the Sabbath we should consider all our tasks completed and give no thought whatsoever to work. Only then can we truly find peace of mind and dedicate ourselves wholeheartedly to the spiritual aspect of life.

Rashi's whole philosophy of life can be gathered from his commentaries. They offer an inspiring presentation of Judaism, with the multitude and variety of its teachings. His philosophy is not expounded in systematic progression, but is spread all through his notes and explanations.

For example, there is purpose in whatever happens. Nothing in life is without its reason, obligation, or compensation. An action not only is the result of past circumstances but is itself the cause of future events. Even though they may not be appreciated at the time they occur, many things unfold and reveal their meaning later. When God liberated Israel out of Egypt, it was not just to redeem the Israelites from servitude and give human beings their rightful freedom. God's action anticipated events to come and alone made them possible. Its purpose and object were Jewry's future duty and task: to become God's messenger on earth.

Everything God ordains has its meaning. Thus, the order to the refugees from Sodom not to look back and watch its destruction was not issued simply to make them hurry in their escape. They themselves were sinful and therefore should not witness the punishment of others and possibly gloat over it, or in self-righteousness consider themselves better.

Common-sense rules can be found all through Rashi's writings. Religious instruction must never be put off. It should commence in earliest childhood, from the very moment a child learns to speak. Times of prosperity are a special danger to man's loyalty to God. The committing of even a small offense imperils the whole moral foundation of life. Once having broken even a minute and apparently insignificant rule, man in the end will be guilty of a serious offense, just as a deviation from the right path, though small at first, will eventually lead us altogether astray. He who refuses help to others will finally need it himself.

Religion is not a mere confession of faith. Judaism is not satisfied with a statement of general rules. It demands their thoughtful and conscientious application in everyday life. Untiringly, Rashi emphasized the manifold implications of simple laws and narrative.

God's blessing was promised to anyone who, having forgotten to gather a sheaf in the field, left it there for the stranger, the fatherless, or the widow. If such reward was the result of an unintentional act of charity, Rashi deduced, how much more would God's blessing rest on him who went out of his way to do good.

When discussing the commandment not to follow a multitude to do evil, Rashi extended his commentary to elaborate several significant thoughts. He set out the legal rules based on this law. Though a man might be acquitted of a capital charge by a majority of one vote, a majority of at least two was needed for him to be condemned. The voting had to commence with the most junior of the judges, who then could not be overawed by the view of a senior colleague. In the interpretation of the law, Rashi expressed an advanced democratic view which, holding that the individual is free, is yet not satisfied with the mere counting of heads: "Do not follow the majority blindly, if in your mind their decision is wrong and a perversion of justice. Give your own opinion openly and fearlessly."

The Bible prohibits the taking of revenge or the bearing of any grudge. Apparently, the law in itself is so clear that an explanation is unnecessary, and yet Rashi felt the need of a further definition. People might avenge themselves and show resentment in such subtle ways that even they themselves might not notice it. Rashi quoted a simple but striking example from rabbinical literature. If a man is denied the loan of a sickle, and on the following day refuses to lend his own hatchet, saying, "I am not going to lend it to you, just as you refused me your sickle!", this already is revenge. If, on the other hand, he agrees to lend his hatchet, but pointedly adds, "I am not like you, because you would not let me have your tool!", he shows resentment and does not live according to God's law. However much we are wronged, there must never remain even a feeling of hurt or enmity in our heart.

Rashi was not only a scholar but a man of deep sympathy and human understanding. Being a Jew, he well knew the mind of a stranger, its sensitivity and susceptibility to become hurt easily. How beautiful in itself, in a world of antagonisms and xenophobia, was the biblical command never to wrong the foreigner in our midst! Rashi added to its warmth of feeling by saying that he who even alluded to a man as being a foreigner trespassed against God's law, for surely such reference alone would make the alien feel inferior and unhappy and thus wrong him. A test of religion is the way in which we act toward the unprotected. We must take special care in the treatment of foreigners, as of necessity they are always so much more sensitive and feel discrimination much more keenly than any national of the country in which they find themselves.

Rashi tried to obviate notes in the Bible passages which seemed to contain the ugly and unpleasant. It was not a harlot, he explained, who gave shelter to Joshua's spies and paved the way for the conquest of Jericho. The word used really described an "innkeeper" or a "hostess." Again, when Moses married Zipporah and the Bible relates that she was one of the seven daughters of a Midianite *Cohen,* the title here did not have the usual meaning of "priest," but referred to a "chieftain." Thus, the founder of Judaism did not choose for his wife the daughter of a leader in pagan worship, but the daughter of the headman of a tribe.

Even the inexplicable, Rashi believed, had its purpose, and this in itself is an explanation. Certainly, there are regulations which are mysterious and inscrutable, without any satisfactory, logical interpretation. Such laws, without apparent foundation and often the cause of taunts from the ignorant, were a test of obedience. The presence of the laws in the Bible constituted an important factor of religious faith, which trusted in God's wisdom even, and especially if, they were beyond man's comprehension.

Rashi's Commentary on the Talmud

Popular in his approach to and interpretation of the Bible, Rashi is purely scientific in method when considering the Talmud. Here, too, he still aims at precision, clarity, and simplicity. As its text was not, like that of the Bible, sacrosanct, or considered God's word, but the result and a résumé of the discussions of scholars at the talmudic academies in both Babylonia and Palestine, Rashi had no compunction in revising it.

His work gave Jewry an authentic text of the Talmud. This made all earlier manuscripts superfluous, and the great majority of them have disappeared altogether. Rashi's talmudic commentary and rabbinical school reestablished a basic uniformity of Jewish belief and practice, which had become varied in many a detail by separate, local traditions. The adoption of his interpretation of talmudic laws gave Judaism back its unity and consistency.

To appreciate fully the greatness of Rashi's achievement, the enormous difficulties presented by the talmudic text must be realized. While the greatest care had been taken in the preservation of even the most minute details of the biblical writings, copyists had been quite careless in the treatment of the Talmud. Errors abounded. The text was in Aramaic, which by then was a dead tongue. There were no punctuation marks of any kind: not even an indication of where one sentence ended and the next began. The language often was obscure and the discussion involved. Customs and views were recorded which had become obsolete and forgotten.

Rashi overcame all these obstacles. He became the Talmud student's ready guide. He pointed to faulty readings and copyists' mistakes, omissions and later additions. He collated different versions. Meticulous in his search for the correct rendering of each passage, he consulted at least eighty older manuscripts and commentaries. Having established the right text, he explained every term and detail with exactitude, finally summing up the discussion itself. He carefully arranged the ideas according to their degree of difficulty, resolved contradictions, and even anticipated questions and doubts on the part of the reader.

He explained Aramaic terms and passages in Hebrew. Where the talmudic text offered merely a string of words, he showed its clauses and differentiated between question and answer. He unraveled confused passages, explained the meaning of obsolete words and of idioms, gave historical background, and quoted examples from sources outside the Talmud.

Rashi's work thus provided a running commentary on this book of two thousand authors. His expositions became so indispensable to its study that, without him, people could truly say, the Talmud would have remained a closed treasure house to generations and thousands of scholars. No one ever tried to supplant Rashi, and historians did not exaggerate when they said that but for him the Talmud would have been forgotten.

Rashi's Influence

Though Rashi gained immortality by his two great commentaries, his authority was not confined to his literary work. It went far beyond. Many of his official replies to a multitude of inquiries have been preserved. These concerned not only difficult scriptural passages and rabbinical decisions but also urgent problems created by the exigencies of the time. In an age of intolerance and fanaticism, he showed leniency and love, even to the sinner. He scorned the narrow-minded. Liberal in his views, he was not only learned but wise.

The Crusades had brought untold suffering and havoc to whole Jewish communities. Before setting out on their mission to the Holy Land, the knights assailed, expelled, and murdered thousands of Jews in the Rhineland. Believing that the slaying of a Jew would bring atonement for their sins, they did not hesitate in their grotesque quest for salvation. Some of their leaders even solemnly vowed not to leave the country unless they had first killed at least one Jew.

Numerous refugees from the threatened communities sought shelter in settlements which were still secure. Other Jews, to save their lives, chose the alternative of conversion to Christianity, though in their hearts they remained loyal to their ancient faith.

Communities were afraid of the influx of newcomers, not only for economic reasons but because of a haunting fear that too many new arrivals would precipitate persecution in their own midst. To protect themselves they issued a ban on settlement. Local authorities arrogated to themselves the right to refuse or grant admission to refugees.

Rashi realized the inhumanity of such legislation. Although unable to have the ban lifted in its entirety, he managed to get it relaxed to such an extent that newcomers could no longer be expelled by an individual locality, once they were within its precincts.

Intolerant and self-righteous Jews frowned upon the readmission of those of their brethren who, under the force of circumstances, had become converts to Christianity. They saw in them only renegades and ignored the tragedy within their souls. Well aware that their apostasy was coerced, Rashi strongly advised that the Jewish community should welcome them back. Nothing should be done to hurt their feelings: "Let us be careful not to take measures for isolating them and thereby wounding them." Their baptism, undergone by compulsion, was only superficial. In their hearts they had always remained loyal to their Jewish heritage. Though baptized, they had never been converted.

In the realm of Jewish-Christian relations (more than eight centuries ago!), Rashi felt the need to do everything possible to create a better understanding and to avoid attitudes that were inimical to mutual friendship.

Ancient prohibitions, which had been well applicable to different circumstances, he considered obsolete and expressed the view that it was essential to change them according to the need of the time.

He disliked extremism of any kind and condemned those whose fanaticism led them to impose on themselves additional and unnecessary hardships, as, for instance, men who felt bound to keep two consecutive fast days. On the other hand, he decried as dangerous any laxity in Jews' observance of the laws. He felt that even if interpretations which made the keeping of Jewish laws easier were justified, they should not be publicized, as they would be liable to be misunderstood and might imperil the whole structure of Judaism.

Rashi's influence is beyond appraisal. He revitalized Jewish life. Through him the Bible became a book even more beloved and better understood than ever before. Talmudic studies received a new impetus. A whole school of commentators grew up as a direct result of Rashi's work and academy. He popularized traditions and teachings and preserved the memory of people and books whose knowledge would otherwise have been totally lost. His descendants and disciples spread the knowledge of Judaism throughout the world. Every worthy edition of the Hebrew Bible included Rashi's writings. No Talmud was published without his commentary, and preachers of every generation used his explanations and similes.

His influence extended far beyond the Jewish community. His commentaries were studied by Christian scholars and theologians, and there is a direct link between Rashi's work and Christian Reformation. The translations of the Bible which emancipated the Christian world from domination by the church, and thereby precipitated the Reformation, were in no small degree based on Rashi's exegesis. Luther, in his historic translation of Holy Scripture into German, depended wholly on the work of the fourteenth-century Franciscan commentator Nicholas de Lyra. Had Lyra not lyred, people punned, Luther never could have danced. However, Nicholas not only had studied Rashi but had adopted his explanations so extensively that he was nicknamed Rashi's ape. The revival of Christianity, too, thus owes an immeasurable debt to Rashi the Jew.

Chapter 11

MAIMONIDES—GUIDE FOR THE PERPLEXED

In 1135, thirty years after Rashi's death, Moses Maimonides was born in the Spanish city of Cordova. He was to become the greatest philosopher of the Jewish people, "a second Moses," and an outstanding authority in the world of thought.

Moslem fanatics forced his family to leave the country when he was thirteen. For ten years they led a homeless existence and visited a great number of places, but finally settled in Fez, in North Africa. But even there the same intolerant spirit among the people did not let them stay. That was why at the age of thirty Maimonides, after a short period in Palestine, went to Egypt. He lived there in Fostat, a suburb of Cairo, for the rest of his life.

He and his brother David went into partnership, trading in pearls. Moses did less and less of the work and devoted most of his time to study. When his brother was drowned in the Indian Ocean on one of his business trips, and the family's fortune was lost, Maimonides was compelled to earn a living and took up medicine. Yet the career of a doctor became much more to him than a mere livelihood.

To him, his profession was his vocation, and he regarded a patient as not just a case but a human being. Still in existence, and a priceless legacy, is "The Physician's Prayer," which has been attributed to him. It is distinguished by its deep humility and understanding of human nature:

O God, Thou hast formed the body of man with infinite goodness; Thou hast united in him innumerable forces incessantly at work like so many instruments, so as to preserve in its entirety this beautiful house containing his immortal soul. . . .

The Eternal Providence has appointed me to watch over the life and health of Thy creatures. May the love of my art actuate me at all times. May neither avarice, nor miserliness, nor the thirst for glory or a good reputation, engage my mind. . . .

Endow me with strength of heart and mind, so that both may be ready to serve the rich and the poor, the good and the evil, friend and foe, and that I may never see in the patient anything else but a fellow-creature in pain.

If doctors more learned than I wish to counsel me, inspire me with confidence in and obedience toward the recognition of them, for the study of the science is great. It is not given to one alone to see all that others see.

May I be moderate in everything except in the knowledge of this science; so far as it is concerned, may I be insatiable. . . . O God, Thou has appointed me to watch over the life and death of Thy creatures; here am I, ready for my vocation.

Maimonides' medical skill soon became known. His practice grew quickly. His fame as a doctor finally reached the highest authorities and led eventually to his appointment as physician to Sultan Saladin's Court. He declined a similar call extended to him by King Richard I of England.

With the passage of the years his responsibilities increased greatly and his life became ever more harassed. But he never neglected his art of healing, which he pursued to the end of his days. Indicative of his sense of duty and of the crowded life he led is a letter he wrote at the age of sixty-five—five years before his death—to Samuel ibn Tibbon, the translator of his philosophical work, residing in France.

Samuel had expressed a wish to visit him to discuss their literary projects. Maimonides replied that, though he would be delighted to see him, it was humanly impossible to do so. "Now God knows," Moses' letter began, "that in order to write to you I have escaped to a secluded spot where people would not think to find me, sometimes leaning for support against the wall, sometimes lying down on account of my excessive weakness, for I have become old and feeble." Then follows a graphic description of Maimonides' average day:

My duties to the Sultan are very heavy. I am obliged to visit him every day early in the morning. And when he or any of his children or one of the women of his harem is indisposed, I dare not leave Cairo at all and must stay during the greater part of the day in the palace. . . .

Hence, as a rule, I go to Cairo very early in the day, and even if nothing unusual happens, I do not return home until the afternoon. Then, when I am almost dying with hunger, I find the waitingroom crowded with people, both Jews and Gentiles, nobility and ordinary citizens, judges and bailiffs, friends and foes—a mixed crowd—all of whom wait for my advice as a doctor.

I dismount from my animal, wash my hands and ask leave of my patients to have some refreshment, which is the only meal I take in twenty-four hours. Then I attend to my patients, writing prescriptions for their various ailments. Patients come and go until nightfall, and sometimes even for hours after. . . . Then, worn out, I retire to bed. Only on the Sabbath have I time to occupy myself with the congregation and my faith. . . . And thus my days glide away.

Maimonides was far more than a medical practitioner. He published scholarly works, which were quoted and translated for more than seven centuries and still today strike the reader with their modern views on sickness and cure. His treatment of disease by scientific principles, rather than by guesswork, is as outstanding as his common-sense approach. Eight hundred years ago, Maimonides stressed that prevention was more important than cure. People should be examined regularly to be kept in good health, instead of calling on their doctor only when they were ill. A proper diet should be kept by the sick person before he was given any drugs. A man's mind had a deep effect on his body, a fact which should be considered by every doctor. Personal hygiene, both physical and mental, was as important as clean living.

It is amazing how Maimonides anticipated some of the most modern principles in the treatment of disease. And yet medicine was merely a diversion for him, not his life.

His religion formed the center of all his endeavors. From earliest childhood onward, his father, a scholar himself, had trained him in Jewish tradition and given him a deep love of all things Jewish. It was because of their fervent faith that his family had left their home, for a mere outward conformity with Moslem faith would have permitted them to stay on. When in North Africa, Maimonides had written to those of his brethren who had adopted Islam, reminding them to remain loyal, at least in their hearts, to their ancient religion, but, if at all possible, to emigrate to lands of freedom. Even his unsettled existence and the life of a wanderer did not make him neglect his studies. On the contrary, wherever he went he made contact with the outstanding local scholars to learn from them. He gathered all available information on every possible subject, whether medicine, astronomy, or biblical and rabbinical lore.

Supremely gifted, and inspired by all the knowledge he had gained, he himself felt the urge to write. At the age of twenty-three he published his first book, a treatise on the calendar. This was soon followed by a booklet on *The Terms of Logic*. But above all it was the Jewish heritage that he wanted to explain to his people. "I love nothing so much," he said, "as to teach one of the principles of religion."

First of all, he wrote explanations on some parts of the Talmud, but the work that established him as an undisputed spiritual leader was his book on the Mishna. Begun in Spain, it was completed in 1168 in Egypt, after he had been working on it for ten years throughout all his wanderings.

Without access to any books, he wrote it in inns, by the roadside, or "while tossed on the stormy waves of the Mediterranean Sea." He called it *The Book of Light,* and, indeed, it illuminated not only the Mishna but the whole Jewish faith. It was not only a commentary but contained inspiring essays on ethics and religion. It included the Thirteen Principles of Faith, which were later to be incorporated in both prose and poetry in the Orthodox Jewish prayerbook and can still be found there.

Once settled in Cairo as a practicing doctor, Maimonides lectured on philosophy and took an increasingly active part in communal life. Through the centuries a tremendous volume of religious tradition had accumulated, the study of which had become exceedingly difficult because of the renewed tribulations of the Jewish people, caused by the fanaticism of both Crusaders and Moslems. People were so absorbed in everyday problems that they had little time left for spiritual values. Scholarship had become rare. Only a few men possessed the depth of knowledge and the peace of mind to devote themselves to the interpretation of Jewish Law. Maimonides felt the urgent need of a book that would give everyone easy access to the whole of Jewish belief and practice, without having to refer to any previous works: a decisive guide to the Jewish way of life, summarizing all that had been written since biblical times. That was why, soon after the publication of his commentary on the Mishna, he started on his second great work, the only one he wrote in Hebrew. This was the greatest attempt ever made until then to condense the whole of Judaism in a clear and systematic manner.

He did his work so brilliantly that he created an unsurpassed digest of Jewish teachings. It commenced with a philosophical statement on the existence of God and concluded with a vision of a universe which was filled with the knowledge of God "as the waters cover the sea." Maimonides included all available material, even if it had no longer any practical purpose, such as regulations regarding ritual purity and the sacrificial cult of the Temple, which had ceased for well-nigh thirteen hundred years.

Anxious to write a code that could be studied and understood by everyone, he omitted from it all references to sources or other cumbersome, scientific data. Because he hoped that the work would make the study of any other book besides the Bible unnecessary, he called it *The Second Law* (*Mishneh Torah*), "for a man should read first the *Written Law,* i.e., the Torah of Moses, and then read this book, and he will know the *Oral Law,* and will not need any other books."

Was it perhaps because of this presumptuous claim that his *Second Torah* became known also by a totally different title, *The Strong Hand* (*Yad Ha'chazakah*), the division of the work into fourteen parts being the cause of the new, and innocuous, name? (In Hebrew every letter is also a figure, *aleph* expressing the value of one, *bet* of two, and so on. Because the numerical value of the Hebrew word for hand—*yad*—is fourteen, the *Mishneh Torah* became *The Strong Hand*.)

It was not long before the code was studied all over the world and Maimonides was recognized not only as the spiritual head of Egyptian Jewry but also as the greatest Jewish scholar of his day. Jewish communities from almost every country corresponded with him, seeking his views and decisions on the most diverse aspects of religious life. Among the great variety of questions put to him were inquiries regarding the borders of the Holy Land, whether scholars should be exempted from taxation, and whether Jews should be allowed to give religious instruction to Christians and Moslems. When Jews were persecuted in South Arabia, he sent them a message of comfort and encouraged them not to lose faith, even in the face of suffering: "Now, my brethren, be unflinching and firm in your devotion to ancestral religion. . . . Bend under temporary oppression, for it is your God Who tries your faith. You can verily prove the strength of your love to Him."

Maimonides' most prominent characteristics were his brilliant mind and passion for truth. As a young boy he had received tuition from distinguished Arab masters, who had introduced him into all the branches of learning of that time and given him a thirst for knowledge that was never satisfied with blind faith.

He did not tire of impressing on everyone the value of reason. It was God's gift to us and therefore meant to be used. It was foolish to rely only on other people's opinion and fatal to think that just because something was written in a book it had to be true.

Many people were deeply perplexed by the impact of current thought upon their faith. Philosophy seemed to contradict the teachings of religion and the text of the Bible. Faith and science appeared to be incompatible. Sincere Jews, Christians, and Moslems who had studied philosophy were perturbed and did not know what to think. To help them and to allay their honest doubts, Maimonides wrote the book which was to be recognized as his masterpiece, and appropriately he called it *The Guide for the Perplexed.*

Its immediate cause was a request of one of his favorite pupils, who asked him to explain the philosophy of his time, the deeper meaning of the Bible, and the outstanding problems concerning God, man, and the world. In his introductory words, Maimonides explained the purpose of the *Guide:*

I have composed this work neither for the common people nor for beginners, nor for those who occupy themselves only with religion in its traditional and ceremonial form without seeking its principles. The design of this work is rather to promote the true understanding of the real spirit of faith in order to guide those religious persons who, knowing the Bible, have studied philosophy and are embarrassed by the apparent contradictions between the teachings of philosophy and the literal sense of the Bible.

Steeped in the philosophy of Aristotle and fully acquainted with its interpretation by Arab thinkers, yet remaining a fervent believer in monotheistic faith and revealed religion, Maimonides undertook the task. He wrote his *Guide* in Arabic, using Hebrew characters. He completed it in 1190 at the age of fifty-five. Within ten years the work had been translated into Hebrew, under his direction, by Samuel ibn Tibbon. It was known as the *Moreh Nevuchim.* A first Latin translation appeared within a few years of his death and was studied avidly by the philosophical writers of his and all later generations. Spanish and Italian translations followed, and during the nineteenth century the work was published in almost every European language. Its standard edition is that in French, prepared by S. Munk (Paris, 1856–1866). M. Friedlander rendered the *Guide* into English. In Hebrew alone, more than thirty different commentaries have been written on the book.

Maimonides fought for freedom of thought. He despised the ignorant masses who, unable to think for themselves, fell easy prey to the written word, the irrational prejudice, or the glamour of outward appearance. Convinced that it was not sinful, but highly commendable, to apply reason to faith, he taught that religion must not contradict understanding. To accept any belief unthinkingly is wrong. The nature of God Himself is rational. Hence, to follow reason means to follow His will and Law.

Religion should not be obeyed blindfolded or be taken wholly on trust. To test its beliefs rationally is not only permissible but desirable. Faith must never be based only on miracles.

For centuries, the existence of God had been accepted without hesitation, without inquiry. The story of His revelation to man had been taken as true unquestioningly, and scores of generations of pious men had prayed to God without ever the slightest doubt in their minds as to His reality. But every age had also known skeptics who had not been satisfied with the evidence of biblical records and refused to subscribe to the veracity of the untested voice of tradition. Their number had greatly increased in Maimonides' time, due to the influence of philosophical thought.

There was no evil intent in their doubts. On the contrary, they were uneasy and deeply perplexed. To them, Maimonides spoke most of all. To him, that God existed was not merely a dogma of faith but could be proved by logical demonstration. There must be a cause of this world, a first, unmoved Mover Who set the universe in motion and gave it its order and design. Step by step Maimonides developed the argument, proving not only the existence of God but the fact that He was an indivisible unity, eternal and spiritual.

Questing man did not stop there. Once convinced that there was a God, he wanted to know more about Him and sought for an explanation of what God was like.

One of the great stumbling blocks in the Bible was that it spoke of God in a way which gave the ignorant the impression that He was just like man. Maimonides spared no effort to refute such a conception. It was true that, when speaking of God, the Bible used words and expressions usually applied to man. But to take them literally was a fatal mistake. They were used only as metaphors and similes to give man some inkling of God's supreme power, wisdom, and goodness. Using finite language to describe the infinite was indeed a dangerous undertaking; but it was inevitable, since we cannot invent words of real significance that can be reserved exclusively for God.

Maimonides constantly reiterated that there was no similarity between the qualities ascribed to God and those belonging to man. Even though the same word was used for both (because of the lack of a better term), its meaning was wholly different in each case. (Somewhat analogous is the way in which, in everyday life, we speak of "the dog" and mean the star Sirius, though the word also applies to our domestic animal.) When the Bible speaks of God's eyes or hands, it certainly never intends that those expressions should be taken literally. It uses this figurative means to portray God as all-seeing and all-powerful.

Maimonides denied the possibility of any man's completely understanding God's true Being: "I declare that there is a limit to man's capacity for knowledge, since so long as the mind is in the body, it cannot know what is beyond nature. Therefore, when the mind tries to contemplate what is beyond, it attempts that which is impossible." Indeed, God is so far above human comprehension that no one can ever say what He is. The only possible approach is negative. Our finite mind can only grasp what He is not. We can define God partially by excluding from Him all the features which we know do not belong to Him.

Many other questions worried the thinking man, and Maimonides faced each one of them. Even if some of his answers no longer satisfy the searching mind and now appear somewhat unconvincing, they rarely fail to stimulate our thoughts.

Faith in God has been tried most of all by the evil which is found in the world. No one can deny its existence. This problem certainly was not mitigated by Maimonides' emphasizing that God was the ultimate cause of all that is. Would it not therefore follow, inevitably, that He was responsible also for all misfortune and pain on earth?

Maimonides did not evade this issue. Often man himself, he asserted, is the cause of much anguish: "We suffer from the evils which we, by our own free will, inflict on ourselves. Then we ascribe them to God, Who had nothing to do with them." In addition, we must remember that our view is biased, distorted, and incomplete. If anything happens to us which we find disagreeable or contrary to our expectations, we conclude that the entire universe is evil. But our perspective is wrong. We forget that man is only a small fraction of the world. If he would properly fit himself into the whole pattern of existence, much apparent evil would dissolve and be recognized as only an illusion. Then we would refrain from rashly decrying the whole world as bad. Much of man's suffering, too, is due to his desire for unnecessary enjoyments and possessions. When we seek superfluous things, we have difficulty even in finding those that are indispensable. We spend strength and ingenuity in pursuit after the worthless and consequently lack force and initiative when we need to obtain something that really matters.

Finally, there was the greatest problem of all: the suffering of the innocent. Maimonides suggested several possible solutions. Perhaps the apparently righteous man had some hidden faults and was being punished for them. Suffering may serve as a test and a discipline, being sent to improve and ennoble man. Indeed, it is a fact that pain has frequently been the source of invention and progress. By surmounting suffering, man can raise himself above this world and gain values which he otherwise would be denied. As the essential part of existence is not material, but spiritual, suffering really cannot touch it, but remains isolated in the world of things. The good and evil befalling man are, therefore, only an illusion of material existence and have no effect whatsoever on man's eternal spirit.

However much anguish and suffering may be inflicted on the pious, he will not be shaken in his belief, because to him there is only one thing that matters: nearness to God. That alone gives supreme happiness, and it is unaffected by anything that might come from the outside world. But in spite of all these suggestions, Maimonides knew that any attempt at a completely satisfactory, rational solution of the problem was bound to fail. Standing on the threshold of the mystery of pain, man cannot be helped by reason, but only by faith.

The average person nowadays accepts the existence of the world as a matter of course. But in other days people were deeply concerned about how the universe came into being: was it created out of nothing or from some preexistent, eternal substance? There were some who believed that the world had always existed and that matter was eternal. Maimonides felt, surprisingly, that such a view would not contradict the Bible, which could be interpreted so as to prove that this world had been in existence for all time. Yet, he thought, it was much more in keeping with our belief in the grandeur of God to assume that the world is His work, created by Him at a certain moment, not because He had to do so, but out of the greatness and goodness of His Being. The world, therefore, owes its existence to Him alone.

Even more significant than the origin of the universe is the question of *why* it exists. Surely, thought people in every generation, it could not be that this world, whether eternal or created, is without purpose or meaning. Maimonides was convinced that it exists for the sake of man, whose final aim is the achievement of happiness, possible only by the acquisition of supreme wisdom, which is the knowledge of God.

In the world of today, most people, without realizing it, are leading a humdrum life. Perhaps it is the tempo of our age that stops them from thinking and asking themselves how far they are guided in what they do—not by self-interest, the laws of nature and heredity, or fear of punishment—but by the great Power beyond which we call God. Furthermore, there is the problem of whether our individual lives matter at all. Is God concerned with each one of us, or does He care only for mankind as a whole, without consideration for the individual?

Maimonides felt that in nature God's providence certainly does not extend to each separate being: "For I do not believe that it is through the intervention of divine providence that a certain leaf drops from a tree, nor do I hold, when a certain spider catches a certain fly, that this is the direct result of a special decree and will of God at that moment." His view could be summarized by the poet's words on nature: "So careful of the type she seems, and yet so careless of the single life."

However, this does not apply to man. In the world of human beings, God cares for each one. But how far His providence extends depends on ourselves and the quality of our individual lives. As this varies in every person, it is obvious that God's influence is not the same for all, but always proportionate to each one's progress toward perfection.

To lead good lives is indeed essential. He alone who is master of himself and not the plaything of passion can get near to God. Nothing can replace man's duty toward his neighbor. He must continuously strive to do justly, to love mercy and show kindness, and to shun all that is callous, unfeeling, and unrighteous. But Maimonides was convinced that moral perfection is not enough and that it is not the final aim. It is only a step toward a higher goal; merely a preliminary, though essential, stage.

The purpose of man's existence on earth is the perception of truth and the fullest development of his intellect so that he can understand the nature of the universe and of God and his own relation to both. This quest, therefore, receives a religious meaning in Maimonides' teachings. Above man's moral being he placed his intellect. By it, we are linked with God. Its fervor and intensity determine not only His influence but even the immortality of our souls.

This is yet another peculiar feature of Maimonides' system of thought. He deeply believed in the possibility of immortality. Yet to him it does not belong to man as a birthright, but is a gift that had to be earned. It is not restricted to certain faiths or races nor dependent on the utterance of a creed. Even good deeds and moral perfection, though essential, are not by themselves sufficient. Only if man by his own effort rises to such intellectual heights that the "acquired reason" becomes his, can he comprehend God and share immortality. Through the action of his soul, man can lift himself to that sublime region. Moral and intellectual discipline, love and longing for the divine light, can lead man from the finite to the infinite. This was exactly what the prophets were able to achieve. Maimonides taught that prophecy is part of the order of nature, and not miraculous. It is not reserved for certain chosen individuals, selected by God. It can be attained by any man who, by a supreme effort of will, reaches the highest degree of moral and mental perfection.

To understand the Bible's true meaning, we must apply our intellect. If properly explained, it does not contradict the teachings of philosophy, but confirms them. As the Bible speaks "in the language of man," it has to be reinterpreted to each generation, thus to become a true and unfailing guide through all the perplexities of life. Many of its passages are not meant to be taken literally, but are pictures or metaphors which our minds should recognize as such. Several supernatural events described in the Bible, such as Jacob's wrestling with an angel and the talking of Balaam's ass, did not actually occur, but were merely seen in a vision.

Using a rabbinical simile, Maimonides likened this true meaning, hidden within the literal sense, to a pearl lost in a dark room full of furniture. There is no doubt that the pearl is there, but we cannot see it, nor do we know where it lies. It is as if the pearl were no longer in our possession, since it is of no benefit to us until we kindle a light. That is precisely what Maimonides did in his masterly and bold interpretation of Holy Scripture included in his *Guide*. His reasoning was the light that illumined the Bible and revealed its profound meaning and message, the circumstances of its laws and regulations. His fearless research led to thought-provoking speculations which stirred the minds of the people.

Maimonides combined scientific method with an intensely religious spirit in his explanations of each part of Moses' Law. With pious sobriety he examined the text and sought for the origin and purpose of all its injunctions. In not a few cases he discovered new and fascinating features in Jewish tradition and custom. But even when merely summarizing old-established convictions, by his genius of expression and the clarity and precision of his style he excelled in presenting the Jewish faith as an intellectual and spiritual force.

A common feature of all Jewish holy days was the desire to promote a feeling of good will among men. But each festival in itself had a specific purpose, apart from its seasonal and historic associations. The aim of the New Year was to make man, lost in earthly pursuits, find again his spiritual bearings and return to God. The ram's horn was blown on that day to stir man's innermost being and wake him out of his forgetfulness. Totally devoted to the soul of man, and therefore excluding every care and thought for his body, was the Day of Atonement. Its fast was meant to create a sense of repentance.

No custom can leave a permanent mark on one's mind unless it is observed for some time at least. Only then will its object lesson be sufficiently clear and become properly absorbed. That is why the Israelites were commanded to keep the Passover as a memorial of their deliverance from Egyptian bondage, not only on the one day of the exodus (which would have been the obvious thing to do) but for seven days.

The counting of the days that separate Passover from the Feast of Weeks has a psychological meaning. The Israelites' redemption was merely completed by God's revelation on Mount Sinai and their acceptance of His commandments, because the latter alone was the sole aim and object of their exodus. Physical freedom is not enough. Liberty is a snare and a danger which soon can deteriorate into license if it be not consecrated by duty. Only to make them a people of religion had God saved Israel from Egyptian bondage. To impress this fact on the Jewish people for all time, they were asked expectantly to count the forty-nine days between "Egypt" and "Sinai," "just as one who expects his closest friend on a certain date counts the days and even the hours."

People quickly forget calamities and do not always appreciate the blessings bestowed on them. The Feast of Tabernacles was instituted to remind man ever to remember his evil days in times of prosperity and thus, realizing his debt to God, to remain modest and humble. The Bible commanded the Israelites to dwell in booths for seven days, because "we shall remember that this has once been our condition, although now, by the kindness of God and because of His promise to our ancestors, we live in comfortable homes, in the best and most fertile land."

Hygiene and the promotion of physical health were the purposes of other biblical laws, especially the dietary legislation. "I maintain," Maimonides said, "that the food which is forbidden by the Torah is unwholesome." The prohibition of eating milk and meat together also had, at least to some extent, an identical basis because "meat boiled in milk is undoubtedly gross and makes overfull." Circumcision not only was the symbol of God's covenant with the Jewish people but was intended to make them moderate and to counteract excessive lust.

The Bible was given to the Israelites at a particular stage in their development and therefore referred to the circumstances of that period. Many laws which today appear inexplicable are pedagogic in origin and reveal the legislator's desire to remove from Jewish life and worship all the traces of ancient paganism which were still prevalent at that time. Because heathen priests used to round the corners of their hair and beards and wore garments made of both linen and wool, the Bible prohibited these practices. Idolaters considered the drinking of blood a sacred rite. They felt that by so doing they acquired supernatural power and communed with their gods. It was to combat this superstition that the Bible stringently forbade the consumption of blood at any time, a law which resulted in the rabbinical order that all meats had to be salted before being eaten, so that one was sure that even the slightest trace of blood had been removed.

Maimonides thus believed that a considerable number of biblical precepts were time-conditioned and included in Holy Scripture merely in order to wean the people from pagan customs. He felt that this especially applied to the Torah's legislation regarding animal sacrifices. Certainly, they possessed no inherent religious qualities. On the contrary, the prophets already had vehemently and repeatedly protested that God desired mercy, and not burnt offerings. But a people who could not imagine any other way of worshiping God had to learn by a slow process of training that prayer, loving-kindness, and social justice were much more welcome to God than the killing of innocent beasts. However, Maimonides explains, "It is impossible to go from one extreme to the other; it is therefore according to the nature of man, impossible for him suddenly to discontinue everything to which he has been accustomed." It was therefore as a concession to man's inability to assimilate a new truth immediately that the Bible still included a really obsolete, sacrificial cult. Yet everything possible was done to limit animal sacrifices to a minimum.

God did not take the Israelites straight from Egypt into the Holy Land, but led them by a circuitous route, for He feared that otherwise their hardships would have been too great. Similarly, in the molding of the Jews as a kingdom of priests, He also knew that the slower way was the better one. He refrained from prescribing what the people, by their natural disposition, would have been incapable of obeying. Instead of revolutionizing their existence and making them abandon at once all the customs in which they had been brought up, He chose the wiser and safer course of slow evolution.

As in the development of the people, so in each individual life there are stages of maturity. Maimonides differentiates between four degrees of human aspiration toward perfection. The lowest of them is man's wish to enrich himself by material goods, to be able to say, "this is *my* house," "*my* servant," "*my* property." But such possessions are only external and of no real value. The second degree is man's striving after physical perfection: to preserve health and obtain strength. Yet here the animal easily surpasses him. Man can never equal the lion in its prowess, the ass in its sturdiness, and the leopard in its agility. To attain moral perfection for the benefit of the community is the third and much worthier step. Even this is outshone by the highest form, which aims at that true wisdom found only in the knowledge of God: "Having conquered this knowledge, you will be determined always to seek loving-kindness, justice and righteousness, and thus imitate the ways of God." It is with this thought that Maimonides concludes his *Guide:* "God is near to all who call upon Him, if they call upon Him in truth and turn to Him. He is found by everyone who seeks Him, if he always goes toward Him and never goes astray."

The Influence of Maimonides

Many centuries before medical knowledge adopted the view, Maimonides had stressed that fresh air, sunlight, and exercise were essential for health. His historical explanations of religious customs anticipated the modern study of comparative religion by half a millennium. When people were convinced that man's actions were decided by the stars and could be foretold by their study, Rabbi Moysis (as he was known among the Christians) denounced such an attitude as totally unscientific and called on the intelligent not to listen to such childish superstitions.

But all these counsels, however significant in themselves and astonishing in their modern approach, cannot be compared with the overwhelming importance of Maimonides as a philosopher. The path he traced in making religion intelligible and reconciling it with philosophic teaching endured through the ages and can still be discerned in some notable features of European civilization.

The great thinkers of the world who followed Maimonides not only adopted his findings but sometimes used his very words. The rabbi's work thus deeply influenced the two most prominent medieval writers of the Christian church: the Dominican Albertus Magnus (1193–1280) and Thomas Aquinas, the "doctor angelicus" (1225–1274). It inspired Spinoza in the seventeenth century and left its distinct mark in the philosophy of Immanuel Kant a hundred years later. Though usually now referred to as Maimonides, he was also known as Rabbi Moses ben Maimon or, by its more usual Hebrew abbreviation, Rambam. In Arab literature he appears as Abu 'Imran Musa ben Maimun ibn Abd Allah.

Maimonides was one of the great spiritual forces in the history of mankind. Some of his views may be outdated, but his contribution to the religious thought of the world is undying, and his *Guide for the Perplexed* can still be described by the words of one of its enthusiastic seventeenth-century reviewers, who called it "a book whose praises are inexhaustible."

Maimonides' life was distinguished by unceasing work, continual new difficulties, and manifold contradictions. A homeless Jewish refugee from Spain, he became the most honored citizen in the home of his adoption and a luminary in the worlds of Judaism, Christianity, and Islam. Using always his powers of reason, he was a man of fervent faith. Though he gave hope and courage to the persecuted, it has been suggested that he himself at one time had been forced to become a Moslem. Though a Hebrew scholar, he wrote most of his works in Arabic.

In spite of his success and fame, he always remained humble. He became the victim of envy, intrigues, and malicious attacks, but never despaired. To him these trials were merely a challenge which, when overcome, made life all the more pleasant: "It is indeed a fact that the change from trouble to ease gives much more pleasure than continued ease."

Most of all, however, it was his *Guide* that created unhappiness and bitter strife. As it prompted a critical attitude of mind, many considered it injurious to faith. They felt that though the work might assist some perplexed students of philosophy to regain their lost beliefs, it would sow seeds of doubt in the hearts of the majority of people who, firm in their faith, were still untroubled by intellectual problems. Some of his views, especially those on immortality, miracles, and prophecy, certainly contradicted established traditions and were therefore decried as heretical. Still, Maimonides was undaunted, and the voice of criticism was quieted by the superiority of his intellect and the impact of his great repute.

He died in 1204 at the age of seventy. Jews and Moslems alike observed three days of public mourning. A general fast was proclaimed in Jerusalem. His body was taken from Cairo to the Holy Land and buried in Tiberias, by the Lake of Galilee. His tomb has ever since been a place of pilgrimage. An unknown admirer originally inscribed it with the lines:

> Here lies a man, and yet no man;
> If you were a man, angels of heaven
> Must have overshadowed your mother.

But soon afterward one of Maimonides' fanatical opponents erased the inscription and replaced it with the words:

> Here lies Moses Maimonides, the excommunicated heretic.

Indeed, all the latent opposition against his teachings, which had smoldered during his lifetime, burst into flames the moment Moses died. Whole Jewish communities split up into opposing camps of Maimunists and anti-Maimunists. His books were publicly burned, and those who read them were excommunicated.

Yet Maimonides' greatness outlived the tempest, and his *Guide for the Perplexed* became a classical work of religious philosophy. Though the Orthodoxy of his time had proclaimed him a heretic, traditional Jews of later generations adopted Rambam's Principles of Faith and found them worthy of inclusion in their daily prayer. An immense stimulus to thought and religious living thus came from this Spanish-born scholar, to whom Christians and Moslems, as well as Jews, appeared as God's servants, preparing His Kingdom here on earth. By his life Maimonides demonstrated the fact that knowledge and religion, faith and enlightenment, need not be opposing forces, but, on the contrary, by combining can enrich life immeasurably.

One of Maimonides' early works, begun at the age of twenty-three in most adverse circumstances and when he was experiencing the powers of darkness, he called *The Book of Light*. The title was prophetic and symbolic of his whole life. No one could have striven more passionately for light. For all time his is the noble plea for the exercise of reason and the value of knowledge in human relationships and in the realm of religion.

Chapter 12

THE *SHULCHAN ARUCH*— THE COMPLETE CODE OF LAW

A unique book, the *Shulchan Aruch,* legislates for righteousness and a society based on spiritual ideas. Its regulations cover systematically and meticulously the whole of man's life. Nothing is left to chance.

It is the "common law" of the Jewish people. To relate everything, without exception, to God is its exclusive and passionate aim and purpose. Indeed, the work is a powerful challenge to our present age, in which religion has become divorced from life and only too often is confined to holy days and hallowed places.

The *Shulchan Aruch* embraces every act and moment of man: the way he talks, walks, eats, drinks, and even thinks, as well as his affairs of business and property and the right attitude for him to have toward his neighbor, his country, his government, and God.

Its many, carefully numbered, individual regulations summarize the heritage of Jewish law, which cannot restrict itself to ritual or even civil and criminal matters, but is concerned with the whole world of man.

As if to make the work even more outstanding, its very publication and adoption were extraordinary. The *Shulchan Aruch* gained world fame against the wish of its author. The carping criticism of a contemporaneous scholar, who opposed the work vehemently as misleading and unsatisfactory, conduced to its enthusiastic acceptance. Published more than four hundred years ago, it yet remains the authoritative code of the Orthodox Jew throughout the world. Far from stifling or externalizing Jewish religious life, as the critic contended it would, it proved itself a dynamic force, a challenge, and a constant reminder to change a humdrum existence into an adventure with God.

Equally fascinating facts distinguish the life and influence of the author, Joseph Caro. A fugitive from oppression, he became the great authority on Judaism. A man with a lucid, logical mind, he was nevertheless a great mystic and claimed to have had visions and revelations. Indeed, his life presented many contradictory features.

Caro was born in 1488 in Spain. His parents fled the country in 1492, that ominous year when hundreds of thousands of Jews were expelled from their ancient Spanish home in the name of religion. After a sojourn in Portugal, his family settled in the European part of Turkey. An avid student, Joseph soon became conversant with every aspect of Jewish law and tradition. He had no equal in this respect, and his fame spread far and wide. He, the unknown refugee who had been carried away from his homeland as a child of four, was soon considered the authority of his age. Communities in every part of the world eagerly sought his decisions and guidance.

After his father's death he moved to Adrianople. There he came into contact with the white heat of Jewish mysticism and with the Messianic visionary Solomon Molcho. Molcho's death at the stake in 1532 impressed Caro so deeply that it created in him a morbid longing to die also "as a burnt sacrifice, an offering made by fire, of a sweet savor unto the Lord."

In 1536, at the age of forty-eight, he settled in Safed, in northern Galilee, to satisfy his longing to live at the center of Jewish mystical thought and rabbinical studies. It was there that he spent the rest of his life and completed the work which was to gain him immortal fame. When eighty-seven years old he died— not as a martyr. His passing was mourned throughout the world. Still in existence are some of the funeral orations and elegies and obituaries composed in his honor.

Caro was widowed twice and chose as his third wife a rich scholar's daughter. He was a man of extraordinary character, combining most incongruous traits. Nothing could equal the clarity of his thought and his realistic approach in all matters appertaining to Jewish faith. Caro possessed remarkable powers of critical examination. His literary work, which helped markedly to give Judaism its unity and strength for survival, is distinguished by its clear-cut definitions, logical thought, and scholarship. In its orderliness there is nothing ambiguous or unintelligible.

It is strange that this rational codifier of Judaism believed that a heavenly voice which inspired him was the spirit of a book. In early youth he had memorized the Mishna, the textbook of the talmudic academies, and had become passionately engrossed in it. It was the personification of this book which he imagined to be his guide and mentor, the voice that dictated his every action, goading him on, praising him, and even more frequently reprimanding him: "I am the Mishna that speaks through your mouth. I am the soul of the Mishna; I and the Mishna and you are united in one soul."

Meticulously, he noted down those revelations in what could be called his mystical diary. It was posthumously published under the title of *The Preacher of Righteousness*. It consists not of one continuous text, but of stray notes, and it makes queer reading. For many years the authenticity of this book was doubted, as its whole content contradicted to such a great extent that of all Caro's other works and his well-known scholarship and logical nature.

But even Caro as a mystic never became lost in a world of the unreal and imaginary. There was always a definite message in his visions and in the heavenly voice he believed he heard in his inner soul. His mysticism never hampered, but on the contrary stimulated his work, driving him on to do better in every way. It was the voice of conscience and duty, urging him to improve his life and to excell in his study.

The mentor angel spoke to him mostly at night, especially after his study of parts of the Mishna. Sometimes the mentor's words were audible even to Caro's friends, who, perhaps not surprisingly, recognized in them Caro's own voice. The spirit admonished him never to speak an idle word, or to indulge in laughter or scoffing, or to give way to anger. "Think about nothing but God's law," it said. "You are strictly watched in whatever you do; therefore be careful."

The personified Mishna commanded him constantly to be conscious of his sins and to mourn for them. It warned him to refrain from drinking too much wine or even an excess of water. Never should he totally satisfy his desire for food, even when breaking a fast. The voice also suggested what he should read and rebuked him for sleeping too long, studying too little, and commencing his prayers too late.

Caro was a man not only of untiring energy but also of great ambition. It was in Safed that he participated in a daring spiritual venture.

From biblical times, when Moses appointed Joshua his successor by placing his hands on him, such ordination had become a solemn rite in the appointment of Jewry's spiritual leaders. It invested them with the right of deciding by themselves practical questions of Jewish law, which once included also the fixing of the calendar. Only he who had himself been ordained could ordain others, and this was possible in the Holy Land alone. However, the ceremony was only symbolic of the bestowal of authority. At no time did Judaism consider the laying on of hands a sacrament.

Historical circumstances made the custom lapse. A thousand years had passed since the last ordination when, in Safed, Jacob Berab, an older contemporary of Caro, had arranged for himself to be ordained by twenty-five outstanding scholars. He justified his extraordinary action by Maimonides' view that even if the chain of ordination were broken, it could be renewed by the unanimous decision of all the sages in the Holy Land.

Once invested with the ancient authority, Berab lost no time in himself ordaining four young rabbis, one of whom was Joseph Caro. Caro thus achieved one of his greatest aspirations: to be officially recognized as a supreme authority. But Berab's death in 1541, and the vehement opposition of other rabbinical leaders to the whole procedure and the way Berab had arrogated the right to himself, condemned this attempt at reestablishing the ancient custom. And so Caro has the distinction of being one of the very few rabbis thus appointed within a millennium.

Although Berab failed to attain his own ambition of creating a spiritual center for the scattered Jewish communities, Caro achieved that end in a different way. Not a chain of authorities of appointed scholars, but a book, was to become the universally acknowledged leader: his book, the *Shulchan Aruch*.

Both Bible and Talmud have formed the secure foundations of the Jewish faith. They have inspired and controlled the lives of its members wherever they lived. It was a natural development, however, for the various Jewish communities throughout the world to create, slowly but inevitably, their own local customs and traditions, varying from country to country. The most marked differences evolved between the Jews within the Spanish and German spheres of influence, divergencies which came to be known, from the Hebrew names of the two countries, as Sephardic and Ashkenazic.

As these groups were living apart and in self-contained communities, nothing interfered with their happy coexistence. On the contrary, color and vitality were added to Jewish life. Then history intervened. Old-established Jewish communities were uprooted, and, especially after their expulsion from Spain, streams of refugees joined Jews in countries where there was still freedom of conscience and an existence without fear.

With few exceptions they were welcomed by the indigenous population, who helped them in every way possible to build up a new life in their midst. But divergencies and cleavages soon became apparent. Though all shared the fundamental ideas of Judaism, they differed in not a few of their customs and in their interpretation of Jewish law. In reality, such variations were only superficial, but in the minds of the people they appeared significant.

Individual migrants from yet other countries brought further variations in details of Jewish observance, adding to the confusion. The position was aggravated psychologically by the fact that the newcomers were much better educated—a fact that seems to have been resented by their hosts. Which was the right way to follow, the people wondered, anxious to live according to God's law. Should the newcomers, being in the majority, impose their traditions on the established order of their host community?

A conflict of conscience arose. Obviously, each national group considered its own traditions to be correct and therefore felt that they should be adopted by the rest of the community. The stability of Jewish life was threatened. With numerous individual congregations within the one community, each following a different pattern, the prospect was that splinter groups would be formed, leading to utter confusion.

The invention of the printing press made the solution of the problem even more urgent. Manuscripts took a long time to write and therefore were rare and expensive, and only a few copies at a time could be distributed. But now the various sets of traditions could be spread worldwide at comparatively little cost, and there was no limit to the number of copies which could be printed. Historical necessity demanded a unified code for all Jews, a "common law" for the scattered remnants of Israel.

Several attempts had been made previously to create such a synthesis. It was for that very purpose that toward the end of the twelfth century Maimonides had composed his *Second Torah*. But mainly because he had made no reference to his sources, and thereby excluded any possibility of others' examining the validity of his decisions, and because he appeared to override all tradition, his work had been violently opposed and finally rejected. Over a century later, Jacob ben Asher (1280–1340) had renewed the effort, learning from and avoiding Maimonides' mistakes. His *Four Rows*—the *Turim* (called after the four rows of stones in the breastplate of the ancient high priest)—duly mentioned previous decisions and authorities. But its fundamental lack was the absence of any final decision on matters where there was a conflict of opinion. Though summarizing talmudic and later rabbinical views on every aspect of Jewish life, Ben Asher had not dared to make a final pronouncement and say which was the right way to follow. Everything else was there; but the most essential element, definite guidance in matters of doubt, was absent.

Joseph Caro sought to meet this need. For more than thirty years he labored incessantly to do so. He accomplished his aim by annotating Ben Asher's *Four Rows*. He consulted every available previous publication, including thirty-two major works, summarizing them and deciding the issue in each case. Wisely, he avoided creating the impression that he did so dictatorially, by his own judgment. His method was simple, and yet appeared irrefutable: he chose three of the best-known and most widely accepted authorities as his guide, and in every instance where there was a controversy, he referred to them and adopted their majority view as "the law."

As his object was the composition of a practical book, Caro left out of it altogether subject matter which once had been of great significance to Jewish worship, but in his time was of mere historical interest. He omitted the great number of regulations concerning the sacrificial cult, which had ceased with the destruction of the Temple in Jerusalem in 70 C.E., but still had occupied much of Maimonides' thoughts.

In spite of this, Caro's work grew to a tremendous size and contained a wealth of material. Indeed, it was a gigantic structure built up out of fifteen hundred years of tradition, with the final decision as the copestone. Significantly, he called the commentary, which was so much more than that word implied, by his own name, *The House of Joseph*. Its first two parts were published in Venice in 1550–1551, the third and fourth in Sabbionetta in 1553–1559. It was his sincere hope and conviction that the Jews throughout the world could not but welcome his work and adopt it as the standard book of Judaism. However, he felt that *The House of Joseph* was too intricate and of too great dimensions to be easily understood by young and still untrained students. Solely to assist them, Caro summarized the work in a digest which he fittingly and graphically called *The Prepared Table—Shulchan Aruch*.

Dealing methodically with every field of Jewish religious practice, at home and in the synagogue, in the street and in court, from birth to death, the decisions and regulations are set out so clearly that they are ready at hand for anyone wishing to know them. Just as a table which is properly set demands no effort from the diner, who need merely stretch out his hand to find each dish in its right place ready to be eaten, so Caro's code presents the final decision on each problem so that everyone can easily find what is needed. Instead of being jumbled together like lumber in an overcrowded storeroom, the whole of Jewish legislation is spread out like a feast. Everything is arranged tidily and logically. Its language is simple, and its sentences are short.

Apart from being less voluminous, this new, abridged version of *The House of Joseph* differed in several important points. Completely omitting discussion and tracing of all previous views, it gave only Caro's conclusion, the authoritative decision. It was no longer published as a commentary on Asher's *Four Rows,* but as a work of its own, and was first printed in Venice in 1565. Implicitly, however, it never denied its origin. It still followed the arrangement of the *Four Rows,* even using their names as titles of its four parts. Each was called by a telling biblical phrase:

1. Orach Chayim—"The Way of Life" (from Ps. XVI, 11).
2. Yoreh Deah—"The Teaching of Knowledge" (from Isa. XXVIII, 9).
3. Even Ha'ezer—"The Stone of Help" (from I Sam. VII, 12).
4. Choshen Ha'mishpat—"The Breastplate of Judgment" (from Ex. XXVIII, 30).

"The Way of Life" deals with the religious observances of every day, prayers and customs, feasts and fasts. It commences with regulations regarding conduct on rising in the morning and leads to a detailed account of the proper celebration of Purim, the Feast of Lots.

"The Teaching of Knowledge" embraces a multiplicity of matters, including the rules governing ritual slaughtering; food; drink; the taking of interest; superstitions; the honoring of one's parents and teachers; the giving of charity; the rite of circumcision; the writing of a Scroll of the Law; the visiting of the sick; death; burial and mourning.

Regulations regarding wedding and divorce form the subject of "The Stone of Help." Indeed, this is a compendium of marriage guidance, legislating for all eventualities, including seduction, jealousy, and the fate of a childless widow.

"The Breastplate of Judgment," as indicated by its title, contains a detailed and concise summary of Jewish civil and criminal law. It deals with the appointment and duties of judges, the question of evidence, the collection of loans, and the giving of mortgages. There are chapters on power of attorney, partnership and agencies, purchase and sale, frauds and mistakes, the treatment of gifts (with special reference to deathbed legacies). Further parts give directions concerning lost and found property, the loading and unloading of animals, the leasing of farmlands, and the hiring of labor. Brief and comprehensive rules relating to theft, robbery, damage to property, and personal injuries complete the colorful pattern of this fourth part of the *Shulchan Aruch*.

The four parts are divided into sections, each numbered and headed by an appropriate title and then subdivided into individual paragraphs, called branches, each of which is devoted to a specific item. Any law can thus be quoted by three distinct references, relating to the book, the part, and the branch.

Once the summarized version of Caro's *House* had reached the people, the obvious happened: the main work remained unread, except by scholars and learned rabbis. But the digest, of which Caro himself had a poor opinion and which he had written merely as an aid to the learner, became world-famous and was studied everywhere. And yet it, too, almost shared the fate of Maimonides' code. Its acceptance was not unanimous, and an ever-increasing opposition seemed to doom the book.

Caro was of Spanish descent. His teachers had followed the Sephardic tradition. Even two of the three authorities he had chosen as his guide in all final decisions were Spaniards. No wonder, then, that the communities which followed the German tradition were opposed to the work from the moment of its publication. They regarded it as unauthoritative, misleading, and suggestive of dangerous innovations, especially as much of their own Ashkenazic ritual was more exacting and scrupulous. In addition, they felt the need to consider prevailing local customs, even if these contradicted ancient authorities—a view Caro did not share.

They attacked him and his *Prepared Table* with great invective. Its dishes were considered unsuitable for German digestion, especially as it left out their national, home-grown specialties. The main center of opposition was Poland.

But the irony of history willed it that the very powers which tried to destroy Caro's work established it throughout the world. One of Caro's most vehement opponents was the Polish rabbi Moses Isserles (1510–1572), best known from his initials as Rema. His criticism extended to a detailed account of all the deficiencies of the *Shulchan Aruch*. In each individual case where Spanish and German traditions were at variance, he supplemented its paragraphs with the different Ashkenazic usage, frequently raising mere local customs to the status of law.

In a number of cases (not relating to ritual and dietary legislations) where Caro's decisions appear stern and rigorous, Isserles shows leniency and a liberal point of view. This is especially reflected in his interpretation of the laws relating to the sanctification of the Sabbath and in his attitude toward science and the Gentile world. The *Shulchan Aruch,* for instance, prohibits the reading of any kind of nonreligious literature on the Sabbath. Isserles permits it, provided the books are written in Hebrew. He even suggests that wherever the literal observance of a law might result in considerable monetary or material loss, rabbinical authorities should show understanding of the special circumstances and be lenient in its interpretation and enforcement.

Isserles called his supplements, rather pointedly, *The Tablecloth,* something he felt was lacking on the so-called *Prepared Table.* But readers misunderstood his intention. They thought that the differing views he voiced were not meant to destroy the *Shulchan Aruch,* but to complete it. It thus came about that the whole of Jewry accepted the *Shulchan Aruch* as the authoritative code. The Spanish tradition followed Caro's decisions, and the German communities made Isserles' glosses their guide.

It was typical of Jewish tolerance and freedom of thought that soon, in 1578, both books—Caro's digest and Isserles' glosses—were not published in separate volumes, but the one was incorporated in the other. Whenever German custom varies from Spanish tradition, Isserles' note is inserted in the text of the *Shulchan Aruch,* distinguished only by a smaller type and the introductory word *Haga* (gloss). A book and its critic thus became one indivisible whole, in which east and west were united, creating yet another unique work of the Jewish spirit, which was universally adopted as "the code" of Judaism.

Apart from the intrinsic value of the book, historical circumstances combined to assure its instantaneous success. The great multitude of uprooted Jews had not yet had time to settle down properly. Fully occupied with establishing themselves in a new home, they did not have the leisure for study. Many lacked the knowledge to go beyond a book as lucid and easily understood as Caro's *Shulchan Aruch.* New academies which could take the place of those destroyed in Spain had not yet been founded, and even learned scholars preferred using Caro's *Prepared Table* to taking the trouble of delving into the many authorities on which it rested. It was an uneasy age, full of uncertainty and unsettled thoughts. Many rabbis welcomed the opportunity of using for mystical speculation the time saved by adoption of a ready-made code.

Caro's work was of inestimable service to the Jewish world. It united the dispersed people of Israel and made them feel at one and at home wherever they were. Most of all, the *Shulchan Aruch* meticulously applied to everyday existence the Jewish principle that only a life which is constantly centered on God is worth living and makes for righteousness. Repeatedly, the work renewed the Jews' strength as a people of religion whose faith did not consist in doctrinal pronouncements, but in a way of life which itself was a confession by deed. The *Shulchan Aruch* ended the diversity of Jewish tradition and unified Jewry for all time. A central book of study and reference, the *Shulchan Aruch* became the subject of numerous explanations, supplements, commentaries, supercommentaries, and digests. Most popular of the latter is Solomon Ganzfried's *Shortened Shulchan Aruch,* which has been reprinted many times and was translated into English by (among others) Hyman E. Goldin and published in New York in 1927.

The *Shulchan Aruch* has not been without its critics. People maliciously chose to quote some of its passages out of context to create the impression that they were typical of the whole work (just as had been done with the Talmud). Modern historians pointed to the danger that a code so rigorously regulating every detail of life could force religion into too rigid a mold.

Yet nothing has ever replaced the *Shulchan Aruch.* It became the unquestioned "common law" for the scattered Jewish communities. Orthodox Jews still consider it their authoritative guide in every aspect of life. Reform Jews do not share this view, feeling that much of its legislation has become invalid through changed circumstances and must be brought into harmony with contemporary conditions. Stressing the significance of the individual conscience, Reform Judaism rejects altogether the possibility of any permanent fixation of Jewish law.

Whichever attitude is adopted, however, no one can deny the grandeur of the *Shulchan Aruch*'s conception, the significant role it has played in the preservation of the unity of the Jewish faith (if not even in its very survival), and, most of all, how it has spiritualized and sanctified every moment and act of man.

The Teachings of the Shulchan Aruch

Outstanding is the *Shulchan Aruch*'s width of vision, the compass of its regulations, and the way it takes into account every eventuality of life. Its legislation ranges from building operations to pornography, from vanity to the true discharge of justice, from marriage guidance to the right arrangements of books. Far from being a mere legal code, the *Shulchan Aruch* is saturated with the spirit of religion. Its scope extends beyond the factual and tangible to the regions of the heart.

All our actions must be prompted and controlled by a feeling of reverence and personal consideration. Out of respect, no child should ever occupy the seat of his father or mother. To make our parents comfortable and happy, we must shirk no sacrifice. Even their death does not absolve us from our duty always to show deference to their wishes. Never should we do anything of which we know they would have disapproved.

At all times we must be careful in conversation and avoid saying anything that might be misunderstood or cause mental anguish. In the presence of a cripple or someone otherwise afflicted, we must not mention his handicap or disease, even if our actual words have no connection whatsoever with him but refer to a totally different person. Similarly, we should never discuss moral wrongs or failings which we know to have occurred in the family of someone present. If we do not contemplate buying an article, we should not inquire after its price.

It is evil to call a man by a nickname, even if it is done only in jest. His dignity would suffer by it, although its use has become a general custom and most people no longer take exception to a nickname. Special care is demanded in our attitude toward people who have done wrong, but have since mended their ways. In no circumstance should we remind them of their past. If they have bad luck, are seriously ill, or have to suffer in any other way, we must never say to them, "It is only what you deserve."

It is wrong to ask anyone a question if we know that he is unable to answer it. This applies especially to debates, when it is sinful to call on a person not conversant with the subject to voice his opinion, as it will either make a fool of him or give him a feeling of inferiority.

Nothing is more painful than thoughtless expressions of comfort. Not only do they increase the mourner's grief instead of easing it, but equally they blaspheme God. We should not say to the bereaved: "What can you do? It is not possible to change God's decree." Words to that effect might infer that were it possible for Him to alter it, He would have done so.

Any kind of slander is a grievous offense, but it is worse still to defame the name of a dead person who is unable to defend himself. The *Shulchan Aruch* rules that a person guilty of such an offense must not only pay a fine but fast and beg forgiveness at the grave of the person whose character he has besmirched.

Men should not dress in front of mirrors, for, though this may be fitting for women, it might make a man vain. When one is piling up books, the Bible must always be placed uppermost, in order to show respect for Holy Scripture. It is forbidden to look at anything which may awaken immoral thoughts.

Everyone is obliged to marry. If at all possible, a man should settle down when he is eighteen years old. A young man should never marry an old woman, nor an old man a young girl. The choice of one's wife should not be influenced by her wealth or physical beauty, but by her piety, integrity, and industry. It is sinful to break off an engagement solely for financial reasons. People about to become engaged should be careful to ascertain first that their future spouse's family is of good reputation, charitable, and imbued with religious spirit. Families which are notorious as arrogant, quarrelsome, and hardhearted should be shunned. No one should marry into a family where there is infectious skin disease or epilepsy. Every home should have a threefold foundation: a knowledge of religious tradition, a spirit of worship, and a life of benevolence.

Study and work demand a sound and strong body. Parents are therefore obliged to look after their children's health. They are responsible for providing them with a balanced diet, suitable clothing, and congenial surroundings. Children should be trained to do regular exercise and should not be pampered. Their religious education is a paramount duty of every parent. If a father is unable to instruct his child himself, he must employ a teacher. If the parents cannot afford to do so, the community at large has to arrange free tuition.

The study of Judaism is never completed. Every Jew, of whatever age, condition, or circumstance, is obliged to continue it throughout his life. At least a short period must be devoted to it daily, and neither poverty nor lack of time is a sufficient excuse.

Convinced of the basic importance of education, the *Shulchan Aruch* tries to ensure by every possible means the efficiency of the teacher. He forfeits his license and has to be dismissed if he ignores any of the rules laid down. To keep himself always alert, he must watch his diet and keep his meals from being either too frugal or too sumptuous. As late nights would impair his faculties, he must keep regular hours and make sure he has sufficient sleep. Nothing exceeds in importance the training of the young. Neighbors must not raise objections to being disturbed by the noise of pupils, just as they must not protest against inconvenience caused by religious observances in adjacent buildings.

A sense of decorum and dignity alone does not assure proper worship. We are qualified to pray only if our thoughts and feelings are free from hatred, envy, or pride and are pure and unselfish. Intensity of feelings, and not length of prayers, makes worship acceptable. All prayer needs concentration and must never be rushed. We should not start a meal, or any new task, within half an hour of the commencement of a service, as it might delay us.

We must attend every service that is being held. To discuss worldly affairs in a house of worship, let alone to jest, is forbidden. However, it is a religious duty to be joyful at heart on Jewish festivals. As always, the *Shulchan Aruch* is not satisfied with a general observation, but makes several definite suggestions on how to give some extra happiness to one's wife and children and, most of all, to the lonely and needy. According to his means, every Jew should celebrate festivals by giving sweets to the young, a new dress or jewelry to the women, and food to the hungry, orphaned, and widowed.

To preserve life is a sacred duty. We must do everything possible to save a person from real or potential danger, even if thereby we break the laws of Sabbath observance. And yet, in spite of the Jew's love of life, there are occasions when he must be prepared to surrender it. The *Shulchan Aruch* decrees that when called upon to deny God's existence, he should refuse to do so and accept death, if need be.

Whoever has escaped from great danger must offer a prayer of thanksgiving at public worship in front of the congregation. Believing in omens of any kind is irreligious.

If we desire help from God, we ourselves must give a helping hand to mankind. That is why whenever we ask for God's assistance we should make a donation to a deserving cause. Every synagogue ought to display a charity box to enable people to contribute their share for the poor. It is every Jew's duty, the *Shulchan Aruch* legislates, to give to the impoverished in just proportion to his own income and property. No one is exempted. Everything should be avoided that might give hurt or humiliation to those in need. The ideal way of giving and receiving charity is that in which neither donor nor recipient becomes aware of the other's identity. No one is permitted to boast of his donation.

The *Shulchan Aruch* contains what amounts to a unique bill of rights for the poor. We owe the homeless person two nourishing meals daily and a suitable place for rest at night. On Sabbaths, we are responsible for meeting all his needs. It is not sufficient merely to pay for his food and shelter in restaurants and hostels. We should invite the poor man into our home and make him feel not like a beggar receiving charity, but like one of our family. This will not only soothe the harassed mind of the poor man but make our children sensitive about the suffering of the stranger.

To ask for charity when there is no real need for it is a grave offense. Whoever does so not only deceives the donor but robs the poor. No effort should be spared to avoid relying on other people's help. To preserve his independence, even the most learned scholar should put aside all false pride and undertake the most menial of tasks.

To look after the sick and visit them, irrespective of the faith or class to which they belong, is a divine command. Even the most noble has to call at the sickbed of the humblest citizens, not condescendingly, but in sincere sympathy and with brotherly love.

Because it is a doctor's duty to treat the sick, he must never refuse to do so. Even if there are other equally qualified doctors available, he still must not send away any patient, as not every physician succeeds with the same cure. Yet a doctor who knows that he lacks the essential knowledge must not treat a man for the sake of receiving a fee, but must send him to a specialist. A doctor should always feel personally responsible for his patient's well-being.

It is forbidden to charge more than the normal price for a drug because it is in short supply. Even if the need of the patient is so urgent and he is so desperate that he promises to pay far in excess of what the medicine should cost, only the usual charge must be made. On the other hand, if the sick person has promised the doctor a higher fee, it must be rendered, as the worth of medical science and knowledge cannot be assessed by a definite sum. Every moment of life is sacred. Nothing must be done to shorten it even by a single breath, as sometimes in mysterious ways it may be used in preparation for eternity.

The highest integrity in commercial life is commanded by the *Shulchan Aruch*. It is prohibited to make goods appear more valuable than they really are, for the purpose of a higher profit. To mix wares of different qualities is a punishable offense. It is not permitted to "top" goods to deceive the customer into thinking that all of them are of the same quality as goods in the upper layer. Without being asked, the salesman is obliged to point out hidden faults in the merchandise. If a man desires to purchase an article for a certain purpose, and the trader knows that it is not suitable, he must volunteer the truth.

It is against the law to overcharge. However, to attract customers, stores may distribute sweets to children. To inflate food prices artificially is criminal, especially if it affects man's staple diet and therefore gives more hardship to the poor. Price control is permissible. However, it should be arranged not by commercial interests, but by the local population. Special officials should be appointed to supervise measures and charges in all shops and stores. Anyone found with faulty scales is to be prosecuted. It is not permitted to try to influence people about to make a purchase at a competitor's store.

Naturally, some of the laws of Caro's code were historically conditioned and can no longer be applied, because of wholly changed circumstances. The best example is the *Shulchan Aruch's* attitude to the taking of interest. At a time when the economy was based mainly on agriculture, this was considered usury and strictly prohibited. Anyone disobeying the rule was branded a criminal legally and a sinner religiously. To reestablish himself as an honest and trustworthy citizen, the moneylender had voluntarily to destroy all records of debts due to him, completely to abandon his business, and to make full restitution of all moneys he had collected in interest. If he was unable to identify individual borrowers, he had to donate to charity the whole amount involved. The use of a pawned object must be avoided, as such action would amount to taking interest.

Both employer and employee must carefully observe each other's rights and responsibilities. Wages have to be paid punctually and in full and can never be withheld. The employee must fulfill his duties conscientiously, and never halfheartedly. Always, and in every circumstance, he should be anxious to look after the interests of his firm. Time set aside for rest and recreation must not be employed otherwise, as this would impair efficiency. It is prohibited to accept an appointment when negotiations are in progress with someone else.

Every state law must be obeyed implicitly and deemed as binding as that of the Bible. Taxes, duties, and levies must be paid scrupulously and punctually. Any attempt at evading them is theft.

No one should be appointed a judge, however great his judicial qualifications may be, if he is ignorant of the Bible. Judges who dislike each other must not sit together on the bench, as their personal animosity may easily interfere with true justice being done. No person or party, witness or officer, appearing before a rabbinical court should be asked to take an oath that the testimony he is about to give is true: "If we cannot believe him without an oath, there is no substance in his testimony."

To appropriate anything which one does not own, even the most valueless object, is theft. A straw is worth nothing to the owner of a huge stack of corn. And yet, we must not take a single straw because, should everyone do so, no stack would be left. The purchase of stolen goods, of course, is condemned. "If there were no receiver, there would be no thief." But the *Shulchan Aruch* extends the prohibition to any article concerning which there is even a presumption that it might be stolen. Sheep from a shepherd, household goods from servants, must not be accepted, for the probability is that the property belongs to their employer.

As complete honesty must rule our lives, there is no room for conventional lies. We must never say what we do not feel in our hearts. The border line between a sham courtesy and an outright lie is exceedingly small. Words or actions designed to create in the minds of others the impression that we think better of them than we really do are decried as an attempt at fraudulently obtaining a good reputation. We must never extend an invitation or an offer to anyone, if we know that it will not be accepted. It is equally a deception to make a person wrongly think, by false pretenses, that a certain action or function was specially meant for him.

The legislation of the *Shulchan Aruch* even includes man's daily meals. No one should sit down to eat without first having seen to his pets and beasts. He must wait for the oldest at the table to start eating, as otherwise he would be nothing short of a glutton. Man must show appreciation of his food, which is God's gift to him. It is not merely ill-mannered but sinful to throw a piece of bread to anyone, instead of handing it to him. Food is degraded if it is fed to animals when it is quite suitable for human consumption.

To throw crumbs away will cause poverty. Instead, we should gather them and feed them to the fowls. To stare at anyone who is eating or drinking, or at the portion put before him, is an offense. When at table, we should not ignore the feelings and desires of those who serve us. If, for instance, a dish or drink is so appetizing, or of such strong aroma, that it must create in the person who waits on us a craving to taste it, we must offer him at least a little of it, for "it is injurious to the person who sees good food for which he longs, if he cannot eat thereof." However, we should offer food only to those who we know will wash their hands first and never eat anything without having blessed God.

To inflict mental anguish equals murder, since it impairs health and thus shortens a person's life. Whoever gives a severe shock to a person—for example, by suddenly shouting at him from behind, appearing out of the dark, or indeed in any other way—is guilty before God, even though he cannot be prosecuted by a court.

Consideration for others must be our perpetual concern. In all our tasks we must be careful and avoid even a suspicion of negligence. Thus, a carpenter who injures anyone with a piece of wood which slips from under his tool is liable even if the person in question entered the premises without permission and was therefore trespassing.

To inflict suffering on an animal or heartlessly to pass by when we could ease its burden is criminal. If one finds cattle broken down under a load, it is a legal obligation to unload them even in the absence of their owner, just as it is a duty to interrupt a journey to assist a traveler who is in difficulties and going your way.

Our diet necessitates the killing of animals. But to prolong their suffering by the slightest delay is evil. Skill in killing animals is insufficient to qualify a man to be a butcher. Only a person of high moral standard and deep religious feelings should be appointed, as he alone will show the requisite care for the beast.

Nothing could summarize the whole philosophy of the *Shulchan Aruch* better than its very beginning, in the words both of Caro himself and of his opponent, who, against his will, became his ally. Using a passage from the *Ethics of the Fathers,* Caro calls on the reader to be as strong as a lion in serving God. From the moment we rise in the morning, all our thoughts, words, and deeds should be worthy of Him and have as their only aim His sanctification. As the lion is the most fearless of animals, so shall we, likewise, in the performance of our duties, fear nothing, but rely firmly on God.

Isserles, annotating this passage, suggests as the most important principle of Jewish faith the verse from the Psalms: "I have set the Lord always before me." Everyone knows how differently we act from our usual way in the presence of a king or other notable personality. Then we take much more care in everything we say and do than normally at home or among our friends. But do we realize that all the time each one of us is in the presence of the King of Kings, Who watches us and surveys our deeds and from Whom nothing is hidden?

If only we would be conscious of this fact, the quality of our lives would be changed. A sense of reverence and humility would permeate all our existence. Prompted by a feeling of awe in the presence of God, we should dedicate ourselves fearlessly and completely to a life that is noble, pure, and worthy of the King of Kings. To give us this sense of God's nearness, and to guide us accordingly, is the fervent and inflexible purpose of the *Shulchan Aruch,* this masterpiece of rabbinic literature.

Chapter 13

THE PRAYERBOOK

Jewish prayer is as old as Jewish history. The very first Jew, Abraham, prayed to God, "the Judge of the whole earth," for the lives of the people of Sodom. The Bible, indeed, contains many prayers: Jacob begging God to save him from the fury of Esau; the servant Eliezer that he might succeed in his romantic mission on behalf of his master's son; King David's supplication to be permitted to build God's Temple; Ezra and Nehemiah pleading on behalf of the returned exiles. The Talmud and the Apocrypha also cite innumerable prayers offered by rabbis and pious men of all walks of life.

Worship was an integral part of Jewish life, as natural and as regular as food and drink. Prayer was never merely an expedient used to attain selfish wishes, but a means of praising God and sanctifying life. Every day of the Jew's existence was to be centered on God, from early morning till late at night, and to ensure this the Jew introduced three regular, daily services. First thing in the morning he had to join in prayer and thus consecrate the work and thought of the coming day. He was not permitted to partake of food until he had done so. His mind was clearest then and best able to concentrate.

Throughout the day the Jew must repeatedly be conscious of God's kindness and never take for granted His manifold gifts. Hence the rabbis early ordained that on a hundred different occasions every day the Jew should make acknowledgment of the blessings of life, praising God as their divine author.

The Greek word for prayer originates from a root meaning "to wish." The German *beten* means "to beg." But in Hebrew the term for prayer is "self-judgment." Sincerity is its first condition. "Man's prayer is not accepted unless he puts his heart in his hands." It must never become a mere routine, "as if a man were reading a document." The rabbis even suggested that every man should offer a new prayer daily. The merit of prayer cannot be judged by its length or its elaborate phrasing. Moses, praying that his stricken sister be cured of her leprosy, used only five words, and the ideal prayer was considered to be that of Hannah—wordless and formless on the lips, but offered from the overflowing of her dedicated heart.

Prayer needs humility and concentration of mind. "When a man prays he must turn his eyes downward and his heart upward." Before offering prayer, "a man should always examine himself. If he can direct his heart to God, let him pray; otherwise he should not do so." A bridegroom prior to his wedding, and a mourner prior to the funeral of his loved one, are therefore exempted from prayer.

Jewish mystics compared the effect of prayer upon the human spirit to that of a flame on coal. Just as the flame clothes the inert, black substance in a garment of fire and releases its imprisoned heat, so does prayer clothe man in a garment of holiness, releasing from him the light and fire implanted in his heart by his Maker.

Originally, all prayers were spontaneous. Their utterance and content depended on the need and emotion of the hour. Then, with the settlement of the Jews in the Holy Land and the establishment of regular, sacrificial services, prayer became systematized and standardized. Originally only accompanying the Temple worship, later prayers were offered outside the Temple precincts and even away from Jerusalem. Such regular worship was held as early as the eighth century B.C.E. It then already threatened to deteriorate into mere outward observance and formality, as the prophecies of Isaiah testify.

With the destruction of the Temple, its place was taken by the synagogue. All emphasis was now laid on congregational prayer, which became the uniting link and most potent force in Jewish existence. Without priest and ritual, it created a totally new type of worship, which exerted an everlasting influence on history.

For a long time prayers were recited from memory only. The frequency and regularity with which they were said, their very conciseness, and the scarceness and costliness of writing material made this a necessity. Just as was the case with the oral law, the writing down of prayer at first was forbidden. Then, as the result of three factors, it became necessary to issue compilations of prayers at least for the use of the leader of worship: the continuous growth of Jewish liturgy, the addition of numerous and often lengthy songs and poems, and, above all, the dispersal of the Jewish community.

Initially, the manuscripts gave only directions to prayer, but eventually they contained the complete text. Even so, stubborn adherence to a great variety of local traditions and customs still created a multitude of different versions. The form of Jewish worship was finally unified only with the advent of the printing press, with its mass production and wide distribution.

In a wonderful way, this unity of prayer has been preserved throughout the centuries and in all countries down to this very day. The essential Jewish prayers are virtually identical throughout the world. As they are said in the same Hebrew, a Jew may feel at home in any synagogue in any country.

Certain minor variations in text and pronunciation have arisen as a result of two streams of tradition, one from the Spanish and the other from the German communities. Appropriately, they are called the Sephardic (Hebrew for "Spanish") and Ashkenazic (German) rites. Throughout the British Commonwealth and in many American synagogues, Orthodox congregations have adopted S. Singer's prayerbook. This was first published in 1890, in London, and then reissued by the late Chief Rabbi, Dr. Joseph Hertz. It follows the traditional Ashkenazic rite and carries with it a literal translation of all the prayers. Reform Judaism published its own prayerbook. It still maintains faithfully the essential prayers of the old tradition, but omits passages which contradict its beliefs and has additional prayers in the vernacular and of modern composition. The most widely used

Reform prayerbook is that of the Central Conference of American Rabbis. It has been adopted by all Reform congregations in the United States, Canada, South Africa, Australia, and New Zealand. The Conservative and Reconstructionist movements also have their own prayerbooks.

The name of the Jewish prayerbook for Sabbaths and weekdays is siddur. This is a most prosaic name for one of the noblest creations of the human spirit. It means "order," the prayers naturally being arranged according to the sequence of the various services. As the holy days recur regularly throughout the year, the collection of their prayers is called *machzor*, meaning "cycle."

The siddur and the machzor combine prayers from the most diverse climes and epochs. There are quotations from Bible and Talmud, compositions of mystics, philosophers, and rabbis, and many anonymous creations sprung from the minds of the people. They stem from the Holy Land, Babylonia, Spain, and Germany. They reflect the yearning of the Jewish soul for communion with God, the fight of the early synagogue for survival, and the affirmation of monotheistic faith in a pagan world. Many of them, full of pathos and poetry, were written not in meditation, mystic communion or fervor, but out of the turmoil and anguish of the Jewish soul. And yet, though the prayers may be centuries apart in origin, divided by thousands of miles, they now form a unity, an integral part of the whole service. They constitute a document of divine inspiration and the Jew's answer to his destiny.

When today the Jew opens his prayerbook, he does not always realize that each separate prayer—almost each page—has its own long and often dramatic history, a knowledge of which would increase the force of its inspiration and add to the intellectual and spiritual appreciation of worship.

The Two Basic Prayers

The foundation and principal prayers of Jewish worship are the biblical Sh'ma and the rabbinical "Eighteen Benedictions."

The Sh'ma, called by the first word of the prayer, is the Jewish proclamation of the unity of God: "Hear, O Israel, the

Lord our God, the Lord is One." It calls on man to love God with all his being and at all times, to make Him an ever-present reality in thought, talk, and action. It stresses the duty of the older generation to teach religion to the young and to surround existence with special signposts to God.

The Sh'ma is recited twice daily in regular service and accompanies also the most solemn moments of the Jew's life. It is said at the taking out of the Scroll, at the completion of the solemn service on the Day of Atonement, and in man's very last hour when he is about to meet God face to face. The Sh'ma was considered so important that its discussion forms the very beginning of the Talmud.

The rabbis ordained that the prayer had to be spoken with intense concentration, putting special emphasis on its last word —God's oneness. Nothing should interrupt its recital, not even the greeting of a king. The Jewish mystical Bible, the Zohar, explains that when man in prayer in love and reverence thus declares the unity of God, the walls of earth's darkness are cleft and God's presence is revealed lighting up the universe.

With the Sh'ma, the Jew sanctifies God's name. It became his inspiration and last, fervent confession. With its words on their lips innumerable martyrs died in the arenas and on the crosses of Roman paganism, on the pyres and torture racks of medieval savagery, and in the concentration camps and gas chambers of Nazi brutality. This one sentence, selected out of the 4,875 verses of the Torah, became Judaism's greatest contribution to the religious thought of mankind and its eternal confession of faith.

The Eighteen Benedictions (in Hebrew *Sh'mone Esre*) became the prayer par excellence. Since the congregation rises for its recital, it is also commonly known as the *Amida* (Hebrew for "standing"). It is a unique group of petitions which deal with the most varied aspects of life and religion and in each case praise God.

The Eighteen Benedictions commence with an affirmation of ancestral tradition, God's power and holiness, and man's immortality. Invocations for human needs follow. They are prayers for wisdom and knowledge, for man's return from his misguided path, for God's forgiveness and help, and for the healing of the sick. Further benedictions plead for the establishment of justice and righteousness and the annihilation of arrogance, evil, and hypocrisy. The prayer concludes with a thanksgiving and a supplication for peace.

Of ancient origin, its various parts belong to different authors and different times, the exigencies of which contributed to their creation. With one exception, the general text of the Amida was finalized in 100 c.e.

The description of this prayer as the Eighteen Benedictions became so fixed in the Jewish mind that even when a nineteenth blessing was added, the old name was not replaced. The prayer was considered so important that a special, abridged version was introduced for those who were unable to find time to say it at length. It became obligatory for each congregant first to recite the prayer silently by himself, after which the cantor repeated it aloud all over again.

The Pagan Who Came to Curse

Right at the beginning of the Jewish prayerbook stands a prayer composed by a pagan seer in the deserts of Arabia thousands of years ago. The author, reluctantly, but in unforgettable words, offered praise to the wandering Israelites encamped in unity and living by faith.

The Israelites were on their way to the Promised Land. Their march was not unimpeded. On the contrary, the surrounding nations tried desperately to exterminate them. Every means was tried, weapons as much as the superstitious incantations of pagan priests.

Balak, King of Moab, was terrified by the repeated victories of the Israelites over other people. He was determined to halt them. Unable to do so by military means, he resorted to magic, which to him seemed inexorable. He summoned Balaam, far-famed seer of the time, and ordered him to curse the Israelites. Balaam undertook this mission, but only after much resistance and with great difficulty. Looking down on the encamped Israelites from an eminence, and wanting to curse them, he had to utter blessings. The words he spoke then have become the opening sentence of every synagogue service: "How goodly are thy tents, O Jacob, thy tabernacles, O Israel."

A Mystic's Welcome of the Sabbath

A much more recent section of the Jewish prayerbook stemmed from a circle of sixteenth-century mystics living at Safed, in Galilee. On the Sabbath eve they used to clothe themselves in white garments, as a sign of purity, and go out into the fields to welcome and lead home like a bride the "Princess Sabbath." On their way, they chanted mystical hymns, most of which contained the refrain "Come, my beloved, to meet the bride." One of these songs, composed by Solomon Alkabetz, became the introductory prayer for every Sabbath eve and is now intoned in every synagogue throughout the world. Its authorship has been perpetuated with an acrostic: the letters of Solomon's name form the initial letters of each verse. The turning of Orthodox Jews toward the doors at the singing of the last stanza is a rarely recognized but most obvious survival of the ancient custom of going out to welcome the Sabbath.

A Family Prayer for the Stranger

The Jew's passion for social justice and his unremitting care for the friendless account for the inclusion of yet another prayer in Jewish public worship and hence its place in the prayerbook.

The eve of every Sabbath and festival was celebrated at home in family union. The father of the house then hallowed the day by praising God with one of His choicest gifts—a lifted goblet of wine. The prayer itself was appropriately named Kiddush (sanctification).

Kiddush was specifically a prayer for recital in the home. However, some occupations obliged many men to be away from home over the Sabbath and even over some holy days. So that they should not feel neglected, the Jewish communities built hostels within the precincts of the synagogue, and to give these wanderers some illusion of the warmth of the home, on the eve of every Sabbath and festival, public worship was beautified by a recital of the Kiddush.

Centuries have passed; the circumstances of its introduction have not only lapsed but been forgotten; yet the "sanctification of wine" is now an irremovable and beautiful part of the "order" of synagogue service: the siddur.

An Orphan Boy's Praise of God

According to talmudic legend the apparition of a dead man led to the creation of the kaddish, best known and most loyally observed of all the formal Jewish prayers: "Extolled and hallowed be the name of God throughout the world which He has created according to His will. And may He speedily establish His Kingdom of righteousness on earth. . . ." It is said daily for eleven months after the death of one's parents and then every year on the Hebrew anniversary of their passing.

Akiba, greatest rabbinical authority of his time (the second century C.E.), was haunted by the apparition of a man who complained that his soul could not find rest. He explained that he was deprived of peace because during his lifetime he had been unkind to the poor, but that his suffering would cease if his son, whose religious education he had neglected, would rise and hallow God's name before the assembled congregation. Akiba located the boy, taught him the rudiments of Hebrew, and so enabled him eventually to praise God at service in the synagogue. The following night the orphan's father appeared once again, declaring that at last he had found peace. The boy's words, originally an ancient, academic prayer used to indicate to students that the lecture had ended, thus became the nucleus of the kaddish, the "prayer for the dead."

Down to modern days, every Jewish service anywhere, whether on festivals or on weekdays, in the morning, afternoon, or night, has ended with the kaddish. Two thousand years old, written partly in Aramaic (the vernacular of that period), not speaking of death, yet spoken in memory of the dead, it is an undying prayer, kept alive even among the most indifferent Jews.

A Rabbi's Penitence

The description of the Day of Judgment forms one of the most magnificent prayers of the Jewish New Year. After its opening words, it is called the *Unetanneh Tokef* (Let us now mightily affirm). A legend first heard in the fourteenth century places its origin in western Germany and ascribes its composition and inclusion in the high holy day liturgy to a rabbi's hesitation and final martyrdom.

Amnon of Mayence, a scholarly and respected rabbi, on numerous occasions had withstood attempts to force him to adopt Christianity. Urged yet again to give up the Jewish faith, he evasively asked for three days for consideration. When he failed to appear to give his decision, he was fetched by the authorities. Pleading guilty, he begged that his tongue should be torn out, as its hesitancy to give an answer had seemed to express doubt in the truth of Judaism. Instead, his feet were cut off, as they had refused to come, also his hands, which had not borne witness as demanded.

It was the day of the New Year. Amnon asked friends to carry him into the synagogue. He interrupted the worship, calling on the congregation to wait. Then he recited for the first time this prayer on God's justice and judgment. No sooner had he concluded than he collapsed and died. This legend, though probably unhistorical, is eternal in its message. It calls on the Jew always to be ready to attest to God's truth, never to be intimidated by the mighty, but, undaunted, to proclaim God's name.

The Only Jewish Rite of Absolution
and
A Tune That Became World-Famous

Not its content, but its music rendered the Kol Nidre the most universally known prayer of the Jewish faith. Its haunting melody inspired millions of people, Jews and non-Jews alike. The first words of the prayer gave to the eve of the Day of Atonement its name. But the misunderstood and even misconstrued meaning of its text caused uncounted suffering.

It is written in Aramaic and is the only rite of absolution known in Judaism. Its words purport to annul vows made during the course of the year, but only insofar as they relate to one's self, as is explicitly stated. In times of stress or distress, people only too easily promise the impossible. In a rash and thoughtless way they vow the unattainable. Then, with the crisis over and a return to a normal way of thinking, they tend either to realize that they are utterly incapable of executing the vow made or even to forget about it. To resolve the conflict of conscience and feeling of guilt which inevitably resulted in the sincere person was the purpose of the Kol Nidre. Publicly it proclaimed null and void this kind of rash promise. But at no time did it apply to a vow beyond one's own self.

It was a dangerous prayer, susceptible of misunderstanding and therefore most welcome to the anti-Semite of all ages. Wilfully ignoring the purpose of the Kol Nidre and misrepresenting its text, he used it in an attempt to prove the unreliability of the Jew and of his oaths. No wonder that from time to time rabbinical authorities have raised their voices against the prayer and that in modern times some Jewish communities, in fear of misinterpretation, retained the music but replaced the text with the words of Psalm CXXX. In a great paradox, they celebrated Kol Nidre without the "Kol Nidre."

Russian Czarist legislation demanded a special Hebrew introduction to the prayer, stating that it referred only to oaths which bore relation to one's own personal life, but in no circumstances to vows made in connection with other people and with the authorities.

There exists another—but untenable—explanation of the origin of the prayer. This places it at the time of the Spanish Inquisition and sees in it an expression of undaunted faith even in the face of overwhelming odds. Jews were then forced to deny their faith and openly to repudiate it. But underground, they continued to worship as Jews in their own way. Every year on their most holy day these crypto-Jews, or marranos (as they were sneeringly nicknamed by the Spaniards), annulled the vow they had made under duress and thereby, with the Kol Nidre, renewed their adherence to Judaism.

The Essence of Judaism

The siddur contains not only this great variety of prayer, renewing in worship the Jew's devotion to God, but also a summary of his faith in order to clarify and daily impress on his mind the teachings of his religion.

Judaism, though a way of life, has its definite pattern of belief. It knows of no dogma, in the sense that acceptance of any doctrine bestows salvation, or its denial, damnation. But in spite of the absence of a creed in the theological meaning of the word, Judaism possesses its definite teaching, implicit in its writings and from time to time summarized by its rabbis. The most famous statement was made by twelfth-century Moses Maimonides in the Thirteen Principles of Faith. They have been included in the Jewish Orthodox prayerbook and are still part of its daily morning service, where they follow the recital of the Ten Commandments.

Maimonides' time was one of religious doubt and disputation. He felt it necessary that every Jew should clearly understand the essence of Judaism. For this purpose, he listed thirteen essentials of Jewish belief as an introductory guide, but not a doctrinal creed. They are introduced by the fundamental of monotheistic religion: "I believe with perfect faith that the Creator, blessed be His name, is the Author and Guide of everything that has been created, and that He alone has made, does make, and will make all things."

The House of Worship a House of Study

Judaism believes that the study of religious literature is itself a means of worship. To learn devoutly was to pray sincerely. To study God's word filled man's mind with divine inspiration and was a command to be obeyed by day and by night. It was a task not to be left to scholars, experts, or rabbis, but a sacred obligation for every Jew. The view prevailed that the ignorant could not be religious. The siddur therefore reinforced its prayers and teachings with excerpts from the treasure house of Jewish literature, most prominent among them being the complete tract of the *Ethics of the Fathers.* To study this became part of the Sabbath afternoon service for six months every year.

It is an anthology of rabbinical, ethical teachings completed in 200 C.E., when it became part of the Mishna. Its wisdom is as apparent and applicable today as it was those many centuries ago. It is outspoken and considers every aspect of life.

Of the many opinions voiced, a few may be cited to illustrate the depth of thought and beauty of language: wars are caused because of delayed or perverted justice; peace is founded on the stability of the world, dependent on the rule of truth and justice; to learn from everybody is wisdom; heroism is the control of one's passions; only he is rich who is satisfied with whatever he possesses.

Every individual, like everything on earth, has his purpose and therefore demands unqualified respect. The attempt to appease in the hour of anger, or to comfort while the dead is still present, is futile. The finest scholar is he who is quick to grasp and slow to forget. A cultured person is distinguished by seven characteristics: he does not speak before one who is greater in wisdom; he does not interrupt his conversation, is not hasty to answer, asks pertinent questions and answers to the point, speaks in the order of things, admits his ignorance in matters about which he knows nothing, and readily acknowledges truth when he hears it.

The *Ethics of the Fathers* warns people against seeking greatness and coveting honors. It advises them to say little, but to do much; to greet everybody cheerfully, whoever it may be, and to remember that a good name excels everything in life.

One of its own quotations most aptly summarizes the very purpose of such teachings in a prayerbook: "He who learns in order to practise, will be given the opportunity to learn, to teach, to observe and to practise." Only applied religion is true religion.

The Hebrew word for worship—*Avodah*—means also "action," as God is best served in our deeds, which are inspired by our prayers.

The existence of the siddur assumes a personal God with Whom one is able to commune and asserts the power of the spirit in life. People often wonder whether there is any need for formulas and definite times of prayer and for specific houses of worship. Certainly, man can pray freely and out of the depth of his heart, with words chosen by himself. All the prayers of the Bible are such spontaneous creations of man's spiritual urge. They are the ideal. For worship to degenerate into mere routine and mechanical performance is fatal. The rabbis warned that "when you pray, regard your prayer not as a fixed task but as an appeal for mercy and grace before the All-present." But it is most difficult for the average person to formulate his own feelings in words. With his heart full to overflowing, his own words are inadequate. In spite of all the developments of science and the increase in knowledge, our needs have never changed. We still require light in darkness, courage in adversity, and God's help when walking in the valley of the shadow. The necessity of spiritual power in our materialist world is greater than ever before. To possess ready-made prayers is, therefore, not a disadvantage, but a wonderful help. They are the creation of deeply inspired men and act as "a lever in spiritual life." Not only do these prayers offer the right kind of words, but through them we link ourselves with the greatest and most inspired geniuses of all times. Nevertheless, the Jewish prayerbook also offers ample room for individual prayer in silent worship and meditation.

The Torah leaves no doubt that God can be served anywhere: "Wherever I cause My name to be remembered, I will come unto thee and bless thee." The rabbis of the Talmud even pointed out that "if it is impossible to pray in the synagogue, then pray in the field. If that also is impossible, then pray on your bed; and if that is equally impossible, then meditate in your heart." But it is a sad experience that if one can do something at all times and everywhere, only too often one does it never and nowhere.

Prayer, to be effective in life as a spiritual force, must have its regular time; otherwise it becomes spasmodic and is finally forgotten altogether. This explains the importance of the introduction in the Jewish prayerbook of three daily statutory services: morning, afternoon, and evening.

Truly, God is everywhere. But to unite in worship in a building specially dedicated to this purpose not only adds mysteriously to the fervor of the individual worshipers but generates its own unequaled atmosphere of devotion. A worshiping community is as different from the same number of individuals praying apart as a bed of coals is from scattered cinders. The very existence of synagogues is a perpetual reminder of man's need and duty to pray. In addition, congregational worship creates a communal and historical consciousness.

The siddur is written in Hebrew, which has always been the essential medium of prayer. It is a language which possesses unique spiritual qualities and is most apt for expressing the emotions of the heart. But it also links the modern Jew with the patriarchs, priests, and prophets at the very cradle of his religion. Today, it is a bond between all Jewish communities throughout the world. Yet a prayer can be said also in any other language. Its efficacy does not depend on its words, but on its sincerity. The siddur, therefore, does not only contain prayers for the government (and in the British Commonwealth for the Royal Family) in modern English, but ancient Aramaic petitions written in the language of the time and place of their origin. One of the earliest manuscripts of the Jewish prayerbook in existence, over a thousand years old, has prayers in Arabic.

In studying the siddur, yet another outstanding feature becomes apparent. The Jew does not pray as a single unit, but as a member of a religious brotherhood. Therefore all the prayers are spoken not as the words of an individual, but of a community. The first person plural always takes precedence over the first person singular. Even in the confession of sins (arranged in alphabetical order), the prayerbook speaks of *our* transgressions and *our* trespasses." Once again, this time in its siddur, Judaism affirms the interdependence of man, the need of mutual aid, and the fact of communal responsibility.

The Jew is the creator of true prayer. He introduced a new way of public worship, quite unknown until then, which has become the mode of prayer of all civilized people. The church is the daughter of the synagogue. The very reason for her existence is one special paragraph in the prayer of the "Eighteen Benedictions"!

The influence of the Jewish prayerbook is worldwide. Just as the Jewish Psalms have become an essential part of Christian liturgy, so the Lord's Prayer combines some of the outstanding Jewish supplications. "Our Father, Which art in heaven, hallowed be Thy name, Thy kingdom come" are well-known Hebrew forms of talmudic prayer and still part of the Jew's most revered kaddish, said daily. "For Thine is the kingdom, and the power and the glory" are words that occur first in the book of Chronicles, but belong to this very day to Jewish worship, when, on Sabbath and festival, the Scroll is taken out of the Ark. Likewise, out of the siddur came the Hallelujah and Amen of the Christian church.

The siddur is a world of prayer. It unites the Jews as a praying fellowship throughout the generations and the world, fostering in them what is finest and noblest. A source of ever-renewed inspiration and intimate communion with the Divine, it spans thousands of years and far-distant continents. It links physical needs with spiritual longing. It leads from the finite and temporal to the infinite and eternal. Through it, God is no longer a distant abstraction, but becomes a vital reality. The Jew's daily companion, its creative power is unceasing.

Chapter 14

HEBREW—A SACRED TONGUE

The Jew has a tendency to relate everything of ordinary, daily concern to his religion. In keeping with this habit, for thousands of years he did not describe Hebrew by the rather nationalistic term "mother tongue," but as *Lashon Ha'kodesh,* the "sacred tongue."

Although contemporary with a score of languages that have disappeared and although, until recently, it had not been the spoken language of a corporate state or people for countless generations, Hebrew has never been, in any sense, a dead language. Throughout the centuries of exile and dispersal of the Jews it remained the medium of Jewish prayer and devotion, and it colored the lives not only of individuals but of entire Jewish communities. Wherever he found a home, the Jew continued to learn Hebrew, if only to enable him to study the holy books. In some communities, indeed, the tongue was in common use as a means of daily intercourse.

It became the language of a vast and impressive literature in such diverse fields as theology and philosophy, history and medicine, astronomy and mathematics.

Moreover, it ranked high among the sources of inspiration which led eventually to the reestablishment of the Jewish national state in Israel. There, after millennia of exile, Hebrew may once again be heard with a precise and vivid vocabulary, articulating not only the life of the past but also the needs of modern society and culture.

Philologically, Hebrew belongs to the family of Semitic tongues, being akin to Syriac, Arabic, and Babylonic-Assyrian. The word "Hebrew" means "beyond" and refers to the fact that the Hebrews came from "beyond" the river.

To the Western eye, Hebrew presents some strange features. Like most oriental languages, it is written from right to left, so that books appear to be opened at the end and the pages to be turned backward.

The Hebrew alphabet, handwritten or printed, has no capital letters and was originally written with no spaces between the words. To make things even more difficult for the reader, there were no punctuation signs, and if the end of a line happened to come in the middle of a word, the writer merely carried on with the ensuing letter at the beginning of the next line.

Thus, early Hebrew documents presented an unending stream of letters, all equal in size, line after line from beginning to end. It is thought that this somewhat excessive economy of space reflected an acute shortage of writing material, whether parchment, papyrus, or clay tablets.

The ultimate complication arose from the fact that the Hebrew alphabet consists virtually of consonants alone, so that the vowel sounds, necessary to a spoken language, did not appear in the written form.

The opening lines of Psalm XXIII afford a visual demonstration of these features:

> The Lord is my Shepherd; I shall not want.
> He maketh me to lie down in green pastures;
> He leadeth me beside the still waters.
> He restoreth my soul; He leadeth me
> In the paths of righteousness, for His name's sake.

This seems to take a somewhat different aspect when printed, *mutatis mutandis,* as it would appear in the style of original Hebrew calligraphy: written backward, with no break at the end of a word and no notice taken of the end of a line and without capitals, punctuation, or vowels:

> mhtnwtnllhsdrhphsmsdrlht
> mhtdlhsrtspnrgnnwdltmhtk
> tdlhlsmhtrtsrhsrtwlltshtdsb
> nshrfssnsthgrfshtphtnmh
> kssm

This situation could not long be tolerated. The first improvement was the invention, unique among known languages, of special final letters. The unknown genius responsible for this innovation selected five letters which often mark the end of a word and devised new symbols, reminiscent of but distinct from the normal form, to be used only if the given letter actually came at the end of the word. Incidentally, although in modern usage Hebrew is written or printed with normal spaces between words, these final letters are retained as a memento of the calligraphic problem of the past.

The next improvement was made about a thousand years after Hebrew came into existence as a written language. This was the invention of written symbols to represent the vowel signs. They were not, as is the case with English, separate letters analogous to the consonants and forming part of the alphabet. They comprised six special arrangements of dots and dashes, and when written under (or in one case over) a consonant, they added to it the sounds, respectively, of *a, e, i, o, ooh,* and *ow*. (It may be significant or merely coincidental that the vowel sound *e* is represented by a single dot and the sound *i* by two dots. Students of Morse code will be interested.)

These vowel symbols were used principally as an aid to the learner or the man of little knowledge; they were not put into use by the better-educated sections of the community, and to this day Scrolls of the Law as used in synagogues are written without vocalization, as, indeed, are modern books and newspapers printed in Hebrew. On the other hand, in prayerbooks the vowels are employed. At various later stages the separation of words came into almost universal use, and certain punctuation marks were introduced, though these, too, do not appear in Scrolls of Law.

The Hebrew alphabet contains twenty-two letters, of which two now are silent, having no individual sound of their own, although being capable of slightly modifying the sound of other letters. There is one letter which is even more guttural than the *ch* of the Scottish "loch." Interesting to note is the fact that each Hebrew letter is also used as a numeral: *aleph* is 1, *bet* 2, and so on. This linguistic peculiarity gave rise to much speculation, and the numerical value of words was employed in Jewish mysticism. Most paradoxical of all, perhaps, is the little-known fact that the present-day so-called "Hebrew alphabet" really uses Syrian square letters, introduced only in the fifth century B.C.E., when the whole of Jewish literature was transcribed from the ancient Hebrew lettering into the "modern" way of writing!

All twenty-two letters originally were pictures, and in some the snake or hand, window or door, oxgoad or fishhook, eye or mouth, can still be recognized.

Hebrew is a very concise language. Two pages of English, when translated into Hebrew and printed in type of comparable size, would occupy only from one-half to two-thirds of a page. This is, in a large measure, due to grammatical differences. In Hebrew, conjunctions, prepositions, and pronouns are represented by prefixes and suffixes. Thus, the word "house" is spelled in Hebrew in three letters, *ba'yit*.* For "in your house" add two letters (and modify the vowel sounds) and you have *b'vayt-cha*.** An even more striking example is the momentous commandment, "And thou shalt love thy neighbour as thyself," which in Hebrew consists of just three words.

Like certain other languages—for example, Latin with its "classical" and "modern" pronunciations—Hebrew is spoken with two quite distinctive intonations—more distinctive, that is to say, than any local dialectical variations. These major divisions are called, respectively, Ashkenazic (from the Hebrew word meaning "German") and Sephardic (meaning "Spanish"). The differences, as with Latin, are not very wide, but quite evident. In the latter case, the Emperor is either *Seezer* or *Kyzer;* that is, one consonant hardened and one vowel modified. Similarly, in the Ashkenazic accent, the name Israel would be pronounced as Yis-ro-ail and, in Sephardic, as Yis-rah-ail. In Sephardic the letter *sov*—the last in the alphabet—is always pronounced as though it were *tov*.

In general, these differences may have developed as dialectical

* בית ** בביתך

modifications, due to the dissimilarity of the German and Spanish languages. When the German Jews were dispersed in the fifteenth century, they took their accent with them to various parts of the world, where it came to be regarded as correct Hebrew. Similarly, when the Inquisition broke up the Spanish communities in 1492, many migrated to Palestine, and the Sephardic accent, surviving through more than four and a half centuries, was adopted as the official pronunciation and so remains in the modern republic of Israel.

The establishment of Israel, indeed, gave great impetus to the movement for the universal adoption of the Sephardic accent. South Africa led the way when, on the day that Israel proclaimed her independence, all congregations, Orthodox and Reform, adopted the official or Sephardic pronunciation.

Quite a number of words in common English usage are borrowed from Hebrew. Thus, in Hebrew, *cider* is a fermented drink (albeit somewhat stronger than a typical English cider); *jubilee* is pure Hebrew, referring in that language to the fiftieth year (of liberation and restoration). *Amen,* in both tongues, has the significance (perhaps not widely known in English) of "it is true," while *Hallelujah* means, simply, "praise God." Even the word "alphabet" could owe as much to the first two Hebrew letters, *aleph* and *bet,* as to the Greek *alpha* and *beta;* certainly the Hebrew are the older.

In existence for almost four thousand years, Hebrew is a language unique of its kind. It never aged, and it has qualities of true spirituality and sanctity. It expresses Judaism even in the formation of its words and the peculiarities of its grammar.

The Hebrew vocabulary testifies to the supremacy of the Jewish conception of God. It does not have any word for goddess, as the very idea behind such a word is totally alien to the Jew. Dry grammar reflects the deep emotional attitude of the Jew. It possesses an intensive mood, where a mere change of vocalization adds special force to the ordinary meaning of a verb.

The etymology of the Hebrew vocabulary conveys the teachings of Judaism. Numerous words cannot be translated adequately into any other language, as no corresponding concept exists outside the Jewish faith. There is, for example, no separate or single word which means "charity." The sense of this word is, in Hebrew, conveyed by the word *mitzvah*, which cannot be readily translated since it means simultaneously "commandment" and "benevolence." Thus, Hebrew indicates clearly that social justice is not a matter of personal inclination, but a social obligation. The language has no direct equivalent for "marriage," which is expressed by the word "sanctification," while "prayer" is "self-judgment," and a "cemetery" is "the house of eternity."

As in ancient days, the newly revived Hebrew of the modern age still reflects this religious quality of a language that reveals the soul of a people. Immigration into Israel is called *aliyah*, which means "ascent," as the newcomer "ascends" to the Holy Land. The act of entering it is like a pilgrimage, the fulfillment of an ideal. It is still an ascent, even when the new settler goes down to the shores of the Dead Sea. People seeking asylum were not refugees, but *ma'apilim*, men who advanced despite overwhelming odds, who "assaulted" hardships. The daily greeting is *shalom*, the ever-renewed prayer for "peace."

Hebrew is truly "the sacred tongue." Israel's historic language, in which God revealed Himself on Mount Sinai, retains insuperable spiritual force and is still capable of molding character and exalting human destiny.

Chapter 15

YIDDISH—A UNIVERSAL TONGUE OF MANY ROOTS

Yiddish is not a jargon or a dialect, but an independent language. It is used all over the world, has established its own culture, and possesses its own literature of both prose and poetry. It is the medium of authors like Sholem Asch and Abraham Reisen.

In the United States, Yiddish is taught at universities and at Jewish colleges. In Soviet Russia, Hebrew was frowned upon, but Yiddish used to be officially recognized as a Jewish idiom and was used in Jewish settlements. Until 1933, Germany maintained a chair of Yiddish at Hamburg University. The Yiddish Scientific Institute of Vilna was known all over the world, and its publications on historical, economic, and psychological subjects were of the highest standard. There still exists a considerable Yiddish press in almost every country. Even the P.E.N. World Association includes a Yiddish section, and the founders of the house of Rothschild conducted all their correspondence in that tongue.

The oldest Yiddish manuscript in existence is a medical treatise of the year 1396. The first Yiddish translation of the Bible dates from 1544. A popular paraphrase of the Torah originated during the same period and for centuries was a source of unending inspiration to Jewish women. Yiddish, indeed, was a language secular and sacred at the same time.

Over a thousand years old, Yiddish basically is Middle High German with an admixture of Slav, French, Hebrew, and even English words. It is always written with the letters of the Hebrew alphabet.

German Jews, fleeing eastward from atrocities during the Black Death in the fourteenth century, took with them the language of their oppressors and preserved it, only adding words of their new environment. Then again, centuries later, when Russian Jews fled from the east with its discrimination and pogroms, they took their "mother tongue" (*Mameloschen*) with them to the countries where freedom was theirs at last. That, briefly, is the way Yiddish spread all over the world. Yet paradoxically, in Germany, where it was originated, Yiddish was little known and less esteemed in modern times.

Through fate it became one of the most emotionally expressive languages. In intensity of mood it reflects the Jewish heart and mind to the full. Its wit and wisdom are unequaled.

A few of its proverbs, chosen at random, may serve as a telling example.

"Man drives, but God holds the reins."

"The publican loves the drunkard, but not for a son-in-law."

"If you are out to beat a dog, you are sure to find a stick."

"Mix with the neighbor, and you learn what is doing in your own house."

"Little children, little joys; big children, big cares."

"When a father gives to his son, both laugh; when a son gives to his father, both cry."

"Hire a servant and do it yourself."

"When a poor man gets to eat a chicken, one of them is sick."

Many Yiddish words can be rendered only approximately in any other language. They possess a nuance of meaning all their own. Among them are *chochma,* for a special kind of sly wisdom, and *chutzpah,* for brazen impertinence. Exclamations like *oy, nu,* and *nebbich* are totally untranslatable expressions of pain, skeptical inquiry, and deep pity. A *schnorrer* is a beggar who is not only resourceful but almost arrogantly demands his alms as though they were his right! The *schlemihl* is a clumsy and luckless person: whatever he touches goes wrong: "He lands on his back and bruises his nose. . . . He kills a rooster, still it hops. . . . He winds up a clock, at once it stops."

For many decades Yiddish vied with Hebrew to become the

language of the Jewish people. A keen struggle took place between the "Yiddishist" and the "Hebraist." But the re-creation of the State of Israel has decided the issue. There, Hebrew has become the mother tongue of over a million Jews, in spite of their Yiddish ancestry. Yiddish will remain a classic expression of the people's soul, but more and more it will be relegated to the past.

Nevertheless, it seems safe to prophesy that throughout the world and for generations to come, Yiddish will survive, and even though they know but odd phrases or single words, Jews from Orient to Occident will manage to make themselves understood by using them among their fellow Jews.

PART III

*Jewish Customs—Their Origin
and Present-Day Meaning*

Chapter 16

THE SYNAGOGUE

The synagogue is the heart of the Jewish people. Once God's fortress in a pagan world, it still fulfills an essential purpose in life. Throughout the centuries it taught the Jew self-discipline and kept his conscience awake. Constantly it renewed his loyalty to God and trained him in the service of man. Without his synagogue, the Jew would have perished. Out of it developed the Christian church and Moslem worship.

The word "synagogue" is of Greek derivation and means "a coming together" or "assembly." It originated in the third century C.E. among the Jews of Alexandria, who in many ways were influenced by the prevailing Greek culture. In Hebrew, three different names are used to describe the synagogue, each stressing a specific aspect of its purpose. It is called "the house of prayer" (*Bet ha-Tefillah*), "the house of assembly" (*Bet ha-K'neset*), and "the house of learning" (*Bet ha-Midrash*).

In the synagogue, the Jew identified himself with the congregation. He who lives unto himself alone denies the fundamental principle of human living: that within the community alone we can realize our being and understand our purpose.

Jews unite in their synagogues for a threefold task: to pray, to study, and to help. All three were considered essential for a truly religious existence.

Certainly it is possible—and, indeed, permitted—for an individual to pray alone, in his home or in the fields, anywhere. But not only does prayer in the synagogue have a most fitting environment, an atmosphere of devotion that seems to envelop the worshiper, but, more than that, in some mysterious fashion the spiritual force of a number worshiping together transcends the total fervor of as many individual prayers. That is why the rabbis of old felt that to constitute a "congregation" for formal worship, it was necessary to have a minimum of ten souls on whom, as they expressed it, "would rest the spirit of God."

Three times every day—in the morning, afternoon, and evening—Jews unite in their synagogues for prayer. They return there, as to a powerhouse, to recharge their spirits for the turmoil of daily life.

An old tradition asserts that the ignorant cannot be pious. Continuously we must learn and study. He who does not add to his knowledge, the rabbis said, inevitably loses it altogether. From the earliest days, the synagogue fulfilled also an educational purpose. This is reflected in the most usual and colloquial name given to the synagogue—*shul*—derived from the German word for "school." Children and parents alike went there to study. The synagogue is, therefore, the oldest institute of adult education. During the service on Sabbaths and holy days, special passages were read from the Bible and then interpreted and used as the theme of the sermon, which forms another integral part of the synagogue service.

Religion must be applied. It must never exhaust itself in prayer alone. In everyday life we must carry out the lessons learned. It was in conformity with this belief that the synagogue acquired its third function, "social service." The stranger was given a warm welcome, and the poor or needy were offered shelter and sustenance. Those who came to a synagogue to pray or to study were automatically enrolled, as it were, as members of a brotherhood.

It is not known exactly when synagogues were first established. It is assumed, however, that they originated during the Babylonian exile after the destruction of the first Temple by Nebuchadrezzar (586 B.C.E.). Sacrifices could then no longer be offered. And as the priests were thus unable to function at the altar, so the Levites could not chant their songs in the courts. The Jews who were exiled felt homesick. They met to discuss their former life and to exchange memories of past glories. Even more, they dreamed of their return to the Holy Land. But in the meantime they were most anxious to keep alive in themselves, and awaken in their children, the knowledge of God. For this purpose they united in prayer and read together from the holy writings. Prophets admonished and comforted them. Then and there, out of the exigencies of their circumstances, arose the synagogue. The improvised service became an established institution, and the occasional meeting developed into regular assemblies.

Thence the idea of community worship spread, and synagogues were soon established wherever Jews settled throughout the world. Nearly two thousand years ago, at the beginning of the current era, there were synagogues in Jerusalem, in Nazareth, in Rome, and in Athens. It is a subject for reflection that, as related in the New Testament, Jesus and Paul visited these synagogues to pray and to preach.

Unique features distinguish the synagogue.

It was born of the people, created by the yearning of the Jewish heart. It has no analogy with the temples of paganism or, indeed, with the Temple of Solomon. Nor was it, as has frequently been found elsewhere in religious history, adopted from other people and then adapted to the specifically Jewish atmosphere. It was created by the Jews to fill an emergent need; it is indigenously Jewish.

It not only came out of the people but belonged to them. In the Temple, power lay in the hands of a hereditary aristocracy of priests, with its ecclesiastical hierarchy and elaborate rules of sacrificial cult. No layman could ever aspire to join their ranks. It is an important factor that within the synagogue a differentiation between clergy and laity is unknown. The rabbi leads the congregation, but no special grace appertains to his office. He is the teacher, the guide, the example, but nothing more. He remains a layman. His only qualifications should be nobility of character and outstanding knowledge. There are no rungs of office. Anyone within the congregation having the required knowledge could step forward out of the body of worshipers and lead them in prayer. It need cause no surprise, therefore, to note that in the early days before the modern cult of specialization, the rabbis of all synagogues were ordinary members of the community—cobblers or doctors, carpenters or fishermen. By those avocations they earned their daily bread, not by preaching the word of God.

Added to this democratic spirit was complete freedom of association. Any ten men could (and still can) start a congregation. They needed no permission of any authority. They were responsible only to their conscience and to God. Whenever synagogues united, they did so voluntarily and mainly for the purpose of organization.

This principle of independence created certain—though restricted—variations in the liturgy and ceremonial of the synagogue. On the other hand, any split into different denominational divisions was prevented. Every synagogue is an organic part of Judaism.

On entering a synagogue, men cover their heads. They do so either with the hat or, frequently today, with a small cotton or silk skullcap specially designed for this purpose. In an Orthodox synagogue, men and women are separated, the latter often sitting in a gallery. This segregation of the sexes is probably Oriental in origin. However, in Reform synagogues, or, as they are usually called, "temples," families sit together, and in most parts of the United States, as well as in some British, Progressive synagogues, men worship bareheaded.

The synagogue is always built facing Jerusalem (at least symbolically), reminding the Jew of the ancient center of holiness, concentrating his mind from the four corners of the earth on this one focal point. "For out of Zion shall go forth the Law, and the word of God from Jerusalem."

A notable feature in most synagogues is the absence of any paintings or sculptures. This is a deliberate outcome of the strict monotheism of Judaism and, further, in deference to the commandment: "Thou shalt not make . . . a graven image or the likeness of anything." God is spiritual, and nothing should divert the mind of the worshiper. Actually, throughout the centuries there has been some relaxation of this total prohibition.

God's spirit and His Law are symbolized by the perpetual light burning in every synagogue. Like the flame of faith which must inspire our whole being all the days of our life, it must never be allowed to go out. "Command the children of Israel to cause the lamp to burn continually . . . before the Lord." This law, once referring to the light in the Temple, is now applied to this symbol in the Jewish house of worship, wherever it may be. And more, light signifies learning, which must never be extinguished.

Behind the perpetual lamp is placed the Ark. This evolved directly from the ancient repository in which the Israelites carried the two tablets of the Law from Sinai to the Holy Land. Executed in beautiful craftsmanship, covered by richly embroidered curtains, today it contains the Scrolls of the Law. These are parchment rolls on which, handwritten in square Hebrew letters, are the whole of the Five Books of Moses. Rolled up around two rods, the Scroll is covered by a mantle and adorned by silver bells, a breastplate, and a pointer in the form of a closed hand with an extended index finger. Every Sabbath morning one of these Scrolls is taken out of the Ark, opened, week by week at succeeding portions, and read, with a special intonation, to the congregation. A definite cycle of readings ensures the complete perusal of the Pentateuch within one year, for "it is a tree of life to them that hold fast to it. Its ways are ways of pleasantness and all its paths are peace."

Most of the prayers are sung in Hebrew by the cantor (called in Hebrew *chazan*), who is accompanied by a choir (and in Reform temples by an organ). The sermon, preached by the rabbi, forms another integral part of the synagogue service. Philo the Jew described his experience two thousand years ago: "The people sit decorously, keeping silence, and listening with the utmost attention out of a thirst for refreshing discourse, whilst one of the best qualified stands up and instructs them in what is best and what is most conducive to their welfare . . . by which their whole life may be made better." In all ages the synagogue pursued a twofold aim: to improve man ethically and to bring him nearer to God spiritually.

Travers Herford, a great English Christian theologian, said:

With the synagogue began a new type of worship in the history of humanity, a type of congregational worship without priest or ritual. ... In all their long history, the Jewish people have done scarcely anything more wonderful than to create the synagogue. No human institution has a longer continuous history and none has done more for the uplifting of the human race.

The Bible had commanded: "Ye shall build me a sanctuary that I may dwell among you." The rabbis explained this passage as meaning: "Ye shall build me a sanctuary that I may dwell in your lives." Such is still the function of the synagogue, and such is the secret of its influence on the Jewish people and of the love in which it is held.

Chapter 17

THE CHAZAN

Music inspires the soul. It exalts joy and allays grief. It is the link between the ephemeral and the eternal. The only universal language, it binds man to man and the finite to the infinite.

From earliest times, therefore, music belonged to Jewish worship. Most of its prayers, and even the lessons from Torah and Prophets, are sung. This explains the importance of the office of the chazan within the synagogue. He intones the prayers and leads the congregation in song. But he is not only a "cantor" in the literal meaning of his modern title. His accomplishments do not end with his mastery of the vocal chords and his knowledge of music.

As early as the second century, one Rabbi Judah ben Illai defined his qualifications as comprising "integrity, modesty, and poverty, in addition to a voice that was capable of inspiring people to devotion."

The chazan must be a true servant of God; proud but not boastful of his voice and humble in spirit. He should know life to the full, not by hearsay, but through personal experience. A family man, he should know the hardships of life encountered in the pursuit of one's daily bread. The Talmud described the ideal chazan as "a man who has heavy family obligations, who has not enough to meet them, who has to struggle for a livelihood, is above reproach, has an attractive appearance, is humble, pleasant to and liked by people . . . and who knows all prayers and benedictions by heart."

No duty could be more joyful than his. To serve God in song was surely the happiest of tasks. No riches could ever compensate for the loss of such an opportunity. Immanuel of Rome, famous Hebrew poet of the thirteenth century, whose *Divine Comedy* surpassed Dante's in the universality of its philosophy, relates how he was the traveling companion of an outstandingly rich man. On numerous occasions they were approached by the luckless, bewailing their fate and asking their help. One such applicant proved to be a chazan. He complained bitterly that his life was unhappy, his talents not appreciated, and his means not sufficient. The rich man was moved and offered to change places and lives with the chazan, who, stunned at the glittering prospect, instantly agreed. Then the flaw was revealed. "You understand," the man of wealth said to the chazan, "that the exchange must be complete. You take my place and my possessions and I take your place and your glorious voice." The bargain was off. To the chazan, disillusioned and discontented as he was, all the riches in Italy could not purchase his gift of song with which he could stir the hearts of men and lift them to the heights of spiritual exaltation.

The word "chazan" has a surprising origin. In this respect it is not unique; the study of the derivation of quite common words is fascinating and revealing. The word "ghetto" is an example. It is, of course, used to describe the part of a city where the Jews chose or were compelled to live; yet according to a prevailing view it is derived from a sixteenth-century Italian word for "gun-foundry." Its present customary usage stemmed from Venice, where in 1516 a Jewish settlement was established near the local arms factory, or geto.

Chazan means "overseer." Neither in the history of his original duties nor in the etymology of his title did the chazan have any relationship to "voice" or "music." The strange fact is that although the profession of the chazan is a very ancient institution, his title descended upon him from a totally different office. It was transferred from the secular post of a government official and synagogue beadle, whose function it was to oversee congregational and communal affairs. Manifold tasks belonged to him, but most certainly not the intoning of prayers. On the contrary, during the talmudic period, the chazan was not even permitted to act as reader unless he was distinguished as a scholar; and then it was only the latter qualification, not his office, which entitled him to do so.

During the second Jewish Commonwealth, the term "chazan" was applied to the caretakers in the Temple. After this was destroyed in 70 C.E., worship continued in the synagogues, which retained the position of chazan as a beadle with slightly wider duties. He was the caretaker of the synagogue and was therefore provided with living quarters on the premises. He acted as a servant of the rabbinical court and had to carry out any penalties it imposed, even flagellation. During services, he had to execute the warden's directions, informing those who were called up to intone the prayers, to read from the Torah, or to deliver the sermon. He had to take out the Scrolls, open them at the appointed readings of the week, and return them to the Ark. From the roof of the synagogue he announced with trumpet blasts the commencement of the Sabbaths and holy days.

Another strange task fell to the lot of the chazan in Alexandria, where the synagogue was so large that those in the rear seats could not hear or follow the service. To enable them at least to join in the responses at the right time, the chazan was placed on a high stand whence, by waving a flag, he gave signals to the remote worshipers.

The great variety of important services rendered the office of chazan indispensable and most honorable. His seat could never be vacated. If he had to leave it, someone else had to occupy his place during his absence. A special benediction was said in his honor at the first meal after funerals.

The final stages in the evolution of the chazan occurred during the sixth and seventh centuries. Oppression and persecution spread through the Middle East; libraries and centers of learning were destroyed; and, faced with the danger and insecurity of daily life, the Jewish communities became almost totally ignorant of their faith. It was thus difficult to find members of the congregation who could lead the services, and it became clearly necessary to appoint men specially trained to fulfill the duties of *Shaliach Tsibbur,* or "delegate of the congregation."

Contemporaneously, the introduction of a new and more intricate liturgy called for men of musical talent and training. In these circumstances it was the chazan, former holder of an almost menial office, who came to the rescue. His standing had already improved, and in most cases he had the qualities of character, training, and tradition of service that fitted him to undertake new responsibilities and discharge them with honor, dignity, and distinction. The truth of the saying in the *Ethics of the Fathers,* that it is the man who honors the place and not the position that gives dignity to the man, was thus exemplified.

And so, thirteen hundred years ago, the chazan finally reached his full stature. His caretaking and other everyday assignments were allotted to the shammash, or "servant," and he himself, though retaining the original but obsolete title, became the cantor, like David of old, "a sweet singer in Israel." The former handyman, ready to wave a flag, birch a sinner, blow a trumpet, or teach a child, now emerged as the musical director of the synagogue service, charged with evoking from the congregation "a sentiment of devotion that the members may hear and fear." In the Orthodox synagogue of today the chazan is an irreplaceable essential.

Chapter 18

THE TALLIT

One article associated exclusively with Jewish religious practice is the tallit, or "praying-shawl," as the word is freely translated. The literal meaning is not definitely known, though it is assumed to be "wrap" or "outer garment." A square piece of cloth with fringes (called *tsitsit*) at its four corners, it is normally of either wool or silk, white in color, but having marginal blue or black stripes.

Every morning when saying his prayers the Orthodox Jew puts on his tallit, either wrapping himself into it, sometimes even covering his head with it, or wearing it like a shawl around the shoulders. At the wedding ceremony it is often spread out to cover the bride and bridegroom, sometimes replacing the *chuppah* (wedding canopy) or being placed on it. Finally, when the Jew is laid to eternal rest, he is wrapped in the tallit which he wore throughout his life.

The tallit goes back to prebiblical times, and, as with many well-established customs, its origin is surrounded with mystery. In general form, it resembles an oriental robe, the abayah, a blanket used by Arabs to give shelter from dust, sun, and rain. Its fringes or tassels may represent an original charm, fixed to the garment to attract good fortune and avert evil. It is also suggested, though on flimsy grounds, that since men and women wore similar robes, the fringe was used by the male as a distinguishing mark to prevent moral laxity.

The tallit derives its religious significance as a Jewish vestment from a passage in the Fourth Book of Moses (Num. XV, 37–41), which in Orthodox liturgy has become the third part of the Sh'ma, the Jewish declaration of faith:

And the Lord spoke unto Moses, saying, Speak unto the children of Israel, and bid them that they make them a fringe upon the corners of their garments throughout their generations, and that they put upon the fringe of each corner a cord of blue: and it shall be unto you for a fringe, that ye may look upon it, and remember all the commandments of the Lord, and do them; and that ye go not about after your own heart and your own eyes, after which ye use to go astray: that ye may remember and do all My commandments, and be holy unto your God. I am the Lord your God, Who brought you out of the land of Egypt, to be your God: I am the Lord your God.

The same law is repeated in the Fifth Book of Moses (Deut. XXII, 12) in much more concise form and without any explanation: "Thou shalt make thee fringes upon the four corners of thy garment wherewith thou coverest thyself." Four facts emerge from these passages:

1. That the garment originally worn by the Jew was a four-cornered robe.

2. That at first no extra vestment was commanded, but merely the addition of the tsitsit or fringes on the four corners of the robe.

3. That the tsitsit were meant to be worn not only at the hours of worship but continuously.

4. That their primary purpose was to be a perpetual reminder to the Jew to obey God's commandment and thereby consecrate his life.

In many of his customs the Jew reflects his environment. This applies especially to peculiarities of food and dress. Certain dishes regarded as being typically Jewish are in reality Russian, Polish, or German in origin.

Similarly, in his long wanderings the Jew has been prone to copy the fashions as they changed, and this very human trait actually led to the revolutionary development in the purpose and, eventually, the form of a tallit.

This, as related in the Bible, was originally his normal, daily garb, but it was modified by the addition of the fringes, with their religious significance. But fashion changed, and the Jew, sensitive to his environment, found himself wearing clothes that had no distinctive corners to which, as commanded by God, he could attach fringes.

Anxious to observe this law, the Jew decided to retain the robe, not as his main garment, but as a shawl, or surplice. This, with its duly fringed corners, he wore throughout the day as part of his religious armament, a perpetual reminder of God's presence. Thus he could continue to wear the tsitsit (fringes), for it was these, and not the robe itself, which were the essential part of the commandment.

Fashion changed again, and the constant wearing of the fringed surplice became somewhat incongruous. It therefore became the practice to don it only while at prayer, whether in the synagogue or at home. But this was not in accordance with the original purpose. Obviously, when praying, the Jew was in communion with God, but the fringes were intended to remind the wearer of God's presence at all other times (and places); lest he forget and "seek . . . after the desires of his heart and his eyes."

Something new was needed, and the Jewish mind, always creative where problems were encountered, devised a miniature tallit, complete with fringes, to be worn under ordinary clothing. This would not conflict with contemporary modes; yet its wearer, metaphorically at least, would be able to contemplate the tsitsit at all times, in accordance with the commandment.

This garment is normally called—the part naming the whole —merely tsitsit or, alternatively, *arba kanfot* (four corners). A rectangular piece of cloth made of linen, silk, or wool, it has an aperture in the center for the head to pass through. It has the four essential corners to which the tsitsit were attached. To this day the arba kanfot is worn by Orthodox men throughout their lives.

It is an interesting question why the Jew puts on his tallit only at morning prayers, never at night (excepting Kol Nidre). This custom is based on the literal interpretation of the biblical passage in which we read that the fringes are meant to "catch our eyes." We must *see* them, the rabbis explained, and hours of darkness were therefore excluded. That is why the Kol Nidre service starts before sunset, so that when the Jew wraps himself in his tallit he can still see the tsitsit!

Such was the interesting development of the tallit. Its history reflects not only the whims of fashion but, more essentially, the role of religion in man's daily existence. A positive symbol of a life dedicated to God fell in stature to the role of a praying-shawl. The tsitsit, once proudly and visibly worn as a signpost to pure living, were relegated to form part of an undergarment, often deteriorating in people's minds from an ethical symbol to a superstitious talisman.

Yet, in spite of such temporal devaluation and displacement, the tallit itself always preserved its potent symbolism. More, the many centuries of Jewish history emphasized and enriched its original purpose. No deterioration could detract from its mission. Today, when the Jew puts on his tallit, numerous thoughtful and incisive messages stir and challenge his mind.

The Jew's Uniform

"Ye shall be My witness—saith the Lord" (Isa. XLIII, 10).

The Jew's battle is not that of bloodshed. He serves the King of Kings. His fight is the more difficult since he strives not for tangible conquests, but for the values of the spirit. To identify himself as God's soldier and to make himself recognizable as such to the world, he dons his uniform, the tallit. Its whiteness symbolizes the purity of his mission. The tallit simultaneously marks God's love for Israel and Israel's determination to battle on for God's ideals, remembering to do all His commandments and to be holy unto the Lord. Because the fringed garment was the specific "uniform" of the Jew, the law forbade its sale to a Gentile, unless its fringes were removed.

The Jew's Festival Dress

When men are summoned before an earthly ruler to defend themselves against some charge, they appear downcast and . . . like mourners. Israel appears before God arrayed in white . . . confident that all who return penitently to their Maker will receive . . . pardon at His hands" (Chassidic saying).

There is no more beautiful and inspiring sight than a congregation in prayer all clad in white. The tallit has become the festival garment of the Jew. He wears it that he may appear dignified when he comes before his God.

The way we are attired influences our mood. André Gide could therefore claim that "if men are more serious than women, it's because their clothes are darker." The tallit is not merely an adornment. As a praying-mantle it expresses and conduces to a spirit of sublime devotion and consecrated meditation. It is meant to inspire within the heart a feeling of awe and reverence.

A Symbol of the Equality of Man

"When two Jews associate on an equal footing and discuss a subject of Torah, the Indwelling Presence of God is with them. But when one of them holds himself superior to the other, God is not there" (Chassidic saying).

Man is susceptible to outward appearance and often misled by the beauty of apparel. Blinded by the glamour without, he cannot see the vacuity within. Thoreau was correct when he said that "there is a greater anxiety, commonly, to have fashionable . . . clothes than to have a sound conscience." "Fine feathers make fine birds," says the old proverb.

Once again Judaism testifies to its democratic character. Every human being is a "child of God," born equal, distinguished by virtue only. The true standard is not the riches of a man, but his righteousness. Before God, rich and poor are alike. The exquisitely appareled counts no more than the austerely clad. It is not the cost of the dress, but only the worthiness of the wearer that matters. That is why, symbolically, all Jews, rich and poor alike, conceal the superficiality and diversity of their everyday clothing, covering them with the identical tallit.

A Pointer to God-Centered Living

"In all thy ways know God" (Prov. III, 6).
"I shall set the Lord always before me" (Ps. XVI, 8).

A simple symbol can be far more eloquent than many words. Herbert Spencer could thus point out that language is often a hindrance to thought. Ideas communicated by signs speak more loudly and intensely. "To say, 'Leave the room' is less expressive than to point to the door. Placing the finger on the lips is more forcible than whispering, 'Do not speak.' A beck of the hand is better than 'Come here.' No phrase can convey the idea of surprise so vividly as opening the eyes and raising the eyebrows. A shrug of the shoulders would lose much by transition into words."

The fringes of the tallit are such silent yet eloquent symbols. They are a signpost toward God; a reminder to consecrate our lives. When desires and fancies tempt our heart, the sight of this symbol of God's commandment urges us to return to His ways. Rabbinical literature relates how a man given to sensuous and riotous living was led back to a life of integrity by the sight of the tsitsit.

To make doubly sure of a continuous awareness of God, early Jewish psychology created an additional "memory aid." It ordained that a blue thread be added to the fringes. By an association of color it was meant to remind the Jew of the sea, which in turn (by its blueness) suggested the sky, inevitably leading his thoughts to Heaven, God's throne.

The dye used to produce this thread of blue was the famous royal purple, extracted from a mollusk found in the Mediterranean. When, for various reasons, this could no longer be obtained, the rabbis decided to abandon the blue thread, deeming no other dye worthy to be used for the purpose. This is yet another example of the influence of temporal circumstances on religious customs.

A Reminder of God's Omnipresence

For wherever I go—You
And wherever I stand—You.
Always You, Only You, Forever You.
—Rabbi Levi Yitzchak of Berditshev

Secularization and specialization—those two tendencies of modern life—have driven religion into isolated pockets. God has been relegated to an infinitesimally small section of human existence and even there is sought only during a small fraction of time. His realm, once the wide expanse of the universe, is now the circumscribed place of synagogue and church; His time is no longer "all the days of my life," but only certain hours of service, already limited and growing ever shorter.

But God cannot be restricted in any sense of space or time. "Wherever I cause My name to be remembered, I will come unto thee and bless thee." Religion must permeate the whole of life or lose its meaning. No place and no task should be without sanctification. Therefore, wherever he went, the Jew always wore the tsitsit. At all times and places his thoughts, words, and actions should be conscious of the Divine and aware of his mission and responsibility.

Metaphorically, the four corners of the tallit point toward the four corners of the earth, for "the whole universe is full of His glory."

A Simile of God's Sheltering Love

"Spread over us the Tabernacle of Thy peace" (evening prayer).

When donning his tallit the Jew not only fulfills a law but accomplishes an act of faith. Symbolically, he puts himself under God's sheltering love, knowing that amid the storms and stresses of life he can there find a haven of safety and peace. "He shall cover thee with His pinions and under His wings shalt thou take refuge; His truth is a shield and buckler . . . because thou hast said, the Lord is my refuge and has made the most high thy habitation."

While donning the tallit, the Jew is asked to recite words from Psalm XXVI, expressing that very idea: "How precious is Thy lovingkindness, O God, and the children of man take refuge under the shelter of Thy wings. For with Thee is the fountain of life, in Thy light, do we see light."

A wide diversity of meaning is thus hidden in the Jewish custom of the tallit, that simple square piece of cloth with a history of thousands of years, which accompanies every Jewish man, literally from the day of his bar mitzvah into his grave.

Everything in the interpretation of the tallit points the same way. The wearing of a uniform demands a discipline of living and self-respect. The tallit is the badge of the army of God's servants, where the only distinction is that of holiness. It is a vestment engendering a feeling of dedication to a life in the service of God. It speaks, too, of the universality of God and the unity of man. It is a perpetual reminder that no pattern of living can be of lasting value unless it is cut from the cloth of religion.

The Jew, through the tsitsit, is made to remember God's command and to follow it. No longer a victim of fate, he becomes master of destiny. When the Jew wraps himself in his praying-mantle, coming before his God in the beauty of holiness, he excludes everything tainted and mundane. Not only is his body wrapped in the tallit, but his soul is absorbed in God's thought. As the tallit envelops the whole of his person, so religion, to be effective, must integrate the totality of his personality. Thus he walks through life wholeheartedly devoted to God, without reservation and without regret. Each day of his life, when putting on the tallit, he can rejoicingly utter the ancient benediction: "Blessed art Thou, O Lord our God, King of the universe, Who hast sanctified us by Thy commandments and hast commanded us to wrap ourselves in the fringed garment."

As the Jew proceeds through the snares and pitfalls of life he may, if he so chooses, be helped and guided by the numerous beacons placed along the path by a beneficent God. Among these, none is more valuable, none more constantly at hand, than the tallit, rich in symbolism and spiritual significance, clearly, definitely, and always pointing the way to a life of holiness in the service of the Almighty.

Chapter 19

THE TEFILLIN

From the time he attains the bar mitzvah age of thirteen years, every Orthodox male Jew is required to "lay" or put on his tefillin every weekday morning of his life. The ceremonial forms part of the morning prayers, whether recited in the home or at the synagogue.

Unique symbols of the Jewish love of God and obedience to His commandments, the tefillin consist of two small boxes, roughly of one cubic inch, sewn by precisely twelve stitches to a square leather basis to which are attached leather thongs of special design. One of the tefillin has to be placed on the forehead above and between the eyes and the other on the left upper arm near the heart. Thus, the thong attached to the tefillin *shel rosh* (for the head) consists of a circlet with a slipknot so that it can be adjusted to the size of the wearer's head. On the tefillin *shel yad* (for the hand), the thong is long and straight and wound by an elaborate yet precise system down along the forearm and on the hand where, finally, it is so arranged as to form the first letter of the Hebrew word *Shaddai* (Almighty).

Within each box are contained four passages from the Bible, handwritten in minute Hebrew characters on parchment. The hand tefillin has the four on a single scroll, but in the head tefillin the passages are written on four separate strips, which in turn are placed in separate compartments within the box.

The first of the passages is the Sh'ma, the Jewish declaration of faith in and love for the one God, not as a philosophical abstraction, but as a personal Father to Whom we offer all the devotion of the heart. The second paragraph emphasizes the important relationship between cause and effect: every thought and every action must be considered in relation to its possible outcome. The third passage speaks of man's duty to express his belief in God in definite action. The final section reminds the Jew of how in the most desperate and hopeless moments in his history God's help has always been nearest.

The wearing of tefillin originated as a literal interpretation of the verse (Deut. VI, 8) which forms part of the Sh'ma: "And thou shalt bind them [God's words] as a sign upon thine hand and they shall be as frontlets between thine eyes." The name *tefillin* is derived from the Hebrew word for "prayer"—an obvious association with the idea that the act of wearing the tefillin should lead man to a life of worship and devotion. In English, they are called, from the Greek, *phylacteries,* occurring first in the New Testament and meaning "protection": a man who was continually reminded of his religious obligation was truly protected from sin. Moses Maimonides, in his monumental work *Second Torah,* stresses this particular aspect: "The holiness of the tefillin is great, for so long as the tefillin are upon the head and the arm of a man, he is humble and God-fearing, keeps away from levity and idle talk, does not conceive evil thoughts, but turns his heart exclusively to words of truth and justice."

Sabbath and festivals inherently direct the whole life of a Jew toward his religion; there was no need, therefore, of specific reminders. Hence there is no necessity to lay tefillin on those occasions. As they were also considered an ornament to the Jew, they were not used during the morning service of the Fast of Ninth of Av. However, so that the commandment may be duly honored, even on that day of national mourning, tefillin have to be worn at afternoon service.

To wear passages from the Bible fixed to one's body (sometimes in early days they were even tattooed into the skin) symbolized a life of dedication. The placing of the tefillin next to the heart and brain stressed that all thoughts and feelings should be centered on God and inspired by the words of His revelation. The winding of one band around the left arm (seven times) and the middle finger of the left hand (thrice) recalled God's protection of the Jewish people under Egyptian bondage when

His "outstretched arm" redeemed a band of slaves and gave them the ideal of a kingdom of priests. Even more so, the use of arm and hand for the fastening of this hallowed strap was a most tangible reminder that all of man's actions should be constrained by the thought of holiness and should aim at goodness and righteousness.

People of outstanding piety used to wear their tefillin not merely during the morning prayer but throughout the day. Two different types of tefillin developed, varying in the sequence of the four biblical quotations. Some Jews, not certain which was the correct one, but anxious to be right, laid the two pairs, either simultaneously, or one after the other.

The rabbis, in their concern to see the law properly executed, regulated every detail and provided for every eventuality. The left-handed may put the phylacteries on his right arm. They are kissed when taken from and returned to the tefillin bag. A sufferer from stomach ulcers, or any other pain which prevents his concentrating, is exempted from the law. Though today the straps of the tefillin are black, the rabbis permitted any color (except blood red). Specimens still exist in blue or purple.

The writing of tefillin was a sacred privilege. Each time the name of God occurred, the scribe had to pause and say: "I am writing this for the sake of the holiness of 'The Name.'" With devout concentration he had to focus his mind on the task. Nothing and nobody must divert his thoughts. "Even if the King of Israel should then greet him, he is forbidden to reply." Women expressed their religious fervor in artistic creation by embroidering special tefillin bags.

The clerical collar and the monk's hood are not worn simply to indicate the wearer's vocation. Rather they are intended to serve the wearers as perpetual reminders of their consecration to a life of holiness and service. In just the same way, the wearing of tefillin symbolizes a dedicated life and a sanctifying force.

To the thinking Jew, tefillin served as spiritual armor, keeping him safe from the danger of sin in thought or action. Positively, they served as a perpetual reminder of his obligation to direct his life toward all that is clean, wise, and sacred.

Chapter 20

MINYAN—THE JEWISH QUORUM

Literally, *minyan* in Hebrew merely means "number." However, it relates to the quorum for any Orthodox public service. It consists of ten males of at least bar mitzvah age. Without their presence, neither a wedding nor even a funeral could be legally conducted.

The idea of minyan stresses the brotherhood of Israel and the communal aspect of religion. Judaism recognizes the great difference between a prayer said in solitude and one uttered within a community, where the fervor of individuals combines in a united spiritual effort, creating its own atmosphere of concentrated devotion.

The minyan implies also the Jewish conviction of the importance of each person in the eyes of God. Every Jew has his claim to be counted. The poorest and the richest, the young bar mitzvah boy and the aged grandfather, the ignoramus and the scholar, all are equal, and no one rates higher than another. A service can be held without a rabbi, but it cannot take place (within the Orthodox synagogue) without a minyan. "Nine rabbis don't make a quorum, but ten shoemakers do."

The knowledge that a quorum was always necessary acted as a stimulus on each member of the community, urging him to attend the synagogue. Each might feel that, in his absence, the minyan would not be present and so, by his own indifference, he would cause difficulty and disappointment to others.

Periods of economic stress throughout the ages led at times to a temporary weakening of religious fervor, and this tendency endangered the holding of the daily service through lack of a minyan. To avoid this, professional "minyan men" made their

247

appearance on the scene. Usually these were elderly, poor, but otherwise worthy members of the community who were paid to be present at all regular services so that no Jew who wished to pray in a formally constituted congregation should be deprived of the opportunity.

The word "minyan" developed a further and unfortunate connotation. After the death of a near relative, Jews meet for services each morning and evening during the week after the funeral at the home of the deceased. In order that the kaddish could be intoned, it was necessary that the full minyan be present, and in the course of time this special service of mourning has come to be known as "a minyan," and in many countries the term can be read in newspaper announcements of Jewish funerals.

Chapter 21

THE COVERING OF THE HEAD

That the Jew covers his head when entering a synagogue is accepted as an old-established tradition. It is considered of such importance and sanctity that in some English and Australian courts of law a Jew is given the option to wear a head-covering when taking an oath. In extremely Orthodox circles men never bare their head, but always wear a skullcap, called a "capple" or a "yarmulka." In the Middle Ages and in nineteenth-century Russia, anti-Semites, ready to use any pretext to abuse the Jew, asserted that the ritual had the purpose of concealing the Jew's horns.

Jewish life abounds in paradoxes. That observation is true even of this simple and innocuous custom. People fought for its observance with fervor and deepest religious conviction. Whether to don or to doff a hat in the synagogue became a most explosive subject of discussion. The custom was regarded as so intensely and eternally Jewish that ever to change it appeared to the Orthodox as the worst possible undermining of the very foundations of Judaism.

The paradox resides in the fact that this practice, deemed to be fundamentally Jewish and hallowed by ancient tradition, is in reality pagan and, in terms of Jewish chronology, comparatively modern. It is not mentioned in the Torah nor ordained by talmudic edict. After only a temporary and partial adoption in Palestine, it was finally copied by the Babylonian Jews from their environment.

In the eighth century C.E., when, through the decline and decay of the Babylonian community, Jewish scholars emigrated and settled in Spain, at the other extreme of the Mediterranean, they took with them their Babylonian custom. There it became so firmly established that four hundred years later, in the twelfth century, Moses Maimonides declared that it was unbecoming for a scholar to study or teach with his head uncovered. Yet at the same time, the Jews in France still knew nothing about it, and a French rabbi of the day, visiting the Spanish Jewish community, expressed surprise when he saw Jews praying in the synagogues with their heads covered. Moreover, we know that in that same epoch boys in Germany were called to the Law bareheaded.

History—and the Jewish fate—intervened and spread the custom farther afield. Expelled from Spain in 1492, the Jews took it with them in their journeyings north and east through Europe. Yet much time was still to elapse before it became firmly rooted in Jewish life, so that as recently as the eighteenth century an eminent authority, Elijah Gaon of Vilna, could still say, "According to Jewish law it is permitted to enter a synagogue and to pray without covering one's head."

An interesting additional illustration is given by the sixteenth-century rabbi Moses Isserles, the famous authority incorporated in the *Shulchan Aruch*. He emphasized that covering the head could not be considered a religious principle. It was merely a matter of good manners, not of ritual law.

When the Reform movement of the nineteenth century tried to reestablish the original form of Judaism as they saw it and to abolish accretions of the ghetto and the diaspora, they demanded that the wearing of hats in the synagogue be discontinued, as a foreign Oriental custom. Aaron Chorin had recommended the same in Prague in 1826, but his advice had fallen on deaf ears. The Berlin Reform Congregation introduced bareheadedness in 1845, but remained the only synagogue in the whole of Europe to do so. The United States anticipated the Berlin congregation by three years, when in 1842 the Temple Har-Sinai, in Baltimore, discarded the use of hats. American rabbis going to England tried to establish the hatless custom there, but succeeded only partially in a very few synagogues. In an unfortunate kind of compromise, they left it to the individual worshiper to don or doff his hat at the service. This created the strange sight of some men sitting with their hats on and others bareheaded.

In the roots of this custom, diverse streams of tradition and history meet and intermingle. Each tells a specific story or reveals an important facet of Jewish living. We find mundane and utilitarian motives next to spiritual explanation. Reflections of past glories and tragedies of Jewish history are mixed with creations of the inventive genius of the Jewish religious mind. The custom, once established, irrespective of its historical origin, was interpreted in colorful symbolism so as to justify it and change what had become an empty gesture into a meaningful habit.

A Health Measure

Like many other religious laws, the covering of the head has implications based on hygienic considerations. The Oriental was easily affected by change of temperature, which was a frequent occurrence. To cover one's head was, therefore, a reasonable protective measure. This is clearly stressed by the Midrash, which said, "Rheumatism will come to the lazy person who forgets to cover his head." Furthermore, Jews used to pray in the open. For obvious reasons, the altar on which the sacrifices were offered had the sky as its ceiling. In the burning sun of the Orient, sunstroke was a real danger. Thus, again, to cover one's head was prudent.

Judaism knows of the close relationship between mind and body. It aimed not only at spiritual fitness but also at physical health.

A Matter of Etiquette

Standards of courtesy and good manners are often geographically conditioned. The very same action might appear decorous and in good taste to one nation and yet be utterly offensive, uncouth, and unfitting to another. While Western man raises his hat out of courtesy, Eastern custom demands the opposite. To honor your host, you remove your shoes, but cover your head.

For an Oriental to appear before his guests bareheaded is a flagrant breach of good manners and would be resented deeply. The hat assumed an almost sacred significance. Western man swears by his Bible; the Arab, by his head cover.

Environment exerted a great influence not only on Jewish theology but on the Jewish way of living. It was thus natural that the Babylonian Jew adopted the local etiquette by covering his head. It was not a religious rite, but an act of courtesy.

The Talmud (Kidd. 33a) relates that when Rabina sat before Rabbi Jeremiah of Diphte, and a man who entered did not cover his head, Rabina remarked: "What an impudent boor is this man!"

Thus, like many another Jewish rite, this custom reveals an Oriental origin. Out of the east the Jew carried the Babylonian practice of covering the head to show respect. Then, with the passing of the centuries, this simple act of civility, by a process of gradual evolution, acquired an entirely new character with implications of great, and sometimes grave, significance.

A Means of Differentiation

New movements struggling for recognition need their own distinctive sign as a focus and a symbol. Moreover, to impress the world with their importance, they often overemphasize superficial differences and ignore, or even defy, much more noteworthy common features.

Judaism experienced this attitude on the part of the two daughter religions, Christianity and Islam. In their desire to appear as something totally new and independent, they went out of their way to underscore differences. No one should ever be able to mistake them as Jewish. The early Christians, therefore, changed Passover into Easter, the Sabbath into Sunday, and made baptism, instead of circumcision, the essential ceremony of initiation. Motivated by the same desire to separate the church from the synagogue, the worshiping Christian from the devout Jew, Paul demanded that every follower of Jesus should remove his hat. He explained to the Corinthians (I Cor. XI, 4) that "every man praying ... having his head covered, dishonours his head."

Theology was helped by history. To keep alive in a world of hatred and intolerance, the Jew had to use every possible expedient. He had to assert his identity to remain different. Once he had become unrecognizable, he was bound to disappear. The greatest danger facing any minority group is that of being swallowed up by the overwhelming force of its environment. Almost superhuman effort is needed to withstand such pressure.

The phenomenon of Jewish survival can be explained, to a certain or perhaps even a greater extent, by this determination to remain apart. Jewish teaching throughout the ages has emphatically forbidden the Jew to imitate other people, to "become as one of the Gentiles." This was, however, no pretentious belief in "Jewish superiority," but a dire necessity in the struggle for very existence. To stay spiritually alive, the Jew had to remain apart! The rabbis, when translating the Chapter of Holiness at the center of the Pentateuch (Lev. XIX), thus deliberately rendered "You shall be holy" as "You shall be different."

The custom of covering the head in synagogue exemplified this principle. As a means of differentiation, it helped the Jew in his fight for survival.

A Symbol of Humility

In ancient Rome, slaves kept their heads covered in the presence of their master as a sign of respect and humility. Bareheadedness demonstrated courage and even defiance! The Aramaic translation of the Bible (*Targum Onkelos*) sought to describe the proud and independent spirit of the Israelites, when leaving the Egyptian house of bondage, by rendering the verse (Ex. XIV, 8), "And the children of Israel went out with a high hand," as "They went forth with their heads uncovered."

Just as in former times the pious mourner put ashes on his head to show his resignation to God's inscrutable will, so does the Jew cover his head as a symbolical expression of his submission to the Almighty. This explanation, indeed, has been cited as a possible origin of the description of the skullcap worn by Jews as a yarmulka. Folk etymology ascribed the word's origin to the Hebrew *yare malka,* "he fears the King." The cap signified man's awe in God's presence.

A Means of Identification

People uniting for a common ideal are rallied in their fight and confirmed in their bond of comradeship by a symbol which they make their own. History shows many cases in which the mere presence of a symbol became a most vital force. The fiery cross, the hammer and sickle, the crescent moon—these are not merely emblems of mass movements. In actuality, they inflamed people with infectious, irresistible enthusiasm.

To the Scots as a nation, the kilt, and to the individual clans, their distinctive tartans, were more than a uniform; they were badges of common purpose. Similarly, the Polish patriots and democrats of 1791 adopted a rectangular cap both as a mark of identification and as a gesture of defiance to the tyrants.

In the same way, when the Jew covered his head for prayer, simultaneously he proclaimed his unity with his fellow Jews and expressed conscious pride in his Jewishness, which he refused to conceal or ignore.

A Sign of Freedom

The history of a custom through the centuries shows that its interpretation changes, that it is adapted again and again to fit the different circumstances of each environment and age. Often the older message is totally forgotten (for example, in the case of circumcision). On occasion it is preserved, and both old and new meanings coexist, making the custom even more colorful and appealing. It may even happen that the new interpretation seems, superficially, not only different but contradictory. Yet in spite of the apparent incompatibility, both explanations are assimilated and then live on together in harmony (as in the case of the matzah).

Consider the problem of the Jew in trying to interpret the tradition of covering the head: in the earliest days a mark of common courtesy, in another age a symbol of humility. In yet another situation this practice was the means by which the free man symbolized his independence.

With characteristic ingenuity the Jew fused these seemingly irreconcilable elements into a new, harmonious, and stable compound. The custom implied humility in man's relationship to God; but at the same time it signified independence, freedom, and a blunt refusal to submit to the dictates of any despotism at any time or in any country. The Jew in this way declared that he was no man's slave. Even when shackled and imprisoned in the hovels of the meanest ghetto, the Jew remained the master of his own soul.

A paragon of freedom, whose very religion began with an act of deliverance from slavery, the Jew aims at the freedom and redemption of all men. Such, too, is the message which the Jew now conveyed when he came before his God with his head covered in respect, in humility, and in defiance!

The Jew and His God

The Jew is distinguished not only by the purity of his monotheism but also by a unique attitude toward his God. He combines utmost reverence with an astonishing feeling of a special "belonging." God's awe-inspiring loftiness and majesty are linked with a feeling of nearness, almost familiarity. To him, God is not just "*the* Lord" but "*my* God," near and most personal. The Jew reveres God with all his heart, but he also knows that obsequiousness is the expression of a pagan mind. "Thou shalt *love* the Lord thy God" is the Jew's creed.

This special relationship between the Jew and his God reappears in the custom of covering the head. Standing before his Maker, submitting to His omnipotence, the Jew still preserves his dignity and self-respect. Thus, the Midrash expressed this very idea (Lev. R. Chap. XXVII): "Israelites, when reverent towards God, do not stand before Him in the attitude of slaves. A human king issues an edict to a province and all his citizens read it, standing uncovered, trembling with fear and anxiety. This, says God, I do not ask of you. I do not trouble you to stand or uncover your head when you read the Sh'ma."

The servile loses his soul. The upright and dignified best serves God.

The Priestly People

The high priest of old, when serving in the Temple in Jerusalem, was conspicuous by his miter, a cloth of fine linen coiled around his head like a turban. A diadem of pure gold was fastened to it with a purple cord. It bore the inscription "Holiness unto the Lord," which summarized the aim and purpose of his office.

When in 70 C.E. the Temple was destroyed and the altar disappeared with it, the offering of sacrifices became impossible, and thus the office of the high priest ceased to exist. Any division between priesthood and laity in Judaism became obsolete. From its early history the whole of the Jewish people (not just a selected class, caste, or family) had received the mission to become "a kingdom of priests and a holy people." With the destruction of the Temple, this ancient task could become a reality. Formerly only the high priest and his ministering clergy wore, as their sign of office, a miter covering the head. Now, all the people, having so to speak assumed the priestly task, do so. Every individual Jew now has a holy office. His is the responsibility to exalt God through loving-kindness and to sanctify Him through righteousness. The simple covering of his head thus links every Jew across the chasm of centuries to the sacred duty of the high priest and appoints him as God's simple servant in our time.

Such are the complex significance and the manifold interpretations of this custom, so widely adopted, but so little understood. Starting as a precautionary measure or a gesture of politeness, it has come to reflect a complete philosophy of living and at the same time to reveal a long story of historical experience.

Chapter 22

THE SCROLL ON THE DOOR

A Jewish home is distinguished by the mezuzah. This is a small case of metal, wood, or glass fixed outside the door on the upper third of the right doorpost, its top slanting slightly inward. It does not contain the Ten Commandments, as many people wrongly assume, but the Sh'ma, the watchword of Jewish faith. This is written by hand in twenty-two lines on a small parchment scroll which bears the word "Almighty" (*Shaddai*) on its back, made visible by means of a small opening in the container. While even the most scholarly scribe must copy his text for all other religious documents from a book, the mezuzah alone may be written from memory.

A Literal Interpretation

Rabbinical Judaism bases the introduction of the mezuzah on the literal interpretation of the sentence in the Sh'ma: "And thou shalt write them upon the doorpost of thy house and upon thy gates." In this context, it is possible that originally the commandment may have been meant in a figurative sense, but it soon became a concrete and visible sign of the Jewish faith. Thus, the *Kitsur Shulchan Aruch,* one of the fundamental guides of Orthodox Jewry, can say:

It is a positive command to affix the *Mezuzah* on every door. Even if one has many rooms, and in every room there are many doors for entrance and exit, all must have *Mezuzot* on them. . . . It is the duty of every man to be careful in performing the precept of the *Mezuzah,* because it is an obligation incumbent on all. Whenever he comes in or goes out he is confronted with His name, the name of the Holy One, blessed be He, and remembering His love, he will awake from

257

his sleep and will cease going astray after the vanities of the time. He will then become aware that there is nothing in this world enduring for all eternities, except the knowledge of the Rock of the world and he will at once repent and walk in the path of the righteous.

The rabbis of old, deeply concerned to direct man's attention to the Almighty, surrounded Jewish existence with numerous signposts toward God. They pronounced:

He who has *Tefillin* on his head and on his arm, fringes on his garment and a *Mezuzah* upon his door, will not sin, because he has many reminders.

Accordingly, the value of a mezuzah was considered to exceed that of the most precious jewel. Obtainable for a few cents, its intrinsic worth outshone everything else. The Midrash relates (Gen. R. Noah XXXV, 3):

Artarban sent to Rabbenu a priceless pearl, and said to him: "Send me a precious object of equal value." Rabbi Judah sent him a *Mezuzah*. He said to him: "I sent you a priceless gift, and you send me something worth a penny." Rabbi Judah replied: "Our respective gifts cannot be compared. Moreover, you sent me something which I must guard, but I sent you something which, when you sleep, will guard you, as it is said: When thou walkest, it will lead thee, when thou liest down it will watch over thee, and when thou awakest it will talk with thee, it will lead thee in this world, it will watch over thee in the hour of death, it will talk with thee in the world to come."

Many a pious Jew, on entering and leaving the house, touches the mezuzah with his hand and recites the prayer: "May God keep my going out and my coming in from now on and for ever more."

The Mystery of the Threshold

The threshold of the home has played a most significant part in the history of humanity. According to ancient superstition it was haunted by demons and evil spirits. People were therefore afraid of coming into contact with it and often jumped across.

By burying stillborn babies underneath it, or smearing blood (as a sacrificial act) on the lintels of the door, the pagans sought to ward off evil and propitiate the demons.

Another widespread and deeply rooted belief was that of the sanctity of the threshold. The household deities were assumed to reside there. Robbers dug through the clay walls of houses because of superstitious dread of the consequence should they pass through the guarded doorway. The custom of lifting the bride across the threshold similarly originates from this early belief of the immature mind, although the carrying itself is a relic of the time when men captured their wives and brought them by force into their homes.

The Hebrew name of Passover, *Pesach,* reflects the ancient custom of jumping across the threshold, as this is the literal meaning of the word. The Temple of Jerusalem had a special office of "keeper of the threshold."

When Marco Polo visited the palace at Peking in the days of Kublai Khan, the mystery of the threshold was impressed on him:

At every door of the hall there stood a couple of big men like giants, one on each side, armed with staves. Their special task was to prevent people from stepping upon the threshold. Did this, nevertheless, happen, they stripped the person of his clothes and demanded a forfeit for the return; otherwise flagellation was the punishment and payment.

In the remote past the mezuzah may have had some connection with this early superstition. Human existence was then thought to be beset by mysterious, inexplicable powers that seemed to threaten man from the cradle to the grave, and even before and beyond. Perhaps at first this scroll was fixed on doorposts as a charm against evil.

Man's progress is in part the story of the conquest of fear. His creative spirit was able to give new meaning to outdated customs and to endow a relic with dynamic and lasting value. The reinterpretation of an amulet made it an invaluable exponent of significant facts.

The Badge of Honor

The mezuzah is a beautiful symbol of Jewish living. Unafraid, the Jew announced to the outside world by the scroll on his door that this was a Jewish home inhabited by children of the Covenant of Abraham and dedicated to the ideals of Israel. Moving stories are told of the time of Nazi persecution when Jews refused to remove this indication of their homes, even though it invited destruction of their property and the greatest personal danger.

The mezuzah was the Jew's badge of honor, the signpost to a Jewish life of courage, not fear; of defiance, not defeatism; of avowal, not disguise. It was the dignified, triumphant affirmation of the indestructibility of the Jewish people.

A Signpost to Judaism

The mezuzah serves another, much deeper purpose. It not merely is a means of identification but is addressed to the Jew himself. It is a constant reminder of the omnipresence of God, and it proclaims our moral responsibility.

Whenever the Jew passes through his doors, entering or leaving, the mezuzah reminds him of his Jewishness, of the great ideals he must never forsake. Whether mixing with the crowds in great cities, apparently unrecognized and unwatched, or in the privacy of his own home, he is still in God's presence. At all times and in all places his life must be permeated by the spirit of morality and integrity, of righteousness and holiness. Thus Rabbi Gedalial of Linz wrote: "When we enter our home, we are reminded by the *Mezuzah* to struggle against the impulse tempting us towards wrong conduct, and to avoid anger and unkindness. When we leave our home, we are again reminded by it to curb our egotism in dealing with our fellow-creatures." This little scroll is thus a sermon in parchment. It is a perpetual charge to the Jewish people to dedicate their lives to all that is noble and worthy.

An Epitome of Jewish Living

As an emblem, the mezuzah is a beautiful expression of the Jewish soul. That the words of the Sh'ma are written in it renders it an outstanding phenomenon. The multitude of ideas contained in its twenty-two lines (chosen out of the 4,875 verses of the Pentateuch) is an overwhelming spiritual force. It bears the secret of the Jewish home, which is the guarantor of Jewish survival.

It is an intriguing fact that although the words of the Sh'ma are inscribed in the scroll, no one is ever expected to remove it from its metal case and actually read it. Yet the spirit expressed in the Sh'ma is always present.

It calls on every man to make an unqualified surrender of all he has and all he is to the love of God. Man is told to dedicate himself to Him "with all thy heart, with all thy soul, and with all thy might."

It reminds man of the moral world order, where every action begets its reaction, every sound has its echo, and thoughts become deeds. Man's individual responsibility is thus implicitly inscribed on the threshold of his home, "that ye may remember and do all My commandments and be holy unto your God."

It emphasizes that existence must be an integrated whole, that religion must permeate man's life on all occasions and at all times, "when thou sittest in thy house, when thou walkest by the way, when thou liest down and when thou risest up."

It accentuates the parents' duty to teach their children the Jewish way of life. They must not delegate this holy task to any outsider, however learned and expert he may be: "Thou shalt teach them diligently unto thy children." Jewish fathers and mothers must find time not only to feed and clothe their children but to mold their spirits, to make them find God.

The mezuzah not only continuously conveys all these Jewish precepts and duties but has captured also the glory of Jewish history and destiny, which echoes through the corridors of time. We know of countless millions of Jews who died the death of martyrs with its words on their lips.

Thus the mezuzah is a most potent religious influence. From it radiates to the "finely aware and richly responsible" a power that makes for excellence. In an acrid and disappointed world, the scroll on the door constitutes to the discerning eye and knowing heart a revelation of timeless reality. It is the affirmation of the superiority of the humane and divine over all the economic and mechanical forces weighing man down today. The mezuzah at the entrance of Jewish dwellings opens up the Jewish life to the spirit of God. It can change a mere house into a Jewish home and render every home a temple of God.

To the unthinking mind, and especially to the uninformed Jewish mind, there is a danger that the mezuzah may be regarded as a mascot or an amulet. Nothing could be farther from the truth. It is a proud affirmation of Jewishness, the essence, as it were, of the Jewish faith. By its mere presence it guides and directs the Jew toward his Jewish heritage of a God-fearing life. No empty decoration, it has profound religious significance. To the Jew who observes it, it offers a constant challenge to live an exemplary life imbued with love and never, in thought, word, or deed, to forget the presence of God everywhere. Thus, this small piece of parchment in its metal case can rouse people with the power of its message to a dynamic and radiant Judaism.

Chapter 23

DIETARY LAWS

We cannot live without food or drink. Their preparation and consumption take up a substantial part of our every day. The way man eats and drinks often reveals his character and the state of civilization. Small wonder, then, that the Jewish religion in no small measure used man's diet to ennoble him and to emphasize or convey specific religious ideas.

On the Day of Atonement the Jew fasts. (Orthodox Jews do so also on the Ninth of Av.) During the first nine days of the month of Av, as an expression of mourning, he abstains from meat. On Passover nothing that is leavened enters his home or diet.

Certain foods became symbolical of the different seasons or days of the year. The matzah became the bread of affliction on Passover, gefillte fish a welcome dish on the Sabbath eve, Hamantaschen and kreplach part of the Purim menu. Honey and apples were eaten on the eve of Rosh Hashanah as a hopeful anticipation that the New Year would bring only sweetness and joy.

Yet all through the year dietary laws appertained to everything eaten. They spiritualized one of the most material aspects of life and introduced an awareness of God where man was most apt to ignore and forget Him. Many of the laws were ordained in the Bible. Others were added in later ages by the rabbis, who asserted that these, too, had been revealed by God, though orally, at Mount Sinai.

The Bible explains the reason for only a few of the regulations. Thus, the prohibition of a certain sinew in an animal's thigh is based on the story of Jacob's wrestling on the banks of the river Jabbok. Most of the laws, however, were ordained as God's will

263

and therefore needed no further explanation. Their observance was considered a test of faith. The rabbis felt that many of their ordinances were implicitly contained in the biblical text and that they were only bringing to light and regulating these laws. Typical examples are the separation of "milk" and "meat" and the regulations of ritual slaughtering.

It is a common misconception that because the Jew may not eat bacon or pork, the pig is the only animal forbidden by Jewish dietary laws. The truth is that the pig, like the majority of other animals, fails to come within the category of "permitted" animals. To be ritually fit for consumption by a Jew, an animal must both chew the cud and have a cloven hoof. The cow and the sheep qualify, but not the pig, which has a cloven hoof, but does not chew the cud, nor the horse, which has neither requirement.

The denizens of the sea, to be ritually acceptable, must possess both fins and scales. Thus, eels and leatherjackets, which have no scales, and all the shellfish are prohibited.

It is not sufficient that an animal or a fish belong to an approved species. The Bible expressly forbids the eating of blood— "for the blood is the life!"—so that the larger animals must be killed by a method that, while being as painless as possible, ensures that the maximum amount of blood is removed. Then, before it is cooked, meat must be properly "kashered"—by salting and soaking in water—to remove the last traces of blood.

Finally, it is forbidden to eat meat or anything prepared from meat (and therefore *fleishig,* from the German) at the same time as anything prepared from milk or its derivatives (*milchig*).

Foods which are ritually permitted are called *kasher,* which really merely means "fit." It is a Hebrew word that could be applied equally well to express the suitability of anything. It refers just as much to the competence of witnesses appearing in a court of law or to the "perfection" of tallit and tsitsit donned by the Jew at morning service. They all have to be kasher. But the perpetual use of the word in connection with food narrowed its application in the mind of most people to this particular sphere. Unsuitable food, on the other hand, is called *trefah.* This word experienced the exact opposite fate, namely, a widening of sense. Originally it only described meat of an animal that was torn by wild beasts. Now, any forbidden food is trefah.

The food laws of the Jewish religion, many and diverse in their regulations, are just as varied in their origin and aim. Their study reveals salient points of Jewish teaching and telling features of Jewish historical fate.

The Bible relates that until the Flood man existed on greens alone. It was only from Noah's days that meat became part of man's staple diet. Originally, the Jew lived mostly on vegetables. He partook of meat only at festivals, when the animals had to be slaughtered at the Temple in Jerusalem, their fat burned on the altar, their blood spilled on its corners, and a specific portion handed to the priests. The eating of meat was then part of the sacrificial service, and therefore only clean animals worthy of being offered to God were acceptable. A close association was thus established between the consumption of meat and divine worship.

Later, when the Temple was destroyed and the killing of animals was permitted anywhere, the early association remained, although the eating of meat was no longer part of a holy communion, but of everyday nourishment. As the whole of the Jewish people were now considered a "kingdom of priests," the priestly rules once pertaining to the Temple service were now applied to the entire community. This aroused and fostered within the Jew the consciousness of his obligation to lead a priestly life, to be a light to the nations and a servant of God.

In the turmoil of daily life it is easy to lose sight of a lofty ideal, and unless it is constantly brought to mind it may be lost forever. Jewish ingenuity found a most unusual but effective way to make religion an unforgettable, everyday reality by associating it closely with eating and drinking. They were essentials of man's existence. They belonged to his daily routine and were always remembered. Now, through the dietary laws, they became a signpost to God. Every time the Jew sat down for a meal he was reminded in a way obvious to himself and the outside world of his dedication and special duty. It was a unique way to make a trivial act continuously bear a message of great importance and value.

To fulfill their mission as a people of religion, the Jews had to preserve the purity of their faith. No compromise whatsoever with the superstitions and idolatry of the surrounding pagan society could be allowed. To combat their rites and uproot any possible traces from the Jewish heart was essential. Only strict prohibition of customs that expressed or accompanied base forms of worship could guarantee the survival of the pure, ethical monotheism taught by the Jew. This aim explains several of the Jewish dietary laws.

The people had to be weaned from the customs of their heathen environment. Pagan worship, for instance, demanded as a sacrificial act the seething of a kid in its mother's milk. Blood was drunk to absorb divine qualities and used for other idolatrous purposes. Judaism, therefore, absolutely forbade both.

Reduced to its simplest terms, Judaism teaches the brotherhood of man under God, the one Father. Since such a creed is essential to the peaceful future of mankind, it is vital that Judaism must be preserved until all men have adopted this tenet. From this it follows that until the millennium—the Messianic era—has been reached, the Jew himself, as the "apostle" of Judaism, must survive. Yet there was never a people in history whose continued existence was more often threatened, either by physical attacks or by the more insidious but no less deadly weapon of assimilation.

Outside the Holy Land, the Jew has always formed only a small minority in the communities in which he dwelt. Thus there was always a temptation to mix freely with his neighbors on the social plane; but in past eras this was deemed to involve the risk of intermarriage which, in turn, might lead to loss of Jewish identity. Accordingly, it was seen to be the unpleasant but unavoidable duty of the Jew to keep himself largely aloof, not to indicate that he was exclusive, but to maintain his singular role as the bearer of a message to the nations of the world. What love and allegiance to its native soil could do for other people had, for the dispersed Jewish people, to be achieved by consciousness of and devotion to his mission to mankind.

The observance of kashrut, whether unconsciously or providentially, acted thus as a separating factor between Jew and Gentile. In the Middle Ages it was often the chief mark of distinction. Undoubtedly this segregation of Jew from Gentile was a powerful means of maintaining Jewish identity. "I have separated you from the people that you should be Mine!"

In Jewish life, cleanliness has always been part of religious observance. To wash the hands was not only a commandment to be fulfilled first thing every morning on waking and before each meal; it had to be consecrated by a special benediction. Not surprisingly, therefore, the Jew's anxiety for a clean and hygienic way of life acted as yet another source of his dietary legislation. To be clean in habit, thought, and word became the Jewish ideal in his personal life, as much as in his dealings with his fellow man.

Modern medical science has shown the influence of food on general health. The importance of the kind of nourishment a man takes is one of the fundamental convictions of dietetics. Psychology teaches the interrelation between body and mind, nurture and nature. The Roman adage of the healthy mind in the healthy body has become a truism. "Der Mensch ist was er isst," says the German pun.

Undoubtedly the food regulations of Jewry early recognized and emphasized this modern conception, and unquestionably they helped in the shaping of Jewish personality. They did so by the control of his physical and mental well-being and the creation of a definite emotional and spiritual attitude.

Every people's existence depends on the preservation of its good health. Jewish dietary law served additionally as a special measure, contributing to national fitness. "I maintain that food forbidden by the Law is unwholesome," wrote Maimonides in his *Guide for the Perplexed*. Foodstuff that was dangerous, and the meat of animals that had unclean living habits or were known as germ carriers, were therefore banned outright. Hence the prohibition of the pig, known in the Orient as harboring parasitic embryos; the banning of blood which often carried dangerous microbes; and of shellfish, which, living at river mouths or near the coastline in probably contaminated surroundings, were considered injurious to health. The separation of carbohydrates and proteins in modern diets points to the relevance in the digestive process of the Jews' prohibition of mixing milk and meat. The meat of animals not killed in the ritual way retained much congealed blood, which was thought to be most unhealthy.

In no small measure the dietary laws account for the Jews' longevity, their lower rate of mortality and greater power of resistance in times of epidemics. This was apparent especially during the Middle Ages, when tens of thousands of people fell victim to the prevailing plagues, but Jews escaped relatively unscathed. This led to anti-Semitic riots and persecutions. The frightened populace, unable to recognize the real cause of the Jews' immunity, accused them of poisoning the wells and of being the Devil's disciples and thus under his Satanic protection.

Deep symbolism is contained in the prohibition of certain foods. It expresses the Jewish abhorrence of violence. It teaches man to abstain from the unclean and cruel, not only in his diet but in his life. By a process of association, a feeling of distaste for the physically repulsive was transferred to the sphere of the unethical and immoral. The Jew, once conditioned to keep away from the unclean, soon learned to avoid the impure.

To be made conscious of such evaluation, even in one's dietary habits, helps to create a sensitive mind and fosters an ethical way of life. God and goodness are brought into every aspect of daily life. A passage in the Midrash is most outspoken on this issue. It posed a question: "What does it matter to God whether or not a man kills an animal in the Jewish way and eats it? It will neither benefit nor injure Him. Or what does God care whether a man eats unclean animals or clean ones?" And—over sixteen hundred years ago, remember—the Midrash replied: "The commandments are only given to purify God's creatures."

Neither birds of prey nor carnivorous animals were thought fit for human consumption. Many of those prohibited not only lived on killing but were obnoxious in their habits and repulsive in their appearance.

The introduction of Jewish ritual slaughtering, similarly, was the result of deep religious concern to foster humane feelings in circumstances where cruelty and hardness of heart might all too easily prevail. Its specific purpose is to alleviate the animal's suffering. Its methods aim at the quickest and least painful death. Only a God-fearing man, therefore, was allowed to execute this task. Before killing the animal he had to utter a special benediction, reminding him of his responsibility toward God and God's creatures. The knife used had to be perfectly smooth and of extreme sharpness. If the obligatory examination immediately before the slaughtering revealed the smallest notch or roughness, the knife could not be used lest it prolong the animal's pain.

To take away the life of another being, though it be a dumb animal, put on man a grave responsibility. The Jew was not satisfied with merely avoiding unnecessary physical pain. His legislation extended to the sphere of emotion. It banned anything that might give hurt to the heart or make man cruel, unthinking, and unfeeling. The Jew objected to hunting. He forbade the eating of blood identified with the life force. Even one drop of it in the yolk of an egg rendered the egg unfit for eating.

A cow and its calf, a sheep and its lamb, must not be slaughtered on the same day. The kid must not be cooked in its mother's milk. Though the rabbis later related this law to the division between milk and meat in the Jewish kitchen and diet, its original basis was humaneness. The mother had produced the milk for her child to live on. Man, taking away the kid and killing it, certainly should not be so cruel as to use the very milk, intended for the kid's nourishment, for its preparation as a tasty dish.

The book of Proverbs had taught the Jew to know the soul of his animals. The rabbis had ordered him to feed his beasts before sitting down to his own meal. Dietary laws and the regulations of the abattoirs continued this tradition of regard for God's lower creatures. Perhaps it was no accident that it was a Jew, Louis Gompertz, who helped to found the Society for the Prevention of Cruelty to Animals.

Ethics is a major part of religion. To train man to live a clean and decent life is one of the essential aims of every faith. Judaism believes in freedom of choice. All through life man faces good and evil. He himself again and again has to decide which way to turn. Temptations abound. To withstand them often demands the hardest possible struggle. Only strong willpower assures the morality of man.

Kashrut has greatly contributed to the training of Jewish self-control. In themselves, the dietary laws may mean little, and, certainly, proper observance of them does not justify anyone in claiming to be "a good Jew." But he who has learned to overcome the greed of his appetite will all the more easily subdue the lusts of the flesh. It is like physical exercises. In themselves, they seem merely a series of muscular contortions. In reality, they strengthen the muscles of the body, enabling it later to carry or to bear any burden.

A talmudic passage stresses this esoteric purpose of food prohibition to steel man in his power of resistance: "Let no man say I do not like the flesh of swine. On the contrary, he should say, I like it, but what shall I do seeing that the Law has forbidden it to me." A man who rejects a certain food merely because he does not care for it shows no moral power. But he is truly religious who, though longing for it, refuses to touch it because of God's law. Once man has acquired the habit of self-control even in only one aspect of life, he will easily be able to apply it elsewhere.

The observance of dietary laws developed in the Jewish people unsurpassed moral strength and self-discipline.

Kashrut has left its impress on the whole structure of Jewish Orthodox life. There is the Jewish ritual slaughterer called the shochet. His is not merely a trade, but a profession. His appointment depends on possession of a rabbinical certificate which can be obtained only by a man of the highest qualifications and finest qualities. He must be efficient in the duties of a normal butcher and, in addition, learned in the regulations of shechitah (the Jewish way of killing). His training, moreover, must fit him to recognize, even in their earliest stages, the symptoms of certain specified animal diseases, the existence of which in a beast otherwise quite acceptable would render it unfit for Jewish consumption—trefah. But, most of all, he must be known as a man of integrity and piety.

The three Hebrew letters of the word *kasher* * are perhaps the characters of the Hebrew alphabet best known among the Gentiles. They appear on the Jewish butcher shop and on the seals which "permit" foodstuff that is declared "suitable." *Mashgi'ach* is the name of the Jewish equivalent of health inspector, whose perpetual duty it is to "watch" the cleanliness and fitness of the Jewish shop.

There is the Orthodox Jewish kitchen with its division into two separate compartments, doubling crockery, cutlery, and sinks for the meat and milk. Thus, Jewish religious influence extends everywhere. It is evident right from the selection of the animal to the washing up of the used dishes: in abattoir, store, kitchen, dining room, and scullery.

Such wide application of dietary legislation obviously presented certain dangers of misunderstanding and overemphasis. At times, the overzealous almost identified the keeping of kashrut with the whole of Jewish faith and replaced a way of living with a way of eating. To them, the observance of those laws became a test of the Jewishness of a Jew. Instead of being only instruments in the achievement of certain goals, they became an end in themselves.

Food regulations attained a most dramatic significance in Jewish fate. The banning of ritual slaughtering was always the first weapon in the hands of the anti-Semite, the dictator who could not bear to see the practice of religious freedom. Instead of recognizing in it the special endeavor of the Jew to be kind to animals and of accepting the testimony of medical authorities and physiologists who described ritual slaughtering as a most humane method, the anti-Semite presented it as cruel and inhuman.

Even the prohibition of the flesh of pigs has its tragic history.

* כשר

The story of Chanukah tells how in the days of the Maccabees, Jews were called upon to partake of the swine in front of the gathered. population of towns and villages as a proof of their apostasy. To the Greek oppressor, to eat pork was the surest sign that a Jew had forsaken his faith. But Jews preferred martyrdom to a piece of forbidden meat, swallowed even under duress. In the Middle Ages, the Jewish people were forced publicly to eat of the swine once again, this time to amuse the jeering masses and to be ridiculed and humiliated. Such was the sadism of the Jew-hater that even innocuous food laws were a welcome instrument for torture and degradation.

Orthodox Jews observe the dietary laws meticulously and completely. They consider them an integral part of God's immutable revelation. To them, no further explanation is needed. "There is no other reason for all the dietary laws than that God gave them," wrote Samson Raphael Hirsch. Their main purpose was to test the Jews' piety and love for God.

The Reform Jewish approach to kashrut varies in different countries. In America, it disregards largely all dietary legislation, stressing the spiritual outlook of Judaism. Elsewhere, however, it differentiates between the laws expressly contained in the Bible and those introduced by rabbinical interpretations and extensions. The biblical laws are regarded as mandatory, but the others are examined in the light of their historical origin and their relevance to contemporary conditions. But even when Reform Judaism prohibits the consumption of certain animals, fish, and birds, it does not insist on the need for ritual slaughtering, holding that modern state legislation closely follows the ancient Jewish regulations. It does not demand the separation of milk and meat or the provision of separate crockery and utensils. The basis of this viewpoint is that the relevant regulations are not explicitly commanded in the Bible.

However, recognizing that apart from their inherent force the dietary laws have a disciplinary value, Reform Judaism teaches them in full and leaves it to the conscience or the conviction of the individual to decide how far to follow them. "There is no merit in the dietary laws unless they can be made a bridge between man and God, a means to spiritualize and sanctify the whole of life for those who maintain them," wrote Sir Basil Henriques.

Dietary laws are by no means exclusive to Judaism. The Hindu will not eat the flesh of the cow. The Moslem is forbidden the flesh of the pig and may not consume alcohol or smoke tobacco. Islam, too, introduced a form of ritual slaughtering under which meat could be eaten only, if, while it was being killed, the name of Allah had been pronounced. This has the curious result that, in Australia, for example, a Moslem will not buy meat at an ordinary butcher shop, but can eat kasher meat over which the shochet would have pronounced a benediction!

The dietary laws have helped to mold the Jewish character and preserve the stability and integrity of the Jewish family. They have contributed to the health and cleanliness of the people and fostered a spiritual outlook. An instrument in the Jews' struggle for survival, the laws have also served as a training in will power and self-restraint.

They have a long and varied history. Some may have arisen out of ancient taboos; others may be explained historically, hygienically, or socially. Yet each of them, in one way or another, expresses the Jews' passionate longing to raise life to a spiritual level and to mold the Jewish community into a people dedicated to God in the service of man.

Chapter 24

CIRCUMCISION

Every Jewish male child is circumcised on the eighth day of his life. The ceremony is called the *Brit Milah* (covenant of circumcision) or, usually, more briefly, the Brit. It marks the initiation of the child into the faith of Abraham and is demanded equally of an adult on joining the Jewish faith.

Its importance is so great that it has to take place on the Sabbath or even on the Day of Atonement. Only illness on the part of mother or child can postpone the ritual. It used to be performed in the synagogue, but now is done at home or in hospital. The ceremony has to be held during daylight.

To perform a circumcision is regarded as an honored privilege or mitzvah, and the profession of mohel (circumciser) is held in high esteem, although nowadays the mohel is mostly replaced by a doctor who has been recognized by a synagogue as qualified to carry out the operation with religious authority. Since the ceremony is looked upon as a religious service, Orthodoxy requires the presence of at least ten men.

It is also regarded as a privilege and sacred task to be invited to hold the infant during the ceremony. The one selected takes the place of the godfather and is called the sandik (from the Greek *syndikos,* "counselor"). Often a separate chair, called Elijah's chair, is placed on the right-hand side of the godfather. It symbolizes the presence of this zealot for Judaism, who was considered the guardian of every Jewish child. The chair, as well as the circumcision knife, were usually artistic creations, and many valuable and magnificent specimens are to be found all over the world.

As on all festal occasions, a special benediction is pronounced over a cup of wine, the symbol of rejoicing. "Circumcision is one of the commandments which, having been accepted with joy, are ever obeyed with joy; because the people gave their lives for them, they are kept with steadfast loyalty," said the rabbis of the Talmud.

All present join in prayer that the boy, thus received into the Jewish faith, may be blessed with true understanding, a worthy marriage, and deeds of loving-kindness. The ceremony concludes with the conferring on the child of his religious name.

This is quite separate and distinct from his ordinary, registered name and is intended for use only—and always—in connection with religious ceremonies. It will be used on the occasion of his bar mitzvah, whenever he is called to offer a blessing over the Torah, at his wedding, and at his funeral. It will be engraved on his tombstone and recalled at his Yahrzeit (the anniversary of his death).

Religious names are almost invariably Hebrew or Yiddish. There is no "surname" in the ordinary sense of the word, but a combination of the child's own given name followed by that of his father and joined by either the Hebrew *ben* or the Aramaic *bar,* both meaning "son of." An example is Yitzchak ben Ya'akov (Isaac son of Jacob). This custom, of course, serves to strengthen the link between the generations.

The selection of the child's name is by no means haphazard. Quite frequently the choice falls on the name of a grandfather, or even a deceased father, whose memory will thus be honored. Often it is merely the Hebrew equivalent of the child's English name (Sh'muel for Samuel, Channah for Ann, and so on). Sometimes the choice is based on alliteration. Thus, a boy named Gordon will be given the religious name Gershon, or Alfred will be called Avraham. In a few cases, the meaning or significance of the English name is translated into Hebrew. A child named Graham, which means "laughter," could be called by the Hebrew name Yitzchak, which has the same connotation.

Traditionally, there is one special reason to give a child a religious name, for it will summon him when he awakes in the world to come. Indeed, lest he forget his religious name and thereby miss that fateful summons, the pious Jewish child is taught a special Hebrew *posek,* or verse, of which the first word begins with the first letter and the last word ends with the last letter of his given name.

Circumcision is known to have been practiced from prehistoric times. References to the rite have been found in Egyptian writing of the period 4000 B.C.E., and archaeologists discovered, in a tomb of the period 1600 B.C.E., the mummified body of a man who had been circumcised.

The custom extends all over the world and is definitely not exclusively Jewish. Less than one-hundredth of the world population are Jewish, but more than one-seventh are circumcised.

There is ample evidence to prove that circumcision did not originate in any one specific country and thence spread elsewhere. On the contrary, it is known to have been practiced by aboriginal people in almost every continent, and it was certainly indigenous in most if not all these cases. It still exists among Christian Ethiopians, African Bantus, and Australian Aborigines. Though not ordained in the Koran by Mohammed, it is obligatory in Islam.

The statutory age for circumcision varies widely from country to country. The youngest age is the seventh day after birth; the most frequently adopted is the age of puberty. In the case of Moslems, the boy may be circumcised at any time between the ages of seven and twelve years.

Similar variations occur in the matter of responsibility for performing the act. In early Jewish times it was the mother who had the task. Among the Falashas it was carried out by three old women, while in the New Hebrides women are not even permitted to be present at the ceremony.

Among many tribes circumcision is observed for all the male (and sometimes female) population, but cases are known where it was the prerogative of only the ruling caste, the rich, or the childless princes.

As widespread as is the custom, so diverse are the explanations of its origin and meaning. They range from tribal and sacrificial to utilitarian purposes.

In many instances circumcision was practiced as a rite of initiation and considered a necessary act of preparation for marital life. Hence its practice at the time of puberty. In Arabic, the same word denotes circumcision and marriage, which clearly demonstrates the early association of both. In Judaism, on the contrary, the custom was divorced from all utilitarian considerations and regarded as of purely religious significance. Thus it was to be performed in earliest infancy.

Others considered circumcision as a test of bravery and endurance. If withstood unflinchingly, the young man could consider himself a full member of his tribe. He had graduated into manhood.

A castration hypothesis sees in circumcision a last remnant of self-mutilation, committed to appease the wrath of the gods. Modern psychoanalysis, for a similar reason, saw in the rite a cause of anti-Semitism, claiming that circumcision unconsciously reminded people of castration, thus generating in them a feeling of repulsion, which they duly transferred to the Jew.

Circumcision served also as a primitive tribal badge, a common mark uniting all the members. Just as the Herreros knocked out their front teeth and other tribes practiced mutilation and tattooing, so circumcision was an indelible tribal marking.

Children were circumcised as a sacrificial symbol to redeem them from the power of the deity who was thought to have given them life.

As with early forms of phallic worship, circumcision served among pagan people as a propitiation of the god of fertility, begging for the gift of children by consecrating the procreative forces.

Circumcision also acted as a substitute for human sacrifice. It expressed man's total submission to divine power. This explains the contempt shown in the Bible to those who, being uncircumcised, thereby defied God. Herbert Spencer pointed out that for the same reason circumcision was used to take the place of annihilation of the enemy. Instead of killing the vanquished, the victorious nation circumcised them.

Regardless of all these various explanations, when Judaism adopted the rite of circumcision, it applied an entirely new set of values. This is one of the earliest examples of the creative genius of the Jewish mind. The finest sign of originality, Goethe said, was the ability to develop an accepted thought so creatively that no one could have easily guessed just how much was hidden therein. The Jew showed this very gift in the way he reinterpreted and sanctified the custom of circumcision and made it a vital and fundamental institution of his faith.

In Judaism, circumcision immediately became a symbol of God's Covenant (Brit) with Israel. Abraham, the first Jew, was commanded to perform it as an everlasting sign of the consecration of the children of Israel. "This is My Covenant, which ye shall keep, between Me and you, and thy seed after thee: every male among you shall be circumcized." It was renewed by Joshua. Leading the Israelites into the Holy Land, he was aware that the children born in the desert had not been initiated into the Covenant. He therefore arranged a mass circumcision of the whole people at a place called Gilgal, whose name was explained by this event.

Circumcision had become a sign of the Jew's loyalty to God. Soon the very word became a metaphor for a life of devotion and selfless service. When the prophets spoke of the regeneration of the people and their return to a life of purity, they called for the "circumcision of the heart." When (in 586 B.C.E.) Nebuchadrezzar exiled the Jews to Babylonia and Temple worship could no longer act as a uniting link, it was circumcision that, next to Sabbath observance, held the Jews together as a badge of unity.

The rite came to express the wish and will to be conscious of one's Jewish heritage. When, centuries later, Hellenist Jews became victims of assimilation, ashamed of their faith, they tried to cover up their Jewishness. They not only changed their names (the Hebrew Moses into the Greek Menelaus and Joseph into Jason) but underwent painful surgical operations to remove the "seal of Abraham" from their bodies, since they took part in physical exercises in the Greek gymnasia, which were performed in the nude. The loyal Jews laid all the more stress on the importance of the rite, and the actual operation was extended to make removal of the "seal" impossible.

Despots aiming at the extinction of the Jewish State felt the necessity to prohibit circumcision. For its preservation, the Jews were prepared to die the death of martyrs.

In 168 B.C.E. the forces of Antiochus IV Epiphanes of Syria executed "the women that had circumcized their children . . . and they hanged their babes around their necks and destroyed their houses." However, the Maccabees undauntedly followed the examples of those valiant mothers. Wherever they went in their underground fight for freedom, they circumcised the Jewish children.

When, three centuries later (in 135 C.E.), Emperor Hadrian of Rome in his turn decided to exterminate the Jewish faith, he not only changed Jerusalem into a pagan city, banning the keeping of the Sabbath and the giving of religious instructions, but made circumcision an offense punishable by death. Secret agents and informers roamed the country to discover offenders. Yet Jews defied the decree all the more and continued to introduce their children into the Covenant of Abraham. Circumcision, from a merely religious institution and a bond of unity, had become a symbol of the fight for freedom and a mark of Jewish loyalty. Hundreds laid down their lives in defense of this rite. Centuries later, the danger of being circumcised was again experienced in the life-and-death struggle under the Spanish Inquisition, and then in Hitler's Third Reich.

The importance of circumcision as a vital symbol of Judaism was heightened by a consideration which arose out of the advent of Christianity. Before that period, baptism had been practiced by the Jews as a religious rite equal to circumcision in importance. Indeed, some Jewish teachers held that if it became necessary to choose one or the other, baptism was the more important. Even in modern times the ritual bath (or *mikveh*) has a special significance as an act of purification among Orthodox women, while females seeking admission to Judaism must, as part of the ceremonial, undergo "baptism" in the mikveh.

Early Christians, on the other hand, knew of circumcision. Jesus himself had been circumcised (as related in the second chapter of the Gospel according to St. Luke), and the Roman Catholic Church still commemorates this important event (on the eighth day after his birth) on the first of January as "the feast of the circumcision of our Lord." But then Paul abolished circumcision, retaining, however, the Jewish rite of baptism as a sacrament. This inevitably facilitated the conversion of pagans (so well prepared by Jewish missionaries), who no longer had to undergo a painful operation which had certainly been an obstacle to proselytization.

The Church soon came to stress circumcision as being a Jewish rite, while emphasizing the Christian aspect of baptism. Jews had no choice but to follow this new distinction and interpretation. For the sake of their continued identity and their very survival, the rabbis of the Talmud were forced to lay ever more stress on the Jewish significance of circumcision as God's eternal Covenant with His people. They did so in numerous ways and in the metaphors and language of their time. They said that only by circumcision did man become perfect and his creation complete. It rescued him from the pangs of hell and was an indication of his love of God. The practice of the rite maintained the stability of the universe: "Heaven and earth are held together only by the fulfillment of this Covenant." Should a father fail in his duty to have a son circumcised, the religious court of the city had to enforce the rite.

The two faiths—mother and daughter—differ widely in their application and interpretations of the ultimate significance of baptism and circumcision. The child born of Christian parents is not regarded as a Christian until baptism makes it so. Until baptized, the child of Christian birth remains outside the Church and, so, a heathen. In Judaism, however, every child born of a Jewish mother is itself Jewish, even without the act of circumcision.

Centuries passed, and wherever Jews went they observed

God's Covenant either in a simple, traditional manner or with the courage of despair in defiance of tyrants. Further and deeper meanings were added to the custom's interpretation. Circumcision was considered not just a survival of ancient symbolism but a means of ruling man's passion and leading him to a life of continence. The New Testament had already explained circumcision as a putting away of carnal lust. Judaism's greatest philosopher, Moses Maimonides, thus saw the rite as an instrument in man's mastery of his instincts.

Judaism does not teach asceticism or celibacy. It has never known monks or monasteries. It demands not the suppression, but the sanctification of man's procreative powers. Circumcision is its symbol. It perpetually reminds man to be master and not slave of the passion that stirs within. In the face of philosophies of hedonism and unrestrained self-indulgence, Judaism taught and practiced self-control and dedication.

Baruch Spinoza, though excommunicated by his own Jewish brethren, held that circumcision would, of its own importance, be sufficient to justify the survival of the Jewish people: "Such great importance do I attach to the sign of the Covenant, that I am persuaded that by itself it is sufficient to maintain the separate existence of the nation for ever."

Modern times revived the rational explanation given two thousand years earlier by Philo the philosopher and Josephus the historian. They saw in circumcision a hygienic measure to safeguard health and cleanliness. At one time it was even suggested as a compulsory operation in the Prussian army, and it is now widely adopted in non-Jewish circles.

Circumcision has thus been the property of the Jewish people from their very birth to this modern age. Adopted thousands of years ago from the outside world, Judaism changed a tribal mark into a dynamic symbol. The Bible made it the seal of the Covenant of Abraham for all times. Throughout the centuries new meanings were added through the exigencies of history and the inspiration of Jewish religious thought. Today, these together make up the multiple interpretation of the rite. First an act of initiation, it became an emblem of resistance against the enemy without and lust within, of loyalty to the Jewish people and to God. Symbol of the Jewish faith, it is a mark of moral training, of the dedication of each individual Jew to his community, and the consecration of the whole of Jewry to a life of holiness.

Thirty days after the birth of their first-born son, Orthodox Jews celebrate his "redemption": *Pidyon Haben*. A Cohen, a descendant of the ancient priestly class, is in charge of the ceremony, which concludes with the threefold benediction and a joyful meal. The custom is based on the ancient belief that all the first-born belong to God and have specially to be redeemed.

Chapter 25

BAR MITZVAH

On the Sabbath following his thirteenth birthday, as reckoned by the Hebrew calendar, a Jewish boy becomes bar mitzvah. For the first time in his life he is called upon in the synagogue to rise before the congregation, to pronounce the blessings over the Torah, and to read from the Scroll of the Law. According to his individual capacity and to the degree of Orthodoxy of his family, a boy may read either one Parsha (portion) or the whole of the weekly Sidra (lesson), each Sidra normally containing seven Parshas. Then, if especially well trained or skilled, he will also render the second lesson, or Haftarah, which comprises a reading from the prophets.

All boys are expected to chant their reading in the appropriate melody (*Nigun*), of which there are two, one for the Torah and another for the Haftarah. If the boy is constitutionally unable to sing or has a voice so poor that singing would embarrass him or his parents (or the congregation), he is permitted to read his portion. In the Reform synagogue, while the Torah may be read or sung in Hebrew, the boy recites the Haftarah in English.

The words "bar mitzvah"—respectively Aramaic and Hebrew —mean literally "son of the commandment," a name which indicates the significance attached to the ceremony. It implies that the boy has, in the religious sense, reached his majority and is now personally liable to keep the tenets of Judaism. From the point of view of his congregation, the bar mitzvah boy has become a "man," responsible for his own religious observances, sharing the rights and duties of all adult male Jews, and in every way a full member of the congregation.

To the boy of an Orthodox family, three specific developments reflect his new status: he is now required to use the tefillin at morning prayer; he has to wear a tallit when praying either in public or in private; he is eligible to form one of the Jewish quorum or minyan of ten men needed for all public religious services.

The ceremony of bar mitzvah may be regarded as analogous to the attainment of citizenship: it is not the matter of a single moment or of one day, but a continuing condition. To become or to be bar mitzvah, therefore, does not, as many Jews mistakenly believe, merely refer to the synagogue ceremonial followed, perhaps, by a "birthday party." Bar mitzvah is more than a ceremony; it is a status and belongs as much to a man when he reaches seventy as it did on the day he became thirteen.

Though popularly believed to be an old-established law, the institution of bar mitzvah is comparatively recent. It was not initiated by any of the recognized Jewish authorities and is not even mentioned in the Bible or in the Talmud. As in the case of not a few other Jewish ceremonial customs, bar mitzvah, an unwritten law, derived its standing and its universal observance solely from its inherent beauty and its deep religious significance.

In the Bible a man reached maturity only when he was able to bear arms. After the destruction of the second Jewish Commonwealth, in 70 C.E., civic responsibility was replaced by religious obligation, and the bearing of arms by the wearing of tefillin. It was Roman influence that then made the assumption of religious responsibility coincide with the commencement of puberty. The term "bar mitzvah" as such came into use only in the thirteenth century.

Originally, the celebration of bar mitzvah consisted of three parts.

1. In front of the congregation and the open Scroll, the father expressed his gratitude to God that his son had reached the stage of personal responsibility and was no longer dependent. It was almost a public pronouncement that thenceforth the father was no longer answerable for the religious life of his son, who must therefore become conscious of his Judaism and conscientious in the fulfillment of its ideals.

2. The boy delivered a discourse, clarifying a difficult passage of rabbinical teaching. This was meant to prove to assembled relatives and friends that he had been properly trained and was well versed in the "ocean of the Talmud." By this thesis he "graduated" to full manhood.

3. The parents arranged a festive meal to emphasize the joyous significance of the day. It was the last religious function they were able to give to their son, as the wedding feast would be the privilege of his bride's parents. All the more did they take every care to make it an unforgettable event. Its central idea was not culinary pleasure, but religious atmosphere.

The ceremony of bar mitzvah is accompanied by a great variety of customs which differ in various parts of the world. In Tetuan, the boy's hair was cut short, and he was presented with a special wig to wear for the occasion.

Perhaps more colorful and certainly more religious in basis was another practice in North Africa, in which the bar mitzvah was not restricted to the celebration on the actual Sabbath, nor the studies to the portion of the Law which was to be read. The boy had to memorize a complete talmudic treatise, in which he had to pass an examination. The rabbis and wardens of the synagogue arranged a special dinner on the Wednesday preceding the Sabbath. On the following morning a service was held in the home of the boy's parents at which, to the accompaniment of a hymn sung by the choir, the Chief Rabbi placed the arm tefillin on the boy's arm and the father put the head tefillin on his son's head. The boy then addressed the congregation partly in Hebrew and partly in the vernacular. Finally, he went round with his tefillin bag to the men, the women, and his parents, who filled it with coins, which he then presented to his teacher. A breakfast concluded the ceremony. Only after this was the boy considered ready to be called up to the Law on the next Sabbath.

The institution of bar mitzvah reveals essential Jewish ideas, and it contributed greatly toward the integration and religious molding of the Jewish community.

Religion demands education. At one period the bar mitzvah

boy's admission to the Jewish community was dependent on his proof that he could think for himself. This was the purpose of his special discourse, consisting not of memorized data, but of perceptive analysis. As every boy of whichever class or background had to be bar mitzvah, a whole people's education was thus assured—something unique in the history of civilization.

Consciousness of one's Judaism is based on knowledge of one's religion. Only he who was generally literate and had entered into the spirit of Judaism could be counted a member of the congregation of Israel. However, responsibility without privilege would tend to dampen enthusiasm (although, in modern times, many nations impose active military service on youths still denied the right of voting). The boy who becomes bar mitzvah acquires complete religious responsibility but is also made to feel that he is a full member of the community, belonging to the ancient faith of his forefathers.

The bar mitzvah thus expresses most potent religious features with essential, present-day meaning, which alone ensure survival of the Jewish religion. It impresses on the boy his religious obligation. Judaism teaches the individual responsibility of each member. No one can take the place or fulfill the task of any other. Now all depends on him; even the rabbi cannot take his place. The boy is reminded of God's presence and his communal obligations, his duty toward his family and his faith. The bar mitzvah, therefore, pronounces the Jewish declaration of faith in the one God, Who is the God of all men. The boy prays for strength to serve God and mankind as a loyal member of the household of Israel.

Above all, the bar mitzvah must be made to realize that the ceremony is not an end, but a beginning. The preparation was no perfunctory training for the one specific event, but a mere introduction into the beauty and grandeur of the Jewish faith, a preliminary glimpse of the totality of Judaism, its literature, its sense of social endeavor, and its emphasis on the universal ideal. Now the bar mitzvah is ready to apply his religion in full, personal responsibility in all circumstances throughout the changes and chances of life.

Chapter 26

MARRIAGE

Marriage is the first commandment found in the Bible. The Jew believes that only in family life and a shared existence can man find true happiness and fulfill his destiny: "This is why a man leaves his father and mother and cleaves to his wife, till they become one flesh." The rabbis of the Talmud went so far as to say that "an unmarried man is not a man in the full sense." He lives "without joy, without blessing, without good."

The Hebrew term for marriage is *kiddushin,* which means "sanctification," as nothing could be more sacred in life than the union of husband and wife before God. To the Jew, marriage therefore became the greatest *simchah,* or spiritual joy, and its celebration has been arrayed with many beautiful customs. Each one of them has an ancient meaning which even today is thought-provoking. All of them possess a permanent symbolism of great depth.

The Veil

In the Jewish faith, the bride's veil dates from biblical times and recollects how Rebecca, in a gesture of modesty, covered her face when she first saw her beloved from afar. Its whiteness stands for the purity of home life, which alone ensures lasting happiness.

Once the covering of the bride with a veil called for a special ceremony, known by the German word *Bedecken.* Four young people spread a four-cornered, white, transparent cloth over the head of the bride.

Far removed from the beautiful symbolism of the present-day

287

custom is its origin outside Judaism, in the very early history of civilization. There it was part of the ancient custom of capturing one's wife, the veil being used so that she might not be recognized and rescued.

Fear of the jealousy of evil forces which might come and threaten her life is yet another reason for the early use of the veil. So as to mislead the demons, the bride was disguised and a cloth placed over her face. For the same purpose, Egyptian brides used to don helmet and sword, and the groom female apparel.

The Chuppah

When a Jewish couple are to be married, whether in the synagogue or, as is permitted, in the home or even a hotel, the groom enters first. He stands, with his attendants, under the chuppah waiting for his bride to come and stand beside him.

The chuppah, or canopy, in its modern form is made of blue or purple velvet or other similar material, heavily embroidered and fringed, and supported on four cornerposts. Originally, the term was used to describe the bridal chamber where, reversing the modern practice, the bride awaited her groom. This is recalled in biblical imagery which describes the rising of the sun as resembling "the bridegroom leaving the chuppah."

It was the duty of each bridegroom's father to build a new chuppah and to adorn it with purple cloth, precious jewels, and beautiful flowers. For the first seven days of the wedding, the bride never left the chuppah.

The medieval ghetto life of the Jewish community, with its cramped space and impoverished life, changed the functional building into a symbolic structure. The bridal chamber was replaced by a canopy in the synagogue. When, in various ages, it became customary to celebrate weddings out of doors, the chuppah was changed into a portable baldachin. Eventually, the solemnization of weddings was again normally conducted in the synagogue, and the chuppah returned to its precincts, but retained its portable, temporary character.

So much for the historical development of the chuppah. More

interesting than its origin is the spiritual lesson which can be gained from its use in the present day.

The chuppah conveys the idea of unity. Bride and bridegroom standing together beneath it, soul bound up with soul, proclaim that they are inseparable. Thus joined together, nothing, and no one, may come between them. Husband and wife, having found each other, complete their lives.

The chuppah is a symbol of God's presence. Like heaven, it shelters bride and bridegroom. It is the *Trauhimmel*. The chuppah calls to mind the sanctity of wedlock: "Without God we cannot; without us God will not." Marriage is not merely a social contract or a legal transaction. It is the most divine task in human life.

Entering beneath the chuppah, husband and wife begin a new life. They vow loyalty to each other and to God. Under His shelter they turn from the vicissitudes of life to the beatitudes of love.

The Ring

The wedding ring originally formed the ransom which a husband paid for his wife. It was a tangible sign of ownership. The wife could easily keep the ring secure by simply slipping it on a finger.

The ring itself was still unknown in talmudic times. Then, the man used to hand his wife a small coin, an obvious development from the original purchase motive. The ring soon gained a new significance. Its bestowal expressed the fact that the giver endowed the recipient—the husband, his wife—with all the authority he himself possessed. It had the same legal meaning as when Pharaoh handed his ring to Joseph, thereby making him his equal in affairs of state.

Today, the ring has become the universal symbol of wedlock. It indicates to the world the reality of belonging, as voiced in Solomon's hymn on love: "My beloved is mine and I am his." The ring is the seal of the bond which unites man and wife.

The circlet is meant to remind the couple of the harmony which must fill their lives and the perfection of living to which they must aspire. Their loyalty and affection must be as unending as the lines of the ring.

> Wear me as a seal close to your heart,
>   Wear me like a ring upon your hand;
> For love is strong as death itself,
>   And passion masters like the grave,
> Its flashes burn like flame,
>   True lightning flashes.
>
> No floods can ever quench this love,
>   No rivers drown it.
> If a man offered all he has for love,
>   He would be laughed aside.
>   —Song of Songs, VIII, 6-7

The Ketubah

The ketubah is the official Jewish marriage certificate. The literal meaning of the word is simply "written." Its language is Aramaic, the vernacular of Babylonian days. The origin of the ketubah goes back to biblical days, the oldest copy in existence being on a papyrus of the fifth century B.C.E. For many years it was the only documentary evidence of a Jewish marriage, but its purpose far exceeded that of a mere certificate. It impressed on the husband his obligation lovingly to care for his wife: "I will work for you, honour you and maintain you in the manner of Jewish men, who work for their wives, honour them, nourish them and provide for them in truth."

The ketubah formed the legal security for the wife in the case of divorce or widowhood, guaranteeing her maintenance in either event: "I will take all the responsibility . . . both for myself and my heirs . . . it shall be paid out of the best and finest of my property . . . even the cloak upon my shoulders shall be security and a pledge that your ketubah shall be paid to you during my life and after my death, from this day forth to all eternity."

The rabbis catalogued a whole series of offenses by which the wife forfeited the money guaranteed. They make interesting reading today. She lost her security if she gave her husband non-kasher food to eat or walked across the street "indecently," namely, with her hair uncovered. Flirtations with strangers, or refusal to join her husband when moving to another place within the same country or to the Holy Land, were further reasons which made a ketubah invalid.

The Jewish artistic genius soon learned to adorn this legal document with exquisitely executed decorations. No Jewish art collection is without specimens of beautifully illuminated ketubahs. Their calligraphy and ornamentation present Jewish craftsmanship at its best. A decorated frame often surrounds the text with biblical scenes, the twelve signs of the zodiac, or even pictures of the bride and bridegroom.

The Cup of Wine

In Jewish faith, wine is the symbol of joy, of that elation of spirit which trusts in the goodness and truth of life. Whenever the Jew lifts the cup of wine, he demonstrates with a visible sign his glad certainty that a great moment of joy has come.

To be permanent and real, joy must be dedicated. With happiness we can sanctify our life. The beauty of holiness enters our finite being. That is why the Jew, in his hour of exaltation, fills a goblet with wine to bless God, the giver and sustainer of happiness. Thus, no longer a temporary focus of excitement, fugitive and evanescent, joy opens up vistas of omnipotence. It is "the eternal, not ourselves, which makes for happiness."

Life can offer no greater joy than when man and woman, having found each other, go forward to unite their lives. Such joy especially needs dedication, a lifting up out of the immediate and finite to the lasting and infinite. The benediction over the wine expresses this consecrated joy. It is the sign which points toward God. With it we pronounce our spiritual earnestness, the inner presence of our soul.

Another most significant message is given with the "Seven Benedictions." By drinking out of the same cup, both bridegroom and bride symbolize their union:

Whilst we pray that God may send you nought but happiness, we are not unmindful that in the cup of life joys and sorrows are commingled. Even as your love will enhance the sweetness of joys, so will its helpfulness lighten the burden of sorrows. All comes from God, and He has inspired you with mutual love, that you may help one another and that you may share all things, even as you share this cup of wine.

Only husband and wife together, united for life, sharing all things, bring the spirit of holiness into their home.

The Breaking of the Glass

At the close of the wedding ceremony the newlywed husband breaks a glass. Numerous explanations and rationalizations have been given for this "grand finale," of which the most modern—and cynical—is that it is the last chance for the husband to put his foot down.

Modern times have given the custom a psychological interpretation, leading us into the dark recesses of the human mind and even introducing Freud into the Jewish wedding ceremony. At the moment of our greatest joy, we are afraid that something might happen to mar it. Evil and jealous forces might try to harm us. A sacrifice to them might ward off the evil. Before the knowledge of psychoanalysis we might have called the breaking of the glass a true superstition. Now it belongs to the "psychopathology of everyday life." Through it we try to forestall any possible misfortune. We "sacrifice" this glass to avert greater misfortune. It must be remembered that in former times glass was a rare and precious object, and its breaking really meant a loss.

Apart from possible psychological aspects, beautiful symbolism renders the breaking of the glass a significant act. With this glass husband and wife consecrate their marriage. It should never be used for any other, especially baser, purposes. To ensure this, the bridegroom breaks it.

Personal joy must not deaden awareness of the trials and tribulations of the people of Israel. When happiness has entered his own personal life, the Jew, always possessed by a social conscience, must not be blinded to the fate of the less fortunate or forget the Jewish people's calamity. Thus, as a reminder and a spur to compassion, the glass is broken. It speaks of the destruction of the ancient Temple in Jerusalem and the vanished glory of the ancient Jewish State. But especially it leads our thoughts to those of our brethren who have lost their way in the world. At the moment of our joy, we are most apt to open our soul in sympathy and charity.

In man's mind, opposites are easily associated. When he speaks of one idea, its contrasting thought immediately arises. Black pictures up white; high, low; and day, the night. Similarly, the breaking of the glass reminds us of the unbreakable bond of wedlock. Man and wife feel that they are bound together. Much may change and pass, but their love will remain, and "aught but death part you and me."

Finally, the custom is a timely warning. The Egyptians introduced a mummy at their feasts to remind the host of his mortality. A Roman emperor, when driving through the streets of the capital to receive the homage of his subjects, had a skeleton placed next to him. "Remember that you are mortal," was the implicit message. "So do not get too proud or too lazy, as your might and joy are not everlasting." Such a message also is conveyed by the breaking of the glass. A damper on the wedding day's festivity, it is designed to prevent an exuberance of hilarity.

Light has its shadow, and happiness its anxieties. Man's love must be prepared to accept both the joys and the sorrows of life. It must see the difference between ephemeral joys, breakable like thin glass, and perpetual happiness, which nothing can ever destroy. Such richness of symbolism is found in that simple and only too often misunderstood custom of breaking the glass.

Mazel Tov

When the sound of the breaking glass is heard and all present call out *Mazel tov,* few are aware that this ancient Jewish wish reflects an obsolete belief in astrology. *Mazel* was the Hebrew term for a constellation. People wished the newlyweds a "good (*tov*) constellation," auguring happy things to come. We do not now believe that stars decide our fate, and *mazel* has become synonymous with luck. Yet still we can wish the couple wholeheartedly that the place, the hour, and especially the bride and bridegroom may be a combination of factors and persons auguring an abundance of happiness and fullness of joy.

To achieve true happiness in our lives, we have to complete a twofold mission. First, we must reach our aim, and then we must learn to appreciate and enjoy it. This is the more difficult task, and many fail in it. Reaching their goal, they forget its significance. To get married is not sufficient. To keep that bond holy, to renew its harmony and love, is the second and more difficult and important aim. The way of achievement is shown by the marriage customs of the Jewish faith.

Jewish tradition has always extolled the blessing of parenthood; yet Judaism does not forbid birth control and the use of the "pill" if, after careful deliberation, economic, social, or medical circumstances justify it. Orthodoxy, however, feels that contraception can be sanctioned by Jewish law only if rabbinical judgment has confirmed its necessity in each individual case. In 1930, the Central Conference of American [Reform] Rabbis adopted a resolution demanding an intelligent birth regulation on the part of parents, to be practiced with a proper sense of moral responsibility.

Abortion is permissible to save a mother's life or health. Her importance to husband and family must be given priority over the life of an unborn child.

It is interesting to note that Jewish authorities debated possibilities of accidental artificial insemination more than seventeen hundred years ago. Certainly, what they considered as such does not stand up to modern scientific knowledge. Opinions on artificial insemination differ greatly, from complete rejection to cautious approval. Orthodoxy condemns it as being against the Jewish law, while Reform, fully aware of its being liable to abuse and complications, advises great caution.

Complex indeed are some of the problems raised, with their many legal, moral, and psychological implications, and little wonder that there is still such lack of unanimity. Nevertheless, all Jewish sections share a common concern to ensure the preservation of the dignity of man and the sanctity of wedlock.

Chapter 27

MOURNING

Man is confronted with the certainty of death. No one can escape it: "For we are strangers before Thee and sojourners, as all our fathers were: our days on the earth are as a shadow, and there is no abiding." The rabbis, adopting this biblical simile, added: "Would that life were like the shadow cast by a wall or a tree. But it is like the shadow of a bird in flight."

Yet to fear death is wrong. Judaism believes in the immortality of the soul. Death is not the ending, but merely the limit of human vision, life as far as man can see it. Death is not the closing of a door, but the opening of a gate to a brighter and fuller existence, the spirit's return to Him Who gave its heavenly spark. The journey done, the summit attained, the barrier falls, and man becomes one with God's love. The body is only a temporary abode for the immortal spirit, something to be used and then discarded, as the butterfly discards the chrysalis.

In everyday language we wrongly speak of the dead as "gone" and "lost." But "only in the eyes of the unwise they seem to have died. . . . They are in peace, and their hope full of immortality."

The sages of the Talmud felt, therefore, that this homecoming should not be cause for grief, but almost for rejoicing. In a parable they contrasted the sailing of a ship, which was given a boisterous send-off by jubilant masses of people, with a boat entering harbor in quiet dignity, with no band playing and no crowds cheering: "You should not rejoice over the ship that has set out as nobody knows what lies ahead of it, what rough seas and storms it may encounter; but when the ship reaches its harbour all should be joyfully grateful that it arrived in safety."

The shortness of life and the inevitability of death should not depress us, but urge us on to ennoble our existence so that when the short span of earthly life is ended we will not have lived in vain. That is why the psalmist asked God to "teach us to number our days" and the *Ethics of the Fathers* reflected that "the day is short and the work is great . . . and the Master of the house is urgent" and that, though it was not man's duty to complete the work, he was not free to desist from it or to shirk his responsibility.

What matters in life, just as in a play, is not how long, but how good it is. The Yiddish poet Abraham Reisen thus uttered in supreme simplicity the wish, not for length of days, but fulness of life, as a shining example, pointing the way!

> Burn out, my life, burn quick,
> Not much is left now of the wick.
> Let there be light on my last day,
> To point the way.
> Don't flicker, life, burn clear,
> Then like a spring-thought disappear.
> I hate to stint! Life blaze away!
> Let me have light at least one day!

An Aid to Self-Expression

When death takes from us someone dear and near, our sense of loss may be overwhelming. It is therefore a psychological necessity to give vent to our feeling of sorrow and distress. Unless we voice our anguish, it may break our body and cloud our mind. But, as in every emotion which is anchored deep down in the heart, we may experience great difficulty in ourselves finding the precise and apposite expression. The most eloquent mind, when confronted by the dire reality of death, may be at a loss for words. That is why, through the wisdom of the ages, religion has developed its own mourning customs. They are the special idiom for the valley of the shadow of death. They are meant to help in the articulation of grief. Growing and maturing through the centuries, they have become the most adequate language to give voice to the inexpressible.

A Help Toward Healing

A wounded soul needs special care for its healing. The rough world outside, with its unconcern and unceasing activity, has become too harsh and too impersonal. The mourning customs thus come to help. They envelop the home of the bereaved with a special atmosphere, soothing the pain and healing the hurt. Not an end in themselves, the customs serve as a buttress against the world without and create a feeling of calm dignity and solace.

A Lead Back to Life

Sorrow can become a poison. It may develop within us a state of mind which paralyzes. Instead of looking forward into the future (as we are intended to do), we may become fettered to the past. Our sorrow may find no ending and lead the distraught soul farther into despondency and world denial: "When we hold sorrow and hug it to our hearts, life will be undone." Here it is that mourning customs fulfill yet another purpose by canalizing grief and limiting it. To exceed them would be blasphemous religiously and fatal humanly. That is why even for a Moses the Israelites were permitted to sorrow only for a limited time, and the rabbis ordained definite periods and stages of mourning—the week of sitting shivah; the "thirty" days of sorrow; the eleven months of kaddish—each one leading into the other and slowly returning man from the solitude of his grief to his duty among men.

A Guide to God

Grief is a religious test. Sorrow may embitter us. In shortsightedness we may turn away from God. With the psalmist we may cry, "My God, my God, why have You forsaken me?" and then lose faith. Thus, in the hour of greatest trial, when we are tempted to flee God, our mourning customs show us the way back toward the Divine. They sanctify our grief and raise us up out of the slough of despond. In humility, we submit to God's inscrutable will. Solomon ibn Gabirol, poet of the golden age of Spanish Jewry, expressed this truth in undying words:

> When all without is dark
> And former friends misprise,
> From them I turn to Thee
> And find love in Thine eyes.
>
> When all within is dark
> And I my soul despise,
> From me I turn to Thee
> And find love in Thine eyes.
>
> When all Thy face is dark
> And Thy just angers rise,
> From Thee I turn to Thee
> And find love in Thine eyes.

Thus Jewish mourning customs serve not only to honor the dead but equally to help the living sustain their grief and renew their faith. Developed through the centuries and in many diverse countries, they were not always the result of ecclesiastical regulations, but often grew out of the soul of the people. They accompany every phase of bereavement, from the moment of greatest anguish, when the dying Jew in his last confession voices the proclamation of Jewish faith—the Sh'ma—to the days of reverent memory, fixed to recur once every year.

The Jew's Last Words

Jewish teaching requires man always to be ready to depart this life. "Repent one day before your death," counseled the rabbis. When their pupils queried this (obviously no one knew when that moment would come), they were informed that that was the very reason to be prepared at all times. Such an attitude of mind gives urgency to every task and value to every hour. It impels man never to put off his duty lest it be too late.

When the hour of death has come, it is the wish of every Jew to die conscious of God's eternal love. That is why his last words proclaim God's unity, which gives peace to all His creation and embraces all men. And if the dying person himself can no longer utter this confession of faith, he who is nearest and dearest to him does so in his presence and on his behalf. At the moment of most personal anguish the Jew is thus lifted up, dying and living alike, to "the Lord Who is our God."

On hearing of the death of a relative or friend, the Jew submits to God's will in a special prayer, and though he may be stunned by the loss, he yet acknowledges the justice of His decision. He says: "Blessed art Thou, O Lord our God, King of the universe, the true Judge."

The Covering of the Mirror

An ancient custom causes some people to cover all mirrors in their home as soon as the loved one has passed away. This is regarded as a sign of reverence. When all is dark, no reflection of light should enter the house. We should be spared the shock of seeing our faces lined with grief and anguish. Most of all, vanity must be excluded. When the spiritual aspect of life is nearest to the heart, we must not be detracted by the mere physical aspect. The invisible now has become so much more important than that which is to be seen. Thus, the mirror is covered. The inner light, the spiritual side of life, and not physical features and reflections, should be the sole concern. We do not want to see ourselves. We must concentrate on the infinite.

In the far distant past the covering of the mirror expressed superstitious fear. People were afraid that if the disembodied spirit chanced to see its reflection in the glass, it would never leave the house, but haunt it forever. Covering the mirror was not merely a selfish precaution but also an act of consideration for the soul of the departed, which, if it remained to haunt its former home, would be deprived of eternal peace and rest. To remove both dangers, all mirrors were covered.

The Holy Brotherhood

The body is never left alone. Originally, this was a precautionary measure against any possible defilement. Now, it is a sign of reverence. And if a near relative is unable to stay, special "watchers" consider it a privilege and a sacred duty to do so.

Traditionally it was "the holy brotherhood" (or, as it is known by its Aramaic name, the *Chevra Kadisha*) which arranged the funeral. Such a society existed in every Jewish community, and almost paradoxically its creation has often been the very first sign of Jewish life.

No description could be more beautiful and apt than its name. Members of the brotherhood were the most pious of the community, who knew that to pay the last respect to the dead was one of the great religious duties of man. They did so not in mere words or gestures but by actually preparing the body for the last rest, washing and clothing it. They gave their services readily to every Jew as though he were a brother, because in death all are akin, and no one is a stranger.

In modern days, even the Chevra (where it continues to exist) has often become an organization of paid officials, doing their task efficiently though impersonally. It retains the ancient name, but it has lost its meaning and message.

The Funeral

Complete simplicity and equality distinguish Jewish burial. All men and women are clad in the same kind of white linen garb, the pious Jew having worn part of it previously each year on Passover night and the Day of Atonement, reminding him of his last hour. Men are also wrapped in their own personal tallit (praying-shawl).

The coffin itself must be of the simplest kind, unvarnished and unadorned. In no circumstances is it permitted to differentiate between the rich and the poor, the "famous" and the "ordinary." Before the coffin is closed, and in front of the dead, the traditional Jew makes a tear in his clothes as a symbol of the rent suffered in his heart, which can never wholly heal again. This custom is called "the cutting of *k'riah.*" It goes back to most ancient times and really is a survival of the custom, frequently mentioned in the Bible, of rending the garment as a sign of grief. King David and Job did so when hearing of the death of their sons. When Reuben thought that his brother Joseph had been killed, he, too, "rent his clothes."

Traditional Judaism developed a whole scale of "tearing" according to the family relationship of the deceased and his general status. The tear must amount to no less than four inches (one handbreadth), be lengthwise and not crosswise, in the cloth of the garment and not at its seams, and be made, if possible, while standing at the open coffin. In the case of parents, all the clothes over the heart have to be rent. Relatives are required to rend only the outer garment.

The prophets of old already realized the danger that mourning might spend itself in mere outward signs. Joel thus admonished the people: "Rend your heart and not your garment." Yet there is deep symbolism in the custom of k'riah.

The interval between death and funeral varies from country to country and is dependent on local custom, climatic conditions, and, in some cases, state legislation. While in the Orient, for obvious reasons, speedy burial is the rule, on the continent of Europe it may not take place earlier than the third day after death. During this time even the most observant Jew is free from the fulfillment of all religious obligation.

Mainly because of their belief in bodily resurrection, Orthodox Jews do not approve of cremation, but insist on burial. Though the Bible itself contains, almost conspicuously, no definite regulation regarding the disposal of the body, the rabbis of the Talmud considered burial as one of the 613 commandments of the Torah and therefore as a religious duty. Yet as early as the thirteenth century, other rabbinical authorities declared that this insistence on burial was only a custom, and not a law. Indeed, they said, an early Midrash related that Isaac requested his father to bring his ashes to his mother Sarah. Reform Judaism, not sharing the Orthodox view on the resurrection of the body, permits cremation and leaves the choice to the family concerned.

At the burial service, the Jew, in devout submission, once again acknowledges God as the true Judge, in Whose hands are all the spirits, Who kills and makes alive and is righteous in all

His doings. A special supplication calling on God's love and mercy prays for perfect rest for the soul of the departed, that it may find shelter forever "under the cover of Thy wings."

When the coffin has been lowered, all present, preceded by the nearest relatives, cast three handfuls of earth into the grave as a last act of piety and respect.

When the grave is filled, the mourner for the first time says the kaddish, the "prayer for the dead," which he will continue to recite daily for eleven months. No other prayer equals it in depth of feeling and strength of faith. It makes no single mention of or reference to death, but every line glorifies God and prays for His kingdom and His peace. In the very hour of grief the Jew thus testifies to his faith. Thinking of his beloved, his heart heavy, he praises God: "Magnified and sanctified be His great name."

It is easy to be "religious" when everything goes well. But man's faith is tested only in the hour of anxiety. To believe in God at the moment of distress and loss, to be able at such a time to say, "Blessed be the true Judge"—this alone is faith, built on a rock!

The kaddish leads man's vision away from self-centered personal grief to higher Reality. Instead of pondering all the time on his own loss in friendship and companionship, it makes him think of the other aspect of death and of what the beloved has gained. *"Ose shalom bimromav* . . . May He Who maketh peace in His high places make peace for us and for all Israel."

The Jew may not always understand its Aramaic wording, but instinctively he feels the inner meaning of the kaddish. It is the Jewish answer to fate. Often the only bond uniting him to his religion, it is the supreme expression of sacred piety, of the loving remembrance of his departed, and of his submission to God's inscrutable will. Through it he echoes Job's great act of faith when this great sufferer, in his loss, still praised God: "The Lord gave and the Lord hath taken away; blessed be the name of the Lord."

Kaddish means "sanctification." Bereavement can hallow our lives and make us dedicate ourselves anew to the service of God.

Shivah

Returned from the funeral, the bereaved (if he follows Orthodox tradition) starts at once to "sit shivah." *Shivah* is the Hebrew for "seven" and indicates the seven days of deepest mourning, starting from the day of the burial, during which time the mourner stays at home (except on the Sabbath) and totally abstains from work and affairs of business. He sits on a low stool as a symbol of his lowliness of spirit. He restricts his reading to comforting religious sources, and friends visit him throughout the week to express their sympathy. They do so with the traditional formula, "I wish you long life," meaning God has chosen to call away your beloved, but may He in His mercy grant you the gift of life. A special Mitzvah, or act of kindness, is to prepare for the mourner his first meal after the funeral, and custom decrees that it include a dish of eggs as a symbol of immortality.

Every morning and night friends assemble at the bereaved's home to join in prayer in honor of the deceased. As this is considered "public worship," the necessary number of ten male adults is required, making up the religious quorum, and this service is actually called a minyan.

We have been shaken to the very depth of our being; darkness envelops us. We ask "Why?" and there appears to be no answer. Like a ship without anchor or compass, we seem to be tossed about on the surging seas of grief and anguish. The shivah is the sheltering bay. After the storm, calm; after the turmoil, the still small voice.

During the seven days the bereaved are meant, while recollecting the beauty of the life of their departed, to regain composure. They must find in God's words soothing balm for their wounds.

The shivah also gives them an opportunity to control their grief. It commands consecrated expression of their loss, yet also demands its termination. After seven days their deepest mourning ends, and they must return, gradually, yet inevitably, to the world of activity. That is why they are led from the cemetery straight to the seclusion of their home—for seven days and for seven days only; and then they must again meet the struggle of life.

Shivah is the eloquent expression of the psychological insight of the rabbis. It is a time of complete inaction. The stress and strain of loss can thus be eased, tension relaxed; exhausted nerves are refreshed and renewed by quiet and calm.

Shivah emphasizes family reunion and solidarity. Relatives, often separated by forgetfulness, find one another again. "The family is one of nature's masterpieces." Too often we ignore this. Yet from the family comes our strength. The gap torn in our ranks by the recent bereavement restores us from the superficialities of a busy life to the reality of the family. Our loss makes us close our ranks. The departure of our beloved to the eternal home urges us to renew our family home, and at least during the seven days the family is reconstituted and reunited.

Perhaps one of the least desirable effects of our epoch of mechanization and urbanization, with its worship of speed, is that it leaves us too little time to think. We rush about busily, talk more than listen, look instead of seeing, chatter instead of thinking. But when the shadow of death has descended on one's home, the shivah provides the mourner with seven days of quiet thought. He stops to think, to consider, and to recollect the life of his loved one. The shivah thus offers one of the few opportunities in life for reflection and thought.

The Year of Mourning

When the shivah is ended, the mourner returns to everyday life, but for twelve months still shuns any joyful gathering.

The wearing of black during this year of mourning was originally not a Jewish custom and was even prohibited in some communities. The tear in the garment, and not its color, was the symbol of grief to the Jew. Later, however, he adopted the custom of his environment and soon found in it deep wisdom and symbolism. To him, the color of mourning was a perpetual reminder of the loss he had suffered. To the people he met, it indicated the state of his soul, making them considerate and reminding them to refrain from anything that might hurt or offend him in his grief. The dark color not only reflected the sorrow of his heart but created inward tranquillity and serenity.

If in modern times both Jew and Gentile alike have again discarded this custom, it reveals a sincere disinclination to publicize grief and the conviction that he truly mourns the dead who lives as they would have desired. Perhaps this is for the better, as the very origin of mourning clothes was not piety but superstition, not respect for but dread of the dead. The clothes were used as a disguise so that the spirit of the deceased might not recognize and haunt the bereaved. The very same purpose, it is thought, applied to the mark of Cain, which was put on him after his brother's death lest he be recognized by his victim's spirit.

The Tombstone

When the year of mourning has ended, the Jew sets the tombstone on the grave of his beloved, well aware that this monument of stone is but a symbol, a token of respect and love. Its inscription contains the name of the departed, in both English and Hebrew, and the date of death according to the common and the Jewish calendars. An appropriate scriptural verse may be added, but the last line on Jewish tombstones comprises the five initial letters of the Hebrew petition that the soul of the departed may be bound up in the bond of eternal life.*

Memory is a matter of the living, not of dead stone. Unless the record of one's life is indelibly inscribed in the minds and woven into the hearts of those we leave behind, it is not worth preserving. In the latter case, the most eulogistic inscription on the most superb monument is futile. The memory of the worthy should be preserved not by dead lettering on cold stone, but by living thought in man's warm heart.

Nevertheless, a monument can convey much more than a mere record. The *matsevah,* as the Jew calls it, can abound in meaning. When the Jews were expelled from Spain in 1492, they were naturally unable to carry much, and many of them chose to take as their most highly treasured possessions the tomb-

* תנצב״ה

stones of their beloved. They acted not in an empty gesture, but with fullness of feeling. They went forth not knowing whither, but imbued with faith. Outwardly broken, they remained immense in passion, pulse, and power. The heavy stone on their bent backs lifted them up. It was symbolic of lasting memory and imperishable piety. Out of the past comes our strength for the future.

Perhaps nothing showed more clearly the deranged mind of the Nazi than when his hordes, unsatisfied with the torture of the innocent and unsated by the blood of their victims, tried to injure even the dead. The desecration of tombstones in Jewish cemeteries is a unique phenomenon of neurosis and psychopathology. Instinctively, unconsciously, the Nazi sensed the mystery of Jewish survival—expressed by the tombstone. Only a people proud of its past is worthy of its future. Those silent tombstones spoke of it. The Jew binds his life with innumerable "ties of love." That is his anchor.

> And thus for ever with reverted look
> The mystic volume of the world they read,
> Spelling it backward, like a Hebrew book,
> Till life became a legend of the Dead.

Our piety for the past guarantees our future. The tombstone is a memorial of that love which abides. Jewish family life has always been the focus of our existence, the axis around which our life has turned. The tombstone, set up by loving children, is its outward expression. Only by preserving the bond from generation to generation can we live nobly and worthily.

We must demonstrate by our lives that we are worthy of our ancestors. Thus, the tombstone stands as a perpetual reminder, immovable, unchangeable: "Look unto the rock whence ye were hewn and the quarry wherefrom you were dug."

Years may pass; wind and weather may even wash away many a letter or whole inscriptions; yet the tombstone's message stands fast. It speaks of heritage and responsibility, piety and remembrance, the chain of generations and the strength of tradition. They are all expressed by the simple stone the Jew erects on the grave of his dearly beloved whom God has called hence. It not only honors the dead but ennobles the living.

The Yahrzeit

The consecration of the stone does not complete Jewish mourning, which in reality never ends, but is renewed perpetually in yet another unique institution of the Jewish faith.

Every year the Jew commemorates the anniversary of the death of his beloved. It is called *Yahrzeit* ("season")—derived from the German—and is a day of earnest reflection and devout prayer.

The custom of Yahrzeit was never commanded in Jewish law. It is not mentioned at all in Bible or Talmud and is unknown even in the *Shulchan Aruch*. It originated in Germany at the beginning of the fifteenth century and spread from there all over the world. What the law left free, piety sanctified, and Yahrzeit has become one of the most widely observed Jewish customs.

On the Yahrzeit the Jew shuns any amusement. He goes to the synagogue and joins there with all other mourners in the recital of the kaddish. He distributes charity among the needy and visits the grave of his beloved. The pious also fast. In his home, he keeps burning for twenty-four hours the Yahrzeit light (a candle, an oil lamp, or even an electric light with a filament in the shape of the Star of David). This is regarded as the symbol of the soul, an expression of undying love, and a beacon to guide us.

Man's soul has been likened to a light: "The spirit of man is the lamp of the Lord" (Prov. XX, 27). The fluttering Yahrzeit candle reminds us that although our dear ones have passed beyond the limit of our vision, their light still shines, their soul is immortal. It is a spark of the never-dying flame of the Divine.

Just as on every anniversary, to the very end of our lives, we kindle the Yahrzeit lamp anew each year, so we affirm our never-ceasing love and affection. Years may pass, but the memory of our parents must never diminish. Distance of time must not lessen in our hearts the flame they kindled. Scripture equated the honoring of parents to the honoring of God. No more divine spirit could dwell anywhere than in the truly Jewish home. Each year, therefore, the renewed lighting of the Yahrzeit lamp wants us, who might have strayed, to turn again toward them and through them toward God.

"In the dark a glimmering light often suffices for the pilot to find the Pole Star and set his course." Every year when we light the Yahrzeit lamp we feel we are in the presence of our beloved parents. We renew our effort and rededicate our will to follow the paths they have shown us. Like a beacon, their light must point our way. We must follow it, be worthy of our parents, and live up to their highest expectations.

The Yahrzeit thus annually renews and never lets fade the memory of the departed whose spirits dwell with God: "And they that be wise shall shine as the brightness of the firmament; and they that turn many to righteousness as the stars for ever."

Jewish mourning customs thus render even death an inspiration and a force for good. "Grief is the agony of an instant: the indulgence of grief the blunder of a life." Life must go on. It is our religious duty to honor in piety our departed, but then to take up the daily round again, undismayed and courageously. Bearing calamity, we must become masters of our sorrow.

The study of Jewish mourning customs not only throws light into the dark recesses of emotion but reveals a most potent force within the mind. They change intense anxiety into calm confidence. Giving healing to wounded hearts, they lead man back to his life and his obligations. When speaking of our loved ones who have passed away, Jewish tradition makes us add the ancient words *Zichronam liv'rachah* (May their memory be a blessing). That truly is the highest meaning and finest purpose of our mourning customs.

Chapter 28

THE SEVEN-BRANCHED CANDLESTICK

Israel said before God: "Lord of the Universe,
Thou commandest us to illumine before Thee.
Art Thou not Light of the World, and with
Whom light dwelleth?"—"Not that I require
your light," was the Divine reply, "but that you
may perpetuate the light which I conferred on
you as an example to the nations of the world!"
—Talmud

The seven-branched candlestick—the Menorah—has been a symbol of Judaism for thousands of years, ever since it was first made in the desert of Sinai. It adorned the Tent of Meeting and then formed an indispensable part of both Temples. It was always placed in the Sanctuary, facing the entrance to the Holy of Holies. But even when the actual candlestick became lost, its emblem remained with the Jewish people in every age as a powerful symbol. This is shown by numerous finds dating back to antiquity.

It was found embossed on coins struck in the pre-Christian era. As an emblem it was discovered in the Jewish catacombs of Rome and in the third-century Palestinian synagogue at Dura Europos. Its motif recurred in private homes and public buildings, on ancient clay oil lamps, tombstones, and sarcophagi. The Menorah was featured in floor mosaics and murals, chiseled in relief on ornamental pillars, capitals, and lintels. Old stone Menorahs have even been unearthed by the spade of the excavator. Moreover, out of the Temple's seven-branched candlestick developed the synagogue's perpetual light (which was adopted also in many churches) and the modern form of the eight-branched Chanukah candelabrum. Finally, when the newborn State of Israel had to choose an emblem, it could find no finer symbol than the ancient Menorah, which spoke of spiritual conquest and the undying and irresistible force of light.

Actually, there has not been just one single Menorah. We know of at least thirteen, treasured by the Jewish people from Moses' time to the destruction of the second Temple. Their shape, material, and even placement differed in the Tent of Meeting, King Solomon's Temple, and—at least three times—in the second Sanctuary. Accordingly, the Menorah is variously described in biblical, talmudic, and historical literature and differs again in some detail in the only replica in existence, found on the Arch of Titus in Rome.

The candlestick is first mentioned in the book of Exodus, where its shape is given in detail, though without measurements. The Bible relates that God revealed its pattern to Moses on Mount Sinai. Later tradition had it that the verbal description was too complicated for Moses to grasp fully and that God therefore showed him, in a vision, an actual model, formed of fire.

Moses then instructed Bezalel, Israel's most skilled workman and the principal artist in the building of the Tent of Meeting, to construct the candlestick itself. It was to be placed there as a symbol of God's presence within the congregation of Israel.

The Menorah was a masterpiece of beauty and craftsmanship. It was not of separate parts welded together, nor was it cast in a mold. It was hammered out of one solid piece of gold which weighed almost 100 pounds (one talent). From a pedestal rose the central shaft, from which spread three pairs of branches, each pair a semicircle, curving outward and upward till they reached the same height as that of the central stem. Bosses in the shape of almond flowers decorated the candlestick. They were spaced out at regular intervals: three on each branch and four on the central stem.

The thoughtful student of religious tradition may wonder how the candelabrum received its peculiar shape, knowing that nothing in life is without its reason and that there is especially deep meaning in the choice of religious symbols. That the Menorah resembled a tree was not chance nor the result of an artist's fancy. It has been pointed out that there was a striking similarity between the candlestick and a Palestinian plant, distinguished by leafless upturned branches. However, far more significant than this natural explanation, it is now believed that the Menorah originally represented the tree of life, a religious concept widely spread among many ancient peoples and found in Babylonian myth, Zoroastrian faith, Hindu belief, and Greek legend. An Oriental tradition regarded this tree as the symbol of fruitfulness.

In Jewish writings the tree of life appears first in the story of Paradise. It became the symbolic expression of joy, inspiration, and vitalizing force and was identified with God's teaching. That is why the two wooden rollers, on which is wound the Scroll containing the record of God's sacred Law, the Torah, are still called "the tree of life."

Thus, even without lights the Menorah in itself contains supreme meaning, a message of God's life-giving force and of the divine foundation of all existence. That the symbolic representation of the celestial tree was placed in the Jews' Sanctuary was meant to convey the fundamental conviction that only a religious basis assures fullness of life and gives lasting security.

The addition of seven lamps gave the Menorah an even deeper significance. They were never meant to serve as an illumination of the dark Sanctuary. This is obvious from the very way the candlestick was placed and, even more so, from its restriction to seven lights, of which only one was kept burning during the day in spite of the fact that the Temple had no actual windows. The lamps of the Menorah were symbolic. Their presence proclaimed a manifold message of light, not only to the Jewish people but to all men.

Light was God's prime work in creation; and man, formed in the divine image, was meant to dispel darkness. A symbol of learning, understanding, and reason, the Menorah's lamps spoke of enlightenment. Knowledge was not to be restricted to a small, selected class of people, to esoteric circles or coteries, but must be made the property of all. Light also expressed joy and gladness. A mood of gloom contradicted true faith and impeded effective worship. Most of all, light was the emblem of spiritual illumination. Only a life that was inspired by the Divine could fulfill its meaning. Individuals as well as nations had to learn that decisive and permanent victories were not gained by material strength or military prowess, but only by God's spirit, Whose teachings should be "a lamp unto my feet, and a light unto my path" (Ps. CXIX, 105). In all those many ways the Jews were meant to be "a light to the nations."

Equally rich in symbolism is the actual number of lamps. Seven was the ancient figure signifying completeness. Only a life fully dedicated to God and suffused with spiritual light can reach perfection. The six lights which were placed on the branches of the Menorah were seen as a reminder of the six days of creation, while the central light, toward which all the others were turned, was considered the symbol of the Sabbath. This universe is God's work, not a soulless mechanism. Our days must receive their value from and be centered on the Sabbath, God's day of spiritual refreshment.

The seven lamps were interpreted also as representing the planets; and mystic thought explained that just as six of the Menorah's branches metaphorically were lightened from the center, so did the planets get their light from the sun and all life received its essence from God.

Other traditions related the seven lights to the seven patriarchs of mankind—Adam, Noah, Shem, Abraham, Isaac, Jonah, and Job—and thereby taught that only a people that honors its past has a future. The sevenfold light was seen to proclaim the blessing brought to the world by righteous action, and the seven lamps were thus regarded as the seven righteous men: Levi, Amram, Moses, Aaron, Eldad, Medad, and either Hur or the prophet Haggai.

Finally, the seven lights were understood to be a reflection of the seven celestial spheres, showing the emanation of the divine spirit and man's laborious path from the mundane to the spiritual, from crude materialism, stage by stage and step by step, to the realm of the sacred, and there, finally, to a meeting with God, face to face.

The lamps were detachable and placed—one each—on top of every branch and of the central shaft. Though the Bible does not give any definite indication, it is assumed that they were receptacles for oil and contained a wick. Originally probably only open bowls with the wick floating in the oil, they were eventually replaced by cups, shaped like elongated shells with a spout or special groove, out of which the wick protruded. Views differ as to the way the wicks were turned. Some believe that they pointed north and thus illumined the opposite wall of the Sanctuary, where the Table of Shewbread stood, vividly contrasting "bread" and "light," man's material and spiritual needs. On the other hand, there was an opinion that the wicks of the six branches faced the central lamp, three from either side, so that the light seemed focused, significantly expressing the one source of all light.

In front of the Menorah stood a ladder of three steps. In Bezalel's Tabernacle it was of acacia wood, but in King Solomon's Temple it was of marble. The priest ascended it when renewing the oil and trimming or lighting the wicks. On its second step were kept the tongs (used to draw out the wicks), the dishes used as receptacles for burnt wicks, and the cruses of oil.

The oil had to be of the finest quality, and its preparation, taking a whole week, was considered a sacred task. Olives were gently crushed in a mortar and the collected oil kept in special jars, each holding sufficient to last one night. Once prepared for the Menorah, the oil could never be used for profane purposes or come into contact with the undedicated.

The priests cleaned and refilled the lamps every morning. The lights on the six branches were relit in the evening and kept burning throughout the night. The central light was never extinguished, but served to kindle the other lamps. It was called "the western lamp," a name easily understood if it is assumed that the Menorah was positioned with the line of lamps pointing from east to south. Then, with all the other wicks turned toward it, the central light alone shone toward the west. Tradition ascribed to it miraculous qualities. Its receptacle did not contain more oil than any of the other cups, which was enough to last the longest night of the winter; yet it continued to burn throughout the day to the following evening without being refilled. Only at the death of Simon the Just, the notable high priest and the last of the men of the Great Synagogue, it is said, did the miracle cease. This happened forty years before the Temple's final destruction and soon was considered a grave omen.

According to other traditions it was not this one lamp alone, but two (according to the Mishna), or even three (as related in the writings of Josephus), that burned through the twenty-four hours of day and night. The everlasting light was a striking symbol not only of uninterrupted worship but of the ever-present God Who neither slept nor slumbered and of the Jews' unceasing duty to be torchbearers to mankind.

When King Solomon built the Temple he was not satisfied with just one Menorah. In his passionate desire to outshine all past achievements and to create a sanctuary worthy of God's greatness and magnificence, he had ten golden Menorahs placed in the Temple—five on either side of the entrance leading into the Holy of Holies. With the destruction of the first Temple by Nebuchadrezzar, the Menorahs disappeared. Possibly they were looted and carried away with other spoil to Babylon. Jewish tradition claims that before the final assault on Jerusalem, priests had secretly buried the Menorahs at an undisclosed spot, where they remain hidden to this day.

When, seventy years later, the returned exiles rebuilt the Temple, they once again installed there a single Menorah, which was cast, and not hammered out, as was the first. This was a sign of an impoverished nation and yet perhaps even more so of a matured people who, through the suffering of their exile, had learned that it was not outward splendor, but spiritual strength, that really mattered.

Centuries passed. The Menorah gave out its light as a perpetual reminder of the spirit of Judaism. When Antiochus IV Epiphanes plundered the Temple, endeavoring not only to gather spoil but to extinguish the light of monotheistic faith, he removed and destroyed the seven-branched candelabrum. When they re-dedicated the Sanctuary three years later (in 165 B.C.E.), the Maccabees immediately restored the Menorah, though it is not known in which shape and of what material. It is believed that at first it was made of wood and later was replaced by a silver one. But irrespective of its material value and artistic form, the Menorah's religious significance was greater than ever before, proclaiming the strength of spiritual power. The Maccabean victory had demonstrated to all the world the triumph of divine light over pagan might.

Although no definite historical data are available, it may be assumed that when, more than a hundred years later, King Herod rebuilt the Temple on a scale of grandiose dimensions, trying to outshine even King Solomon's splendor, he had a new and exquisite Menorah made, befitting the glory and luster of God's house. It is the design of this candlestick which is described in the Talmud. Its height was 6 feet (18 handbreadths) and its width across the top of its branches, 3 feet. The branches themselves were 4 inches thick. The Menorah was ornamented with cups, knobs, and flowers, spaced out in definite proportion and elaborately executed. The cups (22 in number) were said to resemble Alexandrian drinking vessels. The knobs (of which there were 11) were spherical and looked like apples or pomegranates, while the flowers (9 altogether) were thought to be replicas of a Galilean species and are sometimes described as lilies. The Menorah's base was triangular, or shaped like a tripod. One foot high, its width equaled that of the candlestick itself: 3 feet. Differing from the talmudic account, the relief on the Arch of Titus shows the base as hexagonal, in the form of two steps.

Once again religious imagination reveled in the symbolic interpretation of all the features of the new Menorah. Fascinating is the use Jewish numerology made of its various measurements and figures. These were related to Holy Scripture itself and seen to refer to the initial verses of each of the Five Books of Moses.

The seven arms of the candelabrum, it was said, corresponded to the seven (Hebrew) words of the sentence which commenced the book of Genesis and therefore the Bible. The first verse of the book of Exodus counts eleven words, equal to the Menorah's eleven knobs. Its nine flowers were seen reflected in the beginning of the book of Leviticus, while its height of 18 handbreadths was paralleled by the eighteen Hebrew words of the first verse of the book of Numbers. Finally, it was pointed out that the number of Hebrew words which open the book of Deuteronomy was identical with the 22 cups of the candlestick.

When Titus destroyed Jerusalem and the Temple went up in flames, he rescued the Menorah. With other sacred objects it was carried to Rome and proudly displayed as one of the chief pieces of booty in his triumphal procession. The Arch which was then erected to perpetuate Rome's victory over Judea, and called after Titus himself, conspicuously showed the seven-branched candelabrum. Strange to relate that this display of an arrogant conqueror has preserved the only detailed and authentic representation of the ancient Menorah. The irony of history willed it that it was from this replica, on a monument specially built to celebrate the annihilation of the Jewish nation, that almost two thousand years later the new State of Israel modeled its national emblem.

After the triumphal march, the spoil from the Holy Land, and with it the Menorah, were deposited in Rome's Temple of Peace. When, a hundred years later, this was burned, it appears that the Menorah was saved. According to a later report, the Vandals, after plundering Rome in 455, took it with them to Carthage in North Africa. But it did not remain there. Once again military conquest decided its destiny. The North African Vandal kingdom fell to the onslaught of King Justinian in his short-lived attempt to restore the glory of the ancient Roman Empire. It is believed that the Menorah was then again looted and taken to Byzantium, the city which was to become Constantinople and today is known as Istanbul, to be treasured in the Emperor's palace. A contemporary historian relates, however, that a Jew saw the sacred vessels and objects and by devious means convinced Justinian that it was sacrilegious to keep the Menorah outside Palestine, for its only rightful place was in the Holy City itself. Whether out of superstition or reverence, it is hard to say, but the Emperor is reported to have ordered the immediate return of the Temple's treasures to Jerusalem, to be kept there in the custody of the Christian community. Thus, 463 years after having been carried away and passed through the world's capitals, Rome, Carthage, and Byzantium, the Menorah was returned to its original home. The wheel had turned full circle.

This is the last we hear of the seven-branched candlestick. In 614 the Persians captured Jerusalem and plundered the Christian holy places, but the Temple's old treasures are no longer mentioned. Were they carried away once again as a conqueror's spoil to an unknown destination, or were they secretly hidden by pious men? Jewish legend claims the latter, a tradition which inspired modern fiction and was responsible for Stefan Zweig's story *The Buried Candelabrum.* Mystery thus envelops its final fate. Perhaps one day archaeologists will unearth the ancient Menorah and thereby prove that the symbol of Jewry's undying light is itself indestructible.

The Eight-Branched Candlestick

As is obvious by its pattern, the present-day eight-branched candlestick, used during the festival of Chanukah, developed from the seven-branched Menorah of the Temple. And yet at first there was no resemblance at all between the two. As they differed in purpose, so they differed in shape. The golden, seven-branched candlestick belonged to the Temple, its worship and symbolism. It was unique and had its place only in the Sanctuary itself. An ancient law distinctly prohibited the copying of it (or any other of the Temple's utensils), whether for ritual purposes or other use. It was feared that copy and original might be confused and that the people no longer would be able to differentiate between the real object and its replica. The Chanukah Menorah, on the other hand, is part of every home and synagogue. It originated in a desire to commemorate the miracle which occurred at the time of the Maccabees. To make the people of every generation remember it, the annual kindling of the Chanukah lights was instituted.

There were two ways to light the Menorah during the eight days of the festival, and each had its advocates. One school of thought felt that on the first night, all eight lamps should be lit and then be reduced in number each successive night by one lamp, till finally, on the eve of the eighth day, one light was left to be kindled. It was an obvious choice, as it fittingly symbolized how the oil of the one cruse became less and less. But then—and this view was finally adopted—the opposite procedure was suggested. As a symbol of the ever-increasing light spreading throughout the world, Chanukah should start with the kindling of one lamp, to be added to nightly till finally an eightfold light should shed its luster.

The form of the Chanukah Menorah also varied from its beginning to modern times. At first, it was a round lamp with the eight flames placed in a circle and the oil fed from the center. A change of style saw the circular arrangement replaced by one line of cups, set along a rail and eventually fixed to it by individual brackets. The row of eight small spoon-shaped or rectangular oil lamps was backed by a panel which, like a sconce, could be suspended from the wall or, by means of little feet, stood on a table. The back panel itself provided a welcome opportunity for pictorial ornamentation, such as clusters of grapes, palm trees, the Ark of the Covenant, the lion of Judah, and the crown of the Torah.

Religious considerations presented specific problems whose solution offered further scope for artistic ingenuity. The Chanukah lamp fulfilled a sacred purpose, and its message was spiritual. Any secular use of the Menorah was therefore excluded. Its lights could be employed neither for kindling each other nor as illumination by which to work or read. At least one other light was therefore needed. This need created the ninth lamp. Sometimes explained as a symbol of the miraculous cruse of oil, its true purpose was to kindle the other lamps and to provide light for the home. Accordingly, it was called "the kindling light" or "the servant" (*shammash* in Hebrew). At first it was a separate lamp. Soon, however, it was attached to the Menorah itself, either above, at the side, or at the center of the panel. There are instances when even two lights were used.

It was only much later that the Chanukah candelabrum assumed its best-known form, modeled after the Temple's seven-branched Menorah, but replacing its three semicircles with four and adding the "kindling light" by means of a special detachable arm projecting at a right angle from the shaft itself.

As the Menorah was needed in every home, there was no end to the variation of its designs. These ranged from the simplest and most utilitarian arrangement of eight used eggshells to the bizarre form of a lion's head with wicks protruding from its mouth; from minute Menorahs for the humblest home to out-size candlesticks for the decoration of public buildings. There were Chanukah lamps which could be placed on the table, fixed to the wall, or suspended from the ceiling. Some burned oil, and others, candles.

Authorities insisted that the Menorah should be a real object of art; that, if not all of it, at least its servant light should be made of precious metal. Every kind of material was used in the making of the candlestick: wood, pewter, brass, copper, silver, and gold. Carvings, reliefs, and miniatures ornamented the candelabrum, its base, shaft, and branches. Their subject matter was symbolic and biblical. The representation of a flame, flower, or animal frequently crowned the central stem, or even the figure of Judith, triumphantly holding a dagger in one hand and Holofernes' head in the other. Her bravery was considered worthy of being remembered on this festival, especially because it was thought that it was during this season that she delivered the Jewish people from their oppressor. Each country and epoch thus added its own style to the making of the Chanukah lamp, in whose shape and ornamentation therefore can be traced, as a subject of intriguing study, the Jews' wandering through the centuries and across the continents.

Whichever shape the Menorah was given, its message remained

the same. It celebrated the rededication of the Temple in 165 B.C.E., but spoke to all ages and people of the light of holy faith which no power on earth can ever subdue and which, like the lights of the Menorah, will grow brighter. Its lamps glowed in the Jewish homes of the ghetto as a beacon of hope and a reminder of God's power, Whose miraculous help is near even in the darkest night. The Chanukah candles were conspicuously displayed in the windows of the free, shining out into the world as a symbol of Jewish faith.

The Perpetual Light

Few people nowadays realize that the perpetual light, burning in every synagogue throughout the world and in many churches, developed out of the ancient Menorah and represents its central, western light. But a wealth of new meaning has been added to the old symbolism.

The synagogue's perpetual light is kept burning primarily in memory of the altar's perpetual fire. It expresses also the Jews' belief in the permanence of Divine Law and the continuous presence of God everywhere on earth. Most of all, however, it speaks of Israel's conviction that, though the ancient Sanctuary lies in ruins, its task has not ended, but is continued by every synagogue as a center of light to spread knowledge and comfort, blessing and peace.

Quite obvious, but nevertheless often unnoticed, is the fact that the symbol of the Menorah is always shown without its lights. This is not an accident and may add yet another significant feature to its manifold meaning. So to speak, the candlestick is there, ready and waiting to be kindled. But its light must be the result of our own effort. We are meant not only to be the keepers of the light of the past but active kindlers of the light for the future. It is up to us to translate a symbolic message into actual deed and make light dispel darkness.

Chapter 29

THE SHIELD OF DAVID

The Shield of David—*Magen David* in Hebrew—is a figure formed of two interlocking equilateral triangles, one of which is inverted. Today, it is universally recognized as a Jewish emblem. Because of its shape it is frequently referred to also as the Star of David. Synagogues display it conspicuously. It is the central symbol on the flag of the State of Israel, and it marks the graves of fallen Jewish soldiers of all nations. In Israel, the Red Cross is represented by the Red Shield of David.

In spite of the emblem's present-day obvious and definite application, deep mystery surrounds its origin and meaning. Before modern times, its use among Jews was rare. Though the Magen David can be seen (next to the swastika!) in the second-century synagogue of Capernaum, none of the medieval synagogues had it. In 1354, King Charles IV instructed the Jews of Prague to display the "seal of David" together with "Solomon's seal" on their flag. Ukrainian Jews used the symbol on their seals in the sixteenth century, and a hundred years later individual congregations made it their crest.

The fact of such isolated instances shows that to begin with, and for many centuries, the two-triangle star was generally not identified as a definitely Jewish symbol. It figured equally as an ancient pagan symbol; Christian communities displayed it in the architecture and ornamentation of their churches and cathedrals; and it appeared on a medieval Moslem flag in Morocco. It could be found in the old town hall of Vienna, as a German boundary mark, and as a Swiss tavern sign.

The emblem's name itself is of comparatively recent origin,

321

documented for the first time only in the fourteenth century. It occurs then in the writings of David ben Judah the Pious.

All this, added to the anxious concern of pious men to invest the mysterious sign with the authority of antiquity, gave rise to much speculation and countless (and at times fantastic) interpretations. The symbol's very obscurity fostered conjecture, and though many of the hypotheses proffered can be discarded, the message they reveal survives.

It was inevitable that by its very description people were led erroneously to associate the Shield of David with King David himself, both as a weapon he used and an expression he coined. The term itself was said to have resulted from his vanity and craving for recognition. Rabbinical tradition had it that one of the principal prayers of Jewish service was already known in David's time. It was the Amida, whose first benediction concluded by praising God as "the Shield of Abraham." The king felt that he should be equally honored, and accordingly he asked God to permit the introduction of yet another benediction in that same prayer, praising Him this time as "the Shield of David." But his request was refused. The king certainly could not be compared in moral stature with the ancestor of the Jewish people. Abraham had passed gloriously all ten tests imposed on him, but David had failed dismally by his sin against Bathsheba. However, to accord him some recognition for his valiant deeds, it was felt that he, too, should be perpetuated in Jewish worship, though not in one of its most sacred prayers. In that way, the rabbis explained, it came to pass that God was praised as "the Shield of David" in one of the benedictions which on every Sabbath and holy day conclude the second lesson, the reading of the prophetic portion—the Haftarah.

On the other hand, it was contended that in his fight against Goliath, David actually employed a shield of the very shape which is now perpetuated in Jewry's symbol. Its special construction seemed well suited to protect both arms and head. But as in many other cases, here, too, the obvious is not the real, as is proved by reference to the biblical text. When young David volunteered to confront Goliath, he first wore King Saul's own armor. But he took this off when he found it encumbered him, and while the giant approached him with sword, spear, and shield, David carried nothing but five smooth stones in a shepherd's bag and a sling.

At all times Jews had to face up to new ideas, religions, and philosophies. Judaism never ignored them. Its reaction has left a mark in Jewish writings, teachings, and customs. That the Bible, for instance, so distinct and definite in its legislation on almost every human aspect, is silent on the question of death and burial is not due to oversight. On the contrary, it is the result of vehement reaction to the Israelites' experience in Egypt, where death was the master of all, expressed most vividly by the pyramids. That circumcision became the outstanding Jewish symbol of initiation into the faith of Abraham again was a reaction, this time to the adoption of the Jewish rite of baptism as a Christian sacrament. The prohibition of the seething of a kid in its mother's milk was similarly explained by Maimonides as a protest against an ancient pagan custom. It is, therefore, not beyond the range of possibility that the Shield of David, too, owes its existence to a spiritual battle and was created in the sixth century B.C.E. during the Babylonian exile, in opposition to the teachings of Zoroaster.

Professed today by only a small minority in India, Zoroastrianism at that time had spread from its source in Persia to become a powerful force which captured the imagination of people far and wide. In its philosophy of dualism it taught that not one God, but two powers, ruled the universe. Ethically speaking, they were good and evil, while cosmologically they were expressed by light and darkness. Each power had its own symbol: a triangle with the apex pointing upward or downward. Man had to choose which power he was to serve.

Such teaching was totally inconsistent with the Jewish conception of life and God. It was a threat to the pure monotheistic faith inherited from Abraham, which taught that there was one God only, Who was the author of all things. Jewish prophecy raised its voice against the dangerous new doctrine. The Bible contains a telling passage which, unmistakably, was written in direct opposition to Zoroastrian influence. The words are those of the great unknown prophet of the exile, commonly referred to as "Deutero-Isaiah" (Isa. XLV, 5–8):

> I am the Lord, and there is none else;
>   there is no God beside Me . . .
> That they may know from the rising of the sun
>   and from the west, that there is none beside Me.
> I am the Lord, and there is none else.
> I form the light and create darkness:
>   I make peace and create evil:
> I the Lord do all these things.

To the forceful voice of prophetic protest was added an even more powerful symbol which united the two separate Persian signs, representing the forces of light and darkness, into one insoluble unity: the Star of David. Its very shape, the combination of the two triangles, denied the belief in two coexistent forces and proclaimed the indivisible unity of God, Who was the creator of light *and* darkness, good *and* evil.

It is a fascinating interpretation. Yet it accounts for the symbol's shape alone, and not its name. It is here that another theory suggests a remarkable explanation.

For centuries the shield served man as a means of defense. But it created one problem. By covering up the soldier, the shield prevented his being recognized, and with the absence of distinguishing uniforms (which were a much later invention), in the heat of battle, it became most difficult to differentiate between friend and foe. Some kind of identification was needed. An obvious move was to mark the shield on the outside with a distinctive sign. Psychological considerations added to its importance. If well chosen, it could serve as a forceful symbol which, in addition to revealing the soldier's allegiance, was able to intimidate his adversary. Like a challenge, it could proclaim, in concise and dramatic form, the cause for which the soldiers fought.

In the memory of the Jewish people there was no greater hero than King David. His figure dominated their thoughts and inspired them in battle, so much so that all Messianic dreams centered on him. David was the ideal king. He had once led the Israelites victoriously in war and established their freedom. Surely, out of his house would arise the new saviour who, this time, would bring final deliverance and everlasting peace. The people could choose no finer symbol than David's name, so full of happy memories and glorious anticipation. To fight under his sign, certainly, would mean victory.

Several difficulties arose. The symbol was addressed not to the Jews, but to their foes, who instantaneously had to understand its meaning. The space of a shield was limited. Conciseness was essential. How could David's name be shortened in a way that at once presented a definite message and a memorable sign?

Each problem was overcome in turn. As Hebrew was unknown to the enemy, his own language, Greek, was chosen. David's name began and ended with the same letter, the *delta*, which consisted of a triangle. Therefore, instead of the king's full name, a combination of two deltas was used. To save space the deltas were not placed next to each other, but interlocked. The result was the Shield of David which, embossed on the shields of the fighters, soon was recognized as the Jews' symbol!

It was natural that a sign bearing David's name would acquire deep Messianic meaning in the minds of the people: the more so because its very shape brought to mind the prophecy in the book of Numbers in which the pagan seer Balaam spoke of "the star" that would arise out of the house of Jacob to destroy the foe. Though the passage probably referred to King David himself, later religious thinkers applied it to a Messianic figure. It was this tradition that led Bar Koziba, leader of the last desperate attempt to throw off the Roman yoke (in the second century, at the time of Emperor Hadrian), to call himself, with the full approval of Rabbi Akiba, *Bar Kochba,* "the Son of the Star." He himself fervently believed in his divine mission, and the people considered him the expected Messiah. Perhaps the fact that the Christian cross symbolized a Messiah who had already come rendered—in direct opposition—the Magen David the Star of the coming Messiah.

Thus a shortened word became a guiding star, and a simple Greek letter, doubled and intertwined, a Jewish symbol of mighty force. Once engraved on the shields of heroes, it remained for all time the Jewish emblem. Shining forth out of the distant past, it led the Jew toward a hopeful future and Messianic fulfillment.

Another explanation, ingenious though even less probable, was suggested by M. Guedemann. This linked the Magen David with Celtic tradition and interpreted it as an ancient sign of the Druids, whose magicians used the hexagram as a charm against the Drudes, the ghosts of the night. Originally, therefore, Guedemann asserts, the sign's name was the Shield of the Druid and not of David. Rendered in the usual Hebrew way of spelling, it consisted of the letters DRVD. When, later, the original meaning of the word became lost and Jews no longer knew of Druids and Drudes, they simply omitted the letter *resh* and discovered in the remaining three letters DVD the name of David; and ever since, they have incorrectly rendered the Magen Druid as Magen David.

Man's development leads from superstition to the conquest of fear. In the early stages of history, and still today in the primitive mind, magic has its definite place in the pattern of life. Man considered himself surrounded by all kinds of mischievous forces which threatened his health, happiness, and very life. Magic alone, he believed, could protect him and ward off evil influences.

Judaism opposed such an attitude. The very basis of magic denied the Jewish belief in God's omnipotence. If God was all-powerful, it was impossible for other forces to interfere, as they, too, had to be subject to His will. Yet there were moments when even the Jewish mind did not remain immune from superstition. This was especially so in times of persecution, when life became almost unbearable, and in places where Jews came into close contact with people and nations whose whole existence was dominated by the occult. Pure monotheistic faith was then at its weakest and the Jews' rational outlook at its lowest. It was in such circumstances that the Jew, in superstitious fear, grasped at anything which might give him security and keep evil at bay. Customs then created still exist, but have been reinterpreted innocuously and have received a new and sometimes even beautiful meaning. However, originally they were the result not of deep religious emotion, but of irrational fears; not of a God-centered life, but of superstition.

Almost every phase of existence was then surrounded by a protective screen. Nothing was left open to possible mysterious attacks. Everything was armed—magically. Bible verses were used as a protection. God's name was inscribed on amulets which in Hebrew were called *kamea,* a word that has wrongly been given the credit for having created the English "cameo." Mystical letters were invented and incantations chanted. When a woman gave birth to a child, special "tickets" were fixed around her bed to keep away Lilith, the demon, who was considered to be seeking the young child's life. Again, at a wedding, evil forces were thought to threaten the couple's happiness, and magic seemed the only safeguard. That is why the bride originally walked seven times around the bridegroom and the bridegroom had to break a glass. An identical reason accounts for the custom of showering the couple with nuts and, today, confetti. But even more so than at a wedding, it was at death that the mystery of the unknown oppressed the mind. Evil forces then seemed to be at their strongest. Insecure and helpless, man once again sought refuge in magic. To frighten away all bad spirits and hauntings, the mourner poured out water, and before leaving the cemetery he threw dust or tufts of grass over his shoulder.

Thus life (and death) were armed with magic customs and habits against unknown powers. Most prominent among them was the use of charms. One of them was the Star of David. The fact that it was so employed may explain its description as a shield. It was thought to ward off evil and bring good luck.

Numerous examples are at hand from the Holy Land and eastern Europe, extending from the days of antiquity to recent times. Some seventeen hundred years ago the Shield of David was used as a magic emblem in the catacombs of Bet Sh'arim. A Russian nineteenth-century mezuzah container displayed it with the telling Hebrew words: "The watchman of the doors of Israel." Countless amulets and talismans bear the six-pointed star. Cabalists had it tattooed or drawn as a cure on the skin of sick people.

The symmetrical form of the Star was explained as a symbolic expression of the identity of the upper and lower worlds, the natural and supernatural. Its six points were seen as representative of God's universality and omnipresence, Whose power extended to north, south, east, west, below, and above. Its twelve corners were interpreted as representative of the twelve tribes of Israel. The intertwined, equilateral triangles were believed to combine mystically the beginning of the world with present-day existence, the six points being the six days of creation.

A vast number of possible and sometimes fantastic explanations thus offer themselves to interpret the Shield of David symbolically, historically, and mystically. They trace its elements back to Greek letters, Persian symbols, and Celtic charms. Some see in it a magic sign and design, others a military expedient employed in battles fought for physical or spiritual survival. Yet all agree that the history of the Magen David started outside Judaism, which adopted the sign and adapted it to Jewish teaching and life.

The Star's possibly pagan origin caused Judah Leib Gordon, in 1884, to protest against its use in modern Zionist aspiration, a warning which was ignored when, fourteen years later, the second Zionist Congress in Basel officially adopted it as a Jewish symbol on the new Jewish flag. Today, it stands supreme. Forgotten is its dark past. After all, however interesting the history of the symbol is, its continued existence depends on the meaning it has acquired and is able to convey with dynamic force. But nothing did more to sanctify it than Nazi brutality and murder. It was chosen to brand the Jew, as a general, compulsory badge of shame or as a tattoo mark on victims of concentration camps. Under its symbol they went to their death.

No other sign could be more powerful than the Shield of David. Today, it speaks of Jewish endurance, heroism, and miraculous rebirth. What the cross is to the Christian and the crescent to the Moslem, the Shield of David has become to the Jew.

Chapter 30

THE ISRAELI FLAG

Theodor Herzl was an inspired dreamer, and yet a realist. In his blueprint of the *Jewish State,* written in Paris in 1895, he expressed the conviction that the Jewish people needed a national emblem of their own. "We have no flag, and we need one," he wrote. "If we desire to lead many men, we must raise a symbol above their heads." He suggested that it should be a white flag with seven golden stars. The white color was to symbolize the purity of the new life the Jewish people were to lead when returned to their ancient home. The stars were meant to represent the seven golden hours of the working day.

Within two years, the modern prophet's enthusiasm and ceaseless striving were rewarded. In 1897, Jewish delegates from all over the world, 240 altogether, met in Basel to discuss the realization of Herzl's vision and to seek a modern solution of the Jewish question. At this first Zionist Congress, as it came to be called, the present Israeli flag was born. It was designed by another man, David Wolffsohn, Herzl's intimate friend and the future president of the Zionist Organization. He had been assigned the task of making arrangements for the conference. Countless problems were his, but he resolved them conscientiously and methodically. Soon he, too, felt the need of a symbol. "What flag should we hang in the congress hall?" he asked. "We had no flag," he recollected in later years. "This difficulty greatly vexed me. A flag had to be created."

Wolffsohn did not follow Herzl's original suggestion. His thoughts turned to a symbol the Jews already possessed, the tallit, their praying-shawl. White and blue were its traditional colors. The white expressed that purity of which Herzl had

330

spoken. The blue, by an association of ideas linking sky and heaven, was to remind the Jew of his sacred task. Indeed, the Jewish State had to be based on God's Law and be pure in its ideals. It was meant to be not just another small country, defiled by arrogant nationalism and political maneuvers, but worthy of a people of religion and an example to mankind.

"Let us take this tallit from its bag and unfold it before the eyes of Israel and the eyes of all nations." Thus Wolffsohn ordered the first Jewish flag. It was of white cloth with blue stripes, and the Star of David was painted in its center. When the delegates met in solemn assembly, they did so under this new banner.

Wherever Jews lived, they adopted the flag created at Basel, though few people ever knew how it originated or even asked whence it came. Many decades passed. Zionists had made the flag their own, but of course it had gained no official recognition among the nations of the world. World War I, meant to end all wars, was followed by the advent of Hitler, inevitably leading to World War II. In spite of the frequent and impassioned requests of the Jewish settlers in Palestine, they were at first denied the right to form their own military units and as such to join the free forces of the world in their active fight against evil. But when in 1944 the Nazi armies dangerously threatened the Middle East, Churchill's statesmanship and imagination at long last resulted in the Jews' being permitted to do so.

The British Prime Minister had voiced his wholehearted agreement with proposals for the creation of a Jewish fighting force in a directive to the Secretary of State for War on 26 July. At the same time, he had expressed his intention of consulting the King about the suggestion that this force should have its own flag:

I will consult the King. . . . I cannot conceive why this martyred race, scattered about the world and suffering as no other race has done at this juncture, should be denied the satisfaction of having a flag.*

* Winston S. Churchill, *The Second World War* (Cassell & Co., London, 1954), VI, 601.

Two months later Churchill proudly announced to the British Parliament the formation of a Jewish Brigade Group:

It seems to me indeed appropriate that a special Jewish unit, a special unit of that race which has suffered indescribable torments from the Nazis, should be represented as a distinct formation among the forces gathered for their final overthrow, and I have no doubt that they will not only take part in the struggle, but also in the occupation which will follow.

Then, for the first time in history, the Jewish flag gained official recognition and was approved by the military authorities as the flag of the Jewish Brigade.

Four years later, the State of Israel was born. On 28 October 1948, its Provisional State Council decreed that the Jewish banner was to become the flag of Israel. Seven feet long and six feet wide, it carried on a white field two horizontal blue stripes about one foot in width, and at its center, also in blue, the Shield of David. The banner of the first Zionist Congress had thus become the flag of Israel almost exactly half a century after its creation by Wolffsohn.

Chapter 31

A HYMN OF HOPE

Optimism has been one of the distinctive characteristics of the Jew ever since Abraham left his home to wander into an unknown future. Nothing could ever destroy the Jew's belief in the goodness of man and the final victory of all that is right and just. In times of greatest anguish, when darkness enveloped his soul and existence and everything that made life worth living seemed lost, not even then did the Jew lose faith. With folly and evil triumphant in the world, he never sank into despair, but fought on heroically to prepare God's way on earth, with the prophet's message in his heart: "And yet!" Thus, the French Jewish writer Edmond Fleg could affirm his faith with the memorable words: "I am a Jew because in every age when the cry of despair is heard, the Jew hopes." In the light of all this it was but natural that *Hope* was the theme and title of the hymn modern Jewry chose for a national song, which inevitably became the anthem of the new State of Israel.

Expressing two thousand years of fervent longing, the hymn itself was then just seventy years old. It was written by an Austrian Jew, who dedicated it, with other poems, to a Christian Englishman.

Naphtali Herz Imber was born in Galicia in 1856. He received the traditional Jewish education in Bible and Talmud, but showed an early love for poetry. As a boy of fourteen he won a government prize for a Hebrew poem he had written on a patriotic Austrian theme. Four years later, he migrated to Vienna, but did not stay there long.

Always restive, he led the life of a wanderer. He traveled through Hungary, Roumania, and all over the Balkans, finally

333

reaching Constantinople. There he met Laurence Oliphant, one of the outstanding non-Jewish Zionists. Born of Scottish parents in South Africa, Oliphant became a member of the British House of Commons. He was a diplomat by profession and a successful novelist. But the aim that dominated his life was to reestablish the Jewish people in the Holy Land. His Zionism was inspired not simply by the desire to give a persecuted people a refuge from oppression but by the conviction that the creation of a Jewish nation would be of inestimable value to progress and civilization, to good government, justice, and peace. After a careful investigation of all possibilities, Oliphant worked out a scheme which was described by the contemporary press as "the most feasible plan that has yet been put before the world." Imber and Oliphant became intimate friends and in 1878 went together to Palestine.

There, Imber continued his literary activities, writing articles and essays for magazines. In 1886 he published his first volume of collected poetry under the title of *The Morning Star.* He dedicated it to Laurence Oliphant, his one true friend. It contained patriotic compositions, all written in a spirit of confidence and pride. Among them was the poem "Our Hope." It was destined to gain world fame. He had written it at the age of twenty-two in admiration of those early settlers of the Holy Land who had gone out into the malaria-ridden swamps to establish the first modern Jewish colony, called by the prophetic words Petach Tikvah (The Gate of Hope). Obviously it was this name which inspired the title and contents of the poem. Consisting of nine stanzas, "Our Hope" expressed the eternal longing of the Jewish heart to return to the land of the fathers and to dwell once again in the city where David set up his camp, to become "a free nation in Zion and Jerusalem."

The poem caught the imagination of the young colonists. No wonder that it did, for it reflected their own feelings and yearnings. After Samuel Cohen, one of the pioneers in Rishon-le-Zion, an adjacent colony, had set the poem to music, its popular appeal led to its becoming the people's hymn. Its tune is that of an old Spanish and Slav folk song which can also be found in Smetana's tone poem *Die Moldau* but was used by Spanish and Portuguese Jews as the melody of an ancient Hebrew prayer, a supplication for dew.

Imber, so restless in his soul, did not stay in Palestine. When Oliphant died in 1888, Imber went to England, where he became a writer. Volumes of his *Topics of Today in the Talmud,* which he had dedicated "To all scholars of all nations," are still preserved in the British Museum. Other writings were published in the *Jewish Standard,* the journal of Anglo-Jewry, whose publisher, Israel Zangwill, the Jewish Dickens, became Imber's friend. He is said to have perpetuated Imber's memory in the character of Malkisedek Pinchas in his *Children of the Ghetto.* Imber was humbly proud of this distinction, though it was caricature, and often quoted the relevant passages, even calling himself by the fictitious name.

But even Britain could not hold him. Now the New World beckoned. In 1892 he left for America, where he continued his travels and literary activities. His treatise on *Education of the Talmud,* which he wrote in this period, was mentioned in an official report.

Associating with American mystics, he became interested in the theosophical movement, whose Boston magazine he edited for some time. In 1903, the world was shocked by the Czarist pogroms at Kishinev. When, two years later, Imber published yet another volume of his poetry, he dedicated it to the Emperor of Japan. He did so because Japan was then at war with Russia, and he hoped that the defeat of the Czar would at long last bring freedom to his Russian brethren.

However successful Imber was in his literary work and grandiose in his dedications, there was no real happiness in his personal life. His marriage to a woman doctor, who for his sake had become a Jewess, did not last. Unstable all through his life, Imber eventually took to drink. Taverns became his haunt. He was rarely sober. Drink did not make him amiable, but quarrelsome. It was a tragic disintegration of a brilliant man.

Even his friends could not tolerate him any longer, a fact which made him even more bitter and cynical. Typical was an incident which occurred at a Zionist meeting where Imber, completely drunk, had become so obstreperous that he had to be forcibly removed. Standing outside the hall, he heard the crowd join in his song, "Our Hope" (Hatikvah) at the conclusion of the gathering. Listening to it, he, the cast-out drunkard, with shaking but triumphant voice, remarked: "They may kick me out, but they must sing my song."

Eventually, Imber became seriously ill. He went on writing, but with increased venom. Now he despised his former friends, turned foe. In sarcasm he wrote his "Last Will," leaving to his enemies his rheumatism and to the editors of Jewish newspapers his pen, so that they should write slowly and avoid mistakes.

Thus, lonely and embittered, he died in 1909, fifty-three years old, in a New York hospital. Friendless and leaving no money, he was given a pauper's funeral. But the hymn did not die with him. It circled the world. First sung by the colonists in the Holy Land, then intoned in every country by Zionist students, it soon became the fervent expression of Jewish national aspiration. No meeting could close without it. The fact that it was sung in 1903 by the world delegates at the sixth Zionist Congress gave "Hatikvah" official recognition. It was a foregone conclusion that at the declaration of independence of the State of Israel this Zionist hymn would become the National Anthem.

In 1953, forty-four years after his lonely death, Imber's remains were taken from the New York cemetery to Israel, to be interred on Mount Herzl, where he now rests, not far from the grave of Theodor Herzl himself. His deathless song will go on reverberating in the hearts of all Jews. Its message of hope, however, may give all men, of whatever race, religion, or color, faith in the future, determination never to succumb to despair, but to face the world and life with confidence, and the will to help in leading humanity to the Promised Land of justice and peace.

PART V

The Jew In the World

Chapter 32

THE JEW AND CIVILIZATION

Almost bewildering is the part the Jews have played in the history of mankind. A small minority throughout the ages and a people of martyrs, they left their imprint on every phase of civilization. Their history reads like the continuing realization of the prophecy given to the first Jew, Abraham, who, on the eve of his going out into the world, was told, "In thee shall all the families of the earth be blessed."

Four Jews—Moses, Jesus, Spinoza, and Karl Marx—were epoch-makers in the history of mankind. But for Jews, Europe would have remained pagan, America undiscovered by the Western world, and the Dark Ages prolonged indefinitely.

The summary which follows does not purport to present a complete list of Jewish attainments, but rather to put on record the phenomenon, perhaps unique in the story of mankind, of a small and politically powerless people, often despised and tortured, holding faithfully to its ideals and finding fulfillment in the service of man. Surely, no rational explanation can be found. In awe and reverence we must recognize it as a divine shaping of destiny, a God-given vocation and purpose.

The Jew provided the religious source from which numberless people have drawn their belief and religion. His faith illumined the entire world. His outstanding contribution of all time is the Bible. From it the world received the conception of a single God and the idea of a personal religion. It also laid on man the obligation to pursue righteousness and justice.

The first Christian was a Jew, and Christianity could not exist

337

without its content of Judaism. The Old Testament is the Jewish Bible, and the New Testament was mainly written by Jews. Nearly all the earliest Christians were Jews. Whenever Jesus defines his religion, he quotes from Jewish Scripture. It was Moses who first said, "Thou shalt love thy neighbour as thyself." The ideas of the Logos and "the only begotten Son" appear first in the philosophy of Philo the Jew!

Paul, who molded Christianity, was a Jew and a disciple of Rabbi Gamaliel. Jewish missionaries paved the way for the Christian apostles.

The weekly day of rest was a Jewish idea, and the church evolved from the synagogue. Baptism is of purely Jewish origin. The wine and bread of the communion service are the Kiddush and matzah of the Jewish Passover. Jewish sacrificial tradition and liturgy constitute the Christian Mass. The "two lessons" of the church service originate in the synagogue readings from Torah and Prophets. The light before the high altar is the perpetual lamp of the synagogue, and the incense comes straight from the days of King Solomon's Temple. The Lord's Prayer is a combination of most beautiful Jewish passages and prayer formulas, just as Hallelujah, Selah, and Amen are Hebrew words regularly used in the synagogue.

Mohammed created Islam on the foundation of Judaism, even calling it "the religion of Abraham." His basic creed, "There is no God but Allah," not only expresses pure Jewish monotheism but echoes Hebrew Scripture. He adopted—and later adapted—the orientation, when praying, toward Jerusalem, as well as the Sabbath and the fast of Yom Kippur. To this very day Moslem worship is based on the service of the synagogue.

Himself unable to write, Mohammed for many years employed a Jewish scribe. In almost every sura of the Koran we encounter either episodes of Hebrew history, familiar Jewish legends, details of rabbinical law and tradition, or arguments indicating that Islam is the faith of Abraham and Moses.

Abraham is claimed as the founder of the Kaaba, Islam's most sacred shrine, and Ishmael, Isaac's step-brother, was the ancestor of all the Arab tribes.

The ancient world found faith through the writings of the Jewish prophets and enlightenment from Jewish thinkers. In the Middle Ages, it was again the Jew who disseminated knowledge and advanced science in Europe. His research and zeal contributed largely to the success of the great voyages of discovery at the beginning of the modern era.

Not only was Rabbi Levi ben Gershon, who lived in the fourteenth century, the ancestor of modern photography through his invention of the camera obscura but his "Jacob's staff" became an indispensable instrument for the navigator and remained in use for more than four hundred years. Most of the early nautical instruments, as well as the maps, came from Spanish Jews. Columbus used them on his voyage, and his interpreter, the first European to set foot on American soil, was a Jew, Louis de Torez. Vasco da Gama, in his discovery of the sea route to India, was guided by the charts worked out by Abraham Zacuto.

Even when still imprisoned in narrow ghetto walls, the Jew's urge to compass the world, penetrate its mysteries, and trace the stars in their courses could never be quenched, and once he found freedom, his ardor knew no bounds. Then, almost at once, the Jew entered to the full extent into every sphere of life.

To serve his country became a sacred obligation. More than forty Jews fought under Washington. Among the patriots who played an eminent part in the early struggle of the American Republic were Lieutenant-Colonels Isaac Franks and his cousin David S. Franks. Haym Salomon, of Philadelphia, was the "Broker to the Office of Finance" who not only raised vast sums for the government but loaned money which was never repaid. His devotion to the cause of American independence was deservedly acknowledged by a congressional committee which described him "as one of the truest and most efficient friends of the country at a very critical period of its history."

Commodore of the United States Navy was Philadelphia-born Uriah P. Levy, who died soon after the outbreak of the Civil War. He is remembered (as he himself suggested he should be) as "the father of the law for the abolition of the barbarous practice of corporal punishment" for American sailors. The words were inscribed in his epitaph. The outlawing of flogging was the result of his zealous efforts. A notable figure in the Civil War was Judah P. Benjamin, who has been called "the brains of the Confederacy." A fiery protagonist of the South, he served in its government both as Secretary of War and Secretary of State.

The part Jews have played with their civic courage, compassion, and honor in the service of the United States is outstanding. Oscar S. Straus, a close friend of President Theodore Roosevelt, has the double distinction of having been the first Jew to serve as a Cabinet Minister in the government of the United States and of having been sent as an Ambassador to a foreign country (Turkey). He represented America on the permanent Court of Arbitration at The Hague. Equally dedicated in the service of their nation were the Henry Morgenthaus, father and son, and Herbert H. Lehman, for many years Governor of the State of New York and United States Senator. Felix Frankfurter, professor at Harvard Law School and a former Associate Justice of the United States Supreme Court, acted as counselor to President Franklin D. Roosevelt during the inauguration of the New Deal.

Bernard M. Baruch, who became a legend in his lifetime, will always be remembered as "the adviser of Presidents." Justice Arthur J. Goldberg was appointed Ambassador to the United Nations. President Lyndon B. Johnson, when making the announcement from the White House, said that it was appropriate to ask this member of the nation's highest court to speak for America in her efforts to promote the rule of law.

All these men undoubtedly made an impact for good on the life of the American nation. However, even its very beginnings were influenced by the spirit of Judaism and its Bible, which inspired the early leaders and fighters for freedom and independence and permeated the country's legislation and institutions. The Pilgrims based their laws on the Hebrew Scriptures, and Thanksgiving Day itself is modeled on the Jewish feast of Tabernacles.

Jews were prominent among the builders of the British Empire, giving her her finest soldiers, lawmakers, and merchants. Typical of them were the Barnatos and Beits in South Africa, Montefiore, Monash, and Isaacs in Australia, the Nathans in New Zealand, the Kadoories in Hong Kong, the Harts, Franks, and Hays in Canada, and the Sassoons in India.

In Britain, Rufus Isaacs, later Lord Reading, Viceroy of India, deserves especial mention, but pride of place must go to Benjamin Disraeli, who, though baptized as a young boy, always considered himself a Jew and proudly asserted his Judaism even in the British Parliament. It was Disraeli the Jew who created the British Empire when, in the face of bitter opposition, he proclaimed his beloved Queen the Empress of India; who assured the life line of the Empire by his bold stroke with the Suez Canal; and in whose honor London still celebrates Primrose Day. Leader of the Conservative party, he was no lover of vested privilege, but brought to his leadership the Jewish principles of liberty and justice, together with an emphasis on the need for progress by historic evolution rather than radical development.

Karl Marx, on the other hand, who also was baptized as a child (at the age of seven) and whose thought and work have revolutionized the world, felt most antagonistic toward his father's faith and people and did not fail to express his dislike in the strongest terms. Yet it was his Jewish heritage which drove him on in a burning desire to help the unfortunate. In a life of tragedy and poverty, Marx sacrificed everything, but he refused to turn his back on suffering humanity.

In the light of their religious inheritance and of the Bible's insistence on social justice, it was inevitable that Jews should have been among the pioneers in the fields of social service. Traditionally, every Jew, even the poorest, is required to devote one-tenth —the tithe—of his income to charity. In their earliest days, when almost the whole world was illiterate, the Jews instituted a system of free and universal education and kept a hostel attached to their synagogues open for strangers.

In his *Golden Ladder of Charity*, Maimonides held that the gift of the hand without the heart was the lowest form of benevolence, but that prevention of poverty was the highest act. The Rothschild and Hirsch families excelled as much in their philanthropy as in their riches. A Jew started the movement which led to the foundation of the Royal Society for the Prevention of Cruelty to Animals (R.S.P.C.A.). Dutch-born William van Praagh introduced lip-reading for deaf mutes.

So extensive is the list of American philanthropists who spent millions of dollars for the good of their fellow men that a few names must suffice. Jacob H. Schiff (instrumental in the building of the great railroads) endowed numerous colleges and libraries, ranging from the Jewish Theological Seminary to Harvard and Columbia Universities. Julius Rosenwald (owner of Sears, Roebuck & Company for many years) was responsible for the establishment of more than five hundred schools and Young Men's Christian Associations in the South for Negroes. Simon Guggenheim's foundations of fellowships enabled students to continue their scientific research without worry about funds or distinction of religion or race.

Nathan Straus, another American Jew, started the movement to provide milk for school children. His greatest treasure, which he carried with him wherever he went, was a slip of paper on which he had noted down the figures of child mortality in New York City before and after the introduction of his scheme. Jews were prominent in pioneering education among the Negroes and in the establishment of London University College, the first university not confined to members of a special denomination or church. It was a perpetual Jewish ideal to combine an open mind with warmth of heart.

The talmudic adage that "truth is the seal of God" epitomized the Jews' untiring quest for knowledge. The influence of Jewish thinkers made itself felt throughout all ages and countries.

At the beginning of our era, Philo, the Jew of Alexandria, was studied all over the ancient world. His humanism was unique. He stressed the oneness of man in the love of God: "Let there be one bond of affection and one password of friendship—devotion to God." He was a pioneer in the history of religious thought, and his was the earliest attempt to reconcile philosophy and religion.

Greatest of all was the work of twelfth-century Moses Maimonides. It exerted a universal influence on the thinkers of all faiths and nations. Through the centuries that followed, his *Guide* was the standard work in religious philosophy, and it molded the thought of Thomas Aquinas and Albertus Magnus. His passion for truth was all-powerful. He never gave way to intimidation and cared nothing for the applause of the masses:

When I have a difficult subject before me—when I find the road narrow, and can see no other way of teaching a well-established truth except by pleasing one intelligent man and displeasing ten thousand fools—I prefer to address myself to the one man and to take no notice whatever of the condemnation of the multitude.

Of paramount importance in the development of modern thought was the work of Baruch Spinoza. This eighteenth-century Jew was born in the Netherlands, where his fervor for independent thought led to his official exclusion from the Jewish community—a form of excommunication. One of the greatest thinkers of all times, he disdained the offer of the chair of philosophy at Heidelberg University, choosing rather to preserve his freedom of thought by earning his livelihood as a grinder of optical lenses.

His *Five Books of Ethics*, the result of fifteen years of deep thinking, were, at his own request, published only after his death, and even then anonymously. Written in "geometrical"—sequential—form, it contains no superfluous word. Every part depends on the preceding passage and leads inexorably to the next conclusion. He called his philosophy *Ethics* to show that moral duty was its ultimate object. His concept of the "intellectual love of God" is the supreme expression of a truly religious quest. Novalis described him as "the God-intoxicated man."

Henri Bergson's philosophy of creative evolution exercised a profound and lasting influence on modern thought. A Nobel Prize winner of Anglo-Jewish parentage, he refused the offer of exemption from restrictive legislation under Nazi-ruled Vichy France, as he was determined fully to share the fate of his fellow Jews. Freud rediscovered dreams; Einstein, space; but Bergson, time. He taught that a life force (*élan vital*), and not dead mechanical laws, ruled existence. It was this higher, godly impetus which penetrated all life, guiding it and making ever new experiments. Solidity lives in solidarity. Obedience to duty means resistance to self. Intellect may falsify truth, but intuition can grasp ultimate reality. The machine can become man's greatest benefactor. If used to free him from daily toil, it will enable him to dedicate the greatest part of his existence to spiritual achievement.

Seekers after truth, the Jews never rested in their endeavors to guide the perplexed, to search for the true fountain of life and—like Samuel Alexander, a son of Australian Jewry—out of the world of space and time to discover a way to God.

It is more than symbolic that the Jews' fundamental religious source, the Torah, is called "The Law." Jews never ceased from striving after justice and from contributing to the fund of legal ideas. The equality of all men before the law is a Jewish concept founded on the Mosaic commandment: "Ye shall not respect persons in judgment, ye shall hear the small and the great alike." Biblical and talmudic teaching established the idea of natural law. It was the Jews who first introduced a law of copyright, and this in an epoch when Europe was still enveloped in the darkness of the Middle Ages.

Similarly, in modern times, Jews continued to exert their influence in the sphere of law. A man of Jewish extraction was responsible for the abolition of torture in Austria. Hugo Preuss drafted the Constitution of Germany's Weimar Republic. The founder of the present English Court of Chancery was Sir George Jessel, a legal luminary. The stanch democracy of American Louis Brandeis gained him the title of "the people's attorney." He spared no effort to attain justice for all: "I know nothing about sacrifice; I know only duty."

The Jew's effect on world literature was exerted primarily through the Bible. Its translations became the "standard of language" in many a country. Its words, idioms, and sayings form an integral part of our common speech. Jubilee, Satan, Cherub, Paradise, and Armageddon—such words stem from Jewish Scripture. The Jews have rightly been called "the people of the

Book." They were never illiterate, and literature to them was much more than reading to pass the time.

The Jew has played a significant part in every field of writing. In Alexandria, the intellectual center of the Hellenist world, Jewish poets, playwrights, and historians, writing in Greek, occupied a prominent place. It was discovered only in the last century that the classic of medieval churchmen, *The Fountain of Life,* which had been studied with religious fervor by many generations, was the work of a rabbi, the "nightingale of piety," Solomon ibn Gabirol.

Enshrined forever in bronze at the base of the Statue of Liberty in New York Harbor is the impassioned poem on "The New Colossus," by Emma Lazarus, whom Emerson called the natural companion of scholars and thinkers. Her poetry, like her whole life, aimed at righting the wrong, helping the needy, and making light triumph over darkness. Among the many writers who occupy a high place in American literature are Ludwig Lewisohn, Louis Untermeyer, Edna Ferber, Ben Hecht, and Bernard Malamud. But none has given a greater impetus to creative writing than Hungarian-born Joseph Pulitzer, who in his will established the highest awards for the finest achievements in almost every sphere of literary endeavor, the Pulitzer Prize.

Sarah Millin is South Africa's outstanding and representative novelist. Marcel Proust's work constitutes a landmark in the history of the French novel. André Maurois excelled in the art of biography and interpreted English history to the French people. Siegfried Sassoon and Humbert Wolf have acquired a permanent place in English poetry. Max Beerbohm was a past master not only of caricature but of satiric prose. Phillip Guedalla was an essayist and historian of great stature.

German-born biographer Emil Ludwig used to keep in a single frame the insignia of his French Legion of Honor, the certificate of his honorary Swiss citizenship, an honorary degree from an American university, and a photograph of the burning of his books by the Nazis in Berlin in 1933. Lion Feuchtwanger shares this distinction of having had his works destroyed on twentieth-century pyres. Their fate echoed the experience, a hundred years earlier, of Germany's greatest lyric poet, Heinrich Heine, whose "Lorelei" still enchants the heart. Then an exile from his ungrateful country, he died a pauper in a Paris attic, his grave to be desecrated and demolished in 1941 by the Nazi invader.

The *Golden Treasury* of English songs is the work of Sir Francis Palgrave. Sir Sidney Low edited the *Dictionary of English History,* and Sir Sidney Lee was coeditor of the English *Dictionary of National Biography.*

Of rabbinic descent, Victor Gollancz became a publisher whose fervor made him an outstanding figure in the social endeavor of the postwar world. Georg Brandes, a Danish Jew, is a most distinguished literary critic of modern times. In 1966 the Nobel Prize for literature was shared by Nelly Sachs, a German refugee who had made her new home in Sweden, and Shmuel Joseph Agnon, the first Israeli thus to be honored. While most of Agnon's characters live by the tradition of Judaism, Nelly Sachs is the poetess of the holocaust under the Nazis. The citation which accompanied the prize spoke of her lyrics and plays "as works in the German language at its best," "works of forgiveness, of deliverance, of peace." Truly, "Let books be thy companion" remained the Jewish motto ever since it was first enunciated in the days of the Apocrypha.

Rembrandt lived in the Jewish quarter of Amsterdam and found much of his inspiration in Jewish tradition and subjects. For centuries, most European painting centered on biblical themes. Jews themselves, in spite of early rigid interpretation of the second commandment that prohibited the making of "any manner of likeness," still excelled in the decoration of early synagogues, as excavations in the Middle East proved to an astonished twentieth-century world. Murals more than sixteen hundred years old were then discovered at Dura-Europos, 250 miles east of the Syrian coast. They not only present some of the most ancient Jewish illustrations of the Hebrew Bible but indicate that early Christian pictorial art developed and borrowed from Jewish sources. A portrait of a priest, possibly intended to picture the prophet Jeremiah, shows a striking resemblance to the early representations of Jesus of Nazareth!

It was inevitable that Jewish painting should be hampered by the destructive zeal of iconoclasts and the constant migration of the Jewish people. Art, more than any other activity of man, needs to take deep root before it can bear fruit. It was, therefore, only the emancipation of the last century which gave the Jew freedom and apparent security and brought his creative genius to full flower. In outstanding measure Jews, once again, soon became not only notable artists but illustrious representatives of their country.

Camille Pissarro is the champion of French impressionism, and his landscapes are regarded as the best of his time. Max Liebermann was considered one of the most brilliant German portraitists: imbued with a deep sense of responsibility, he shunned no effort in the execution of his work. Typical is the reply he gave to famous surgeon Professor Sauerbruch, who, tired of many prolonged sittings, asked how much longer the portrait would take. "My dear Professor," Liebermann said, "when you make a mistake in treating a patient it is covered over by a grass mound, but when I make a mistake it continues to hang on the wall for centuries."

Marc Chagall, whose impact on modern painting is profound, felt that the artist must penetrate into the world, feel the fate of human beings, of peoples, with real love. There was no art for art's sake, he wrote. Rather, the artist should be concerned with the entire realm of life. His stained-glass windows at the Medical Center near Jerusalem, the ceiling of the Paris Opera, and the mural which adorns the Grand Tier promenade of the Lincoln Center Metropolitan Opera House in New York are true examples of his renowned and powerful work. He himself explained his paintings as a pictorial arrangement of the images which possess him and which, like poems on canvas, diffuse "the light of freedom" and "the color of love."

An irresistible humanity dominates the work of Jacob Epstein, the most controversial sculptor of modern times. "The deeply intimate and human were always sought by me, and so wrought that they became classic and enduring." Of eastern European origin, he was born in New York and studied in Paris, but settled in London. Practically all his creations started bitter feuds, and his "Christ" and "Adam" almost a scandal. The knighthood conferred on him by Queen Elizabeth II confirmed the outstanding qualities of his monumental work, so full of emotional vigor, truth, and sincerity.

Eric Mendelsohn is a Jewish genius in architecture. Great buildings in many lands are monuments to his vision and integrity. His credo, to make the most of aesthetic virtues of unadorned geometry and of the intrinsic beauty of the materials, has been adopted all over the world.

Church music developed from the ancient Temple tunes. The Kol Nidre is perhaps the most famous melody of the synagogue and has become the property of the heart. Beethoven called music the mediator between the spiritual and material life. The Jew has always been a wanderer between these two worlds, and music naturally became almost his passion. He fostered, interpreted, and composed it.

Richard Strauss acknowledged the world's debt to the Jew in the sphere of art, saying that "without our Jewish friends all our opera houses and concert halls would be more than half empty." Rossini was helped by James de Rothschild; Wagner, though an outspoken anti-Semite in later years, owes much of his success to the Jew Levi. Handel, at a time when he was ignored by many, was sponsored by London Jews. Mozart's librettist was an Italian of Jewish descent.

The music to the *Midsummer Night's Dream* and the oratorio *Elijah* were written by the grandson of the "Jewish Socrates," Moses Mendelssohn—Felix Mendelssohn-Bartholdy—who died at the age of thirty-eight, when thirty thousand people attended his funeral. Jacques Offenbach, to whom we owe 102 works of music, was the son of a synagogue cantor in Cologne who emigrated to Paris. Composer of *Les Huguenots* and a prodigy pianist at the age of seven, Giacomo Meyerbeer, as a boy, wrote melodies for his father's private synagogue. He is buried in the Jewish cemetery in Berlin.

Swiss-born Ernest Bloch went to America at the age of thirty-six, during World War I. Speaking of his compositions, he confessed that he had "hearkened to an inner voice, deep, secret, insistent, burning"; a voice which seemed to come from far beyond himself and his parents; "a voice which surged up in me on reading the Bible." In fact, he felt that he transcribed into his music the venerable emotions of the Jewish people that slumbered in his soul.

The *London Times* described Irving Berlin as the composer who "has set more feet dancing and more mouths whistling than any other single person." George Gershwin's music and Al Jolson's songs conquered the modern world.

Jewish violinists who won world acclaim include Bronislaw Hubermann, Jascha Heifetz, Fritz Kreisler, Yehudi Menuhin, and Isaac Stern. Among the acknowledged leading virtuosos of the piano are Myra Hess, Benno Moiseiwitsch, Artur Rubenstein, and Solomon. Joseph Schmidt was a former synagogue choirboy of a Berlin Liberal synagogue, and Richard Tauber's parents were Jewish. Jan Peerce's family name was Perelmuth, and, curiously, he started his career not as a singer but as a violinist in an orchestra. Toscanini discovered him as a "star" and would not believe that his forebears went to America not from Italy but from eastern Europe.

Jewish artistic genius and patronage did not fail in the world of drama. Sarah Bernhardt, recognized as the finest actress of the nineteenth century, was of Jewish birth. Surmounting every difficulty, from sickness and frailty in childhood to the amputation of a leg in later life, "In Spite of Everything" was ever her motto. Max Reinhardt's productions revolutionized the theater.

Only a few examples can be given of Jewish enterprise and talent in the world of films. Among the film directors are Samuel Goldwyn and Louis B. Mayer, of Metro-Goldwyn-Mayer; Harry Cohen, former head of Columbia Pictures; Adolph Zukor, founder of Paramount; and the Selznicks, father and son. The Warner Brothers were pioneers of the talkies. Theirs was "The First Name in Sound." In 1926 they presented the first full-length talking picture, *The Jazz Singer*. Some of the many Jewish stars of the screen are Elisabeth Bergner and Pola Negri, Paul Muni and Eddie Cantor, Leslie Howard and Edward G. Robinson, Louise Rainer and Judy Halliday, Danny Kaye and the Marx brothers. With the advent of television, Jewish talent found a rich new medium of expression, and names such as Jack Benny and Phil Silvers became household words.

The ancient book of Sirach expressed the Jewish respect for medicine. It spoke of the honor due to the physician, "for the Lord has created him." The Bible itself introduced measures of utmost significance to health. Outstanding among them are the legislation on regular rest and preventive medicine. The latter provided a meticulous system of prophylaxis, with isolation and methodical medical inspections of the infected. The Jews introduced Arab medicine into the world at large. "Alcohol" and "arsenic" are Arab words brought into medicine by Jews. The European universities used Jewish medical textbooks right into the eighteenth century. Jews founded the medical schools of Montpellier and Salerno. Maimonides' medical works anticipated modern methods of treatment. He believed in the curative power of nature and the importance of the right mental attitude of the patient. He advised exercise, sport, and utmost cleanliness and— seven hundred years ago—he stressed the supremacy of prevention over cure and the beneficial influence of diet and sunshine.

The alleviation of suffering became to the Jew almost an obsession. Innumerable hospitals have been endowed, and vast research has been fostered by Jewish philanthropists. It would demand a book by itself to list all the work done by Jewish doctors in the field of discovery and healing. Once again, only a few contributions can be quoted as examples.

A persecuted Russian Jew, Waldemar Haffkine, discovered serums against cholera and bubonic plague—scourges of mankind—and thereby saved countless millions of potential victims. He did not merely work in the isolation of the laboratory but personally tested his discoveries in the plague-infested provinces of India. The Jew Paul Ehrlich, by his discovery of salvarsan, was the first to make any real progress in the fight of yet another most maleficent disease, syphilis, the diagnosis of which was made possible by another Jew, Wassermann, by whose name the test is called.

The investigations of Cesare Lombroso on the heredity of crime and the relationship between genius and lunacy opened up new vistas in criminology. Ferdinand Cohen is the father of modern bacteriology, and Moritz Romberg of neurology. O. Minkowski paved the way for the discovery of insulin for the treatment of diabetes. Knowledge that the irregular working of the thyroid gland caused cretinism was due to the investigations of Moritz Schiff. Countless lives have been saved following the discovery of streptomycin by Selman Waksman and by the Salk vaccine whose name honors Jonas E. Salk. His achievement in conquering the scourge of poliomyelitis was further advanced by the development of an oral vaccine by Albert B. Sabin. Unending is the Jew's fight against suffering and ever-renewed his zeal in the art of healing.

It would be difficult to point to any sphere of modern progress in which Jews did not play some important part. An eloquent indication is the number of Jewish Nobel Prize winners, which is out of all proportion to what one might expect from so small a fraction of the world's population.

Jews invented the microphone, sewing machine, amplifier, and safety match. They designed the calculating machine and the keyless watch. They created color photography. The experiments of Heinrich Hertz in the production of electromagnetic waves prepared the way for radio and television. The first electric telephone was constructed by Philipp Reiss in 1860, anticipating Alexander Graham Bell by sixteen years. Emile Berliner, it has been claimed, also was instrumental in the development of the telephone, the invention of one of the earliest gramophones, and a method of duplicating records. The first benzine automobile was built by Siegfried Marcus in 1875. David Schwarz constructed the first rigid airship. When he was summoned by the German War Ministry to display his invention, he was so overjoyed that he fell dead of apoplexy, but the later Zeppelin was the direct result of the genius of Schwarz. Nobel prize winner Albert A. Michelson, of Chicago University, was the first to measure the length of light rays and the velocity of light, feats formerly considered impossible.

Some of the most significant ideas and institutions of the modern world which have become bywords and symbols of everyday existence stem from the Jew. They are an integral part of the pattern of life and speech.

Esperanto was invented by the Lithuanian Jew Ludovic Zamenhof. Inspired by the Jewish ideal of one humanity, he tried to pave the way to the brotherhood of man by his synthetic international language. Hopeful that his dream might come true, he signed his articles with the pseudonym *Esperanto,* which became the name of the new language. "Break down the walls between the people, make the curse of Babel a myth of the past," was the motto, which urged him on in his intensive search for man's happiness.

The world's greatest news agency, famed for its accuracy, objectiveness, and independence, bears the name of its German-born founder, Julius Reuter. A man of ingenuity and never-flagging energy, his story leads from the days when he flew his messages by pigeon post to the era of the fastest news service, reaching the ends of the earth. Joseph Pulitzer founded the School of Journalism at Columbia University and the New York *World*. The New York *Times* became one of the world's greatest newspapers through Adolph S. Ochs, who acquired it in 1896. He had started his career as a humble newsboy.

Humanity owes the knowledge of vitamins (and even their name) to a Polish Jew, Casimir Funk. In 1912 he detected a substance in food which he considered so "vital" to health that he called it "vitamin." The genius of Sigmund Freud discovered the unconscious mind and founded the science of psychoanalysis. Alfred Adler, another Viennese Jew, gave twentieth-century vocabulary and society its "inferiority complex." Greatest genius of modern times, if not of all times, was Albert Einstein, the German refugee who became a professor at Princeton University, discoverer of the theory of relativity, and herald of the Atomic Age.

With undying faith in the ultimate victory of truth and goodness, the Jew pursued his unselfish quest for man's happiness. In the tangled web of life and its never-ceasing vicissitudes, he held fast to his ideal. Injustice never intimidated, but rather infuriated him. Repeatedly himself a victim of adversity, he fought the harder for peace and justice for all. But whatever Jews contributed to advancement, individually or collectively, as fervent enthusiasts, solemn seekers, or devout servants, it was from an innate and almost unconscious compulsion to help and to build a better life.

Isaiah told the Jew that it was his duty to be a light to the nations. Jesus had been convinced that "salvation is of the Jew." Humbly, but deeply aware of his responsibility, the Jew feels that his mission is not yet ended, that more than ever before he is required to make the wilderness blossom as a rose, and that for humanity he must be a pathfinder and a willing servant.

Chapter 33

THE STATE OF ISRAEL

Thus saith the Lord God: I will gather you from among the people and assemble you out of the countries where ye have been scattered, and I will give you the land of Israel.

More than 2,500 years ago a dramatic, dynamic chapter of modern twentieth-century history was written by a Jewish priest of no official standing, one indeed who, because of his outspoken criticism, was not especially popular with either the leaders or members of the community. The fortunes of the Jews, even then no strangers to misfortune, had rarely been at a lower ebb. Because the people had forsaken the laws of God, the Temple had been destroyed, Jerusalem laid waste, and the king with his people carried captive to Babylon.

Then it was that Ezekiel, the son of Buzi, inspired by God, spoke to the people of things that had been and of things that in the fullness of time would come to pass. There was nothing vague about his prophecy, none of the ambiguity of the pagan oracles. In plain and unmistakable words he foretold the inevitable doom of Egypt, Assyria, Persia, and "the men of the land that is in league."

Moreover, perhaps even foreseeing the charnel houses of Hitler's Europe, Ezekiel was set down in a valley which was full of bones. And God said to him: "These bones are the whole house of Israel; behold, they say, Our bones are dried and our hope is lost." And Ezekiel prophesied again: "Thus saith the Lord God: Behold, O My people, I will open your graves and cause you to come out of your graves and bring you into the land of Israel."

The creation of the State of Israel must stand as the greatest contribution which the Jews have made to history since the canonization of the Bible. This modern miracle of a people re-born and of a new society built in the ancient homeland and on the ideals of an ancient faith cannot be explained in any rational terms. Had such an event occurred in the days of old, the rabbis surely would have deemed it worthy to be given a place in the Holy Scriptures.

The people of the world of today have been privileged to watch the fulfillment of prophecy, to see a people condemned to death rising from the holocaust of an unprecedented martyrdom to stand up as free men, regenerated, vital, and ready to face any eventuality. As for the Jews, it would be difficult to find words that better describe their incredulous exultation than the lines of Psalm CXXVI:

> When the Lord brought back those that returned to Zion,
> We were like unto them that dream.
> Then was our mouth filled with laughter,
> And our tongue was singing;
> Then said they among the nations:
> "The Lord hath done great things with these."
> The Lord hath done great things with us;
> We are rejoiced.

The birth of modern Israel provides a fascinating study of history and divine destiny. The Holy Land, cradle of the Jewish people and of Judaism, became the center of three world re-ligions. Throughout the centuries it remained the focus of Jewish aspiration and prayer. The yearning of the Jewish soul was poignantly echoed by the psalmist's words: "If I forget thee, O Jerusalem, let my right hand forget its cunning. Let my tongue cleave to the roof of my mouth, if I remember thee not, if I prefer not Jerusalem above my chief joy."

From remote antiquity to the present day Palestine has been a tempting prize for ambitious nations. Strategic link between west and east, its military significance often overshadowed the spiritual uniqueness as the Holy Land. Jerusalem—ironically the name signifies "the city of peace"—again and again became the center of bloodshed and strife. Conquest followed conquest. Assyria ousted Egypt. The Babylonian Nebuchadrezzar destroyed the Temple, only to be struck down himself by the Persians. Alexander the Great conquered the whole east, but his death spelled ruin to all his dreams. Again Palestine became the plaything between east and west. Syrians followed the Ptolemies. Cross and crescent clashed in the Holy Land. Finally, Sultan Selim annexed it in 1517, and for exactly four hundred years Palestine languished under Turkish rule.

Suffering has been the badge of the Jewish people: "If there are ranks in suffering, Israel takes precedence of all the nations." Truly could Byron say:

> The wild-dove hath her nest, the fox his cave,
> Mankind their country—Israel but the grave.

Far from Palestine, dreamers in the ghettos of Europe began to have visions of a new life, a reborn Jewish Palestine. "Zionism" became the name of their striving for the reestablishment of an autonomous country in the Holy Land.

Moses Hess was the first Zionist in the modern sense. In his *Rome and Jerusalem,* published in 1862, he urged the creation of a new Jewish life in the old homeland, on the basis of Mosaic principles. The literature of the Jew appeared to him as the historical plan for the development of mankind, and he visualized the solution of the Jewish problem as a steppingstone on the road to universal brotherhood.

Leo Pinsker viewed the Jewish situation with the eyes of a pathologist. Two diseases, he felt, were responsible for the misery of the Jews: loss of self-respect and "Judeophobia," the psychic aberration of mankind. Both would disappear as soon as the Jews had again become a healthy and free nation. "We must not persuade ourselves that humanity and enlightenment alone can cure the malady of our people. That we may not be compelled to wander from one exile to another, we must have an extensive productive land of refuge, a center which is our own."

Pinsker expressed his thoughts in a manifesto which bore the significant title *Auto-Emancipation* and was published in 1882. As his motto the author used the words of Rabbi Hillel: "If I do not help myself who will help me? And if not now, when?"

Jewish students in Russia became the first modern "lovers of Zion." Out of the anguish of the Czarist pogroms they traveled to Palestine, inspired by the biblical phrase: "O House of Jacob, come, let us go." Their movement was known as *Bilu,* the initials of the four Hebrew words of that particular verse. In 1882 they started the first modern Jewish colony in Palestine.

Ascher Ginzberg, writing under the pseudonym "Ahad Ha-Am" (One of the People), proclaimed his philosophy of a spiritual center in the Holy Land. He refused to believe in the optimism of the zealous Zionists who saw in Palestine a panacea for all the political, economic, and social ills of the Jew. He contended that a mere political solution and mass immigration were "not the way." The return to Judaism had to precede return to the Promised Land: "There is no room here for compromise." The creation of an invincible faith and indomitable will were necessary for a great and constructive national effort. The Jew, therefore, had first to be prepared spiritually and intellectually. Palestine was to be the refuge of the Jew's soul rather than his body. Then would arise in that small country, in an atmosphere of unhampered freedom, a "centre of emulation" for Israel and all mankind.

The superhuman zeal of one man, Eliezer ben Yehuda, created modern Hebrew. He was convinced that only a Jewish tongue in a Jewish land could ensure Jewish life. Born in Lithuania, he went to the Holy Land in 1881, and for twelve years his was the only Hebrew-speaking family. Considered a madman by the early colonists and a blasphemer by the zealots, he was taunted, excommunicated, and imprisoned. But he persevered. With his wife he traveled all over the world to read every available Hebrew manuscript. On a million index cards he gathered every Hebrew word in existence. He himself invented all terms that were missing. His dictionary, covering all the requirements of life, created the modern tongue.

At the time of his death Ben Yehuda had finished only five of eleven projected volumes, but the rest of the material was ready and needed only final editing by his widow. He had thus virtually completed his chosen task. Thirty thousand Jews followed Yehuda's coffin. However, a dead language come to life again is his everlasting memorial and the symbol of the power of an ideal.

The greatest prophet of Zionism was Theodor Herzl. His *Judenstaat*, published in 1896, became the blueprint of the land of Israel. He wrote it in Paris under the spell of a rapturous emotion, asserting: "We are a people, one people." In splendid vision he looked into the future:

We shall live at last as free men on our own soil and die peacefully in our own homes. . . . The world will be freed by our liberty, enriched by our wealth, magnified by our greatness . . . and whatever we attempt there to accomplish for our own welfare, will react powerfully and beneficently for the good of humanity.

Ridiculed and humiliated, Herzl fought on undaunted: "If you but want it this is no dream." By 1897 he had gathered enough followers to make possible the first World Zionist Congress at Basel. After it had finished he wrote in his diary: "What I have done today is to found a Jewish State. . . . If I spoke these words out aloud I should be laughed at. But I am certain that in fifty years' time from now everybody will see I am right." His prophecy was to be fulfilled almost to the precise year.

The critical opportunity emerged from the welter of World War I when, after the "glorious failure" of the Dardanelles, Britain engaged the Turks in the desert of Sinai. It is credibly reported that at about this time Dr. Chaim Weizmann, a brilliant chemist, had presented the British government with his own process for synthesizing a vital munitions material. He was offered rewards, both in money and in honors, but to all these offers he replied, "All that I ask is that Great Britain should help my fellow-Jews to find a homeland."

Whether *post hoc* or *propter hoc*, it was on 2 November 1917 that, in the form of a letter to Lord Rothschild, the famous British statesman issued his historic "Balfour Declaration" which declared that "H.M. Government view with favour the establish-

ment in Palestine of a National Home for the Jewish People."
Little more than a month later, on 9 December (during the Jewish festival of Chanukah), General Allenby entered Jerusalem at the head of British, Australian, and Indian forces. Before the campaign ended nine months later, Jewish forces, too, were to play their part in the conquest of Palestine.

Meantime, at a service of thanksgiving held in London, the then Chief Rabbi of the British Empire had said: "And now, on the very day when Judas Maccabeus rescued Jerusalem from the heathen, the Holy City has passed into British occupation. A new future with undreamt-of possibilities opens before this Eternal City of the Eternal People." Five years later, in 1922, the League of Nations handed to Great Britain the mandate for Palestine.

In ever-increasing volume, streams of young Jews entered Palestine to build and to plant. Spurred on by a holy zeal and inspired by a sacred enthusiasm, they turned the malarial swamps into fragrant pastures and made the desert flower like a garden. Settlements and villages appeared, and the first all-Jewish city for two thousand years, Tel Aviv, the "Hill of the Spring," became a landmark.

The advent of Hitler in 1933 changed Jewish history more profoundly and tragically than the history of the rest of mankind. The concentration camps, the jack-booted storm troopers, the Streichers—these became the symbols of Nazi culture and "Nordic" civilization. Though some nations opened their doors to a restricted number of refugees, it was to Palestine, the "National Home of the Jewish People" promised by Balfour, that the vast majority looked for a haven. The arrival of these hunted people, in hundreds and then in thousands, created new problems, and the Arabs, who had given trouble in earlier years, launched a fresh wave of violence and terrorism. Attacks on the new agricultural colonies and the murder of settlers occurred daily, and the "watchtower" became the symbol and safeguard of the settlements. Indeed, it was at this time that Britain authorized, trained, and armed the Jewish defense force, *Haganah*, of which so much was to be heard in later, even unhappier years.

The Arabs threatened to start a holy war to extend wherever

Islam was practiced; and, with the threat of a European war becoming ever more imminent, royal commissions and round-table conferences having failed to pacify the truculent Arabs, the mandatary power issued a White Paper—on the very eve of World War II, in 1939—setting a limit on Jewish immigration of another 75,000 persons within the ensuing five years, after which Jews might enter their "National Homeland" only with Arab approval.

Then indeed it seemed to the Jews that the cup of succor had, at the most tragic hour of their history, been dashed from their lips. But war broke out, and Jews throughout the free world had to table their own problem while pursuing the common task of crushing the Nazi tyrant. Even, or rather especially, the Jews in Palestine—the Yishuv, or "those who had settled"—mobilized their resources to the utmost. Denied at first the right to bear arms against the Nazi in their own fighting units, they enlisted in the regular British forces. They also labored willingly to build and helped to man naval bases, cantonments, airfields, and hospitals. They established laboratories and factories to supply urgently needed munitions, medicines, and supplementary foodstuffs. Then, at last, on the personal orders of the greatest Briton of them all, Winston Churchill, they were permitted to create their own Brigade Group, and Jewish soldiers under the British High Command fought with gallantry and distinction under the Union Jack and the blue and white Shield of David.

Six years of bitter struggle ended. The liberating armies of the West and the East unlocked the doors of "Festung Europa" and, to the horrified eyes of all mankind, revealed the gas chambers and the mass graves where six million Jews had died. Some few had survived, and the Jews dared to hope that justice would at last be done to the stepchild of humanity. Unfortunately, during the hours of peril, promises had been given or commitments made to the Arabs, unworthy though they had proved themselves to be. More commissions, more inquiries, more negotiations, took place. All were fruitless.

At last, in 1947, with all the evidence before them, the United

Nations, by thirty-three votes to ten, decided that Palestine should be partitioned between the Arabs and the Jews and that the British mandate be terminated before 1 August 1948.

The Arabs protested and threatened. Violence again raged in the Holy Land, and tensions, bitter and often tragic, arose between the Yishuv and the mandatary power. But Britain had accepted the decision of the United Nations and, on the night of 14–15 May 1948, relinquished the mandate and left Palestine, avoiding the Arab Scylla and the Jewish Charybdis by transferring authority to neither one nor the other.

Within the hour an event occurred without precedent in the recorded history of mankind. A homeless people came home. Exiled for nearly two thousand years, since the day of the Roman Caesars, the Jewish people returned. In the new Jewish city of Tel Aviv, the new Jewish Commonwealth of Israel was proclaimed "by virtue of the natural and historical rights of the Jewish people and of the Resolution of the General Assembly of the United Nations." The dreams and prayers of two thousand years, the prophecies of the ancient seers, had been fulfilled, and what Field-Marshal Smuts had declared to be "an historical necessity" was at last an accomplished fact.

A provisional government was selected by the Jewish Agency which, under the mandate, had represented major Jewish interests. Among its first proclamations, the new government declared that as a sacred principle the State of Israel would be open to the immigration of Jews from all countries and:

It will promote the development of the country for the benefit of all its inhabitants; it will be based on the precepts of liberty, justice and peace taught by the Hebrew prophets; it will uphold full social and political equality for all its citizens, without distinction of race, creed or sex; it will guarantee full freedom of conscience, worship, education and culture; it will safeguard the sanctity and inviolability of the shrines and holy places of all religions, and will dedicate itself to the principles of the Charter of the United Nations.

In 1949, Israel was accepted as the fifty-ninth member state of the United Nations, and in 1950 the Israeli government announced that its capital and seat of government would be in Jerusalem.

As its first President, the government proudly and logically selected the aged but still intellectually great Chaim Weizmann, lifelong Zionist and long-time leader of the world-wide Zionist Federation, the man whose genius in two wars had been at the disposal of Britain and her allies. Weizmann, student of world history, fully realized that the state would not be handed to the Jewish people on a silver platter. The right to nationhood, as recent experience had shown, must be earned or it would be lost. That there would be difficulties had been anticipated, but few observers could foretell how immediate and how bitter they would be.

Hemmed in to north, east, and south by various Arab nations of disparate degrees of civilization and political unity, and with a large and mainly hostile Arab majority within their own boundaries, Jewish leaders had well realized that when they attained independence they would need to be alert against possible attack, most likely from the east or from the south. Actually, within a few days of the proclamation of the state, no fewer than five Arab armies marched on Israel, violating its frontiers on all sides. Egyptian planes showered bombs on Tel Aviv and Jerusalem, and marauding commando bands pounced on undefended settlements and massacred their entire populations.

An improvised Israeli force sprang into existence. It was based on the Haganah and was manned by officers, noncoms, and men who had served in the famous British Eighth Army. To them were added young and old men and women untrained in the arts of war, but armed with a religious and patriotic fervor, though with little else. Armored cars and tanks were improvised, and a few planes and some modern weapons were purchased in Europe.

Israel's "War of Liberation" was a triumph of strategy and tactics. Fighting on internal lines, but assailed from three sides, with the Mediterranean forming the fourth, it often happened that a unit scarcely knew which battle it was fighting and in which direction was its opponent. Miracles of valor were performed by individuals, by units, and by cities. The Jews' heroic stand in the siege of Jerusalem by the well-equipped and highly trained Arab legion of Glubb Pasha is itself an epic of masterful improvisation and unconquerable determination. The spirit of the Maccabees was again abroad in the hills and on the plains of Israel.

One by one the battered and frustrated Arab armies were flung back to and beyond the proclaimed boundaries of Israel. It was reported that so far were the Arabs unaware of the extent of their defeat that the Egyptian representatives at the eventual armistice convention demanded immunity for a village which had been captured by Israel weeks earlier and was by then fifty miles behind the southern front line.

Thus the victory was won, though at a price in blood and property that the young state could ill afford. Yet from this, too, a lesson was derived by David ben Gurion, first Israeli Premier, when he proudly declared: "It was as well for us, for history and for the world to know that we were not made a present of independence but paid a supreme price for it with the lives of our dearest sons. We set up our State with our own hands."

Victory did not bring surcease from struggle. The strain of a war, literally for life or death, would have taxed to the full the powers of any people; but when the war ended Israel was confronted with a problem of different character but equal gravity. Through the gates of Israel, now for the first time widely opened, there flowed in hundreds and thousands of immigrants who had to be absorbed at once. Such a problem would have been almost beyond solution had it involved only people who were healthy and vigorous; but the vast majority of the newcomers were wounded in body or mind. They were men, women, and children who had escaped death as if by a miracle and were still haunted by memories of the horror camps where in most cases they had witnessed the murder and the martyrdom of their families. Without hope for so many years, they felt too weak to cope with the problem of living.

Indomitably, Israel faced the task of adjusting, rehabilitating, and salvaging this pitiful human wreckage. The problem was further complicated by another factor. Israel was no longer the land flowing with milk and honey of biblical days. Even the former smiling agricultural settlements had, for the greater part, been ravaged by war, and the soil was barren and arid. Yet food, as well as clothing and other necessities, had to be found for the thousands who had come and continued to come from the starvation of the camps. Israel itself, the Yishuv, wrought miracles of economy and economics and in this area found help from the Jewish communities throughout the world and from some great and humane governments who realized that Israel was entitled to help. This was offered unstintingly.

Thus Israel overcame the enemy without and the crisis within. As the patriarch Jacob in ancient days had done, so his modern descendants wrestled with their fate and prevailed to merit the biblical phrase: "Thy name shall be ... *Israel;* for thou hast striven with God and with men and hast prevailed."

The creation of the State of Israel transformed Jewish fate and gave the individual Jew a different outlook. No longer did he need to live in lands of persecution and discrimination, haunted by fear that he might again be driven from his home, to wander as a refugee without a haven. To the pitiful initials of the "displaced person" (D.P.) was given a new and dynamic interpretation: "Destination Palestine." Now banished for all time is the figure of the Jew standing in his hundreds as a supplicant at the doors of foreign embassies, seeking an entry permit which might be given or refused at the whim of an uninterested official. In his place stands the proud and upright figure of a man who knows that, whether in case of need or at his own free will, he can go to a land which will be his own, where on wharf or at airport he will cease to be a foreigner and will see a banner saying: *B'ruchim Haba'im*—"Blessed be ye who come." At one port of entry another sign once said poignantly: "The ghetto ceases at the gate of Zion." By such signs, and even more by the warmth of welcome which they found in the hearts of the Yishuv, were the new arrivals made to feel that no longer were they refugees or displaced persons, that they were not subjects of suspicion and distrust bound by police regulations and alien restrictions, but brothers who had returned to the home of their ancestors.

Israel has given the Jew self-respect and gained him renown all over the world. No one could ignore its achievements or deny the heroism of its armed forces, the idealism of its pioneers, and the selfless devotion of all its citizens. Profoundly interested, the world watched the unique features of Israel's life develop. The Jews, for so long considered as uprooted wanderers and described as a people of merchants or an idle intelligentsia, proved to be hard workers, breaking stone, paving the streets, tilling the soil, and sailing the seas.

In ancient Hebrew literature Israel was called "the country of the stag." Modern Israel permitted the Jew once again to hold his head high like the stag. As of old, the Jews became an upright people, full of dignity, pride, and self-respect.

Theodor Herzl had spoken of the insuperable force of an ideal, how the raising of a symbol could lead a people anywhere, even into the Promised Land. The young state justified his prophecy. It showed the power of a common ideal which gives sublime fortitude to even the weakest and binds together the most diverse people, overcoming all hazards and obstacles.

The Jew's long history and spiritual heritage have prepared him for the task of realizing eternal ideals in the modern world. The spirit of the pioneer dominated his people. His innate optimism and Messianic zeal imbued him with unsurpassed strength to surmount seemingly impossible odds. The Jew's fervent belief in the equality of man and in human freedom are conditions of pioneering.

A capacity for great intellectual and scientific effort enabled him to apply technological advances in his efforts to restore what had wasted away, to water the desert, and to create the most out of the least. His religious training in self-control made him the ideal pioneer, never surrendering, but, forgetting self, building for the sake of future generations.

The wide opening of the doors of the Promised Land to mass immigration was the supreme test of the Jews. Inevitably it meant hardship and tremendous sacrifice on the part of the old settlers. Yet they did not resent the newcomer. They were happy to bear the burden, to go short of even the necessities of life, to see the "ingathering of the exiles" fulfilled.

Jews came to Israel from sixty countries. Among them were every type, class, and race. They varied in language, customs, tradition, and social condition. They were primitive Yemenite Jews, German university professors, Russian mystics, American business magnates, English technicians, and South African youths. They came either as refugees from lands of tyranny or as free men impelled by a dream and a mission. In spite of their great diversity, they achieved unity. They were molded into one nation and learned to speak with one tongue because above and beyond their differences of dress and language, of thought and outlook, of features and coloring, they were fired by the common ideal to rebuild their ancient homeland and create a model state of society and a citadel of goodness. No wonder, then, that entering into Israel, which has always been regarded as a pilgrimage, is rendered in Hebrew not prosaically as "immigration," but symbolically as an aliyah, or "ascent."

In former days, aged Jews went to the Holy Land to die; now the young go there to live. "Youth Aliyah" became the greatest child migration movement in history. Henrietta Szold, whose sympathies were as wide as the whole world, became the "mother of Israel." Out of the hell of Nazi Germany she rescued 33,000 children and gathered the dispersed and frightened little ones to give them a new home, to restore their belief in human love, and to provide them with care and faith.

Modern Israel became the country of the young. Its motto is Froebel's maxim, "Let us live for our children." Infant mortality in Israel's settlements is among the lowest in the world. The first houses built are always the nurseries and the children's homes. One day in every year is Children's Day, when all adult settlers give up their rest to make toys. One of the foundation stones of the Hebrew University was laid by children on behalf of the young generation. The Israeli-born youth is nicknamed "sabra," after the cactus bushes growing in the land. Like the cactus, he is hardy and prickly. His patriotism is not narrow or intolerant, but inspired by self-sacrificing zeal and wide visions. He is a good and devoted Jew, but he hates to talk about it.

Unique achievements have distinguished the Jewish State from its beginning.

Its most fascinating romance is how Hebrew, the sacred tongue of ancient days, became the everyday language, not of a few extremists but of the whole people. The Jew succeeded in re-creating the speech of King David and the prophet Isaiah in twentieth-century terms. He did so not by government laws or state direction, but by pure idealism. Through conviction that no other language could better convey the Jewish spirit, Hebrew was revived and rejuvenated. Young and old shirked no effort to master it, and a sacred tongue welded the lives of selfless pioneers in the Holy Land.

Unparalleled in history is the "law of return" passed by Israel's Parliament. This guarantees admission to the country to every Jew. The mere fact of his Jewishness entitles him, not as a favor but as a right, to enter Israel and claim Israeli citizenship. Hundreds of thousands of Jews have done so and started a new life. Before the creation of the state, the Jewish population was 650,000. Within three years this number had doubled, representing a growth rate of more than 200,000 a year, more than 4,000 a week, more than 600 a day, every day for three years.

Entire Jewish populations from persecuted countries were transplanted to Israel. "Operation Magic Carpet" will be a legend for future generations. It is like a tale out of the Arabian Nights. As on eagles' wings, modern transport planes wafted Iraqi Jews out of an existence of squalor, danger, and degradation and carried them "home."

The intake of migrants from all over the world has continued throughout the years in fantastic proportion to the population already in the country. Significantly, a vast number of newcomers have not been absorbed into existing communities, but accommodated in completely new territory where the desert has been pushed back into regions once considered uninhabitable.

Within twenty years, five hundred new settlements were established in the small country in this way.

Israel refused to apply any restrictive or selective immigration policy. It did not favor the useful and exclude the burdensome. On the contrary, priority was given to the old, the stricken in body and mind. Poetry exists in the very name Yishuv, as the Jew came to call his settlement, meaning literally "sitting down." At long last the wandering Jew had found his rest.

Attainment of security for himself did not satisfy the Jew. History had taught him that only service to others gave dignity and meaning to life: "If I am for myself alone, what am I?" The teachings of his Bible had become humanity's guide. Throughout the centuries he had enriched the sum total of man's happiness by innumerable individual contributions. But even against his will, his mere existence among the nations had acted as a perpetual conscience which could not be silenced. Now, in Israel, Jews once again became actively, creatively, and collectively torchbearers and servants of humanity. They became such in most diverse ways: in simple habit and important legislation, in unparalleled experiments, and powerful institutions.

The project of the Jewish National Fund to restore Israel's arid lands and prevent soil erosion by the planting of trees (started as early as 1905) was to prove profoundly important. Reafforestation became not just a national program but almost a sacred pursuit. Other countries confer titles and orders on people they wish to honor. The Jews show their esteem by planting trees in their name in the ancient land. Israel's Martyrs' Forest thus commemorates each of the six million men, women, and children exterminated by the Nazis. Forests honor Queen Elizabeth II, Sir Winston Churchill, John F. Kennedy, the Australian and New Zealand servicemen who fell in the Middle East. A boy's bar mitzvah, a couple's wedding, the passing of a friend—in fact, any moment of joy or sorrow—is perpetuated by planting a sapling, a living monument that one day will grow into a mighty tree. He who plants a tree, a Jewish tradition says, plants the future.

By the application of highly scientific methods, Israel increased agricultural productivity sixfold in two decades despite numerous arid areas, and the country's cattle, sheep, and poultry are among the most prolific in the world. Harnessing the wind, the sun, and the atom, Israel's progress in every dimension is unending. "In Israel we are realists," Chaim Weizmann once said; "that is why we believe in miracles." Israel is one of the few nations which have developed a system of accelerated social and economic advance without losing the democratic way of life.

Israel was the first and remains the only country in the Middle East where men and women share all civil rights and responsibilities, where education is free and compulsory, where absolute freedom is given and guaranteed to all men to follow their own faith. The Arab was no friend to the Jew, and during the war of liberation the majority of Arabs fled the country, thus causing, by their own action, yet another problem. They had no need to flee. Those that remained are Israeli citizens with full and equal rights. Arab men and—for the first time, perhaps, in the history of the world—Arab women have full voting rights, and in the Parliament of Israel a number of Arab representatives sit, still dressed in their native robes and speaking to the members in the Arab tongue.

Dire necessity forced the system of compulsory military service on the community, but unique in this, as in many other matters, the Jew so legislated that his citizen-soldiers, young men and young women alike, devote part of their period of service to learning and practicing the art of agriculture.

In social legislation, too, Israel was a pioneer. First of its kind in history, a "village of the blind" was established in 1950. In it, blind Jews from all over the world, Orient and Occident, found a new existence. Its objective was to help blind men and women to help themselves, so that they need not rely on charity and pity, but find happiness and their own place under the sun. There are pure poetry and a revelation of tender piety in the name given to this village: Or Adonai (The Light of God).

To grow old is the inevitable lot of mankind. To be old is no hardship of itself, but to be old and to feel unwanted and useless is a tragedy that befalls all too many in this, the "age of youth." "Cast me not out in old age" is an ancient Hebrew supplication reflecting a haunting fear in the heart of many. Modern Israel has answered this fervent prayer in yet another of its unequaled achievements. In its "village of the old," the aged no longer lead a lonely and empty existence or become objects of charitable impersonal institutions. They have been given a life of their own. Each of them has some kind of constructive, daily occupation. The library, the workshop, and even the local post office are run by the old people. Israel, a country built up by the young, has offered a sanctuary for the old.

Bernard Shaw is reputed to have said, "The Jew is born civilized." Israel, though beset by numerous problems, felt from the outset that art is not a luxury, but a vital and indispensable necessity for any nation. The new state soon developed a number of distinguished artistic centers where art belonged to the people and was not the property of a small coterie. *Habimah,* once a wandering company of struggling actors, has become, as its name implies, *"the* stage," with great acting as a sublime medium of religious fervor. *Ohel* (the tent) was started as an experimental progressive and democratic workers' theater.

The Israeli Philharmonic Orchestra, founded by violinist Bronislaw Hubermann, has rightly been called "an orchestra of soloists." The Hebrew National Opera is an essential part of the cultural life of the Holy Land. No name could be more appropriate than that of the School of Arts—*Bezalel*—called after the artificer of biblical days who was described as being inspired by God in the craft of fabricating in gold, silver, brass, stone, and wood.

Bezalel now forms part of the gigantic complex of the Israel Museum in Jerusalem which presents Israel's spiritual heritage, thereby fulfilling Herzl's dream of displaying "the tangible evidence of a people's culture." The Shrine of the Book is its very center. It preserves the most precious of recent finds, the Dead Sea Scrolls, and reveres the greatest gift of the Jewish people to mankind, the Book of Books.

Beyond and in many ways above all these achievements, Israel offers promise of infinite benefit to mankind through two other institutions: the kibbutz (collective settlement), a purely Jewish innovation in the field of rural community life, and the Hebrew University, which affords an unprecedented concentration of Jewish genius in one focal center.

The kibbutz may well become one of Israel's most prominent contributions to the advance of mankind. It has been called the most exciting undertaking in the world, the translation into tangible reality of the spirit—a spirit which comes down from oldest times, yet looks forward to the future. In the kibbutz the Jewish ideals of human equality and social justice are realized in a society based on freedom and passionate belief in the dignity of personality.

Social pioneers combined in collective groups in the country of their adoption. All members joined, not under state coercion, but of their own free will and out of the urge to serve. They owned nothing themselves; everything was shared. Their labor belonged to the community; yet the value of the individual within the group was recognized and respected. The opportunity of sacrifice for a cause and of service to the community sanctified their existence.

Vibrant with the joy of life and assimilating the cream of European culture, the kibbutz created a unique kind of peasant who was idealist, scholar, and pioneer in one. Accepting the discipline of a common task, his manner of living taught him to bear and forbear. It demanded cooperation, loyalty, efficiency, and moral integrity. There was no place for the selfish and mediocre.

In the kibbutz, everybody gives of his best and receives what he needs, with the complete exclusion of the profit motive and the spur of economic competition. A pride of achievement and a missionary zeal have taken the place of the incentives of materialist society.

Every kibbutznik (settler) feels himself or herself a partner in an enterprise destined not only to feed the population of Israel but by way of idealistic example to prepare the way for a better world. Thus inspired, each strives to the utmost, not for fear of reproof or in the hope of higher wages and better conditions, but in a burning, religious belief in the inherent dignity and greatness of his quest.

Since 1909, when the first collective settlement was established and named Dagania (the place of corn), hundreds of new settlements have been formed—the majority, naturally, since the birth of the state.

There are several variations of the common plan. Some settlements are almost purely communal, with common ownership of land, livestock, implements, and the profits of the united effort. From colonies of this type, any settler may withdraw (though few do so) and claim his share from the common pool. Provision is made for the higher education of children who show exceptional promise, and all settlers may, in rotation, go for holidays to the bigger cities or to the seaside.

On the other end of this scale are the almost purely cooperative settlements, where each individual owns his own land and livestock. More costly implements are purchased cooperatively, while crop programs and the marketing of produce are handled on a democratically decided plan.

The colonies vary in their degrees of religious adherence. Some are of the most complete Orthodoxy, while others express equally sincere Jewishness in their love for the spirit of the new Israel.

Many colonies are based on former common nationality. There are "German," "Russian," "South African," "American," and "British" settlements, but their adherence to their various designations is purely one of sentiment or tradition, and their love and loyalty are for Eretz Yisrael.

Scattered throughout Israel, these settlements may vary in emphasis and philosophy, but their basic ideals are the same. As a compromise between state direction and uninhibited free enterprise, they offer the world a new pattern of life that combines respect for human personality, social ardor, and communal responsibility.

Cardinal Newman, famous theologian and lecturer, once envisaged the creation in Jerusalem of a university which would exercise an influence as potent and as worldwide as the spiritual influence of mankind's Holy City. In 1918, while the sounds of war could still be heard but a few miles away, a site was selected and the foundation stone laid for the Hebrew University in Jerusalem. To a notable assemblage, including leaders of the Christian and Moslem communities and Jews from Palestine, America, England, Egypt, Australia, and many other countries, General Allenby described the mere fact that the ceremony was held at a moment when fate was still in the balance as an act of faith that must give heart and courage to his army and to all the allied powers.

The selected site was on Mount Scopus, where Titus once pitched his camp when he conquered Jerusalem and destroyed the Temple. Symbolically this expressed Jewish conviction that history had come full circle; where formerly the enemy of their faith had seen his triumph, they would build a new shrine dedicated to truth, to the great truths of culture. This was to be no mere gesture of restoration but a positive determination that the Jewish people should again become creative. No longer was the Jew to be a wanderer on the face of the earth; here would he settle and aim to offer service to all mankind.

Seven years later, in 1925, Lord Balfour inaugurated the Hebrew University. He reminded his audience of the contribution to thought made by three Jews of his generation: Einstein, Freud, and Bergson. So far, humanity had known only the separate efforts of separate individual Jews, men of science, doctors, theologians, and philosophers, scattered all over the world. Now, in the Hebrew University, Jewish genius and talent could combine in a supreme quest for truth and knowledge.

Nothing in history has ever paralleled such an accumulation of zeal, ability, and intellect. The first lecture in the university was given by Professor Einstein. He spoke on his theory of relativity and used Hebrew for his opening sentence. He presented the library of the university with its greatest treasure, the manuscript of his treatise on relativity.

Today, the Hebrew University occupies a unique place in the State of Israel and the pattern of Jewish life. Its development has been phenomenal. As prophesied, it gathered Jewish talent from the four corners of the earth and not only contributed largely to the development of the young nation but served as a source of enlightenment and progress in the Middle East. Its horizon is worldwide and its endeavor the realization of the ancient Jewish ideal to contribute to the welfare of all men and nations.

Jewish learning has been restored to its citadel in Zion in the framework of modern research. Bible, Talmud, and Jewish history are approached in a scientific manner. Discoveries, especially in archaeology, and not least the finds of the Dead Sea Scrolls and of other manuscripts in the ancient fortress of Masada, have had a radical effect on the teaching of these subjects and have stirred the world.

The school of Oriental studies is distinguished by the brilliance of its scholars. Medical research has found new ways to combat the endemic and epidemic diseases of the Middle East. The department of social studies has aided immensely the absorption of new immigrants. The determined efforts of the university's chemical and geological research have made the desert bloom and converted areas, arid and barren for centuries, into orchards and forests.

Through the Hebrew University, the Jew, so old in soul, is renewing his mind. In its ever-expanding growth, the Hebrew University is well on the way to becoming the focal spiritual center for world Jewry and, perhaps, a mighty power for goodness to all humanity.

It has always been Israel's wish to hand on the benefits of its own hard-learned experience by sending its best pioneers and workers abroad to give help wherever it has been needed and wanted. Thus, in 1958, the young state launched a program of international cooperation which went far beyond mere economic assistance and technical aid.

Within ten years, nineteen hundred Israeli experts had served in sixty-two countries, ranging from the rapidly emerging new African nations and the Mediterranean region to Latin American republics and far-off Asia. Their advice and work covered such diverse spheres as rural planning (particularly in connection with arid zones), cooperative markets, economic organization, establishment of pioneer and youth movements, vocational training, medicine, social adaptation of immigrants, and community development in the form of the admired Israeli kibbutz. Wherever they went, Israel's dedicated experts were able to arouse enthusiasm in tackling difficult tasks, training the people in new skills, and establishing appropriate organizational methods for new countries with limited resources.

Israel's efforts at selfless "colonization" for other people was vastly different from anything that had been done before. The Israelis never stayed on or gathered riches for themselves. All they acquired was the knowledge that they had given of their best and forged bonds of friendship. They initiated a program of what has become known as integrated projects. When the Israeli expert visited a distant country, its nationals were invited to Israel to be trained there. On their return they could, as key personnel, easily take the place of the Israeli pathfinder. For example, when a team of Israeli doctors was establishing an eye clinic in an African country, one of its doctors and a team of nurses were simultaneously being trained in Israel, with the result that the clinic is now entirely under the supervision of an African staff. The motto of its program of international cooperation is symbolic of Israel's modern mission: "To teach, to serve and to leave."

The cessation of hostilities in 1949 did not bring final peace and security. The Suez campaign of 1956, and the six-day war in 1967, demanded new sacrifice in the face of a foe who had sworn the annihilation of Israel. Indomitable in a struggle that left them "no choice," the Israelis won reunification of Jerusalem and the return of the Western Wall, that sole remnant of the ancient sanctuary, into their hands. The figure of the victor of Sinai, the dashing Moshe Dayan, with his eye patch, became a romantic symbol of Israel's military leadership, and strategists all over the world came to regard his lightning campaign as a classic.

However, the Jew does not want war. Bloodshed of any kind

contradicts his entire philosophy of life and faith and only delays dismally the realization of his dream of a world worthy of God and man. In Spain, Jews and Arabs once lived together in friendship and jointly created one of the world's highest civilizations. Today, hope has not died that the time will come again when Jew and Arab, both Abraham's children, will dwell together, not as pawns of power politics, but as dedicated servants of the One God they both worship, peacefully and in brotherhood.

In Israel, the Jew attempts to build up a society in which social justice, liberty, and religion combine. Its aim is the creation of a state so clean and perfect that its very being will radiate a new spirit and a new morality to the farthest corners of the earth. The Jews are known as the people of the Book. Their only justification for existence is their religion. In Israel, they apply Judaism. Thus, the Jews' contribution to humanity is no longer confined to the glorious tenets of a book or the separate efforts of gifted individuals. It extends to the supreme example of a life and a people. "For out of Zion shall go forth the Law, and the word of God from Jerusalem."

Chapter 34

IN SEARCH OF THE TEN LOST TRIBES

Modern Jews trace their origin to the ancient Israelitish nation. This was composed of tribal groups who were said to be the direct descendants of Jacob's twelve sons and who therefore bore their names. They were:

Reuben	Judah	Dan	Naphtali
Simeon	Zebulun	Gad	Joseph
Levi	Issachar	Asher	Benjamin

On their way through the desert from Egypt to Canaan, the Israelites marched and pitched camp according to their tribal divisions. After they had conquered the Holy Land, Joshua apportioned a definite territory to each tribe, with the exception of Levi, who was charged with the care of the Sanctuary and "wholly given unto the Lord on behalf of the children of Israel." For that reason this tribe owned no fixed area, but had forty-eight cities in various parts of the land reserved for their residence. On the other hand, "Joseph" was subdivided into the descendants of his two sons, Ephraim and Manasseh, each of whom was allocated a separate district.

For many years the tribes remained independent, often fighting their own battles and going their individual way. They were ruled by Judges, a title which implied much more than judicial authority. Yet they soon learned that all of them were members of one people and that only as a united nation with a central government could they survive.

Eager to imitate other people, they desired to have a king. Unwillingly and against his better judgment, Samuel, the last Judge, anointed Saul (in 1040 B.C.E.), who thus became the first king of Israel. He consolidated the state and unified the nation. His reign was marked by many wars. He himself was deeply unhappy and suffered from frequent moods of depression. When he fell in battle against the Philistines, David succeeded him. Beloved by the people, David became the ideal king. He was a military genius and the greatest conqueror in the history of Israel. Thanks to his vision, Jerusalem became Jewry's capital. He was followed by his son Solomon, who will always be remembered as the last king of the united nation and the builder of the first Temple, which he dedicated as a house of prayer for all men, "that all the people of the earth may know Thy name."

Noted for his sagacity, Solomon was not concerned with new wars. He consolidated his father's conquests, and his reign was notable for its preservation of peace. But within the nation itself seeds of grave disaffection were sown, aggravating the already existing tendency of the northern tribes to regard the south with jealousy and suspicion. On several previous occasions, this had led to a temporary disruption of the kingdom. People watched with ever-increasing disgust the luxurious life of the king and his wasteful expenditure of huge sums of money on the extension of an already enormous royal household. They resented the lavish building program and the adornment of Jerusalem at the expense of all other tribes. Most of all, however, it was their conscription into unpaid labor battalions and the unprecedentedly heavy taxation that roused their anger.

An attempted rebellion was suppressed. Its leader, Jeroboam, a former captain of the task force, fled abroad and found shelter as a political refugee in Egypt.

In 933 B.C.E., King Solomon died. The people felt that at last their opportunity had come to assert their rights and gain their freedom. They were no longer willing to be used as chattels and exploited as a source of money and labor. Jeroboam returned from his exile and confronted Rehoboam, the king's rightful heir and successor. He voiced the people's demands clearly, but the young and impetuous son of Solomon was not prepared to listen. However, at a public gathering of all the representatives of the entire nation, the people refused to acknowledge his kingship unconditionally. First of all they insisted on a declaration of his intentions and future policy. The counsel of his friends, all lusting for power, but inexperienced in rulership, confirmed him in his determination to establish his reign by a show of force. To make any concessions then, he felt, would be a wrong start. Arrogantly he proclaimed that if his father's rule had been hard, his would be even harsher.

The great mass of the people, consisting of the ten northern tribes, rejected Rehoboam and chose Jeroboam as their king. Since they embraced almost the whole nation (with the exception of Judah and part of Benjamin), they retained the old name and continued to call themselves the kingdom of Israel. The south, however, remained loyal to Solomon's son and enthroned him. Predominantly made up of the tribe of Judah, the new—remnant—state became known by its name. This is still borne today by the Jewish people, the sole survivors of the kingdom of Judah, for *Jew* means a person from Judah.

Thus, the cleavage between north and south, latent for so many years, became real and lasting. The Jews were divided: the one people had become two separate states. The kingdom of Judah, in the south, continued to choose its rulers from the house of David. Israel, embracing ten of the twelve tribes, went its own way. Though exceeding Judah three times in area and twice in the number of its population, the Northern Kingdom lacked cohesion, spiritual force, or any sense of social justice. Immorality was rife; idolatry and all kinds of pagan customs vitiated the purity of monotheistic faith. The poor had no rights and were exploited by the rich. The prophets' voice went unheeded. Israel became the plaything of pagan nations. The priests and other citizens left the country and migrated to Judah. Afraid that the people might still visit Jerusalem for worship and be won back into allegiance to the Judaic dynasty, Jeroboam established his own two national shrines (in the extreme north and south of his kingdom) and put golden calves in them as a counterattraction to Jerusalem's Temple.

Except for short-lived periods, the two brother states fought each other bitterly, and most of their contacts were collisions.

They did not even shrink from allying themselves with neighboring nations against each other. None of Israel's dynasties was able to establish itself for long. During the 210 years of its existence, it was ruled by nineteen kings, seven of whom reigned only two years or less, and eight of whom were assassinated or committed suicide, with a consequent change of dynasty.

Lacking a moral purpose and loyal allies, with its manhood weakened by a licentious life, drunkenness, and perversions and its leaders playing the dangerous game of power politics, Israel inexorably moved toward its doom. In 722 B.C.E. the Assyrian armies annihilated the state, and thus 210 years of turbulent history came to an inglorious end.

The Bible contains only a brief report of the fate of Israel's population. It states that in the ninth year of the reign of King Hosea, the Assyrian king carried Israel away captive into his land "and placed them in Halah and in Habor on the river of Gozan and in the cities of the Medes" (II Kings XVII, 6). Contemporary Assyrian inscriptions corroborate this statement, the last authentic mention of the ten tribes. Ever since then their fate has become the subject of numerous legends and fantastic claims, all of which reject what is obviously the most probable consequence of the deportation: that once dispersed and settled in foreign surroundings, the Israelites intermarried, losing their identity for all time, and thus no longer exist. Yet it was asserted that the ten tribes did not stay long in the country of their exile, but, anxious to regain their freedom even if unable to return to their ancient home, soon left Assyria to wander on to more distant lands where they were assured of survival.

This is precisely the claim of the Apocrypha, where (in Esdras XIII, 40–46) it is related that the ten tribes, after having been carried away as prisoners,

took counsel among themselves, that they would leave the multitude of the heathen and go forth into a further country where mankind had never dwelt, that they might there keep the statutes which they had never kept in their own land. And they entered by the narrow passages of the river Euphrates. . . . Then after a journey of a year and a half's duration they came into a region called Artzaret. Then dwelt they there until the later time.

For many centuries nothing further was heard about the Israelites. But distance of time did not lessen the mystery of their disappearance or the hope that one day the ten lost tribes would be rediscovered.

Ancient Jewish tradition believed in the existence of a legendary river called Sambation. Its name was thought to have been derived from the Sabbath, for obvious reasons. It was said either that its waters flowed throughout the six days of the week, but, out of respect for God's creation, rested on the Sabbath, or that, on the contrary, the river remained dry for six days, but then developed into a torrent. Another explanation was that it consisted not of water, but of sand and stones, which it cast up throughout the week. Whatever the "facts" were about the Sabbatical river, it soon became closely associated with the ten lost tribes, who were believed to dwell safely behind its sheltering barrier (whether of stones or water). However absurd this assertion may sound to the modern mind, scholarly men and even potentates accepted the legend as factual, and men went out to look for the river in countries far beyond the Middle East: in India, Africa, Spain, and China. Indeed, to seek for it became synonymous with the search for the ten lost tribes.

In the tenth century, a worldwide sensation was caused by the appearance of a Jewish traveler and merchant who called himself Eldad *the Danite*. By his very name he claimed to belong to Dan, one of the lost tribes, several of whom, he related, he had visited in the interior of East Africa. They lived there, he said in his fantastic claim, behind a sevenfold mountain barrier and the river Sambation.

Though there were some who doubted Eldad's words and considered him an untrustworthy adventurer, the majority of people were spellbound and eagerly accepted his story. Men and women to whom he spoke, whether in Spain, North Africa, or the Middle East, were fascinated. His account spread all over the world, first by word of mouth and then in numerous pamphlets which were avidly read and believed.

It may be that after all Eldad was not an unscrupulous man who took advantage of man's credulity. There is a possibility that he came into contact with the Falashas, that isolated and forgotten group of Jews in Africa who were rediscovered only in the nineteenth century.

As soon as the legend of the ten lost tribes was no longer a tale of the distant past, but, once again, through Eldad, a topic of conversation and controversy, of religious fervor and heated debate, among Christians as much as among Jews, fiction and fact were confused more than ever. It was not just historical interest, thirst for sensation, or the fascination of tracing a long-lost group of the early Hebrews that fired the imagination of the people. Most of all, it was a Messianic yearning that made men of deep piety look for the ten lost tribes. It was believed that only when these had been found (and thus the whole of the scattered Jewish people could be reunited, in fulfillment of Ezekiel's prophecy in Ezekiel XXXVII) could the Messiah come and bring peace to mankind.

When, in the seventeenth century, Rabbi Manasseh ben Israel of Amsterdam sent his petition to Oliver Cromwell to readmit the Jews into England, whence they had been expelled for almost four centuries, he, too, sincerely believed that the lost tribes still existed. He was equally convinced of the authenticity of the Sambation legend. "Lastly, all thinke," he wrote in his *Hope of Israel,* "that part of the ten tribes dwell beyond the River Sabbathion or Sabbaticall."

Little wonder, then, that as people were looking for the ten tribes all over the world, fantastic claims were made from the Far East to the distant West, from the Middle Ages to the present time.

Manasseh himself had finally become convinced that the American Red Indians constituted part of the lost Israelites. It was a view which was to be voiced frequently in the centuries that followed, and it is expressed in a huge volume of literature. In his abortive attempt at creating a Jewish state on American soil, Mordecai M. Noah in 1825 invited Red Indians to the inaugural ceremony, as the representatives of the ten lost tribes. Joseph Smith went further, considering the American nation the heir of Israelite immigrants of biblical times. He expressed his conviction in his famous *Book of Mormon,* which became one of the holy writings of the American Church of Jesus Christ of Latter-Day Saints, whose adherents are best known by their original nickname of Mormons.

In Russia a Jewish group, the Karaites, explained that they were the descendants of ancient Israel. Their claim had an important bearing on their personal fate. Czarist authorities, accepting as true the alleged genealogy, exempted them from all anti-Jewish legislation as, having left the Holy Land many centuries before Jesus' time, they could have had no part in his condemnation.

Ancient Irish legend and history have been associated with Hebrew tradition, and early Irish names were identified with biblical figures. Tara, the High Place of the Kings, was variously explained as being called after Terah, Abraham's father, and the Hebrew Torah, Jewry's Law. Hibernia itself, Erin's alternate name, was said to perpetuate the memory of Heber, the son of Shela, whose genealogy is given in the eleventh chapter of Genesis. Early Irish settlers were traced back to the Hebrew Bible. The Scoti and Gaels claimed to have descended from Magog, the son of Japheth. Wild fantasy placed Ur of the Chaldees in Ireland and saw in the round towers the result of Oriental workmanship.

The prophet Jeremiah was said to have settled in Ireland. A tradition related that he had gone there from Egypt, where he had fled after the destruction of the first Temple, and that he had taken with him some of the treasures of the Sanctuary, including the Ark, David's scepter, and the mysterious Urim and Tummim. Another ancient report stated that Hebrew women had been stranded on the Irish shore and had become the wives of the later-arriving Milesians. Even sacred institutions in Erin's life were related to the Israelites, especially the Stone of Destiny on which the kings of Ireland were consecrated and which came to play such an important part in English history. It was claimed to be the very stone on which Jacob rested his weary head by the wayside when he had the famous dream of the heavenly ladder, on which angels were ascending and descending. Refugees from Palestine were said to have carried the stone to Ireland.

It is not surprising, therefore, that with this background of tradition the Irish also came to consider themselves as the remnant of Israel. A ready support to their claim was the passage in the Apocrypha which spoke of the deported tribes, after further migration from Assyria, having eventually settled in Artzaret. This term is merely a contraction of two Hebrew words meaning "another land." It actually refers to the passage in Deuteronomy (XXIX, 27) which spoke of God's rooting out the Jews from their home and casting them into "another land." But a fantastic explanation now identified the word with Ireland, pointing out that *Ar* meant Ire and *Aret* was the Hebrew word for "land."

Of all claims, however, the most fascinating and obdurate is that of the British Israelites. They believe fervently that the Anglo-Saxons are the lost tribes and the true children of Israel. Nothing can shake their conviction, which they base on absurd calculations and manipulations of biblical data, prophecies, and etymology. These first appeared in late seventeenth-century writings, were systematized in the eighteenth century, and clearly expounded by John Wilson in 1840 in *Our Israelitish Origin*.

The British Israelites are convinced that without a doubt the prophets of the Bible were referring to Britain as the eventual home of the Israelites when they spoke of the glorification of the divine name "in the isles of the sea" (Isa. XXIV, 15). Equally, it was the British Unicorn and Lion to which Balaam pointed in his prophecy as related in the Fourth Book of Moses (Num. XXIV, 8–9). The name of the Saxons itself, they contend, was derived from "the sons of Isaac." These had arrived in the British Isles after journeying from their Assyrian exile through many lands in which they had left their traces even in nomenclature. Thus, the tribe of Dan was responsible for the naming of the Russian rivers Don, Dnieper, and Dniester and even of the Danube. The very name of the Danes revealed their Danite origin. But part of the tribe already had reached Ireland in the time of the prophet Jeremiah, led there by his scribe Baruch. With them they had brought the Stone of Destiny. An Israelitish princess who had been among the early migrants had married an Irish chieftain, and the sacred stone was used for their coronation. From this alliance the present Royal House of Britain was descended.

The stone itself did not remain in Ireland. First it was taken to Scotland to serve at Scone in the coronation of Scottish kings. In 1296, King Edward I (six years after he had expelled the Jews from England) had it placed under the coronation chair in Westminster Abbey. There it has been resting ever since (except for a short period when it was removed by Scottish patriots) and has played an important part in the ceremony of the crowning of the sovereign.

If further evidence was needed to prove the Israelite origin of the British people, it was supplied by their very language, which could not deny its many Hebrew roots. For instance, not only did the English berry come from the Hebrew for "fruit" (*p're*), and the kitten grow out of the Hebrew for "little" (*katan*), but, to leave no doubt, the very name of the British was also Hebrew and proclaimed for all time that they were of "the Covenant Man" (*B'rit-Ish*).

Yet another hypothesis is that the ten lost tribes found their way to Japan. N. McLeod, in his *Epitome of the Ancient History of Japan,* the third edition of which was published in Nagasaki in 1875, was the first to draw the world's attention to striking parallels between Japanese traditions and institutions and those of the ancient Hebrews.

Was it an accident, he asked, that the last king of Israel was Hosea (who died in 722 B.C.E.) and that the first-known king of Japan was Osee, who was enthroned during that period? Was it not an obvious conclusion that the Israelitish refugees had established themselves in the Far East and, renewing their kingdom there, had continued their ancient tradition, including their last ruler's name? Even if the proximity of the dates and the similarity of the names were merely coincidental, though in an astonishing degree, other facts appeared to the writer as irrefutable proof of his theory. The Shinto temple, like the Temple in Jerusalem, was divided into a Holy and a Holy of Holies. A linen dress, a miter, and breeches were among the garments of both Israelite and Japanese priests. To support his arguments further, McLeod supplemented his *Epitome* with a volume of illustrations, one of which shows the alleged rafts that carried the Israelite tribes to Japan.

Other writers and scholars added more so-called evidence, which they regarded as concrete facts, gained from a great variety of research ranging from linguistic studies to investigation of comparative religion. Attention was drawn to a Japanese temple called Ohosaki, a word whose meaning—"beloved"—was identical with that of King David's name. Significantly, therefore, it was referred to as "the Temple of David." Other astonishing features were quoted to support the proposition of the Israelite origin of the Japanese. They included the occurrence of the word "Israel" on a stone parapet and the existence of two ancient villages in Japan named Goshen and Menashe and of a city called "River Crossing and Journey Cake," names certainly reminiscent of Israel's redemption from Egypt and Passover.

There is no doubt that Judaism reached Japan very early and that its influence can still be recognized in ancient relics, names, and customs. But whether this is due to the ten lost tribes or a later migration of Jews is a question which will be answered differently by the lover of historical romance and the factual historian.

Fact and fiction thus compete in the solution of a mystery which probably will never be solved beyond all doubt. Though many of the theories advanced are as far-fetched as the suggestion that, because of their practice of circumcision, the Australian

Aborigines were the lost tribes, other claims have features that cannot be ignored.

It is more than 2,500 years since the kingdom of Israel vanished. Part of its population can certainly be accounted for and survives in the Samaritans. But what happened to the Israelites who were deported to Assyrian lands? Were they totally absorbed, leaving no trace at all? Or did they migrate farther "to the ends of the earth," to live on there in isolation and obscurity to this day? And if so, where did they go to? Was it to the east or to the west, the isles of Japan or Britain, the interior of Africa or America, or the shores of the huge subcontinent of India? Without doubt the numerous attempts to trace and identify the ten lost tribes present one of the most fascinating quests of history.

Chapter 35

ORIGINS OF JEWISH FAMILY NAMES

Most Jewish family names are only a little more than 150 years old. Originally, people called themselves simply by what is known as "first names." However, as these were restricted in number, it was inevitable that frequent use of the one identical name led to confusion. A further description was needed to identify a person properly.

Obvious possibilities presented themselves and were duly adopted. They are already found in the Bible, the Gospels (which follow Jewish tradition), and the Talmud. They included the addition of one's occupation, native town, a personal characteristic, and, most frequently, one's father's name. It was Joshua "the son of Nun" who was appointed Moses' successor. In the New Testament six different women bear the name of Mary, but only one of them resided in Magdala and was therefore appropriately identified as Mary Magdalene. Two of Jesus' disciples were called Judas. To distinguish them, the one who came from Keriot was referred to simply as "the man of Keriot," which in Hebrew is *Ish Keriot*—Iscariot. Abba "the tall" was the founder of the rabbinical academy at Sura on the Euphrates, and it was Rabbi Eleazar "the asphalt merchant" who taught that asceticism was a vice.

All these names, however, were only the property of the individual to whom they applied. They were not passed on to the next generation. Happily, Jews bore their own personal name and deemed it superfluous to identify their family by any common denominator. Their sense of tradition was so deeply rooted, and their cohesion so strong, that there was no need of any outward sign or link. Everyone knew where he belonged. Even when in later centuries surnames were generally adopted by the Gentile world, Jews still considered them unnecessary. The only exception was countries where Jews lived in small numbers, such as England, where by a process of natural assimilation they followed their neighbors' example.

Circumstances changed, and the time came when adoption of family names was no longer a personal matter, but was regarded by governments, quite apart from judicial and political considerations, as essential for the efficient administration of registration, conscription, and taxation where correct identification clearly was all-important. It was therefore made obligatory for people to acquire a hereditary surname. Indeed, to enforce the new law on the Jews, their attainment of full civic rights was made conditional on their having first registered a proper family name.

Decrees to that effect were issued by Emperor Joseph II of Austria in 1787, by Napoleon in 1808, and by the Prussian government in 1812. The small, yet significant, variations which appeared in the relevant legislation of the different countries provide an intriguing study. To facilitate implementation of the law, some governments published official lists from which Jews could choose the name that most appealed to them. In Galicia, the authorities used the occasion as a welcome opportunity of boosting their funds. They catalogued names in various groups, according to "value." The most expensive names were those which referred to flowers and precious metals, such as Rosenthal and Goldstein. Steel and iron—Stahl and Eisen—were offered at a cheaper rate; animal names and terms of abuse were free of charge.

The kingdom of Westphalia demanded registration of surnames within three months from the date of publication of the decree. There Jews could choose any names except those of towns and well-known families. Strange to relate, Napoleon's edict, which applied to the whole of the French Empire, forbade "the people of the Book" to employ biblical names. Prussia, adopting the French resolution, added to it a rider that whoever had not adopted a surname within six months would forfeit his citizenship and, irrespective of the length of his domicile in the country, would be considered an alien. Government officials could veto sought names within eight days of the filing of the application. Jews who already possessed a family name could not change it without a proper permit. Outdoing the laws of other countries, Poland in 1821 made the nonacquisition of family names a punishable offense.

A mass adoption of surnames within the Jewish communities of Europe was the inevitable result. The long-hoped-for freedom depended on this simple action. The way Jews chose or did not choose their names revealed the diversity of human nature. It showed concern or indifference, a sense of beauty or of its lack, deep affection or a factual approach to life, a mind steeped in Jewish tradition or a desire to get off cheaply. No matter how the names were selected, for better or for worse, the result was permanent, as we, their heirs, know only too well. To inquire into the origin of our family names is thus not only an interesting study but a most personal affair.

Paternal Perpetuity

From biblical times onward, an individual's name was linked with that of his father. This undoubtedly was first of all the result of a practical consideration. There might have been many Balaams, but only one Balaam "the son of Beor." To identify a certain man by the name of Saul may have been difficult, but it was no longer so once he was described as "the son of Kish."

This early tradition received additional emphasis in the Jewish conception of family life. When the nineteenth chapter of Leviticus summed up the Law of Holiness, it put as man's first duty reverence for his parents. This was deemed so important that it was included as one of the Ten Commandments. Filial affection has been a Jewish characteristic ever since.

Only a people that shows piety toward its past has a future. The bond between the generations was the Jew's security in an unfriendly world. With pride and affection the Jewish child remembered his parents. Indeed, to honor them at all times was his supreme aim in life, and honoring of them did not cease with their passing. The Jew considered all his achievements as the outcome of his parents' striving and sacrifice. It was to "the merit of the fathers" that Jewish teaching attributed God's guardianship over their children and children's children.

It is thus not surprising that when Jews had to choose permanent names they could think of nothing better or more worthy than perpetuation of their father's name. Abraham's children called themselves Abrahamson, and those of Jacob, Jacobson. It was only natural, and indicative of the Jews' assimilation into their environment, that the word "son" appears always in the language of the country in which they lived. Most famous of all, perhaps, became the name of Moses "the son of Mendel." As Moses Mendelssohn he is known as the founder of German Jewish enlightenment and ancestor of the celebrated composer.

Surnames thus honoring a father's memory are termed patronymic. They are so frequent and easily distinguishable that further examples are superfluous.

Maternal Monuments

It has always been the Jew's conviction that whatever blessing dwells in a home comes from the woman who molds it. Her influence is the most decisive factor in man's life. According to biblical tradition, God created her in order to complete man, to give him happiness which he could not find on his own; and throughout the ages the Jew saw in her a symbol of all that was noble and great. Her most sacred vocation was the training of her children for a worthy life. A woman's wisdom and dignity, her modesty and trust in the future, her innate kindness toward all, her untiring industry and deep faith, form the inspiring subject of one of the chapters of the book of Proverbs. The custom of reciting this poem weekly in the family circle at the beginning of the Sabbath is an indication of the Jew's loving care and fondness for his wife and mother.

It is little wonder, then, that many Jewish female names were really expressions of endearment and admiration: Liebe (beloved), Gute (good one), Schöne (beautiful one), Süsse (sweet one), and Edel (noble one). Unaffected and unsophisticated, they were the most simple and obvious words, coming straight from the heart. They were not empty, meaningless phrases, but truly felt. All of them belong to every man's vocabulary of courting and feelings of love, but the Jew not only used them in short-lived moments of affection, or merely as pet names, but chose them for permanent use.

In the molding of their new surnames, many Jews could find no better material than the names of their mother and wife. This is the origin of the Frats and Freudenbergs—from *Freude* (joy)— and of Mirkin (from Miriam). Hannah gave her name to the Henschels, Hannemanns, and Chankins. The Perlmans and Perls grew out of the *Perle* (pearl); the Rosemanns, Roses, and Rosens from *Rose;* Beilas from *Bella (Schöne)*; the Liebmanns, Lipkovits, and Lipmanns from *Liebe;* and the Goodmans and Gutmanns from *Gute*. All these names are monuments to the fine qualities of womanhood and a happy home life.

Ancestral Geography

Jewish history is a story of wanderings. It gave the Jew his special philosophy and wide horizon.

It is only in comparatively recent times, and probably as a result of their unhappy experience of people's narrow-minded dislike of foreigners, that Jews have become reticent or even ashamed of saying where they came from. Once it had been exactly the opposite, and a feeling of true affection and almost humble local pride caused Jews, rather than hide their place of birth, to reveal it conspicuously. They made it their name.

Frequently, they thereby merely confirmed a development which had already taken place. It was only natural that in small communities a newcomer who had arrived from Warsaw was referred to as Warschauer and the man from Moscow as Moscowitsch. No opprobrium was attached to such expressions. People used them as the easiest way to describe the new neighbor who had arrived from another city or a foreign land.

That is how the Breslauers, Brodys, Dancygers, Deutschs, and Schlesingers were born. The Schapiro and Spiro hailed from Speyer; the Bachers came from Bacharach; Zunz from Sons of the Rhine; and the Laskis from the Polish town of Lask. The

Bohemian city of Horovice found a place of honor in the names of Horowitz, Horwits, and Gurvitch. The Ginsbergs reveal their Bavarian origin, and the German town of Trier is recalled in the French, Trèves, the Alsatian, Dreyfus, and the Russian, Trebitsch. The Montefiores, Soncinos, and Luzzattos proudly called themselves after their Italian home towns.

This group of names not only yields a compendium of geographical sites but, more significantly, reveals the origin and journeyings of numerous Jewish families, wherever they may reside now.

Occupational Guidance

There was no better way to distinguish between two people of the same name than to refer to their different occupations. After some time the use of the combination of name and occupation became an established custom, and what originally was only an aid to identification assumed an inherent value, linking a man's proper name and occupation for all time.

These names were thus not so much the outcome of thoughtful, personal choice as a result of a natural process of daily living. It was much easier to remember a man as the tailor or baker than to call him by a sometimes almost unpronounceable name.

The number and variety of occupational names found as early as talmudic times are surprising. Well distinguished from Rabbi Jochanan the cobbler was Rabbi Jochanan the son of the smith. There were Abba the bleeder, Dan the tailor, and Honi the chariot maker. The frequency and diversity of such names show that early in their history the Jewish people followed every kind of occupation. The view is thus confirmed that only later, unfortunate Gentile legislation forced them into unproductive channels. Another significant phenomenon revealed by these names is the fact that all these men, earning their living as workers, artisans, or doctors, were famous rabbis. A rabbi's calling was honorary, not salaried. The thought of payment for preaching and teaching God's word never entered a rabbi's mind in that period.

Carlyle thought that the giving of a name was a poetic art.

Yet it can also be a most practical way of advertising one's trade or profession, a fact which was not forgotten when Jews had to register surnames by order of the state. The cantor became Mr. Kantorovitch, Kantor, or Sänger. A rabbi's family presented themselves as Rabbinowitz. The Hebrew word for tailor created Mr. Chayat and Chait, finally to be assimilated in the Scottish Keith. The student of German easily recognizes Drucker the printer, Schnitzer the carver, Goldschmidt the goldsmith, Schimmelberg the horse dealer, and Steinschneider the mason.

Alas, the men who chose those names could not foresee that in our modern world little is inherited and that with the passage of long years many professions and aptitudes which were once a family heirloom no longer would be followed by the family's descendants. Today, it is more often the exception than the rule for sons to follow their fathers' footsteps in the workaday world. Thus honored occupational names have become a misnomer. Many a Schneider now sings, and many a Tailor teaches.

Inherited Characteristics

Well known today are the facts of heredity: that certain physical and mental qualities can be transmitted from parents and even remote ancestors to their progeny. Opinions may still differ as to what extent chromosomes pass on specific characteristics from generation to generation and how far those may be modified by environmental influence. There is no doubt, however, that many a family has perpetuated in its name a conspicuous peculiarity of one of its ancestors, of whom its members may not even know. But because at the period of enforced or voluntary "naming" a forebear was Small (*Klein*), Young (*Jung*), Black (*Schwarz*), or Fat (*Fett*), descendants have to bear those names, though they may be tall, old, blond, or slim.

Atavistic Totemism

Common to all peoples is the use of animal nomenclature in the coinage of men's names. Nicknames bestowed on men because of some real or fancied resemblance to a particular animal's distinguishing characteristic frequently remained the property even of his children and children's children, a legacy which was not an asset, but a burden. Thin-legged people were compared with birds. A hasty man was called a hare, a crafty person or a redhead a fox.

Such animal names were not always the uncharitable gift of critical neighbors. Originally, some were a man's own choice, a product of ancient, superstitious traditions which joined the creation of names with totemism, one of the archaic forms of all religions. This believed that a specific animal was the ancestor of every tribe and clan, which considered it sacred and inviolable. The clansmen never killed the animal or ate its flesh, but worshiped it and chose it as their emblem and name. Every member of the group felt that his own life was mysteriously bound up with that of the totem and that to bear its name was therefore a distinction, clothed with sanctity and respect.

Man, of course, became more enlightened, but the original feeling of reverence associated with an animal's name lingered on and was inherited by the Jewish people. One chapter of the Bible—Genesis XLIX—fostered the Jew's love of animal names and was even responsible for definite combinations of first name and surname.

When, on his deathbed, Jacob blessed his sons, he compared five of them with the beasts of the field: Judah with a lion's whelp, Issachar a large-boned ass, Dan a serpent on the path, Naphthali a hind let loose, and Benjamin a tearing wolf. There were no thoughts of totemism in Jacob's mind. These descriptions were mere metaphors, expressions of character. He chose them to express nobility (lion), physical strength (the large-boned ass), the gift of instantaneous and deadly action (the serpent), swiftness (the hind), and warlike qualities (the wolf). Nevertheless, thousands of years later when Jews anxiously sought for appropriate family names, they took Genesis XLIX, with its ready-made associations of animal names, as their guide. Benjamin called his family Wolf or *Sief,* which is its Hebrew translation. Naphthali chose Hirsch, the German stag, as his name, and Judah selected Loeb, Leibel, Liebovitch, or Lew—all meaning lion. Incidents related in other parts of the Bible, too, assisted the Jew in finding the right kind of animal name. Jonah's sojourn in the belly of a big fish, for instance, led many a modern Jonah to become a Mr. Fish or Fishl. Though Jews, therefore, share a common tradition in their choice of surnames, as a people of religion they are distinct in making the Bible their guide whenever possible.

Synthesis of Initials

Modern society has grown accustomed to the use of an abundance of abbreviations, from the call sign of radio and television stations and the title of the United Nations Organization (UNO) to radar (for *ra*dio *d*etecting *a*nd *r*anging). A novel term (first used in 1943) refers to such "words formed from initial letters of other words" as acronyms. Yet to the Jewish people this peculiar kind of economy in speech has been an old-established custom, a shorthand of the spoken word, which saved time and paper. More than fifteen hundred years ago the Talmud employed it as a matter of course. It was then already popular to combine the initials of several words and to replace the original phrase with them. The phrase "worshippers of the stars and constellations" was thus compressed into the one term AKUM and the abbreviation SHAS substituted for the "six orders"—*shishah sedarim*—of the Talmud.

In such fashion a whole group of words could be rendered in one short term which, though artificial, by frequent use eventually was considered a real name or word. Whole lists of such abbreviations would follow at the end of any good Hebrew dictionary. The conscientious writer or printer, however, always put two slanting strokes before the last letter as a clear indication that the word was not a word and the name really not a name. Yet it was by this method of abbreviation that for centuries many Jewish names were created.

As a mere fusion of consonants was unpronounceable, the genius of language, wherever necessary, added a vowel sound (mostly that of an *ah* or *eh*) as a link and thereby cemented a row of initials into a smooth and easily uttered sequence of letters: a newly coined, perfect word.

Rabbi Moses ben Maimon, Jewry's illustrious philosopher, is best known nowadays as Maimonides. A combination of his initials, RMBM, was useless, for it could not be pronounced. But pronunciation was easily made possible simply by the addition of the auxiliary vowel. Thus Rambam became his accepted name and still is today. Similarly, the Bible's most popular commentator is known as Rashi: the welding together of his title with his own and his father's name: *Rabbi Sh'lomo Itz'chaki.* The founder of Chassidism was famed for being able to make occult use of the divine name, an alleged faculty which gained him the title of "master of the good name," or, in Hebrew, *Baal Shem Tov,* a designation which finally was contracted into its abbreviation, *Besht,* which has become his established name.

Accustomed to this method of coining words, Jews were quick to employ it when the adoption of surnames became a legal duty. Numerous families thus not only literally called themselves their father's son but did so by way of an abbreviation. The word "son" was not always rendered in the vernacular, but sometimes by the Hebrew *ben.* There were the children of Rabbi Shalom. Contracting the three Hebrew words Ben Rabbi Shalom, and again making use of a filling vowel, they called themselves Brasch or Brash. The same synthetic principle applied to the construction of such names as Brill (Ben Rabbi Judah Loewe), Baeck or Bak (Ben Akiba), and Bud (Ben David).

This method of creating names extended to titles, offices, and even cities. Amsterdam created the family of Ash and Asch. Sax or Sachs has nothing to do with Saxons or Saxony, but traces back to a family of martyrs in the small German town of Stendhal. They are, in an abbreviated form, "the holy seed of Stendhal," *Sera Kadosh Stendhal.* The leader in prayer at a synagogue used to be called "the delegate of the congregation," which in Hebrew was *Shali'ach Tsibbur.* Using the initials of his title, he gave himself the name Schatz, which therefore has no connection whatsoever with (German) valuables. That the Segals, on the other hand, originated out of the (contracted) "head of the Levites"—*S'gan L'viyah*—reflects only on the coinage of their name and has no relationship with Greek mythology and its well-known claim that Athena, the daughter of Zeus, had sprung fully armed from the head of her father.

Puzzling claims are explained, and misconceptions avoided, by knowledge of the Jews' use of abbreviations in creating their names. Jewish people called Bach have nothing to do with the German Bach, whether composer or brook. The Jewish Bach is not original, but synthetic, and it owes its existence to something much more substantial than flowing water; namely, to a house. New homes are conspicuous. It was therefore inevitable that, in search of identification, the happy family who had moved into a new abode should become known as "the new house"—in Hebrew *Bet Chadash*—which was duly shortened into the combination of its initials, Bach.

It has always been considered a privilege and an honor to be descended from the ancient priests. A Cohen could not be mistaken, as the very word meant "priest" and is used as such in the Hebrew Bible. How was it, then, that people named Katz (or Catts) claimed priestly heritage and, in the Orthodox synagogue, the right to be the first called up to the Law and to redeem the first-born son? The obvious interpretation is not the true story in this case. In spite of all appearances, the Jewish Katz bears no relation to the German word for "cat"; it actually consists of the initials of the two Hebrew words *Cohen Tsedek,* which describe "a priest of righteousness." If such nobility can be hidden in a simple name, it is not surprising to find that a man called Shalit has the distinction of bearing a name which is the direct result of a prayer. His name is the shortened version of the supplication: "May he live for long and good days," *Sh'yich-yeh l'orech yamim tovim.*

Jewish Heraldry

Long before the introduction of the numbering of houses, it had become customary, especially in southern and western Germany, where many Jews had settled, to indicate one's home with a badge fixed outside. The badge depicted a well-known object which thus could easily be recognized, and in many cases it was linked with the dweller's occupation or profession. To find the house with the shoe was child's play.

Conspicuously attached outside the door, the house sign eventually was identified with the family residing there. People living in the house with the nut tree thus became known as Nussbaum, and those who exhibited the replica of a boat were called Schiff or Kahn.

That is the way in which the Rothschilds got their name. A simple red shield was displayed outside their home at No. 148 on the Judengasse in Frankfort-on-Main.

Numerous families, now far removed from their original homes, maintain what was once their outward mark of distinction. The (Hebrew) ox turned into Schaur, Schor, Scheuer and its (German) head into Rindskopf. The Flaschs preserve a bottle, the Stiefels a boot, and the Gans a goose.

It was one of the Levites' duties to pour water on the priest's hands before his blessing of the congregation. Recollecting this task, they identified their homes with a jug, and it was this professional symbol which gave them their name: Krug or Kann (both German jugs).

Immortalized Moments

Names date. Some people, at least, must have felt the urge to perpetuate a moment of their lives for future generations, whether as an ordinary day, a festival, or a whole month. The circumstances of their choice are no longer remembered and can only be guessed at. Perhaps the occasion was the birth of a child or a happy hour. Perhaps the name merely recalls the time when one's ancestors had to adopt a name, possibly without much time for reflection. For reasons unknown, people are still called after Pesach, the feast of Passover (Peissachovitch or Bettsack), the month of Nisan (Nissen), or, just generally, a holy day (Yontef or Jandorf) from the Hebrew *Yom tov*. The Jewish name Bondi is not derived from the famous Australian Bondi Beach, which is the aboriginal description of "the noise of water rolling in." It means "a good day," and it has passed down the years through good and evil times.

A Question of Aesthetics

Shakespeare was right when he pointed out that a rose by any other name would smell as sweet. Yet the choice of a name is not insignificant. Its very sound and meaning may influence people's reactions and unconsciously create definite feelings and attitudes in their minds. It was only natural, then, that when it became necessary to adopt a name, those concerned were anxious to acquire one which was dignified and attractive and might even add to their status within the community. To them, there could be nothing nobler than to be called a Prince, Duke, or King. More frequently their selection was guided by a sense of beauty. They wished to bestow on their family an ornament, something that was graceful and exquisite like a flower (Blume or Bloom). Nothing could excel the rose: whether just as a single specimen (Rose) or a whole bunch (Rosen or Rosenstrauss) or its blossoming bush (Rosenstrauch) or merely one of its twigs (Rosenzweig).

When these names were chosen, they were beautiful. But beauty is time-conditioned. What appeared graceful and attractive to one age may become ugly and gaudy to another. Ideas once considered refined degenerate; the exquisite changes, by frequent use, into the commonplace.

Indifference Penalized

A name? If the party had a voice,
What mortal would be a bug by choice,
Not to mention many a vulgar name,
Which would make a door plate blush with shame,
If door plates were not so brazen.

Not all Jews cared about their surnames. Some felt that, as everyone knew them by their first name, it did not matter what the authorities called them. Totally indifferent, they left the choice to the local officials, who in many cases did not hesitate to have their fun at the Jews' expense and inflicted on them names which were most colorful, but terms of ridicule and abuse.

Rarely found nowadays, they were abundant in every list of the Polish nineteenth-century ghetto. Typical examples are Wohlgeruch (good smell), Eselskopf (donkey's head), Nussknacker (nutcracker), Fresser (glutton), Tintenpulver (ink powder), Butterfass (butter vat), Geldschrank (money chest), and even Hintergesitz (bottom).

For generations the Jew bore those names which, after all, could do him no harm, as his own dignity and way of living overcame the ridicule.

> Sticks and stones
> May break my bones,
> But names can never hurt me.

Emancipation and Assimilation

The multitude of methods used in the fashioning of the new names vividly reflects the variety of human nature and the ingenuity of man's mind. Though generally the names follow the pattern of the Gentile world, many of them record a specifically Jewish sentiment and tradition, even apart from the use of the Hebrew acrostic. More significantly still, they bear also the mark of Jewish fate. They carry with them the history of a people which has wandered through many lands.

Less than a century after the adoption of the new names, a peculiar development took place. The Jew had become completely emancipated and had fully adapted himself to the life of his environment. Yet often he felt that his very name was an obstacle. It made him appear different and alien. Most oddly, names which sounded most Jewish were pure German. There was nothing indigenously Hebrew or Yiddish in Stern, Rosenstrauss, or Adler. But because these names were favorites among the Jewish people, they became "tainted" with Jewishness. Out of a feeling of insecurity, or in a wish to appear just like all other people, many Jews began to discard their foreign or Jewish-sounding names and to replace them with Gentile ones.

This was nothing new. It repeated an identical experience in the period of the Jews' first (and only) names two thousand years earlier. Then, under the influence of Hellenistic civilization and in his zeal to be totally Greek, a Moses had called himself Menelaus, a Joseph, Jason, and an Isaac, Isidor—the most pagan name he could choose, as it signified "the gift of the goddess Isis." Now, twenty centuries later, Avronsky became Veronique and Cohen Keith or Cullen or Owen; Rabinovitch changed into Robin, Reichheim into Reigate, and Eppenheim into Elton. Mr. Levy became Mr. Leigh (or Lee) and Mr. Baruch, Mr. Bernard. Isaac's metamorphosis was Irvin and Moses', Morris or Hitchcock.

To add to the confusion, some brothers were so anxious to change their names that they did not wait to consult each other, but selected each one his own: a sad development in a people who once could pride themselves on strong family bonds and traditions. On the other hand, and paradoxically, non-Jews often adopted as their family names those found in the Hebrew Bible and proudly bore the only truly Jewish names. It was a phenomenon which can easily be understood if it is remembered that Gentiles did not have to experience persecution for their names' sake.

The Wheel Turns Full Circle

Not all countries welcomed the development. Once anxious to force the Jews to adopt names, now they insisted that these should not be changed. From 1787 onward special decrees were issued in Bohemia, Prussia, and Russia prohibiting the adoption of non-Jewish names. Then anti-Semitism waned, the laws were forgotten, and Jews shared all rights and privileges equally with their fellow citizens, including freedom to call themselves what they liked. Modern Turkey went even further and demanded that Jews, like all other non-Turkish minorities, should adopt Turkish names.

Then Nazi Germany arose and in 1938 renewed the forgotten laws, enlarging their scope with callous efficiency. Once again, German Jews were forbidden to alter their names. If they were not sufficiently "Jewish," a middle name (Israel and Sarah, respectively) had to be inserted and duly registered with the authorities. To remove any doubt as to what constituted a Jewish first name, German thoroughness compiled a list of permitted names —185 for men and 91 for women—which, absurdly, excluded Abraham, David, Joseph, Ruth, and Miriam. To make doubly sure that no Jew should escape identification, his passport was conspicuously stamped with the capital letter J.

The Third Reich collapsed after twelve years. The renascence of Jewish consciousness created a new life and a new pride. The State of Israel was born, and as Jews returned to their ancient homeland they felt the urge to discard their Gentilized names, often chosen out of a feeling of insecurity or in an exaggerated wish to appear like all other people. Names were replaced with Hebrew ones. Shertok became Sharett (the servant); Torczyner, Tur-Sinai (Mount Sinai); and Bergmann was translated into Harari. David Green turned into the famous Ben Gurion, and Golda Meyerson, on her appointment as Foreign Minister of Israel, called herself Golda Meir. The wheel had come full circle.

Rabbi Simon said: "There are three crowns: the crown of learning, the crown of priesthood and the crown of rulership. But the crown of a good name excels them all."

Chapter 36

PROFESSIONS WITHOUT AN EQUAL

A wit once remarked succinctly, yet most appropriately, that Jews were just like other people, only more so. Indeed, just as they shared with their fellow men identical hopes and desires, joys and anxieties, so they followed the same kind of work and occupations. In ancient times, they earned their livelihood as shoemakers, blacksmiths, doctors, farmers, and fishermen. In the Middle Ages, Jews were well known as lion tamers, jugglers, and tightrope walkers. Modern times have seen Jewish generals, prime ministers, governors, ships' captains, coal miners, and wrestlers. Yet Jewish life and fate produced occupations which were specifically Jewish. Obvious examples are the mohel (circumciser), who initiates the Jewish child into the Covenant of Abraham, and the shochet (ritual slaughterer), who is responsible for the religiously proper killing of animals. And the Jews' inventive spirit created still other professions, unknown elsewhere and full of fascinating features.

The Schulklopfer

The chiming of church bells invites the Christian to worship. The Moslem community is informed that service is about to commence by the chant of the muezzin from the top of the minaret of the mosque. To ensure prompt attendance at synagogue, the Jew created his own profession: the *schulklopfer,* a title derived from a German Jewish word meaning "synagogue knocker," whose specific duty it was to call daily on every Jewish home in the district, long before the service was due to commence. Knocking at either door or window, he called out: "In Schul herein" (To synagogue!).

As synagogue services were held daily at sunrise throughout the year (which was indeed at a very early hour during the summer), the schulklopfer was both a walking church bell and an alarm clock for the sleeping community. His "badge" of office was a mallet which was often shaped like a shofar, the ram's horn whose sounding, according to rabbinic tradition, was one day to awaken the dead. As the Sabbath could not be desecrated by carrying anything, on that day the schulklopfer used his bare fist. But in keeping with the solemnity and grief of the occasion, on the Fast of Av the congregation was not summoned to synagogue, but arrived there uncalled and in subdued mood.

The usual number of knocks was three or four, spaced rhythmically. They were reduced to two whenever a death had occurred in the congregation. Understandably, families waited anxiously each morning for a third knock to signify that all was well and that the angel of death had not descended on any of their friends' homes. An ancient manuscript describes the suspense and apprehension roused in the mind of the writer every morning on the arrival of the schulklopfer and his intimate sharing of all the joys and sorrows within the community: "When he only knocked twice I sighed; but when thrice, my heart leaped with joy."

Indeed, in a period when no daily press existed, with its personal columns, the schulklopfer also acted thus as a walking newspaper. Apart from giving information about births, marriages, and deaths, he added his own welcome gossip concerning communal affairs. Some Jews, possibly heavy sleepers, employed their personal schulklopfer to make sure that they would not miss the service.

To the Jew, religion was always something most intimate. Perhaps that is one of the reasons why he replaced the general call from church steeple and minaret by the personal summons of his friend, the schulklopfer, a Jewish identity who now is merely a historical oddity.

The Schnorrer

All people have had their poor, but no other community has had its schnorrer, so that his name cannot be translated into any other language. He was a good deal more than an ordinary beggar. His poverty seemed to him not so much a personal plight as a matter for communal concern. Far from soliciting alms, he demanded them. His existence appeared to him not as a misfortune, but as a privilege, which the community should recognize and honor. He considered his profession not degrading, but highly respectable. Small and insignificant gifts he would reject indignantly as an insult. To sing hymns of praise to his benefactors was far from his mind. On the contrary, he almost expected thanks for being gracious enough to offer the rich an opportunity of performing a worthy deed by making a "contribution."

Such a peculiar attitude was not due solely to the arrogance of the ignorant. It revealed one of the most beautiful aspects of the Jewish faith. To help the poor was the Jew's duty. The giving of alms was not something left to one's personal mood or initiative, but a divine obligation. Thus, in Hebrew the word *mitzvah* came to mean simultaneously both "charity" and "commandment." For the Jews, benevolence was not a voluntary act, but a sacred charge.

The whole earth belongs to God. Whatever man possesses is not his own, but merely lent to him for the sole purpose of helping the needy. The only reason why a beneficent and all-powerful God permitted poverty to exist on earth was to give all men a chance of doing good.

One of the central prayers of the Day of Atonement service pronounced charity as one of the three essential ways to induce God to forgive sin. The story is told that two lambs had to cross a stream: one was shorn and the other heavy with wool. The shorn lamb got across safely, but the unshorn, its body soaked with water, perished. To give of one's best saves from death. The rabbis felt that no beggar who called on us ever came alone, but that God accompanied him. To refuse him his due was to reject God.

Only a gift handed to the poor with a cheerful spirit was acceptable. Anyone who gave grudgingly or sullenly was considered not to have given at all. Jewish tradition suggested that all charity should be bestowed secretly: "Better give no alms at all, than give them in public." If at all possible, the poor man should never know who helped him, nor should the donor be able to identify the recipient. The ancient Temple contained as one of its unique and sacred rooms "the chamber of secret charity." It was there that God-fearing people left their contributions, anonymously and unknown to anyone, and the poor collected them, unseen also. Thus the rich did not feel false pride, nor were the poor humiliated.

Though it was Jewish law to give one-tenth of one's earnings to the poor, many people exceeded this minimum and in most thoughtful ways humanized charity. To invite the poor to one's home became a sacred tradition and a joyful task. No holy day was deemed rightly observed if one did not have a homeless or needy person as an honored guest at table. A Jewish butcher in Prague used to weigh his children three times a year and then give their weight in meat to the poor. It is said that a mother who hoped that her son would one day become a rabbi used to put the child on the scales daily and each time distributed the increased weight in gold to those in need. Again, a scholar of the Talmud, whenever buying meat for his family, purchased an equal amount for those who could not afford it.

Maimonides, always eager to express Jewish teachings as clearly as possible, designed "a ladder of charity." Leading from the lowest step to the highest rung, he differentiated eight ways of giving:

1. He who gives grudgingly.
2. He who gives less than he should, but with good grace.
3. He who gives only after he has been asked to do so.
4. He who gives without having been asked.

5. He who gives without knowing the recipient's name, but makes sure the latter is aware where the gift came from.

6. He who gives secretly, knowing who the recipient is, but not revealing his own identity.

7. He who gives without knowing who receives it or being known himself.

8. He who helps the poor to become self-supporting either by means of a loan or by taking him into partnership into his own business or profession.

It was no wonder that a people whose faith had thus made charity an essential part of its religion produced the schnorrer, who had his own rules, traditions, and "ethics." He did not go about his business haphazardly, but organized it efficiently. Keeping to definite routes, he had his own clients, on whom he called at regular intervals. His "contributors" became his vested right. Any other schnorrer who dared to interfere was soon made to feel the ignominy of his unprofessional conduct. Schnorrers who settled down, or moved elsewhere, sold their "good will" to the highest bidder or donated their "business" to a deserving case. Sons inherited the benefactors from their schnorrer fathers.

Incidents abound which are typical of the schnorrer, his wit and wisdom, self-confidence and impudence. Never awed by a man's wealth, to him the richer Jew was never the better Jew.

Eloquent of the schnorrers' subtle wit is the story of how one of them attended the funeral of a Rothschild. He appeared overwhelmed with grief. People, anxious to comfort him, pointed out that after all he was not a relative. "That's exactly why I am so upset," he replied; "I shall inherit nothing of his riches."

Israel Zangwill immortalized *The King of the Schnorrers*. One conversation stands out from the wealth of incident described in the book as characteristic of the Jewish beggar's psychology. A well-off benefactor was trying hard to impress on the schnorrer all the good he had done to him and how he had freely given him of his hard-earned fortune. But his ward, quite unmoved, arrogantly suggested that the rich should be less boastful. He should remember that there was a wheel always turning in the world and that he who was rich today might easily be poor tomorrow: "God lowers and lifts up."

The Shadchan

One of the most venerable Jewish professions was that of the matchmaker. He was called by the Hebrew word *shadchan,* which describes a person who "persuades" and "influences." Not just an ordinary professional "marriage broker," he was a deeply religious man (often a rabbi) who was convinced that true and lasting happiness could be experienced only in married life. But husband and wife must be of the right type and "match." Marriages should not depend on mere chance meetings or the passing feeling of a moment. The shadchan's help could unite suitable men and women who, meant for each other, would never meet without his good offices, but would pass through life joyless and with their purpose unfulfilled.

Forty days before the birth of every boy, according to a talmudic parable, a divine voice announced in heaven whom he would one day marry. Though legendary, this belief expressed the Jewish conviction not only that marriages were made in heaven but that divine destiny determined human happiness. And so the shadchan believed in all sincerity that he was helping God in the execution of His will. Arranging a marriage was held to be so important that for its sake it was permissible to sell even a Scroll of the Law.

There is a fascinating report in Jewish writings of a discussion that took place two thousand years ago between a rabbi and a Roman matron on the subject of God's activities. The Bible taught that divine power had created and completed the world in six days. If that were so, the woman was anxious to know, what had He been doing ever since? "Only one thing," the rabbi replied. "He has been arranging marriages." But the lady scoffed. Certainly, God was not necessary for that, she claimed. Anyone, even herself, could do it. Still, the rabbi strongly disagreed. To match the right people, he said, was as difficult as the parting of the Red Sea.

Unconvinced, the matron was determined to prove her point.

She summoned two thousand slaves, an equal number of men and women. Dividing them into groups, she then paired them off. Within one day she had "matched" them all. However, when the newlyweds appeared before her next morning they were not happy, grateful couples, but dejected and cheerless, seeking help and separation. One had a broken leg, another a bruised face, and a third a black eye. Completely stunned, the matron wanted to know what was the matter. She was told in no uncertain terms that they did not like the partners she had chosen for them and felt most unsuitably matched.

Calling on the rabbi, the matron admitted her mistake and agreed that to unite the right man and woman was a task beyond her power, that it undoubtedly required supreme wisdom and divine guidance.

The shadchan, indeed, considered himself God's instrument. His was a well-known office and an established institution as early as the twelfth century. Only people of the finest character and integrity were permitted to act in this capacity. They possessed all the qualities needed for their responsible mission, were highly respected within the community, and had a deep knowledge of human nature and a wide circle of friends. They kept confidences and were reliable in all their information. Conscientiously, they followed the counsel given them by an early Jewish writer: "Whenever you are arranging a marriage between two parties, never exaggerate but always tell the truth."

The shadchans, in their enthusiasm, spared no effort to find the right match. To them, their task was not just a business transaction but a pious mission, carried out for love of God and the creation of happiness. Though in the great majority of cases only men filled the position, there were also some female shadchans.

The mere knowledge that they were the cause of happiness seemed sufficient reward to the shadchans, many of whom worked without pay. Eventually, however, communities introduced fees, which fluctuated between 1 and 3 percent of the dowry. In most cases the fee was payable as soon as the match had been arranged, irrespective of whether the marriage eventuated. But in some communities the money was due only after the marriage ceremony had actually been performed and the success of the shadchan's efforts proved beyond doubt.

At first the matchmaking of the shadchan was merely a happy and helpful occupation, but historical circumstances changed his office into an almost indispensable institution. Times of persecution brought social life among the Jewish people to a standstill, and without the shadchan's help boys and girls would never have had an opportunity of meeting. He became a pathfinder and a link. His importance further increased among the many scattered communities and Jewish families living in isolation, with no other Jewish people to mix with or to meet. They all relied on him. Untiringly, he moved between villages and congregations, established contacts, suggested meetings, and arranged weddings. His travels were often undertaken at grave personal risk, but nothing could dampen his zeal.

Modern times again changed the ancient and respected office. Unscrupulous men frequently replaced the former reliable agents. Business acumen, and the wish to "sell" quickly as many marriages as possible, took the place of good character and desire to spread gladness. All kinds of salesmanship were employed, including exaggeration of the bride's beauty, the bridegroom's learning, and the parents' prominence and fortune. On the other hand, worthless matchmakers glossed over or explained away any obvious defects on either side. A sacred profession thus deteriorated dismally. It became something which evoked fun and ridicule and finally degenerated into fully commercialized, legally registered "Associations of Shadchans" and insurance schemes which provided for any possible breach of promise.

The Mezuzah Fixer and the Meat Salter

Not all Jewish professions conjure up happy memories. Dire necessity, indeed, was the mother of their invention. The occupations of the mezuzah fixer and the meat salter are typical examples.

There was no art in salting meat before cooking it, and every housewife, trained from childhood in the proper ritual preparation of food, used salt mechanically. Even in the most luxurious home a specially trained servant was not warranted for the purpose of salting food.

While the salting of meat was a daily occurrence, the need for fixing a mezuzah arose rarely, actually only once, when moving into a new home. Certainly, no one could ever make a living as a mezuzah fixer. Nothing was easier than to nail the little scroll onto the doorpost of the home. Even the youngest child could do it without the slightest trouble.

Thus, both occupations were apparently wholly unnecessary. Yet, in fact, they were needed. For many centuries Jewish existence was most insecure. In some countries the Jew was only tolerated, at best. A change of government or a sovereign's whim might render him a wanderer. Only too often laws issued without warning made a settled community rise in panic and grasp at anything to be permitted to stay on.

Such crises abounded in the Austrian Empire at the end of the eighteenth century. The Jewish community lived in continuous tension as harassing new laws followed each other without respite. Some restricted the Jews' domicile: others prohibited it altogether. Further clauses, again, provided for exemptions and exceptions. To ensure that no Jew should become a burden on the state, a law was issued demanding the immediate emigration of all Jews without an occupation. It did not matter that they might be well looked after as members of family groups. The mere lack of employment necessitated their prompt departure. To have an occupation became a question of life and death. As a measure of survival, the Jew had to create professions unheard of, until then, in Jewish history. So long as a Jew could register some calling as his own, the authorities were satisfied, and his continued residence on Austrian soil was not threatened.

That is how the mezuzah fixer and the meat salter were born: as fictions of the Jewish mind, created to justify their very existence. Perhaps in no other time did a mezuzah so literally guard the homes of the Jewish people, their going out and their staying in.

The creation of professions and occupations unique of their kind—this, too, belongs to the picture of the Jew in the world, with its laughter and tears.

Chapter 37

STRANGE CONTRADICTIONS

Few, if any, experiences are unknown to the Jews. Ever since Abraham left his home in the quest for God and freedom, Jews have wandered the earth. They have seen powerful nations collapse and new kingdoms arise and have watched many a civilization, after a brief stay in the sun, condemned to a long night in the dust. Welcomed and expelled, praised and calumniated, they have survived all the cataclysms of history. They have been the scapegoats of numerous people; they have been the pioneers of progress and have known man at his best and worst.

The Jews never wavered in their resolve. Even when cast on the pyres of the Inquisition or into the ghettos of medieval Europe and the concentration camps of twentieth-century savagery, they remained loyal to their divine mission. They lived in Orient and Occident; among pagans, Christians, and Moslems; in the shadow of the pyramids, Moorish castles, and Gothic cathedrals; on the highways of history or in hidden corners of forgotten continents. But wherever they were, Jews added to their knowledge of man, his cruelty and his kindness, his indifference and friendship.

Not surprisingly, therefore, the wealth of the Jews' experience, throughout three thousand years and in every part of the world, is unsurpassed. So, too, is its variety. It follows, then, that many odd features and the strangest possible contradictions mark Jewish life and faith, giving much food for thought. Examples range from the Jews' peculiar way of uttering thanks to the explanation of such oddities as a horned Moses and a Jewish nose which is not Jewish. They also include the story of fateful errors when people, unable to grasp the Jew's spiritual outlook or merely the correct meaning of a simple Hebrew word, were gravely misled. Some added further hardships to an existence of already unparalleled suffering.

All these oddities and contradictions arose in various ways, and there are many of them. Together, they help make up the uniqueness of the Jew in the world.

The Jew's "Thank You"

When the religious Jew says, "Thank you," he uses no stereotyped formula which, however sincerely meant, only acknowledges services rendered. His thanks are a wish. But, far from being flattering or obsequious, it contains almost a challenge. "May your power always be used justly," is the meaning of the Hebrew "thanks"—*Y'yasher kochacha*. There could be no nobler desire for any well-wisher than that his benefactor's capabilities should only and always be used in dealings that are "straight" (the literal meaning of the Hebrew word "just"). Far from feeling hurt, a person thus thanked gratefully responds, "May you be blessed." This is a vocabulary of etiquette worthy of a social order where justice and righteousness prevail.

The Jew and the Crucifixion

It is proverbial that appearances can deceive. That they can lead to peculiar misconceptions is a misfortune Jews have experienced in the most diverse ways. For instance, the so-called Jewish nose, with its aquiline shape, is not Jewish at all, but distinguished the ancient Hittites.

It was natural that pagan nations could not grasp the spiritual outlook of Judaism. Their mind was unable to comprehend the idea of an invisible God. When they watched the Jewish people at prayer and saw them looking heavenward, they misinterpreted the gesture and were convinced that the Jews worshiped the clouds. They drew an equally wrong conclusion when they observed that no smoke ascended from Jewish homes on the Sabbath. They assumed that the Jews fasted on that day. It did not occur to them that in the fulfillment of the commandment which prohibited any kind of work on the Sabbath, Jewish people did not light fires on that day even to cook their meals, which were prepared previously. The Jewish custom of always keeping the head covered was erroneously and maliciously explained by the assertion that, as the Devil's disciple, the Jew grew horns and was anxious to hide them.

To our enlightened mind interpretations as these are so absurd that it seems incredible that they ever existed. Nevertheless, they were once widely accepted. Most of them were innocuous and had no evil intent or effect. They might have ridiculed the Jew, but they did not actually harm him. However, in one instance an error of judgment and a misconception brought untold suffering to the Jewish people. They were hated and persecuted as "the killers of Christ." Yet it is an established fact that not the Jews, but the Romans, crucified Jesus.

Thousands of Jews were crucified at the time. They died on the cross as national heroes and martyrs. When Rome invaded the Holy Land and a reign of terror began for the Jewish people, crucifixion fulfilled the purpose of the modern firing squad. It combined a painful death with a ghastly display of the executed as a warning to others. Above all, it was intended to humiliate the condemned: the Roman Empire originally reserved crucifixion for slaves and foreigners, unworthy of the treatment accorded free citizens.

Jews who fought for their freedom and tried to drive out the invader were crucified, and their bodies, hanging on the crosses around Jerusalem, became a horrifying everyday sight.

One of the Jews put to death in this manner was Jesus. He was one of those thousands of Jews who died on the cross. Repeatedly, the Jews had tried to shake off the Roman yoke. It was a period of great unrest, and the occupying forces, tense and apprehensive, applied ruthless measures against revolt. Anxious to put down at once any movement which might endanger their foothold in Judea, the Romans saw in Jesus just another rebel. He had attracted some of his coreligionists. They had called him "the king of the Jews," a claim which implied high treason. There could be no king but the Emperor of Rome. That was why Jesus was arrested and tried. He was sentenced to death as a rebel against Rome, not as a heretic among the Jews. Military insecurity, not any religious controversy, was the background of Jesus' execution. This also explains why Roman soldiers mockingly crowned him with thorns and why the superscription on his cross (which always indicated the reason for execution) read: "Jesus of Nazareth, *King* of the Jews."

At the time of his crucifixion, Judea was a conquered country, and Jews had no power whatsoever to inflict capital punishment on anyone. But even when the Jews were still a free nation, death by crucifixion was totally unknown and repulsive to the Jewish mind. Jewish legislation provided four kinds of execution. They were strangulation, beheading, burning, and a combination of precipitation and stoning. But in spite of their legality, a rabbi called any court murderous which had passed a death sentence during a period of seventy years. Many of the circumstances of Jesus' execution were contrary to Jewish law, possibly purposely so, in order to offend Jewish religious feelings. Execution on a holy day, or its eve, was considered sacrilegious: but Jesus had to die on the eve of the Sabbath and Passover. Jewish law forbade several executions at the one time; but Jesus died with two others.

Certainly, the Gospels put the blame on the Jewish religious leaders and point out that Pontius Pilate himself, the Roman governor, had only yielded to their pressure and in symbolic action washed his hands of the deed. But it is Jewish conviction that the account given does not conform with the actual events. No invading power—and especially not a man as cruel and ruthless as Pilate—would ever have given heed to the voice of a people they had come to subdue. The death of Jesus was not the result of a Jewish conspiracy. The Gospels could not deny the fact that Pilate had consented to the execution, as he had done in the case of many other crucifixions of so-called Jewish rebels. But to appease Roman opinion and gain Roman favor, the New Testament vindicated him and condemned the Jews.

Yet, even had the accusation been correct, it should have led not to the persecution of the Jewish people, but to exactly the opposite. Christian theology teaches that Jesus' sacrificial death on the cross alone can save a man from original sin, inherited from Adam, and from the actual sins of his life; that only he who believes in this dogma can find salvation; that it was God's will that Jesus should die for the sake of mankind. Inevitably it follows that had Jesus not been crucified, sin would still be unatoned and would condemn man to damnation. Does the Christian, therefore, not owe deep and lasting gratitude to those, whoever they were (and they certainly were not the Jews), who crucified Jesus and thus, however gruesome his death, enabled him to suffer for mankind and bring salvation to all those who believed in him and his death?

Furthermore, if Christians had so much as honored Jesus' last prayer on the cross, they would have forgiven as he did, and the whole question of who did what and why would have been resolved into a tragic episode of impersonal ignorance.

It is one of the greatest paradoxes of all Jewish experience that the Jews not only were accused of having killed Christ but were persecuted and hated for it for well-nigh two thousand years by those who had forgotten that his death alone, according to Christian belief, could redeem man from sin. It was Jesus who had said that "salvation comes from the Jew." He, himself a Jew, had asked forgiveness for all those who had harmed him, saying that they knew not what they were doing. Well known became the verse of a modern writer, W. N. Ewer, which said:

> How odd of God
> To choose the Jews.

More justified was the stanza which was later added as "A Reply" by another author, Cecil Browne:

> But not so odd
> As those who choose
> A Jewish God
> Yet spurn the Jews.

History was made in the declaration adopted in 1965 by the Vatican Council II. Symbolical of the turning point in the evolution of the Catholic Church, it adopted the declaration (by a final vote of 2,221 in favor, 88 against, and 3 blanks) which absolved the Jewish people of deicide.

In the Protestant church, it was Billy Graham who, speaking of the Jews' role in the crucifixion, recognized many of the facts related here. He declared: "The Romans killed Christ. All of the people of that day had a part in the tragedy. It was man's sin as man, that was responsible; not the sin of man as Jew or as Gentile. Even God played a role in the drama, for it was God's will that Jesus be sacrificed, as a reconciling atonement for man with God."

Exoneration of the Jews from blame for the death of Jesus, after almost two millennia, certainly could not undo the tragedy of persecution, social ostracism, anti-Semitism, and killings perpetrated as a direct result of the false accusation. However, it showed courage, nobility, a quest for truth, and determination to open up a new, genuine, and positive understanding between the Christian church and the Jews.

The Pharisees

It would be a major error to accept as objective and in accordance with the facts an opponent's view on his foes, especially when made in the heat of controversy. But this is exactly what has happened in the case of judgment of the Pharisees. What the name now conjures up in the minds of most people is not the reflection of their true lives and character, but a false picture resulting from enmity.

The Pharisees derived their name from the Hebrew word *parush*. Though this has been explained as referring to their being "apart" from the crowd and "divided" from the rest of mankind, according to its classical interpretation it means "separated" from sin and pagan abominations. Indeed, the Pharisees became the great nonconformists who, undeterred by calumniations, suffering, and temptation, remained true to their mission to be loyal servants of God, standing alone among the nations—misunderstood, derided, despised, and rejected.

Of all the misconceptions about the Jew which have survived the centuries, perhaps none is more typical than this derogatory attitude toward the Pharisee. His name has become synonymous with the hypocrite who looks upon himself as holier than other men. Yet historical facts prove exactly the opposite. The Pharisee was distinguished by deep humility, religious spirit, and inwardness. He taught that any given act has value, moral or religious, only if it is performed with the sole purpose of serving God. To love Him and one's fellow man is the fundamental basis of all religion.

Two thousand years ago the Pharisees formed the great majority of the Jewish people, and it was their teaching that molded Judaism and Christianity and enabled the Jew to survive. The Pharisees differed from the Sadducees, who denied the value of oral tradition and the existence of life after death, and they did not share the asceticism and communistic tendencies of the Essenes. As the Pharisees preached righteousness, holiness, and the imitation of God, so they practiced virtue, kindness, and sincerity.

What was it, then, that made their name, which should have become the description of all that was noble and great, a byword for bigotry and hypocrisy? It was through the writings of the New Testament, where condemnation of the Pharisees is expressed with remarkable invective and hostility. For nineteen centuries no further evidence was sought for passing sentence on them. It was a foregone conclusion that a Pharisee was a hypocrite. Yet it was modern Christian scholars who pointed out that the accusation was unjust, historically incorrect, and a dangerous, one-sided generalization.

It is undeniable that the ethics of the Gospels are largely identical with those of the Pharisees, frequently not only in general thought but also in detailed expression. Christianity developed not in opposition to, but in conformity with Pharisaic Judaism. When Jesus was asked to define his faith, he gave the Pharisaic reply, quoting the Hebrew Bible's demand to love God and one's neighbor. Paul himself was a Pharisee and proudly professed it.

Certainly, just as in any other group of people, there were bad Pharisees, and the rabbis themselves condemned them. They compared them with chameleons which took on all kinds of color, and they spoke contemptuously of "the shoulder Pharisee" who anxiously tried to display his piety for all the world to see. But the rabbis stressed that the true Pharisee shunned all religious exhibitionism and was motivated in whatever he did and said only by love of God.

However, it was those exceptions among the Pharisees whom Jesus denounced scathingly, but then wrongly identified with their whole party. It was to them, the black sheep, that he really referred when he spoke of the offspring of vipers, the whited sepulchers which outwardly appear beautiful but inwardly are full of dead men's bones, and the blind guides who strain at a gnat, but swallow a camel.

Later generations, ignorant of the historical circumstances and generally prone to disparage the Jews, welcomed those passages and, without inquiring into the validity of the judgment, assumed that all Pharisees were evil, bigoted, narrow, and intolerant. Just as the good deed of one Samaritan came to reflect glory on all his people, so Jesus' censure on a small section of men was extended to their whole group. There have been insincere people in every faith; yet no one should condemn it because of them. Nevertheless, it is one of the sad experiences and contradictions of Jewish life that a judgment, addressed to just a few Jews, condemned by their own people, was applied to the whole group and that a false generalization became accepted as truth. The misrepresentation of the Pharisees was thus taken as their true image and as such entered the vocabulary of all nations.

Though the facts about the Pharisees are now fully known, it is doubtful whether the new and correct appraisal will replace the fallacious description of almost two thousand years' standing. Claude G. Montefiore, a great Jewish scholar, well known for his studies of the Gospels and commentaries on them, wisely remarked:

A fierce light beats upon the Jew. It is a grave responsibility this— to be a Jew; and you can't escape from it, even if you choose to ignore it. Ethically or religiously, we Jews can be and do nothing lightheartedly. Ten bad Jews may help to damn us; ten good Jews may help to save us.

The Horned Moses

One of the most famous statues of Moses stands in Rome. It was carved by Michelangelo and was part of a memorial begun at the request of Pope Julius, but left unfinished through the death of the Pope and lack of finance. Only three figures were completed. The other two are of nude slaves, which were placed in the Louvre in Paris. The statue of Moses is now in the Church of San Pietro in Vincoli.

It was not only the fact that the statue was one of the great sculptor's masterpieces that made it renowned all over the world, but one striking, unique feature. Moses is horned!

Several explanations have been given for this. Some saw in Moses' horns simply the fancy of a genius. Others considered them symbolic of the lawgiver's spiritual force, a materialization of the divine light that inspired him. Critical scholars pointed also to obvious parallels in pagan mythology, the horned representations of Babylonian and Egyptian deities, and claimed that Michelangelo had copied them. Even a passage from the Koran in which Alexander the Great was called the "two-horned" was quoted.

Yet none of these answers is correct. Neither a supernatural miracle nor the adoption of pagan tradition grew Moses' horns. They are the result of a mistake, of one misunderstood word in the Hebrew Bible.

The vocabulary of any language has its difficulties. The same word may describe completely different ideas, various roots eventually having become blended in the one expression. For the proper understanding of a passage the mere use of a dictionary is thus insufficient. Only the study of the context can determine which of the various meanings was intended in each specific case. "He saw the host" may describe a variety of experiences, religious, social, and martial. It may refer to the communion service of the church, a party, a parade, or a battle. Only the circumstances of its application will make the meaning clear in each individual instance. If these pitfalls exist in all languages, they are multiplied many times in Hebrew by the fact that all its words were originally written without vowels. It was left to the reader's discretion and scholarship to add these to the skeleton of consonants which alone constituted the texts.

The combination of three consonants—KRN *—spells out two totally different Hebrew words, one meaning "to shine" and the other "to sprout horns." Actually, it is the latter which forms the root of the Greek *keras,* the Latin *cornu,* and the English *horn,* all of which have thus developed from Hebrew.

The three unvocalized consonants appear in the text of the Bible where Moses' second descent from Sinai is described. He had stayed on the mountain forty days and nights. In communion with God, he had inscribed the second pair of tablets, to replace the first which he had broken in his anger at the people's early apostasy. Filled with spiritual fervor, he descended from the mountain for a second time to present to the people the testimony of God's Law. It is at this point that the Bible relates: "and it came to pass, when Moses came down from Mount Sinai with the two tablets of the testimony in Moses' hands . . . that Moses knew not that his face KRN."

Jewish tradition, and the fact that farther on in the passage it is told that Moses had to cover his face with a veil, leave no doubt that the true meaning could only be that his face *shone.* He did not know then that in the exaltation of the moment he was radiant. It was as if a supernatural light emanated from his inspired countenance. So strong was the light, indeed, that the people were afraid to approach him.

Yet the word was misunderstood and the wrong alternative chosen. It was perhaps because of his pagan background that Aquila, a second-century convert to Judaism, when translating the Hebrew Bible into Greek, rendered KRN as meaning "sprouted horns." The later Latin translation of the Bible, the Vulgate, which, in the sixteenth century, was to be authorized as the official Roman Catholic version, copied this error and interpreted the word as denoting *cornuta erat.* Michelangelo naturally used the text approved by his church, and that is how he

* קרן

came to create his "Horned Moses," a unique piece of art, but distinguished even more by its perpetuation in stone of an early translator's mistake.

Names

Obviously, a Jew cannot have a "Christian" name. Yet some Jews refer to their first name as such. Christian names are given at baptism, which explains the use of this term. On the other hand, so-called typical Jewish names have a pagan past. Esther comes from Ishtar, the Babylonian goddess of love, and her companion, Marduk, the god of the sun, still hides himself in Mordecai. The name of Moses himself, though often explained as "drawn out" of the water (in Hebrew), is really an Egyptian "child," present in not a few of the pharaohs (such as Tutmosis and Ramses). A Cohen is not necessarily of the priestly tribe, even if to all appearances his name claims he is. His apparent noble ancestry may be an illusion, though not a deception. There is evidence that in several cases a Cohen did not inherit his name from the ancient priesthood, but had it bestowed on him by impatient government officials in modern times. When, during the nineteenth-century migrations, Jewish people on entry into a new country had to give their names, immigration officers not rarely found these so unpronounceable that to obviate further difficulties they registered the newcomer simply as "Cohen," which they considered a most appropriate Jewish name.

Originally, names were not mere labels, designed to identify and differentiate between persons, things, and ideas. It was believed that, in a most intimate way, they belonged to the object they described. That is why Naomi, "the lovely one," after her husband's death called herself Marah, "the bitter one," and why Jacob, after having prevailed in his struggle with the mysterious being on the bank of the river Jabbok, thereafter became Israel, "he who strives with God."

Even magical power was attributed to names. To know the name of a being conferred the power to rule it. Thus, even today members of primitive tribes are still loath to reveal their true names to strangers and use every means to disguise, hide, or fake them. A worldwide custom, known also among Orthodox Jews, is the changing of the name of a person who is critically ill. It was not only hoped that the angel of death, sent out to gather him in, would be confounded but also assumed that the changed name changed his identity and fate.

If, in the imagination of people, the destiny of a man could thus be closely linked with his name, it is not surprising that early in the history of religion knowledge of God's name was considered a potent possession. It could limit and influence divine power and even be used for selfish or evil purposes.

In reality, however, it is obvious that God cannot have a name. There is no word that could ever describe Him, His grandeur, omnipotence, and eternity. God is incomprehensible and infinite. To call Him by any name, therefore, is merely a concession to man's yearning to express the indescribable and know Him Whose very Being is far beyond understanding and can never be encompassed in a mere word.

The Bible relates that when God called on Moses to go to his people and prepare them for redemption from Egyptian bondage, he asked what he should say if the Israelites wanted to know who had sent him and what his name was. "Say to them," God replied, " 'I AM' has sent me," a passage which has been the subject of much thought and interpretation. It is followed by the very word which came to be known as the mysterious symbol of the name of God. As it is a four-letter word, consisting of the Hebrew consonants JHVH * (*yod, hay, vav,* and *hay*), theologians call it by the Greek *tetragrammaton,* meaning "the (word) of four letters." Though it is usually rendered in the translations of the Bible and the prayerbook as "the Lord" or "the Eternal," its meaning and even pronunciation can only be suggested. All we possess is the way God's name was written, and this is without its vowels.

During the existence of the Temple, it was used only once every year when, on the most sacred of Jewish days, the Day of Atonement, the High Priest uttered God's ineffable name in the

* יהוה

Holy of Holies. But even then he spoke it so softly that it could not be heard. As its pronunciation was never entrusted to writing, but carefully handed down by word of mouth among the priests, it will never now be known definitely.

Today, Jews still do not pronounce the four-letter word. From earliest childhood they have learned automatically to replace it with a totally different word, *Adonai,** meaning "my Lord." They do so not only because they are ignorant of the actual pronunciation of the original name but out of piety and a desire to obey the third commandment not to take God's name in vain. It was this same concern which made pious Christians always refrain from spelling out God's name and merely to write instead its first and last letters: G–d.

Eventually the very word which came to take the place of God's name acquired equal sanctity in the minds of the people, and they sought to avoid using even the substitute. Each time God's name occurred in prayer, literature, or conversation, they did not even use the less awesome *Adonai*. They simply paused in reverence and referred to "the name," *ha-Shem*.

It does happen, however, that, absent-mindedly or forgetful of Jewish tradition, some people (especially young students of Hebrew) do read out God's name as it appears in prayerbook or Bible and, pronouncing it, call God *Jehovah*. Indeed, Christian scholars frequently refer to the God of the Hebrew Bible as such. The name was also adopted by the Christian sect, Jehovah's Witnesses. But all those who think that they use God's real name by literally pronouncing or transliterating into English the present-day spelling of the word are mistaken. They have been misled by an early rabbinical precaution which envisaged exactly those possibilities and wisely guarded against them so that those who apparently pronounced the title of the Deity did not do so in reality. The explanation of this contradiction makes an interesting study and exemplifies how religious fervor influenced the development of language.

It must be remembered that originally Hebrew was written

אדני *

without any vowels and that these are a comparatively recent addition. They were invented as an aid to the ignorant masses at a time when Hebrew had changed from a spoken tongue to a language of prayer. For many years several systems of vocalization competed for official adoption. Eventually, our present way of spelling, with the help of dots and dashes, prevailed. These were then duly added to the whole text of the Bible, always accurately reflecting proper pronunciation and the right grammatical forms. But there was one exception to this. It concerned the spelling of God's name.

Those who vocalized the Hebrew Bible were not mere dry linguists, interested only in the correct way of spelling and the right application of grammatical roots. Nor were they simply traditionalists, anxious to produce an exact phonetical record of the text of Holy Scripture as it had been handed down. They were rabbis, fervent Jews, steeped in the spirit of their faith. To them, their work was not just a scientific undertaking but a holy task, and they were especially concerned with preserving the sanctity of God's name for all generations. They knew of the pitfalls of life and realized how easily in the fervor of prayer, in the concentration of study, or even in mere absent-mindedness the unwary might, instead of substituting Adonai for the four-letter word, accidentally read it out and thus, by voicing the unutterable, blaspheme God. To prevent any such mistake, the rabbis took a most ingenious (but to the ignorant, misleading) precaution. The vowels they added to the consonants had nothing to do with the actual pronunciation of the word. They belonged to its substitute, Adonai. That means that the rabbis transferred the vowels of the one word to the consonants of the other, so that even if the absent-minded spelled out literally JHVH as it was written, he really pronounced a nonexistent word and most definitely not God's name. That is how *Jehovah* was born: a hybrid formed out of the consonants of JHVH and the vowels of *A*donai. [The initial *a* in Adonai becomes *e* in Jehovah for phonetic reasons.]

Christian theologians who studied the Hebrew Bible learned its language, but ignorant of its spirit, faltered. Transliterating the text, they misread (by properly reading) the vocalized tetragrammaton and erred by spelling it out literally as *Jehovah*. The first-known example of this erroneous pronunciation is found in the work of Raymond Martin, written in 1270. Ever since, the mistake has been repeated innumerable times so that *Jehovah*, as the name of the Hebrews' God, appears in Christian Bibles and theological treatises. But the frequency of its occurrence has not changed its absurdity.

Modern scholars, guided by ancient traditions among non-Israelite tribes, have suggested that the name originally bestowed on God was *Yahveh*. But even this is only a guess. Whatever the name may have been, no single word could describe God the Indescribable. No one will ever penetrate the mystery of God's nameless name.

Contradictions thus abound in Jewish life. Some are expressive of Jewish conviction; some, the result of deplorable mistakes. That a grateful person expresses thanks by wishing more strength to his benefactor is indeed an intriguing feature. A nonexistent Jehovah and a horned Moses show the lasting effect of a simple error in the vocalization of two Hebrew words. An unjustified generalization in the judgment of a group of people and Jesus' crucifixion—these have left their mark in the dictionary of all nations and the persecution of innocent men and women for almost two thousand years.

Altogether, these many facts make up a colorful pattern, delightful and sad, cause for both regret and gratitude. Some have enriched Jewish life greatly, and others have added to its burden. Yet all have contributed strikingly to the character of a people who, in spite of being condemned to perish innumerable times, with grim persistence went on to exist—perhaps the greatest contradiction of all. It explains the reply given to a well-known monarch who had demanded a convincing proof of the existence of God. Nothing could demonstrate it more plainly and forcefully, was the immediate answer, than the miracle of the survival of the Jew.

INDEX